METHUEN'S
MANUALS OF MODERN PSYCHOLOGY

General Editor   *H. J. Butcher*

Perception Through Experience

Perception Through Experience

M. D. VERNON

BARNES & NOBLE, Inc.   NEW YORK

Publishers   Booksellers   Since 1873

First published in 1970
© 1970 *by M. D. Vernon*
Printed in Great Britain by
T. & A. Constable Ltd
Edinburgh

SBN 416 12470 4

Distributed in the USA
by Barnes & Noble Inc.

Contents

Acknowledgements

Acknowledgements for permission to reproduce figures are made to the following:

Academic Press

Fig. 9, from the *Journal of Verbal Learning and Verbal Behavior*, Vol. 2, p. 449, by W. R. Garner and D. E. Clement.

American Psychological Association

Fig. 3, from the *Journal of Comparative Physiology and Psychology*, Vol. 55, p. 898, by E. J. Gibson *et al.*; Figs. 11 and 14, from Vol. 56, p. 893, by R. G. Rudel and H.-L. Teuber; Fig. 12, from Vol. 63, p. 360, by J. Huttenlocher.

Fig. 7, from the *Psychological Review*, Vol. 61, p. 185, by F. Attneave; Fig. 22, from Vol. 62, p. 36, by J. J. Gibson and E. J. Gibson.

Fig. 8, from the *Journal of Experimental Psychology*, Vol. 46, p. 363, by J. Hochberg and E. McAlister; Fig. 28(b), from Vol. 53, p. 25, by I. Rock and I. Kremer; Fig. 39, from Vol. 32, pp. 336 and 337, by R. Schafer and G. Murphy.

British Journal of Psychology

Figs. 17 (a) and 20, from the *British Journal of Psychology*, Vol. 59, pp. 25 and 27, by G. H. Fisher; Fig. 21(a), (b), (c), (f), from Vol. 57 pp. 313 and 314, by W. H. N. Hotopf; Fig. 32(a), from Vol. 49, p. 32, by L. S. Penrose and R. Penrose.

Canadian Journal of Psychology

Fig. 26, from the *Canadian Journal of Psychology*, Vol. 15, p. 206, by B. R. Bugelski and D. A. Alampay.

Holt, Rinehart and Winston

Fig. 32 (b), from *Contemporary Theory and Research in Visual Perception*, edited by R. N. Haber, 1968, p. 314; Fig. 37, from *Modes of Thinking in Young Children*, by M. A. Wallach and N. Kogan, 1965, p. 156, after T. R. Sarbin.

Journal Press

Fig. 6, from the *Journal of Genetic Psychology*, Vol. 77, p. 222, by L. Crain and H. Werner.

Nature

Fig. 17 (b), from *Nature*, Vol. 207, p. 893, by R. H. Day; Fig. 33, from Vol. 200, p. 612, by R. T. Green and E. M. Hoyle.

Nauelwerts

Fig. 35, from *La Perception de la Causalité*, by A. Michotte (Publications de Louvain), 1946, p. 28.

Dr. E. Newson

Fig. 13, from *The Development of Line Figure Discrimination in Preschool Children*, Unpublished Thesis, University of Nottingham, 1955.

North-Holland Publishing Co.

Fig. 30, from *Acta Psychologica*, Vol. 11, p. 347, by G. J. W. Smith and M. Henriksson; Fig. 38, from Vol. 20, p. 218, by P. B. Defares and D. De Haan.

Professor J. Piaget

Fig. 4, from *Archives de Psychologie*, Vol. 34, pp. 211, 216 and 224, by J. Piaget and B. Stettler von-Albertini; Fig. 16(*b*), from Vol. 33, p. 4, by J. Piaget and B. Stettler von-Albertini; Fig. 16(*c*), from Vol. 34, p. 159, by J. Piaget, F. Maire and F. Privat.

Presses Universitaires de France

Fig. 15, from *Les Mécanismes Perceptifs*, by J. Piaget, 1961, p. 223.

Quarterly Journal of Experimental Psychology

Fig. 17(*c*) and Fig. 21 (*d*) and (*e*), from the *Quarterly Journal of Experimental Psychology*, Vol. 20, pp. 294 and 295, by H. J. Jeffrey; Fig. 17 (*d*), from Vol. 19, p. 209, by B. J. Fellows; Fig. 19, from Vol. 20, pp. 212 and 215, by G. H. Fisher.

Routledge & Kegan Paul and Humanities Press

Fig. 1, from *The Child's Conception of Space*, by J. Piaget and B. Inhelder, 1956, pp. 54, 56, 57, 58 and 75.

Society for Research in Child Development

Fig. 2, from *Child Development*, Vol. 31, p. 342, by F. K. Graham *et al.* Fig. 18, from Vol. 36, p. 443, by C. Hanley and D. J. Zerbolio.

University of California Press

Fig. 36, from *Perception and the Representative Design of Psychological Experiments*, by E. Brunswik, 2nd ed., 1956, p. 101.

University of Illinois Press

Fig. 5, from the *American Journal of Psychology*, Vol. 69, p. 580, by L. Ghent; Fig. 10, from Vol. 69, p. 516, by I. Rock; Fig. 23, from Vol. 65, p. 436, by W. Bevan and K. Zener; Fig. 27, from Vol. 74, p. 608, by R. W. Gardner and L. J. Lohrenz; Fig. 29, from Vol. 42, p. 444, by E. G. Boring.

J. Vrin

Fig. 21(*g*) and Fig. 24, from *L'Organisation Perceptive*, by E. Vurpillot, 1963, pp. 93 and 101.

Foreword

The number of experiments and controlled observations which have been performed on visual perception during the past fifteen or twenty years has been very large. It would probably be impossible for any author to describe these within the compass of a single book. Thus he is faced with the choice of selecting a limited number of key experiments and discussing these fully; or of endeavouring to cover a wider range in less detail. The first task has been admirably performed by, for instance, Forgus (1966) and Neisser (1967). The present author has chosen the second alternative. Nevertheless it would seem desirable, in discussing so extensive a range of psychological functions as those which may be covered by the term 'visual perception', to discriminate and select certain of these functions and the related experimental data for consideration, while omitting others. In this book certain important topics, such as the psychophysiological processes and signal detection processes, are not discussed, since each in itself requires a whole volume which the author is not competent to write. Even with the topics which are included there must be numerous experiments which the author has overlooked and omitted. Again, the author has done little more than allude to the various theories which have been advanced in connection with the experimental data, since in her view a reasonably extensive knowledge of the latter should precede detailed theoretical argument. But it is hoped that students taking degree courses in psychology may profit from a general outline of a large number of experiments on visual perception, their findings and some of the conclusions which may be drawn from them. This outline may at least map out the field of knowledge. Moreover, anyone who is about to embark on a research investigation into problems of visual perception may also find that the book affords some direction to his enquiries to be provided by the study of an outline of the literature relating to his particular sphere of interest.

I

Introduction

(1) Basic Processes

The title of this book requires some explanation. It is not intended to demonstrate that all perception is based solely on experience, and that innate capacity for perceiving is non-existent, or at least unimportant, as is sometimes suggested by, for instance, the 'transactionist' school of psychologists (see Solley and Murphy, 1960). Rather, it would appear that there is a first order visual mechanism comprising the eyes, optic nerves, lateral geniculate bodies and striate cortex, which is innately constituted in such a manner as to mediate the discrimination of brightness, colour, movement and simple form, irrespective of any learning through experience. Nevertheless, from infancy upwards these functions are increasingly subordinated to higher order cognitive processes taking place at other levels of the cortex, and interacting with the arousal functions of the reticular formation of the brain stem and thalamus. Thus simple form and movement perception are integrated with and supplemented by processes of identification, classification and coding through the operation of perceptual schemata which depend to a considerable extent on learning, memory, attention, reasoning and language. Undoubtedly the simple perceptual processes do still function, and indeed provide sensory data on which the operation of the more complex processes depends. Yet laboratory experiment has perhaps tended to isolate and over-emphasize these simpler perceptual processes, and has sometimes failed to take into account the more complex processes which normally determine our understanding of and response to the environment.

The simple processes may, however, be legitimately studied in the perceptual responses of infants and young children, who have not acquired the more complex. During recent years extensive studies of these responses have been made by Fantz, Bower and many others, which will be discussed in Chapter II. However, we shall see that these simple percepts lead on, even during the first year of life, to the more complex perceptual processes associated with the identification of objects, and schemata relating to these begin to be formed through learning by experience, especially through manipulation, and the memorizing of previous events.

(2) Natural Settings

It is the author's view that some of the most interesting and important observations of perceptual phenomena and of behaviour in response to these have been obtained in naturalistic or quasi-naturalistic surroundings. Obviously such situations are difficult to investigate since they provide a wealth of 'redundant' information, and the factors involved are hard to isolate or control. Nevertheless, in laboratory experiments we are in danger of selecting for study only a limited range of stimuli, and we may fail to include conditions of vital significance to our understanding of the essential processes involved. This is nowhere more obvious than in studies of perception of the spatial surroundings, and in estimates of distance and of the appearance of objects in relation to their spatial location.

Perhaps the first psychologist to draw attention to the value of experiments carried out in natural conditions was Egon Brunswik*, who used the technique of 'ecological sampling' to investigate size constancy in natural surroundings. Somewhat unfortunately, perhaps, he employed only one observer. But this observer was required to make very extensive 'sample' judgments, in the course of his everyday life, of the distances and apparent sizes of a large number of natural objects. In this way, a wealth of valuable data on size constancy was obtained. Brunswik pointed out that, through the innumerable 'ecological samplings' he makes, an observer builds up strong probabilities as to many expected features of the environment, which greatly affect the particular environmental cues he selects at any one moment for perception and judgment. Moreover, through 'feedback', that is to say, by checking the accuracy of his percepts through his actions, he is enabled to select those cues which are most likely to provide him with veridical information as to the nature of objects and their surroundings. This is particularly evident in judgments of distance. The observer is then able to identify objects rapidly and judge their spatial locations, on the basis of partial and imperfect information, though he may fail to do so with complete accuracy. However, there is usually a redundancy of information which

* The experiments and theories of Egon Brunswik, together with work of the same kind by other psychologists subsequently, are described and discussed at length in *The Psychology of Egon Brunswik* (Hammond, 1966).

minimizes error. The distal characteristics of the environment must be transmitted through proximal characteristics of the image projected on the retina, and there is no one-to-one correspondence between these. Impulses from the retina cannot carry to the cortex all the information necessary to produce veridical knowledge. It is essential that the observer establish stable relationships, or invariances, with the distal aspects of the environment, but this can be performed only on a probability basis. The simple characteristics of form, colour and movement must be systematized and processed schematically, as we noted above, to produce correct identification. There may be some loss of complete accuracy, certain features being ignored, distorted or over-emphasized. Hence over-constancy of size as the result of over-compensation for distance in natural surroundings, as contrasted with under-constancy when the number of cues to distance is greatly reduced. Though in some circumstances there may be a conflict between a rapid and slightly incorrect impression and a more accurate set of percepts which are too hesitant and long-drawn out as an effective guide to behaviour, yet usually a satisfactory working compromise is achieved.

A long series of investigations has been performed by J. J. and E. J. Gibson in which data obtained in natural surroundings have been supplemented and extended by exceedingly ingenious laboratory experiments. Many of these will be described below. In his latest book (1966), J. J. Gibson has provided a summary of all his findings and has propounded a theoretical setting for them. His general approach has been to stress the close correspondence between what is perceived and the 'invariant' sensory data related to certain physical properties of objects and their spatial settings. But although he minimizes the functions in relation to perception of memories and ideas, he stresses the importance of learning to employ sensory data in a way which is most effective to the improvement of discrimination. Moreover, he discusses the development of 'perceptual systems' within which these data, often forming highly complex patterns, are organized and integrated together. In the visual system, he has particularly emphasized the organizations on which are based the perception of form, position and movement of objects interrelated with perception of the position and movement of the body in space. The experiments which he and his collaborators have performed, and the discussion of the manner in which the perceptions investigated are related and organized, are of enormous importance to our understanding of adjustment to our normal surroundings.

Also of great significance to our knowledge as to the adjustment of the body to its spatial setting are the experiments carried out at Innsbruck by Kohler and his collaborators on adaptation to prolonged inversion and reversal of the visual field by means of special lenses and mirrors. These will be discussed fully in Chapter VII. Though these observations were perhaps insufficiently systematic and not always adequately documented, they nevertheless demonstrated the value of studying ordinary behaviour in natural surroundings.

(3) Variation and Change

An important aspect of the perceived relationship of the body to its spatial surroundings and to the objects situated in these is the stable framework constituted by the surroundings. We shall see that in numerous perceptual phenomena change in stimulation may be minimized or may be anchored to the spatial framework. Indeed, it was stated in an earlier book by the present author that 'the individual constructs his perceived world as far as possible in accordance with the maintenance of the maximum stability, endurance and consistency' (Vernon, 1952). This may still be true as regards concepts of the environment and the perceptual schemata related to them. Yet more recent experimental investigation has shown that in immediate perception change and variation are essential to the maintenance of normal perception, and even of the cognitive faculties generally. Realization of the importance of variable stimulation began through the remarkable series of experiments initiated under the direction of D. O. Hebb at McGill University on the effects of sensory and perceptual 'isolation'. These, which will be discussed in Chapter VI, demonstrate the profound changes that may result from exposure to homogeneous and unvarying stimulation over a long period of time. Remarkable short-term phenomena resulting from homogeneity in the field have been demonstrated in experiments on the '*Ganzfeld*' and the 'stabilized retinal image'. Comparable, though less striking, effects were obtained by Mackworth, and many others after him, in experiments on the decline in 'vigilance' – the tendency for accuracy of perception to decrease – during long periods of observation of and response to monotonously repeated stimulation. Such situations occur frequently in many everyday occupations in industry, etc. – for instance, in watch-keeping, inspection and other repetitive work.

It was clear from these studies that one of the most obvious effects of unvarying stimulation was a decrease in alertness and attention. Much light has been cast on the physiological basis of these processes and their variability by the discovery of the reticular formation of the brain stem and thalamus, its variation in functioning with different types of stimulation, and the control it exercises on the cortical functions on which perception depends. Again, it is probable that the direction of attention to various aspects of the environment is closely related to the functioning of the reticular formation, which may in turn be affected by motivational processes (see Chapters V and XI). Here then is a type of modification of primary perception which is of the greatest importance in the more complex perceptual processes.

(4) The Effects on Perception of Other Cognitive Processes

It is also increasingly clear that other cognitive functions may be involved in these complex perceptual processes. It has been argued by Neisser (1967) and others that information is seldom derived merely from instantaneous perceptions which fade immediately from awareness; but that impressions are prolonged at least for a short time in the primary memory image. This both makes for continuity in our perception of the environment, and also facilitates the utilization of memories of past experiences and the application of reasoning and judgment in evaluating events before reacting or deciding how to react. Such processes are particularly apparent in the coding of single stimuli and the classification of isolated events, and they form the basis of the perceptual schemata which determine our general moment-to-moment grasp of the nature of the environment. It must be realized that in everyday life behaviour is comparatively seldom a function of the perception of isolated stimuli and events, but is determined by the whole continuity of knowledge and experience with which such perceptions are associated. Knowledge and experience are particularly involved in the inferences we commonly make as to the nature of objects and events.

In many situations immediate perception may be incorporated in and supplemented by deliberation, judgment and decision. This modification of perception through judgment is particularly likely to occur in the performance of laboratory experiments in which the observer is required to make specific responses, either in words or by other actions. Thus we shall see that, for instance, in making assessments of size and shape in constancy measurements (Chapter VIII), it is difficult to ascertain what in fact the observers initially perceived, because it is almost certain that they utilized memory and judgment in processing these percepts in order to produce the somewhat artificial type of assessment which is required in these experiments. And effects of this kind must be taken into account in considering the findings of many other perceptual experiments, for instance, on the effects of motivation (Chapter XI) and personality qualities (Chapter XII). Thus factors in the environment and in the experimental design and instructions may be affecting not so much the immediate perceptions as the subsequent judgments and decisions. In recent years there has been much discussion as to whether such factors, for instance in the direction of attention by set, are modifying responses tendencies rather than initial perceptions. In everyday life situations, perception and response are so integrally related that it is as impossible as it is unnecessary to differentiate them. But in laboratory experiments problems of some importance arise; and we shall discuss some of these in Chapters V and XI.

(5) The Basis of Individual Differences

Although it has long been recognized that in many types of perception individual differences are clearly apparent, the study of these has been carried out systematically to only a very limited extent. The exact nature of these differences is often difficult to infer, because inadequate reports have been obtained from observers as to what in fact they perceived. It is true that people may perceive and react effectively to stimulation without clear awareness of their total operative percepts. Nevertheless, the phenomenal aspects of perception are interesting in themselves, and reports on these, together with inferences and judgments related to percepts, may be of considerable value in elucidating the variations in reaction to the total situation by different observers.

Such information is nowhere more important than in connection with the effects of motivation and emotion on arousing, directing, facilitating or inhibiting the perception of relevant situations and events. Motivation may be extremely variable in different individuals, and cannot be determined simply by the experimental design and instructions. Yet reports of such varied motivation are obtained only infrequently. Motivational effects will be discussed fully in Chapter XI; but it now seems possible that they may not be very far-reaching except in ambiguous or restricted conditions. It is unfortunate that little investigation has been made of the relation of perception to long-term interests, since motivation, ability and acquired knowledge associated with such interests might well have powerful effects especially in the direction of attention towards specific objects and events.

It is possible also that differences in knowledge and acquired skills, of intelligence and ability, are of greater importance than are motivational influences in for instance directing attention and promoting efficiency of discrimination. But the experimental work on the former has been inadequate to explore them fully.

It has also been argued that perception and other related cognitive faculties may be based upon enduring personality qualities. The work of the most important recent experiments on this problem, by Witkin and his colleagues and by the psychologists of the Menninger Clinic, is discussed in Chapter XII. The outcome of this work is however somewhat disappointing. It is not clear whether the individual differences in modes of perceiving which they have studied are basic and fundamental. And it is still more doubtful what are the personality characteristics to which these could be related. However, these studies may well have suffered from the lack of any exact, reliable and systematic knowledge as to what *are* the basic characteristics of personality. Therefore, one is left with the impression that the whole situation is so complex that at present the hypotheses as to consistent individual differences in perceiving and their causes are highly speculative. Furthermore, veridical perception of the environment is essential to the preservation of life. Thus although perception may be partially selective, the selection cannot vary with individual disposition to more than a minor extent if it is to perform its essential functions efficiently.

II

The Origin and Development of
Visual Perception in Infancy

(1) Reflex Responses

That the visual mechanisms are sufficiently well developed at birth to provide a basis for vision is shown by the variety of reflex responses which occur in response to stimulation (Pratt, 1960). A bright light produces blinking and the pupillary reflex, and is fixated monocularly. If it is exposed peripherally, the head turns in order that the eyes may look at it. In the *optokinetic reflex*, the eyes follow an object dangled and moved to and fro, or a moving light. The optokinetic reflex is produced by moving stripes subtending angles as small as thirty-three minutes of arc, indicating a high degree of visual acuity (Gorman *et al.*, 1957.) A series of moving black dots gave rise to a succession of fixations and saccadic* movements in infants from eight hours old, demonstrating a fixation reflex (Dayton *et al.*, 1964). But not all infants tested were capable of this response. It was also found that a set of brightly lit panels lit up in succession produced following movements, showing that apparent movement was perceived by newborn infants in much the same way as is real movement (Tauber and Koffler, 1966).

There has been some disagreement as to whether *accommodatory reflexes* of the lens of the eye in response to changes in distance of a stimulus take place in newborn infants, or whether they do not develop until later. Haynes *et al.* (1965) made retinoscopic observations of changes in accommodation to targets at different distances, and claimed that in infants up to two months of age accommodation remained fixed at a distance of 19 cm. It began to adapt to differences in distance during the second month, and became comparable to that of adults during the third month. However, Hershenson (1967) considered that the failure to accommodate during the first month may have occurred because the targets of black marks and dots were inadequate to stimulate the infants'

* Saccadic movements – a series of short rapid eye movements from point to point in the visual field, with fixation pauses between them.

attention. Though very similar results were obtained by White *et al.* (1964), the evidence presented below suggests that accommodation is sufficient for form discrimination during the first month. Again, Fantz *et al.* (1962) found that infants of one month directed their gaze significantly more frequently at striped surfaces than at plain grey surfaces when the stripes subtended an angle of forty minutes of arc. This suggested that acuity for motionless patterns also was considerable even at this age; although it became greater with increasing age, the minimum angle being as low as ten minutes at four months.

Monocular fixation of stationary objects is reasonably stable by the sixth week. Accurate convergence and binocular fixation would appear to develop more slowly. According to Gesell *et al.* (1949), convergence appears during the second month, but only gradually becomes smooth and accurate. At first it is intermittent, and varies according to the type of object at which the infant is looking; presumably with the degree of attention accorded to it. It might seem that a confusing binocular rivalry would occur if the two eyes were gazing at different objects. However, it is possible that one eye is not fully accommodated, or that the information transmitted from it is repressed, so that clear vision is derived from one eye only (Hershenson, 1967).

(2) The Beginning of Form Perception

It was hypothesized by the *Gestalt* psychologists that the perception of form is innate and basic, the fundamental constituent of form being its contour or outline. Until recently, no evidence was available as to the age at which infants perceived form. However, research work carried out within the last eight or ten years has provided some evidence for the *Gestalt* hypothesis. In the first place, it has been shown by Hubel and Wiesel that there exist built-in mechanisms in certain animals which respond selectively to certain simple contours. By recording the responses of single cell units in the striate (visual) cortex of cats (1962) and monkeys (1968), Hubel and Wiesel demonstrated differential responses in different cell units to visual stimulation by slits of light, edges between bright and dark surfaces and dark bars. Moreover, these responses were maximal for particular spatial orientations of these line stimuli, and varied if they were rotated. Responses to moving edges were maximal when the direction of movement was at right angles to these orientations. There was also some generalization of response to stimuli of the same form with different retinal sizes and positions. The responses to patterned stimuli in kittens a few days old were similar to those of adult cats (1963), though somewhat slower and less well defined. These kittens had not previously been exposed to patterned stimuli, which suggests that the capacity to differentiate between simple forms develops early in life, and without previous experience. However, early exposure to patterned stimulation appears to be essential for the normal development of these responses. Wiesel and Hubel (1963) found that if a kitten was deprived of patterned visual stimulation for two to three months after birth, the functional organization of the striate cortex described above disappeared.

It seems possible that a similar organization exists in the human striate cortex, and that therefore infants possess similar mechanisms for *response to patterned stimulation*. However, Teuber (1966) considered that the cell units in man responded to a wider area of the field than the small area directly projected on them; hence the phenomena of closure and continuity especially for straight lines. However, we shall discuss these more fully in Chapter III.

The second body of evidence as to the early development of form perception in infants, obtained from direct observation of their gaze, indicated that they could discriminate a form or pattern from its background, though possibly in a somewhat blurred fashion, and also two patterns from one another. Thus Fantz (1958) found that infants in the first few weeks of life developed a tendency to look longer and more often at patterned surfaces, such as a checker board pattern, than at plain unpatterned surfaces. The method he used was to present a pair of different stimuli above the head of an infant who was lying prone, and to observe the direction of his gaze at one stimulus or the other. Thus it could be determined which of the two stimuli he looked at first most frequently, and for the longest time. In later experiments by other psychologists, the corneal reflection of the stimulus shape was recorded photographically (Hershenson, 1964). And in some cases stimuli were presented from in front to older infants who could sit upright with support (Spears, 1964).

It was then shown that infants as young as two to four days differentiated stimuli of different *brightness* (Hershenson, 1964). They looked longest at surfaces of medium brightness; then at those of greatest brightness; and least at the dimmest. Infants also looked more at vertical lines than at other simple line stimuli, suggesting the operation of the visual mechanisms described by Hubel and Wiesel (Kessen *et al.*, cited by Hershenson, 1967). Recording the eye movements of newborn infants indicated that they followed with their eyes the contour of a brightly coloured triangle (Kessen, cited by Bruner, 1966). Differentiation of *shapes* also appeared early, first with very simple shapes, and later, with increase in age, with more *complex* ones. Thus Hershenson (1964) found that newborn infants looked longer at a half-white half-black surface than at a plain surface or at a checker board with two black and two white squares. Then Brennan *et al.* (1966) presented, in pairs, a plain grey surface and a checker board pattern with 4, 64 or 576 squares, to infants aged 21-25 days, 51-61 days and 93-103 days. The first group looked increasingly more at the patterns as they decreased in complexity, and indeed did not seem to differentiate the most complex from the grey surface. The second group looked longest at the 64-square pattern and least at the 4-square pattern. The third group looked more with increasing order of complexity. It is possible that the youngest infants looked longest at the simplest pattern because their accommodation was not adequate to enable them to see the more complex patterns clearly. In fact they may have perceived two rather blurred patches, with light and darkness shading into each other. However, Brennan *et al.* repeated their experiment using smaller patterns with the same numbers of squares at shorter distances, and obtained similar results.

Other findings have been that as early as two months a checkered pattern with fourteen squares was looked at for longer than a pattern with two stripes (Thomas, 1965). At about eight weeks a bullseye pattern was looked at more than a striped one (Fantz, 1958). At four months, a bullseye pattern was looked at for longer than were random patterned and unpatterned coloured surfaces (Spears, 1964).

That infants spend an increasing amount of time, as they grow older, in examining patterns of *increasing complexity* seems to show that their capacity for differentiation improves steadily, possibly because they become increasingly able to scan more complex patterns thoroughly, and to attend to whole patterns and not merely to parts. This does not occur in very young infants. Thus newborn children to whom large black triangles were presented looked mainly at one corner; different infants, however, looked at different corners (Salapatek and Kessen, 1966). When the infant is able to perceive complex patterns clearly, it would seem that he spends more time in examining the complex rather than the simple in order to grasp all their details. The complex patterns vary more than the simple, and there is more uncertainty as to their exact nature. However, there has been some argument as to the aspects of form which determine its complexity. Hershenson *et al.* (1965) adopted a definition of complexity proposed by Attneave (which will be discussed fully in Chapter III), namely, that it is determined in silhouette shapes by the number and variation of angles or turns of the outline. They then carried out an experiment in which they paired silhouettes with five, ten or twenty angles, and found that infants of two to four days looked more frequently at those with ten angles than at those with five or twenty angles. Thus they inferred that medium complexity was preferred by infants of this age. However, according to McCall and Kagan (1967), the duration of the first fixation, which they considered a better measure of attraction of gaze than is the total duration of regard, varied with the length of the contour rather than with the number of angles, at four months of age. But even if Attneave's definition of complexity is applicable to perception in adults, its use for infants is scarcely justifiable. The infant's endeavours to obtain visual information is affected by a number of different factors.

It might well be supposed that perception in infants would be concerned with *colour* and colour variations. However, the extent to which young infants can differentiate colour has been disputed. Stirniman (1944) claimed that new born infants looked longest at blue and green, less at red and least at yellow. Hershenson (1967) considered that these differential responses may have been due to intrinsic brightness differences of the different hues. This hardly agrees with the results of Chase (1937), who found that infants showed ocular pursuit movements of a coloured spot moving across a differently coloured background, but not of a colourless spot moving across a background of different brightness. However, Staples (1932) showed that infants of ten to twenty weeks, though they looked longer at a coloured than at a grey disc, did not seem to differentiate between different colours. It was not until over six months of age that colour preference began to appear. The infants reached out most frequently for a red object, then yellow, blue and green. This seems to reverse the order of preference noted by Stirniman.

Finally, Hubel and Wiesel (1960) obtained differential responses to different colours in the optic nerve of the spider monkey; but differentiation was less in the cortex (Wiesel and Hubel, 1966). Thus it may be that in the young infant rudimentary differentiation between chromatic and neutral (grey) colour takes place, but preferences for different colours do not develop till later. Spears (1964) found that four-month-old infants looked longer at red and blue than at grey surfaces, but showed no preference for yellow. Again, plain coloured surfaces were looked at less than were patterned ones.

(3) Attention

Clearly, before any discrimination can occur, the infant's attention must be attracted, so that he observes an object and differentiates it from its background. We noted that even at birth attention is aroused and gaze attracted by bright lights and moving objects; and a little later by certain types of pattern. Nevertheless, prolonged gaze at an object is not necessarily accompanied by perception. The infant may stare passively; he may even drowse with his eyes open, as indicated by the sleep pattern of the EEG which has replaced initial arousal (Hershenson, 1967). But increasingly the infant looks around him and searches his environment. As he does so, his attention is caught and held by particular stimuli; and at the same time there is a decrease of other bodily activity (Gesell *et al.*, 1949). As age increases, periods of visual fixation and visual examination of objects become longer. But it would seem that in the early months impressions are extremely fragmentary. There is little capacity for memory storage, and each new appearance of a stimulus is perceived as a new and unrelated event. Thus it was shown that if a moving stimulus passed behind a screen and re-emerged in altered form, this alteration was registered by cardiac acceleration in two-month infants only if the stimulus reappeared within about a second (Bower, 1965). With longer intervals, the infants were not aware of any change because they did not remember the first stimulus. Again, Fantz (1964) presented pairs of patterns to infants, one of which patterns varied while the other remained the same, at intervals of one minute. Infants over two months of age ceased to look at the repeated pattern, which had become familiar and therefore attracted less attention. But younger infants showed no decline in fixation of the repeated pattern, because they did not remember that it had been shown before.

As age increases and with it memory span, *novelty* and *uncertainty* become increasingly effective in attracting attention. Fantz and Nevis (cited by Schaffer and Parry, 1969) found that preference for novelty emerged gradually and became prominent at three months. This is indicated in the appearance of the '*orienting response*', the direction of gaze and the arousal of the central nervous system to novel stimulation. Charlesworth (1966) presented the model of a face made of white cloth, preceded by the sound 'ah', to infants of five to ten months, either consistently to right or to left; or in regular alternation between left and right; or in random alternation. Persistent orientation towards the model was greatest for the third condition, less for the second and least for the first. In the third condition, uncertainty was greatest. But complexity may have effects on attention similar to those of novelty. Caron and Caron (1968) showed infants of fourteen to sixteen weeks a series made up of several different patterns and one repeated pattern, a red and white checker board which in some cases had four squares, in others

144 squares. The total time during which the infants looked at the patterns decreased steadily, but markedly more for the repeated than for the varying patterns; and more for the simpler than for the more complex checker board. But the duration of looking increased again when, at the end, two new multi-coloured patterns were shown. It was clear that both the decline in attention to the repeated pattern and the recovery from this effect with a new pattern were greater with the simpler repeated pattern. Moreover, cessation of attention was also demonstrated by increase in restlessness and in vocal protest, which decreased when the new patterns were presented. Schaffer and Parry (1969) found that when an irregularly shaped coloured solid was presented several times in succession to infants of six and twelve months, visual fixation time decreased steadily. The older infants, who were slow at first to reach out and grasp the object, and sometimes showed signs of fear, gradually did so more quickly. But the younger infants quickly reached out for the object even at its first presentation, showing that discrimination of novelty was not associated with avoidance until the latter part of the first year.

Attention to and interest in novel and complex stimuli vary also the infant's on-going and previous *experience*. Infants two or three days old showed more alerting and scanning of the environment if propped up and held in a sitting position than if they were merely lifted up (Korner and Grobstein, 1966). White and Castle (1964) investigated these processes in infants brought up in hospital and normally given little personal attention. But in one group each infant was taken up, held and rocked by a nurse for twenty minutes a day over thirty days. Records over periods of three hours at fifteen-day intervals from the thirty-seventh day to the tenth week showed that these infants spent, especially at first, more time in looking round their surroundings than did infants who had not received handling. At three and a half months all the infants were removed to a more complex visual environment, and thereafter showed considerable increases in visual attention. Again, infant monkeys reared by the mother and tested shortly after birth showed readiness to press a bar which opened a window giving them a view through it (Green and Gordon, 1964). Readiness was greatest when the view was of the mother; then of another infant; then of food; and lastly of meaningless objects. But infant monkeys reared in isolation showed no such behaviour. The experiments of Harlow and Zimmerman (1959) showed that infant monkeys who were allowed to cling to a 'cloth mother' – a wire framework covered by soft towelling – were more ready to explore novel and potentially frightening objects than were those who had only a 'wire mother' – an unpadded framework. Thus it would appear that attention to and exploration of the environment may depend not only on its variety and complexity but also on the adventurousness of the infant, related to social encouragement and support.

(4) The Identification of Objects and the Development of Schemata

We have considered the development in infants of the capacity to discriminate between two different patterns. This, however, does not mean that younger infants are able to identify either patterns or objects, in the sense that they remember them from one appearance to another and can therefore recognize them when they reappear. Obviously this is impossible until memory capacity is adequate for the storage of impressions. It seems probable that the *earliest identification* is of very familiar meaningful objects, and particularly the mother. She not only constantly appears in the infant's surroundings but also her appearance is associated with pleasurable experiences of being taken up, handled, cuddled, soothed and fed. Undoubtedly the infant pays great attention to his mother's appearance. Robson (1967) noted the intent gaze of the infant at his mother's face when she looked at him, beginning at about the fourth week; and considered that this eye to eye contact was a very important constituent of the relationship between mother and child.

We noted that infant monkeys preferred looking at the mother's face to any other object; and the same seems to be true of the human infant. Carpenter and Stechler (1967) measured excitatory reponses (movement of the head, direction of gaze, smiling and vocalizing) in infants aged one to eight weeks when shown the mother's face, a manikin's head and a meaningless solid form. Throughout the period there was a regular increase in response to the mother's face, but responses to other stimuli were variable.

There can be no doubt therefore that true identification of the mother's face develops at an early age. But also surprising discoveries have been made as regards responses to *pictures of faces*. It would appear that they may not only be discriminated as patterns but also that there is some element of identification as related to real faces. Now up to a year of age infants responded little if at all to most pictures (Smith and Smith, 1962; Bower, 1967), although from twenty months they looked at a succession of different pictures more than at a single one; and more at the latter than at a variably lighted screen (Weisberg and Fink, 1968). But Fantz (1961) claimed that infants as young as four days looked longer at a picture of a face than at a half-black half-pink shape. However, they looked almost as long at a face with 'scrambled' features, that is to say, with the features scattered at random. This experiment is not well documented, however, and its results are contraverted by later experiments. Thomas (1965) found that at two to four weeks infants looked longer at a checker board pattern than at a picture of a face, presumably because the latter was too complex for them to grasp. At two and a half months there was no discriminatory preference between a face with normal and with scrambled features. But at about three and a half months infants looked longer at a face than at all other patterns. At four months, the pattern which most clearly resembled a face was looked at for longer than were other patterns with less resemblance (Haaf and Bell, 1967).

It has been suggested that in these experiments the duration of the first fixation is a more sensitive measure than the total duration of regard (Lewis *et al.*, 1966), although once the infant begins looking at one stimulus of a pair, he tends to return to it frequently. Using the measurement of duration of first fixation, McCall and Kagan (1967) found that in infants of four months who were shown pictures of faces, faces with scrambled features and solid black shapes, the first fixations were longest with the faces, then the scrambled faces and then the random shapes. Moreover, degree of cardiac deceleration, indicating a pleasurable reaction, followed the same order. Kagan *et al.* (1966) compared the effects of presenting in pairs a normal face, a face with features transposed or scrambled, a face with no eyes and a face with no features. The durations of first fixation and of total fixations during a thirty second period were about the same for the normal and scrambled faces, and longer than for the third and fourth faces. The greatest amount of cardiac deceleration occurred with the normal face for girls but not for boys.

Kagan *et al.* pointed out that fixation time was a somewhat ambiguous measure. Prolonged fixation could result both from the attractiveness of the stimulus and the pleasure it caused, and also from attempts to explore the stimulus and discover its nature – that is to say, to overcome their uncertainty as to what it was. Better measures of attractiveness were cardiac deceleration and the amount of smiling, and these were greatest for the normal face. Thus it may be concluded that the infants were pleased by the normal face, but puzzled by those with scrambled features. We noted that Haaf and Bell also found the greatest amount of smiling with the most face-like patterns.

It would naturally be supposed that when infants smiled at pictures of faces, they were identifying them in some manner as representing or as related to real faces. Indeed, it is often thought that *smiling* is essentially a social response, first evoked by a human face or voice, especially those of the mother. It is true that infants smile readily at any human face. The response to a nodding face emerged at two to three and a half months, reached its peak at three and a half to five months, then declined and disappeared as an automatic response at six to eight months (Polak *et al.*, 1964a). Thereafter smiling became more discriminating, appearing only with familiar faces. However, the early type of smiling may occur in younger infants in response to other stimuli which attract the infant and cause him pleasure. These might be supposed to resemble a rudimentary human face. Kaila (cited by Ambrose, 1961) obtained a smiling response to a horizontally arranged pair of bright balls; Ahrens (cited by Ambrose, 1961) to a drawing of two eyes; and Spitz and Wolf (1946) to a grotesque mask. But Salzen (1963) reported a smiling response in an infant during the period of eight to eleven weeks of age in response to a flashing light and a rotating card with black and white sectors. Moreover, at about two months there was no discrimination between a moving photograph and a nodding human face (Polak *et al.* 1964b). Discrimination between these emerged at about three months. Thus the earlier smiling appeared to be caused by something attractive and interesting.

Ambrose (1960) found that smiling at a human face occurred about a month later in infants brought up in institutions than in infants brought up at home. Rheingold (1961) on the other hand showed that at three to four months infants brought up in institutions responded better than did those brought up at home to the experimenter, as shown by their smiling and vocalizing. In this case it seems possible that the institutional infants, who were accustomed to being handled by several different people, responded more readily to strangers than did those brought up at home.

These responses to faces may then indicate that at about four months the infant is able to identify a particular class of objects which afford him pleasure. It would seem that at about the same age he is beginning to realize that identifiable objects can be a source of more than one type of sensory pattern; hence identification is facilitated by the *co-ordination of two or more sensory patterns* originating in the same source. Indeed, the co-ordination of visual and auditory patterns begins earlier. Thus Piaget (1955) noted that at two to three months an infant turned his head in the direction of a voice and looked attentively at the person who spoke. This association between visual and auditory patterns thus develops in relation to identification firstly of the mother, and afterwards of other human beings. We have noted that the tactile and kinaesthetic sensations produced by the mother's handling are also of considerable significance. These may operate in the clinging of Harlow's infant monkeys to the cloth mother (Harlow and Zimmerman, 1959).

But these sensory patterns enter also into the identification of other objects from the third to the fourth month.

There is much *tactile exploration* during the early months of life. The infant touches his own body and any object he can reach, and frequently puts the latter in his mouth. But it would seem that he does not for some while realize the identity of the object seen with that which can be touched, handled and mouthed. Both Gesell *et al.* (1949) and Piaget (1952) have described how this takes place.* Although the age at which this behaviour develops seems to vary somewhat in different studies, the stages appear the same. The earliest may be that in which the infant visually perceives his hand moving and also feels it move. But according to White *et al.* (1964), the infant of two and a half to three months glanced repeatedly to and fro between his hand and a toy held in front of him, and hit out at the toy with his closed fist. At three to three and a half months both hands were frequently raised towards the toy; and at four to four and a half months the object was sometimes grasped if one hand touched it accidentally. Finally, at four and a half to five months, he looked steadily at the toy, lifted one hand out of his visual field, opened the hand and grasped the toy. Thereafter prolonged and forceful manipulation began without hesitation as soon as the object was within reach. Yet, as we noted, Schaffer and Parry (1969) found that some children of twelve months were slower to manipulate strange objects than were children of six months. And children brought up in an institution were slower to grasp and manipulate objects than were children brought up at home (Kohen-Raz, 1966).

We owe our knowledge of the next stages to take place in the identification of objects and the understanding of their nature mainly to the observations of Piaget (1952, 1955). Although these observations are not derived from systematic experimental studies, yet there are numerous observations which corroborate each other. The infant continues to explore objects by touch and visual examination; moreover, he manipulates them by hitting, rubbing, pushing, balancing them, and so on. He lets them fall, makes them slide and roll, floats them in water. Thus he learns that objects with a certain visual appearance are soft or hard, slippery or rough, penetrable or resistant to handling. He develops *schemata*, organizations related to particular familiar objects in which are associated, not only their sensory qualities, but also knowledge of what they do – if for instance they move spontaneously or only when pushed – and also what he can do with them. Piaget has particularly

* Excerpts relevant to this and the following discussion from Piaget (1952, 1955) are quoted in Vernon (1966, pp. 421-30).

stressed the significance in formation of schemata of the child's actions in relation to objects. But also he begins to investigate the characteristics of objects as such, independently of the effects on them of his own actions. New objects may be assimilated to existing schemata, any unfamiliar characteristic being ignored; and familiar actions are applied to them.

A very important stage in the development of a schematic association between the visually and tactually perceived shape of an object is the realization that although the visual pattern varies with *orientation*, as a solid object is turned round in space, its tactile pattern remains the same. Therefore the visual pattern given by an object of specific identity may vary, although in a lawful manner related to its orientation in space, yet its identity remains unchanged. Moreover, an important characteristic of three-dimensional objects is their perceived *depth*, as shown by the relationship of the shapes of the receding sides to the front side. Now Bower (1966b) showed that an infant of about eight weeks, who had been taught to recognize the shape of a board tilted through 45° to the line of sight, could easily recognize this board when it was placed upright. However, it may be that this recognition requires prolonged experience of a particular object in a particular situation, and does not lead to a general realization that objects retain their identity in different orientations. Certainly this does not occur with complete reversal from back to front. Thus Piaget (1955) found that at seven and a half months his son continued to recognize his bottle when it was merely tilted; but failed to do so when it was completely reversed so that he could see only the bottom. But at nine months he obviously expected that the nipple was there, and rapidly reversed the bottle to the correct position.

Another factor which must enter into the schematized notion of objects is the *change in size* of the image projected on the retina with its *change in distance*. In fact this seems to develop at an early age; and it is possible that from the first the recognized identity of an object includes a range of projected sizes. Thus Bower (1966a) found that infants of six to eight weeks, trained to respond to a 30 cm. cube at one metre, made a similar response to the same size cube at three metres, but not to a cube three times the size at three metres. In other words, they recognized the object's 'real size'. Cruikshank (1941) showed that infants of six months reached for a rattle of the same size at three times the distance without special training in recognition of this object. However, Piaget's observations (1955) seemed to indicate that infants continued to experiment with the relation between projected size and perceived distance until nine to ten months, as if to assure themselves how these were related.

What is important here is that the infant realizes that the same object can exist in different spatial positions. Thus its identity is independent of its spatial position, and changes of position are differentiated from changes of state. However, the understanding of the *permanent existence of objects* when they are hidden from sight is a somewhat later development. Piaget (1955) made extensive observations on the development of this realization. An infant who dropped an object out of sight did not try to search for it at seven months, but at eight months he did so. However, if an object was hidden from sight by someone else, the infant did not try to search for it until about nine months. We may conclude that infants were aware of some continuity in objects they handled themselves before they realized that objects, over the appearance of which they had no control, continued to exist even when they could not be directly perceived. This does not mean that they forgot the object altogether, as younger infants would do, but that they could not conceive of the continued existence of something not apparent to the senses. Now clearly our whole commerce with the environment is based on the assumption that it is stable and continues to exist in its known identity unless and until we have reason to suppose otherwise. As we shall see, this expectation of continuity plays an important part in the perception of adults. But it would seem that infants have to learn by experience that certain aspects of the environment are permanent, although their appearance may vary from time to time according to their distance and spatial orientation. We have suggested that this happens through the development of schemata relating together the sensory impressions of objects which vary in different situations, although in a lawful manner. Although these schemata are fairly well established by the age of a year, they must nevertheless undergo modification as the child's intelligence and experience of his environment increase.

(5) Further Development of Object Identification: Classification

It would seem that from the latter part of the first year of life the child is interested predominantly in the identification of objects and their characteristic situations and activities, together with their effects on him and their usefulness to him. His perceptions of objects involves schemata which include not only their appearance and behaviour, as conveyed by vision and touch, but also these further 'meanings' in terms of his own activities. Indeed there is comparatively little interest in the formal qualities of shape, colour, etc., and these are perceived only in so far as is necessary to identification, which is derived from a minimum of perceptual cues. Thus we find that children are often not clearly aware of formal qualities and small details. A child may recognize an animal in a picture book, but be unable to point out its characteristics separately. Or in other cases he may perceive what we should regard as irrelevant details, in so far as these do not serve to discriminate one object from another.

It is difficult to trace exactly the development of object perception, since children between the ages of one and four years are too active and restless to be amenable to controlled experimentation. Thus our understanding is necessarily based on sporadic observations of natural behaviour made by Piaget, Werner and others. There seems to be general agreement, however, that from the time the child realizes that objects continually reappear and continue to exist even when they are not visible, he makes use of some form of *imagery* by means of which he is able to identify that an object he is now perceiving is the same as one he has experienced in the past. The utilization of this imagery is particularly important at the ages of one to three years, before language develops sufficiently to enable the child to identify precisely by naming. Piaget (1951, 1952, 1955)* considers that the image of an object does not represent simply its appearance but is an interiorization of his own actions or those made by others in relation to this object. It thus precedes the object concepts which develop later when language is available. But the image is often insecure, labile and subject to the influence of the child's emotions and desires; and it may be tied to specific temporal and spatial aspects of the original perception.

Although in general at this age schemata are attached to specific objects rather than to classes of objects, they may be based upon erroneous notions of what constitutes the essential nature of the object. In particular, there may be a failure to differentiate the object from the setting or *surroundings* in which it commonly occurs. Thus the child may fail to recognize familiar people when they appear in strange clothes. This failure may persist even after language develops, when the surroundings change. Thus Piaget (1951) noted that a child of two years, while she was in the garden with her father, heard the bath water running upstairs and said: 'That's daddy up there'. Again, after seeing her uncle drive away from the house, she went into the drawing room where he had been earlier saying: 'I want to see if uncle has gone.' Thus for

---

* It should be noted that these dates refer to the English translations. The French originals are dated in a different order: *La Naissance de l'Intelligence chez l'Enfant* (1936); *La Construction du Réel chez l'Enfant* (1937); *La Formation du Symbole chez l'Enfant* (1945).

correct identification the child needs to be able to differentiate what constitutes the essential identity of the object from its variable qualities and its surroundings. We shall find that such differentiation is even more difficult with meaningless forms.

The correct identification of objects becomes easier when the child is able to *name* or use a word for them, since the word signifies the essentials of the object. Nevertheless, according to Piaget, words originate in the earlier symbolic images and are not merely acquired through social influences. The importance to perception of using words has been demonstrated in several experiments by Russian psychologists (see Simon, 1957). Thus Liublinskaya found that children of one to two and a half years learnt to find a sweet under a red paper cup more quickly when the word 'red' was spoken at the same time. A butterfly with stripes on its wings was recognized by rather older children only when they were given the word 'stripes'. Other single words may be used accurately and effectively as names from the time they are acquired. But again they may be too general. Thus at a year one of Piaget's daughters used the name 'Tch-tch' for a train passing her window; later, for vehicles and a man walking, also seen from the window; and even for a noise in the street (1951). In other words, a single word covered several associated objects and events. So also at one and a half years she used the word 'panana' not only for her grandfather, who often played with her, but also to indicate that she wanted something to amuse her when he was in no way concerned. Werner (1948) noted that an Italian child used the term 'qua-qua' (acqua) both for water and for the duck on it. On the other hand, a name may be used too narrowly. Thus Lewis (1936) reported that his son, at nine months, learnt the name 'ballie' for a small white ball; but he did not respond to this name for a large coloured ball until he was over a year of age. Liublinskaya also found that, at a year, the name 'cup' was used for a small pink cup but not for a large white one.

Thus it is necessary for the child to learn that some names are used for single objects, but others for *classes* of object, since in many cases a common name is employed by adults for a category of objects, such as 'dog', rather than for a single example such as 'Mummy' and 'Daddy'. It seems probable that in the first case names are learnt in their most frequent type of employment (Brown, 1958). Subsequently the child learns either to narrow down their use, for instance from calling all friendly males 'Daddy'; or to widen it, and apply 'ball' to all types of ball. In so doing it becomes clearer to him how *conceptual categories* operate and are delimited; and this marks one of the most important stages in the development of perception and thought. Clearly as the child encounters more and more objects, the accumulation of schemata of single objects would become excessive. In the identification of any new object, it might be necessary to have recourse to the schemata of all similar objects previously experienced. However, when a schema can be attached to a class of objects, any new object encountered may be identified by relating it to this class, and its principal characteristics, including the actions appropriate to it, are then known.

However, the establishment of adult classifications and the attribution of their accepted names is a gradual process, not fully developed in the child until the age of six to seven years, and in some cases even later. For in order to understand the manner in which objects are categorized, the child must first be able to discriminate from the numerous qualities of similar objects those characteristics which indicate their essential nature and similarity; and then generalize from these as to the fundamental properties of the whole category. Of course he does not do this entirely through his own efforts. Adults name objects to him; and when he is sufficiently mature, he realizes that a common name signifies a class of objects. But in all probability the name is learnt before the child fully understands what are the essentials of the category to which it is attached. Thus he is liable to use the name incorrectly, and to make false identifications. This is well illustrated by Lewis's son (1967). At first he used the name 'ti' not only for the cat, 'Timmy', but also for dogs, cows, sheep and horses. Later he learnt the name 'goggie' for dogs and 'hosh' for horses; but a large St Bernard dog was called 'hosh'. In this case again, therefore, conceptual categories were only gradually delimited correctly. Furthermore, even older children may apparently fail to recognize that there exists more than one instance of a class of objects. There is a well-known story of Piaget's daughter (1951) who at the age of two and a half years saw a slug on the path, and then another one about ten yards further on, and said 'There's the slug again.' Even after going back to see the first one, she seemed doubtful if there could be more than one slug.

It has been claimed by Kuhlmann (cited by Bruner, 1966) that children with good imagery are more likely to associate a name with a single object; whereas those whose imagery is poor are better able to attach a name to a category of objects with similar attributes.

There is fairly general agreement that in the early stages of conceptual categorization children may classify and name objects in accordance with superficial and relatively unimportant perceptual characteristics, or under the influence of some egotistical emotional reaction. Werner

C

(1948) in particular stressed the frequent occurrence of personal connotations in the identification and classification of objects by young children. Thus the use of the names 'panana' and 'qua-qua' (see p. 22)
is an example of an early attempt at such classification. Again, the word
'hot' was employed for anything the child was forbidden to touch
because touching might lead to pain. Personal use may occur in slightly
older children; for instance, 'bench' and 'hammer' were classed together
because 'you can make a bench with a hammer'. The same tendency to
emphasize use may appear also in definitions; thus at five to six years a
bottle was defined as : 'There's lemonade in it'; 'where you put water';
'where you pour something out of'.

But also from the ages of six to eight or nine years superficial characteristics of appearance and similarity are often employed in classification.
Thus Olver and Hornsby (1966) asked children to group together
pictures of objects which 'belonged together' or were alike, and found
that nearly half the six-year-olds and a quarter of the eight-year-olds
stressed perceptual characteristics such as shape, colour or location.
Personal use also appeared; and association as subject and object, for
instance in 'the bunny ate the carrots.' In another experiment with
models of real objects similar effects were observed in children of seven
and nine years (Sigel, 1953). The majority of the seven-year-olds and
more than half of the nine-year-olds made perceptual groupings, for
instance through similarity of structure. The seven-year-olds often constructed a group by including objects in a story, or by associating them
with particular situations, for instance, 'they all belong in a house'.

Kagan et al. (1964) found that although there was a general development between the ages of six and twelve years in the ability to form
analytical concepts, there were also marked individual differences. The
children were required to pick out from three pictures of familiar objects
those two which were alike. Concepts were said to be analytical when
two objects were selected with similar attributes; for instance, 'the
watch and the ruler have numbers on them'. The production of such
concepts was associated with delay in making decisions, which was more
noticeable in the more reflective than in the more impulsive children.
The former were generally superior in the analysis of complex visual
material.

However, it is probable that adequate conceptual grouping, in which
objects are classified together in accordance with their essential characteristics, is not really effective until ten to eleven years. This is indeed
the age at which Piaget's 'formal operational' stage begins, when the
child is able to reason verbally without recourse to concrete situations.

It seems probable therefore that younger children cannot perform these tasks adequately because they are incapable of the necessary abstract verbal reasoning. But they can form classifications of a practical kind at a much earlier age, which are adequate for rapid perception and identification of objects, at least in normal circumstances. However, identification may break down when perception is made unusually difficult; and analysis of percepts, such as would be necessary for conceptual classification, is also unreliable.

Thus we may conclude that perception of objects, particularly in the complex environmental settings with which we are normally concerned, develops comparatively slowly, and is dependent on the capacity to analyse out the essential aspects from a multitude of irrelevant detail. It would seem that the child explores and discovers for himself the nature and identity of new and unfamiliar objects by applying not only his habitual activities but also variations of these, in order to find out what can be done with the objects. Thus he watches carefully to see what happens to something when he lets it fall. He also images to himself what actions to perform and what may be their outcome. Schemata are involved which cover categories of object associated together, not merely by appearance, behaviour or use, but related in complex organizations of these. Thus immediate perception is interpreted in the light of conceptual reasoning.

Further instances of this occur in the capacity to extract general qualities, such as number, size, volume and weight, and to judge these irrespective of the objects and settings in which they occur. This is essential in judgments of what Piaget has termed '*conservation*': the realization that these attributes may remain constant in spite of changes in appearance, setting, etc. For instance, the volume of water remains constant when it is poured from a wide vessel into a narrow one in which it reaches a higher level. The child perceives a change in the most obvious aspect of the situation, the height of the water level. His judgment as to the volume of water in the vessels is overweighted by this perception, and he reports that the volume of water is different. In other conservation situations, judgment is similarly determined by immediate perception, uncorrected by reasoning. But a detailed discussion of conservation would go beyond the scope of this book.

The ability to modify immediate perception through reasoning is generally supposed to develop through maturation, although at the stage at which it begins to develop experience and learning may affect it considerably. So also we may suppose that the capacity to identify and recognize is to a considerable extent determined by maturation. Nevertheless, experience plays a major part in providing the information as to the nature and characteristics of objects on which identification is based. So also does the ability to name general qualities of objects, as well as the type of object. Thus Spiker *et al.* (1956) found that children of three and a half to five and a half years who could understand and use the term 'middle-sized' were able to select the middle-sized from among three objects in a variety of different sets of objects; whereas those who could not use this term were less adept.

III

The Perception of Form

(1) Development of Form Perception

According to the Gestalt psychologists, Wertheimer, Köhler and Koffka, perception of the environment is based fundamentally on the perception of form. Completely homogeneous surroundings cannot be perceived; they appear vague, indefinite, without location in space. Perception occurs only in so far as some form or pattern arises and is discriminated by virtue of the contour which segregates it from its background. This is known as the '*figure-ground*' experience, which is fundamental to all perception. In the last chapter we considered evidence which showed that the central nervous system in animals was directly responsive to simple forms and their spatial location. Infants also appeared to discriminate patterns from each other. However, the discrimination of patterns would seem to precede the discrimination of single shapes. Thus Fantz (1958) found no differential responsiveness at three to four months to a cross and a circle.

Moreover, as we have noted, the ability to discriminate between two forms or patterns presented simultaneously, although it may provide a basis for *identification*, does not necessarily produce it. Some memorization is required in order that the child may identify a shape as such. An early experiment by Ling (1941) showed that at six months an infant could learn to discriminate shapes such as a circle, oval, square, triangle and cross, presented in pairs. One shape was movable, and covered with a sweet substance, and could be picked up and sucked. At first learning which shape to select was very slow indeed, and there were considerable individual differences between different infants. The rate of learning increased rapidly from seven to twelve months. But the task was more difficult when several shapes were presented together; and if the correct shape was similar to one of the others, for instance a circle and an oval. It would seem that during this period the infants were gradually learning to identify particular simple forms. Babska (1965) investigated the further development of identification. She required children to memorize the shape of a real object or a shape such as a circle, square, etc., and recognize it afterwards when it was shown with three other shapes. At two to three years, the response was one of chance; but it improved subsequently, and nearly all choices were correct by five years. Thus it could be concluded that simple identification of shape was by then well established. However, the problems of memorizing form discrimination go beyond the scope of this book; they are fully discussed by Fellows (1968a).

The exact discrimination and identification of shape, when a number of different shapes is presented, develop only slowly. Thus Meyer (1940) studied the behaviour of children of one and a half to five and a half years, required to nest boxes inside each other and to pull them through holes in a board. Clearly these tasks were impossible unless the shapes fitted each other accurately. Children up to two and a half years used a pure trial-and-error procedure, banging the boxes together and never succeeding in fitting them. At three to four years children began to try and fit the shapes to each other, but they did not work out beforehand how to match the shapes until over four years. A similar result was obtained by Venger (1964), who also found complete trial-and-error behaviour at two years, but some direct matching of shapes between two and three years.

It would seem that in younger children, using vision alone, perception is *global*, and even with quite simple shapes the characteristics of outline cannot be analysed from the whole pattern. Thus Ames *et al.* (1953) found that in responses to the Rorschach ink-blots children of two years perceived the forms of the blots as wholes, in an inexact and vague manner. But children often assist their visual perception of shape by *tactile perception*. In particular they trace the outline with one finger, which calls attention to its form. Thus Gellerman (1933) showed that a two-year-old child could learn to identify the shape of a triangle by tracing it with her finger, and could subsequently recognize it when it was turned upside down or reversed from white to black. Luria (1961) also found that children under five years had great difficulty in remembering the differences between pairs of shapes unless they handled them and felt their contours. If they did this, and also named the shapes, errors even with confusing shapes such as irregular quadrilaterals were almost eliminated at three to four years. Thus it would seem that tactile handling is of assistance in the identification of shape in so far as it reinforces the exact *perception of contour*. But the tactile impressions are not very important in themselves, after the period of early infancy in which they convey information about solidity, surface texture, etc. Tactile percep-

Original   Copies

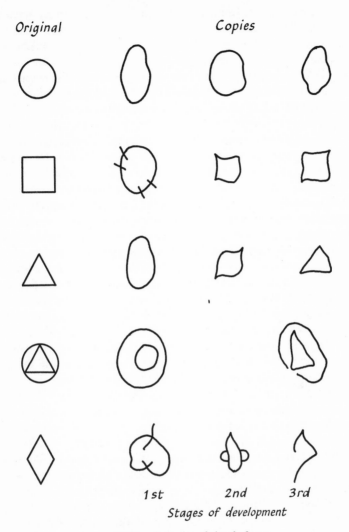

1st   2nd   3rd

Stages of development

FIG. I Children's copies of simple forms
(*After* Piaget and Inhelder (1956) pp. 54, 56, 57, 58, 75)

tion of form is always less efficient than is visual perception, which in adults completely predominates over the former. Thus when the tactile perception of a shape conflicts with a distorted visual perception, it is the latter which determines the observer's impression of shape.

It might be supposed that *copying of shapes* would also stress their outline and lead to accurate perception. But this is not so. Children can usually match shapes more correctly than they can copy them. They begin to identify simple shapes like circles, squares and triangles at an early age, as we have noted. Yet Piaget and Inhelder (1956) found that copying of these was notably deficient in young children. Up to four years there was some representation of form in copying only with so-called 'topological' shapes, in which there was a distinction between that which is inside and that which is outside (see Fig. 1). At four to five years some distinction appeared between circular and straight line figures; and at five to six years the square, circle and triangle emerged clearly. But the diamond could not be reproduced accurately until six years or over. Now it may be argued that these errors are made because the child lacks drawing skill; and indeed Lovell (1959) did find that straight-sided figures could be reproduced correctly, using match-sticks, at an earlier age than by drawing. Lovell did not indeed confirm the order of development obtained by Piaget and Inhelder. Thus among the children he studied, circles were reproduced correctly as early as topo-logical shapes, which, he suggested, were easily characterized by their gaps and holes. However, it is probable that the difficulty of copying depends not so much on lack of skill in drawing as in the necessity of observing accurately all the attributes of the model, to an extent which is unnecessary in discrimination or even in identification. In the case of the diamond, angles and slant of sides must be accurately observed and reproduced; and this seems particularly difficult for young children.

The gradual development of the capacity for accurate perception and copying of outline forms was systematically assessed by Graham *et al.* (1960), who presented children aged three to five years with the shapes shown in Fig. 2. They did not state which forms were correctly copied at which ages. But the difficulty of copying increased more or less in the order in which the shapes were given, that is to say, with increasing complexity. Beery (1968) also found that accuracy of repro-duction decreased with the complexity of irregular outline figures between the ages of six to ten years, whereafter it remained more or less constant.

Graham *et al.* also assessed the accuracy with which certain charac-teristics of shape were copied, as shown in Table 1. Here 'form' means anything more than a scribble. Then came the distinction between open and closed figures; straight and curved lines; whether the right number of parts was shown; whether they were organized together in their correct spatial relations; whether they were correctly orientated to the background; whether size was correct; and whether angles were correctly reproduced. From these data it would appear that improvement with increasing age was gradual, without any sudden jump as indicated by

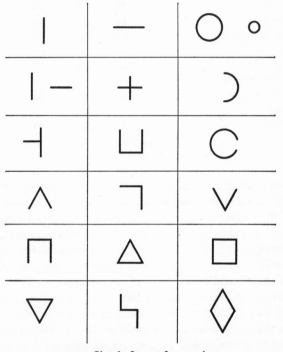

FIG. 2 Simple figures for copying
(*After* Graham *et al.* (1960) p. 342)

Piaget and Inhelder. However, it is interesting that the open-closed distinction developed particularly early. But also some arrangement of the parts in relation to one another appeared before the child was able to reproduce these accurately, suggesting an early appreciation of essential configuration. Even orientation was fairly well observed, and it was only the reproduction of angles, and especially acute angles, which continued to be notably inaccurate.

These findings may be compared with those of E. J. Gibson *et al.*

(1962), who employed the technique of shape differentiation. They selected twelve 'letter-like' forms (see Fig. 3), and presented each of these with twelve 'transformations'. The transformations employed changes from straight to curved lines and *vice versa*; from broken to

Shape characteristic	Per cent correct at year				
	3	$3\frac{1}{2}$	4	$4\frac{1}{2}$	5
Form	51	61	83	88	88
Open-closed	50	62	75	77	84
Straight-curved	54	61	65	66	77
No. of parts	36	44	55	62	71
Organization	53	69	76	78	86
Orientation	41	41	57	60	67
Size	36	29	49	52	53
Angles	8	16	25	35	39

TABLE I

closed lines and *vice versa*; and changes of tilt, rotation, reversal and inversion. Children aged four to eight years were then required to match each of the original standard forms against a group containing the standard form and its transformations. The errors in matching decreased from fifty-eight at four years to twenty at eight years, but they varied considerably in kind. Errors of break and close were few throughout; errors of straight and curved lines, of rotation and reversal were high at four years, but decreased to nearly zero at eight years; and errors of tilt remained high throughout. Now these shapes are considerably more complex than were those of Graham *et al.* But because discrimination and matching are easier than copying, accuracy was good at an early age, and only orientation remained uncertain at eight years.

(2) Form Perception in Adults

We see then that perception of form becomes increasingly more accurate and rapid with increase in age; although, as we shall discuss in Section (6) of this chapter, notable inaccuracies persist in perception of the visual illusions. Adults of course perceive and identify simple forms immediately in normal conditions. But in 'impoverished' conditions, for instance in low illumination, brief exposure or exposure at a distance, perception is delayed; and it is then possible to investigate the comparative ease of perception and identification of even very simple forms such as the circle, square, triangle, etc.* It then appears that different experimenters disagree as to which of these is the easiest to perceive. Hochberg *et al.* (1948), presenting silhouette forms, found that the threshold for recognition was lowest with the simplest form, the circle; then for a

FIG. 3 'Letter-like' forms
(*After* E. J. Gibson *et al.* (1962) p. 898)

rectangle and then for a cross. Bitterman *et al.* (1954) using the same technique, also found the lowest threshold for the circle, and then, in order, triangle, T-shape, square and diamond, cross. Casperson (1950) measured the number of times that forms were correctly recognized at a distance, and obtained the order of correct recognition as: triangle, cross and rectangle, star, diamond. Though it is possible that some differences in results occurred as the consequence of differences in experimental technique, the principal factors involved would appear to have been size (figures should be equated for area) and *simplicity versus complexity*, as measured by the ratio of perimeter to area. This is minimal

* The majority of the data presented in these and following chapters were obtained by means of tachistoscopic exposure. Either the material was first presented in very short exposures with durations of a few milli-seconds, the time of exposure then being gradually increased until the material was perceived. Or in other cases, intensity of illumination was gradually increased. More complex material was sometimes presented initially with rather longer exposures, and the number of correct responses or the number of errors scored. Other techniques employed were variation in the distance of the stimulus, and variation in the degree of blur.

with the circle. Whereas Hochberg *et al.* and Bitterman *et al.* found that the simplest figure, the circle, was most readily perceived, Casperson considered that more complex forms were easier. When complexity is measured by the dimension, the number of sides, of an irregular polygonal figure, it would appear that ease of perception is greatest with figures of medium complexity. Thus Crook (1957) exposed four-, eight- and sixteen-sided polygons in decreasing degrees of blur, and found that the eight-sided figures were the most readily perceived.

But with other types of shape, the amount of *critical detail* may be a more important factor, which seems to influence comparison between figures such as the circle and rectangle, and the cross and star. It may well be that in some circumstances the simplicity of the former is the most important factor, and in others the form quality, the characteristic details of outline of the cross and star. Hence the disagreement between the results of Hochberg *et al.*, Bitterman *et al.* and Casperson. A similar conflict of results appeared between Fox (1957), who found the threshold with increasing illumination to be higher for the cross than for the circle, square and triangle, and Kristofferson (1957a) who found that a star was more easily identifiable than a square and triangle, these being equal to the cross.

Finally, it should be noted that in all experiments in which a gradual increase of intensity of illumination or decrease of blur are employed, the factor of *contrast* between figure and ground may play an important part in the discrimination of the former from the latter. According to Adams *et al.* (1954), contrast is a more important factor than any other when identification with increasing illumination is involved. But in other experimental settings, form quality may again be found to predominate. Thus Boynton and Bush (1956) showed that when a critical shape had to be picked out from a number of other 'confusion' shapes, the cross was more often detected correctly than were the triangle, quadrilateral or pentagon.

(3) Gestalt Qualities

We have noted that according to the Gestalt psychologists the first stage in perception is the emergence of the *'figure'* from the *'ground'*. Until this has occurred, no real perception is possible, and therefore it is usually considered to be primary and fundamental in the perception of form. However, experiment has shown that children may be less well able than are adults to differentiate figure from ground. Thus Gollin (1956) presented pictures of real objects, with cross-hatching over the contours, each for a period of four seconds. The number of these perceived and identified increased from one at two and a half to three and a half years, to five at four and a half to five and a half years. Adults, given only a one second exposure, identified eleven. Munsinger and Gummerman (1967) found that ten-year-old children were better able than were seven-year-olds to detect shapes which were obscured by lines drawn across them, either regularly or at random. However, once the figure is identified, it may be less labile and open to modification in children. Thus Elkind and Scott (1962) found that reversal of ambiguous figures, for instance of the Gestalt vase or profile, were perceived to an increasing extent as age increased from four to eleven years.

However, another important feature of Gestalt theory is the postulation that there exists an inherent tendency to organize what is perceived into *configurations*, in accordance with certain principles, in such a manner that what is perceived may not accurately correspond with the external stimulus. Organization takes place in accordance with the *Law of Prägnanz* ('goodness'), which states that configurations tend to appear as clear, impressive and stable as possible. This may take place through simplification whenever possible, and one form of simplification is through increase of symmetry and regularity. With other stimulus forms, the factors of closure, continuity, inclusiveness and good articulation may operate in such a manner as to integrate the parts of the stimulus figures into unified wholes.* Even when the stimulus consists of scattered parts, such as a number of dots distributed over the field, there will be a tendency to associate these either through *proximity* (stimuli close together will be grouped together) or through *similarity* (similar stimuli will be grouped together) (Wertheimer, 1923).

Wertheimer demonstrated the effects of similarity and proximity in his 'fence' figure. These have also been investigated using rows and columns of dots, the distances apart of which can be varied. Hochberg and Hardy (1960) exposed rows and columns of translucent dots; the proximity of the rows could be varied, and the relative brightness of alternate columns. When the rows were near together, there was a tendency to perceive the figure in terms of rows, but if the brightness differences between columns was increased, similarity operated to produce the perception of columns. The nearer the rows together, the greater was the brightness difference necessary for perception of columns through enhancement of similarity.

In another experiment with rows and columns of dots, Krech and

---

* These factors are discussed more fully by Vernon (1952).

Calvin (1953) investigated individual differences in the perception of organization according to proximity. They presented the figure with the rows slightly further apart than the columns, and required their observers to reproduce these on peg boards, arguing that reproduction in an undifferentiated mass showed less capacity for organization than reproduction as in the original. In fact they found that observers who made the former type of reproduction were of lower intelligence than those who made the latter. This result was confirmed by Pickrel (1957). This finding seems to contradict the theory that perception of configurations is a fundamental and basic capacity, suggesting that some types of perceptual organization necessitate a higher level of ability.

However, it might be supposed that young *children*, who perceive the exact characteristics of form less clearly than do adults, would be particularly prone to the effects of the Law of Prägnanz. As regards simplicity, this is probably true; excessive detail is overlooked by them. The ability to copy complex irregular outline figures decreases in accuracy with increase in the number of sides, and increases with age, thereafter remaining more or less constant, as we noted in the experiment of Beery (1968). However, simplification may not be a straightforward process. Osterrieth (1945) found that in copying a very complex form, details were reproduced without relation to each other or to the total structure until eleven to twelve years. Graham *et al.* (1960) also found little evidence with their much simpler forms as to a gradual decrease in the effects of Prägnanz, that is to say in tendencies to simplification and closure (continuity); and there was only a slight decrease in the tendency towards symmetry. But although in these experiments correct reproduction of open and closed forms appeared at an early age, Rosca (1959) found that children of three years were unable to detect lack of completion in fragmented pictures and in figures with gaps. As regards globality of perception, Elkind *et al.* (1964) presented to children of four and a half to nine years pictures in which both the whole figure and also the parts of which it was constructed were representational; for instance, carrots and leaves were grouped together to form an aeroplane. The youngest children saw the parts more readily than the whole. This tendency decreased up to nine years, more of the wholes being seen. However, the parts appeared more integrated as figures than did the wholes.

That children do not always find it easy to *close* and *complete* forms also appeared in an experiment by Gollin (1960), who presented drawings of real objects with incomplete outlines in a series with the most incomplete shown first. The points at which the children were able to identify the objects were recorded; and it was found that these occurred later in the series for the younger children. Piaget and Stettler-von Albertini (1954) carried out an extensive investigation of the procedures adopted by children required to complete and identify figures with mutilated outlines (see Fig. 4a). Naturally the more complex the figures, the harder they were.to identify. In completing the mutilated figures, the younger children tended to draw a straight line across the gap, regardless of the appearance of the remainder of the figure. But others made fanciful additions, sometimes in order to make the figures represent real objects. Figures with large pieces of the sides missing were seldom recognized until six years (Fig. 4b); but those with dotted outlines were somewhat easier. Interlaced discontinuous forms were harder again, and were generally not recognized until seven to nine years (Fig. 4c). The outlines of the separate shapes were joined up in an irregular manner; or else parts of these outlines were joined to produce a large number of small forms, in accordance with the effect of proximity.

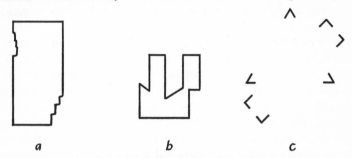

a   b   c

FIG. 4 Mutilated and incomplete forms
(*After* Piaget and Stettler-von Albertini (1954) pp. 211, 216, 224)

Equal difficulty was manifested by children in the *analysis of the parts of complex configurations*, and the discrimination of parts within the

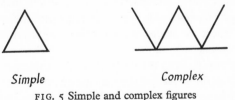

Simple   Complex

FIG. 5 Simple and complex figures
(*After* Ghent (1956) p. 580)

whole. In certain circumstances, as with Gottschaldt's original figures (1926), it may be very difficult for adults to extract simple *embedded figures* which form continuous parts of complex wholes. But this failure to analyse out the parts of a pattern is even more noticeable in children. Thus Leuba (1940) showed that children of one and a half to five years found it more difficult to pick out a box containing a piece of chocolate when it formed a continuous part of a line, a circle, a square or a triangle, than when it stood just outside these figures. Only when the box was at the end of the line were they usually able to find it. Ghent (1956) used a technique similar to that of Gottschaldt, though considerably easier to perform and with less complex material (see Fig. 5). She presented the simple and complex figures simultaneously, and asked the child to trace out in the complex figure the part which looked like the simple figure. Children of four years could seldom do this and errors were numerous even at eight years. Goodenough and Eagle (1963) used meaningful figures, such as a man, a car, a boat, each constructed from wooden pieces, one of which, the simple figure, could be removed by pulling a knob attached to it. The mean number of failures decreased from 37 per cent at five and a half years to 19 per cent at eight years. Thus even with this apparently easy task, perception of parts within the whole is difficult for children.

The same difficulty is apparent in *uncultured peoples*. Thus Schwitzgebel (1962) found that Zulu adults were significantly slower than were Dutch-speaking Caucasian (white) adults to extract simple from complex Gottschaldt figures, although both groups were relatively isolated and uneducated. The capacity to perform this task is in fact related to intelligence in American adults (Teuber and Weinstein, 1956).

The experimental data then seem to show that in some circumstances there is a tendency towards globality and failure of analysis in children; but in other conditions, *integration* of whole patterns is equally defective. Thus Furth and Mendez (1963), comparing the reproductions of various Gestalt forms by children aged nine and sixteen years, found that the younger children tended to see the figures more globally, with less differentiation of parts; whereas the older organized them more effectively in terms of similarity and closure. That older children were better able to grasp the organization of and inter-relationship between parts of complex figures was shown by Crain and Werner (1950), who required children of six to twelve years to reproduce patterns made of marbles (see Fig. 6), by placing similar marbles in a frame. Whereas the younger children reproduced parts of these patterns piecemeal, the older ones analysed the whole pattern into its fundamental constituents and reproduced these. The amount of perceptual organization increased from 18 per cent at six to seven years to 48 per cent at eleven to twelve years.

When we study the operation of Gestalt tendencies in *adults*, we find again that they do not always function as universally and straight-forwardly as the Gestalt psychologists suggested. We saw that in the perception of simple figures (see p. 34) the factor of simplicity was paramount in some cases; but in others critical detail defining form quality was more significant. There can be little doubt that perception is facilitated by figural properties such as symmetry and regularity; though a somewhat different explanation of these phenomena will be discussed in the next section. With more complex line figures, *good*

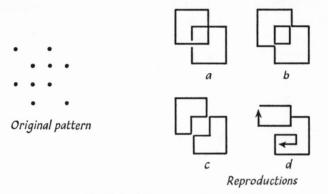

Original pattern

a *b*

c *d*

Reproductions

FIG. 6 Marble-board pattern and reproductions
(*After* Crain and Werner (1950) p. 222)

articulation would appear to be important; that is to say, the relevance and coherence of the internal detail with the pattern as a whole (Asch *et al.*, 1960). Indeed, it was suggested that the rapid and easy perception of real objects may be related to the invariant coherence and relevance of their peculiar properties to their total form.

(4) Uncertainty and Redundancy

In recent years the problems of perception of forms and patterns have been reformulated in terms of 'information theory'. The principle concepts utilized are those of 'uncertainty' and 'redundancy'. The amount of *'information'* conveyed in any percept depends on its uncertainty, that is to say, the number of possible alternatives which might be perceived.* But if different aspects of the percept convey the same type of information, they are said to be redundant. For instance, in figures

---

* Only a brief outline is given here as to the application of 'information theory' to perceptual problems. There is a fuller discussion in Forgus (1966) and the whole topic is presented in detail by Garner (1962).

D

symmetrical about an axis, the form characteristics of one half of the figure are identical with, and therefore redundant to, those of the other half. But redundant information is given by any area homogeneous in colour and brightness; and by any contour consistent in direction or shape (Attneave, 1954). On the other hand, essential and non-redundant information is given by a delimiting edge or contour, where colour and brightness change abruptly, and at points in a contour where direction changes. This is relevant also to the holes in Piaget's topological shapes. The main characteristics of form are provided by these points of change of direction. Even forms of real objects can be convincingly represented by plotting the points of maximum change in direction of contour and joining these by straight lines (see Fig. 7). Attneave (1957) prepared a set of irregular silhouette forms by joining points at random on a large

FIG. 7 Cat
(*After* Attneave (1954) p. 185)

grid, with straight or curved lines. He then presented these to a large number of observers who judged them for *complexity*. It was found that the principal factors making for complexity were, first, the numbers of independent angles (of straight-line figures) or turns (of curved figures); secondly, the degree of symmetry; and, thirdly, the differences of angle between successive turns. When these factors were held constant, no difference in complexity appeared between the curved and straight-line figures.

Now if these different aspects of complexity are taken into account, some of the findings described earlier may be explained. With a variety of other complex forms, however, it has been demonstrated that the effects of redundancy and of complexity may differ, according to the type of task in which they are operating. In a number of tasks it was found in general that in discrimination the more random, unconstrained and heterogeneous patterns were differentiated more quickly than the more regular and symmetrical, because the former possessed more distinctive cues, which were reduced by redundancy (Anderson and Leonard, 1958). However, redundancy might facilitate discrimination in the presence of visual 'noise'; that is to say, when patterns were obscured by blur, random dots, etc. (Rappaport, 1957). Redundant figures were also easier to identify than irregular figures (Anderson and Leonard, 1958; Attneave, 1955). The latter were particularly difficult to identify in short exposures when there was insufficient time to observe all their details (Garner, 1962), and if presented at a distance, when details were not clear (Krulee, 1958). In matching irregular forms obscured by visual 'noise' to a standard, an intermediate degree of complexity was found to be optimal (Crook, 1957). Eight-sided figures were matched more easily that were four- or sixteen-sided figures. But it is possible to vary complexity and redundancy independently. Thus Deese (1956) presented irregular and regular forms, some of which were simple, possessing few turns of contour, and others complex, with many turns. Among the regular forms, the more complex were most readily identified in immediate recognition. But when the forms had to be remembered for recognition subsequently, the simple were more accurately identified.

Thus it appears that with certain kinds of form, discrimination and identification are to a great extent functions of complexity or redundancy. But other functions may be important, for instance compactness, as determined by ratio of perimeter to area; elongated and compact figures are readily discriminated from each other. Another factor making for ease of perception is the jaggedness of the outline (Michels and Zusne, 1965). In making judgments of similarity of figures, number of turns (complexity) might be the main factor involved, but some observers used angular variability and compactness in addition (Silver *et al.*, 1966). There are considerable individual differences in making these judgments, which may also be reflected in variability in the ease of perception of different types of form.

It is obvious that a good Gestalt is characterized by a high degree of internal redundancy, and is inversely proportional to the amount of information required to define it. Not only symmetry but also good articulation, continuity and similarity of parts all reduce uncertainty. On the other hand, uncertainty and complexity may be increased by increase in the number of discriminable different parts within a complex pattern (Terwilliger, 1963). Nevertheless, as Heckhausen (1964) has pointed out, there are considerable difficulties in treating such patterns solely in terms of information theory. They may be perceived in accordance with a breakdown into 'natural parts'. Thus Arnoult and Price (1961) found that, although errors in matching complex dot patterns increased with increasing similarity, the actual confusions made depended on the sub-patterns in which observers grouped the dots.

Experiments by Hochberg and McAlister (1953) and Hochberg and Brooks (1960) suggested that with ambiguous figures the particular figure perceived might be that which required the least information to define it. Hochberg and McAlister exposed the figures shown in Fig. 8, and required observers to state whether these were perceived as two- or three-dimensional. The percentage of two-dimensional responses increased from about one per cent with the first two figures to 60 per cent with the fourth. This figure shows a high degree of goodness and redundancy as a two-dimensional pattern, but the first is redundant only if perceived as a three-dimensional cube. This result was confirmed with other figures by Hochberg and Brooks. But Dinnerstein (1965) found that when the second of these figures was rotated through 180°, it appeared two-dimensional to 79 per cent of observers when shown alone, though to only 38 per cent when it followed the first figure, which appeared predominantly cubical. It may be therefore that the manner in which the first two figures are perceived does depend to some extent on their identification as reproductions of cubes.

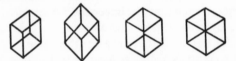

FIG. 8 Two- and three-dimensional forms
(*After* Hochberg and McAlister (1953) p. 363)

Uncertainty is also related to the number of possible *alternatives* in the set of figures presented. Figures chosen from a small set could be discriminated more quickly than could figures in a large set (Hyman and Hake, 1954). Garner (1962) pointed out that goodness may be related to the small number of possible alternatives; hence the goodness of the circle, which is a unique figure. Garner and Clement (1963) presented a set of dotted patterns which varied as to the number of possible alternatives, and found that goodness was judged to be less for patterns belonging to very numerous groups of similar patterns. Thus Fig. 9a is unique in the sense that it appears the same whatever its spatial orientation; but Fig. 9b varies with rotation.

It is obviously difficult to apply concepts of information theory to the perception of natural objects in the normal environment as they have been applied to the perception of meaningless patterns. The number of possible alternatives is very large, but so also is the redundancy of information provided by any one object. Moreover, objects cannot be differentiated from each other in quantitative terms, as in information theory, but vary qualitatively; so also do the constituent parts of different examples of the same type of object. Thus it is necessary to consider separately the perception of meaningful objects and material. In adults such perception is closely related to verbal processes. Therefore in the next chapter we shall discuss the effects of meaning and verbalization.

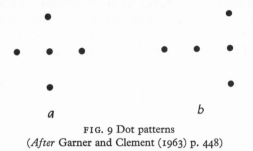

FIG. 9 Dot patterns
(*After* Garner and Clement (1963) p. 448)

(5) Orientation of Form

But we must now consider an important and debatable aspect of form perception, namely its relation to the orientation of the form, and the problem of alteration in perceived form with change in orientation. Now we know that forms preserve their essential characteristics and are readily recognized if their size is altered; so also are forms projected on to different areas of the retina. Indeed, Dees and Grindley (1947) found that often transpositions of size and retinal area were not noticed by observers. But forms may cease to retain their identity if their orientation is changed – if they are tilted, inverted or reversed in relation to the spatial coordinates, for instance, of the page on which they are printed. This can be seen by comparing the shape in Fig. 10a with its tilted version, Fig. 10b. The former is usually identified as a 'dog', the latter as the 'head of a chef'; whereas orientation at 45° is ambiguous, and either identification may be made, or neither. Rock (1956) found that it was the position in relation to the margin of the page which determined the identification. Observers who looked at Figs 10a and 10b with the head tilted through 90° still saw them as a 'dog' and a 'chef's head' respectively.

There has been considerable discussion as to the effects on *children's perceptions* of variation in orientation. Do they recognize objects and shapes equally well whatever the orientation, and do they notice if orientation has been changed? Or do forms and objects appear to them different, and therefore harder to recognize, in altered orientation? Again there seems to be some conflict of evidence. With regard to *inversion*, Hanton (1955) found that children of two years had no more difficulty in naming pictures of people, houses, etc., when they were upside down than when they were upright. But whereas all the older children remarked on the inversion, few of the younger ones noticed it. Nevertheless, they usually turned them right side up when asked to sort them. On the other hand, according to Ghent (1961), children of three to four years recognized inverted realistic pictures more slowly than non-inverted, from among a set of pictures. With meaningless shapes, Ghent and Bernstein (1961) found that recognition of inverted shapes

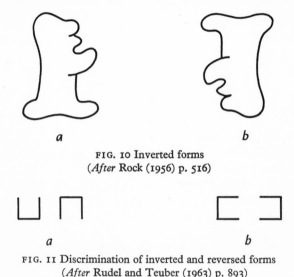

a   b

FIG. 10 Inverted forms
(*After* Rock (1956) p. 516)

a   b

FIG. 11 Discrimination of inverted and reversed forms
(*After* Rudel and Teuber (1963) p. 893)

was harder for three-year-olds, but less so for four to five-year-olds. And Wohlwill and Wiener (1964) showed that confusion of inverted shapes seldom occurred at four to four and a half years. Thus it would seem that during the early stages of learning to identify objects, children may learn that objects retain their identity even when inverted. The perception of inversion in pictures and meaningless shapes may be somewhat more difficult; but even this develops quite early.

More confusion would seem to occur with *reversed* shapes, as Wohlwill and Wiener (1964) found. Rudel and Teuber (1963) showed that in three- to four-year-olds discrimination between the parts of Fig. 11a was readily learnt; but discrimination in 11b was not perfect even at eight years. But Huttenlocher (1967) found that it was the mirror image discrimination which was difficult to learn. Thus discrimination in Figs 12a and 12d was difficult, but in 12b and 12c relatively easy.

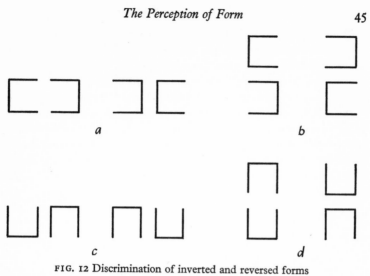

FIG. 12 Discrimination of inverted and reversed forms
(*After* Huttenlocher (1967) p. 360)

Newson (1955) also showed that in a matching task five-year-old children were particularly liable to error with mirror image reversals. The hardest figures to discriminate were those which remained unchanged when rotated through 180° (Fig. 13a). Asymmetrical figures were less difficult (Fig. 13b). Nevertheless, it is obvious that confusion between reversed shapes is more persistent than that between inverted shapes; it is very likely to occur when the child begins to learn to read, for instance

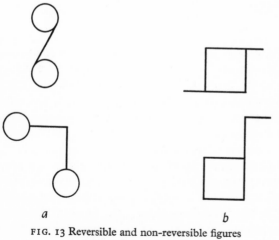

FIG. 13 Reversible and non-reversible figures
(*After* Newson (1955))

between the letters 'b' and 'd'. Although special training may enable children to respond correctly to a particular set of reversed shapes, such as Newson's, this is not necessarily transferred to others.

We noted that E. J. Gibson *et al.* (1962) found that discrimination between *tilted* shapes was ineffectual even at eight years. Possibly the same type of confusion is that which occurs with oblique lines sloped in opposite directions (Fig. 14). Rudel and Teuber showed that only one four-year-old learnt to make this discrimination. Over (1967) found that even when children could discriminate between these two tilted lines placed side by side they could not match them correctly against other

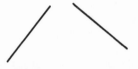

FIG. 14 Reversed orientation
(*After* Rudel and Teuber (1963) p. 893)

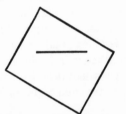

FIG. 15 Effect of framework on perceived orientation
(*After* Piaget (1961) p. 223)

lines, nor could they identify them from memory (Over and Over, 1967). Children are also liable to be confused by the orientation of lines relative to a surrounding framework; for instance, they could not judge correctly the orientation of a line contained within a slanted framework, as in Fig. 15 (Piaget, 1961). Thus the immediately contiguous framework of the tilted square excited a stronger influence than did the framework of the page on which it was printed.

Adults would appear to be more strongly affected by *inversion* and *reversal* than by tilting. Thus it is possible to read a page of print, though slowly, when it is tilted through a considerable angle, but not if it is inverted or reversed. Though the habit of discrimination between reversed letters such as 'b' and 'd' is, as we noted, acquired slowly, once acquired it operates strongly. Even capital letters are difficult to identify when inverted or reversed (Robinson *et al.*, 1964). Complex meaningless shapes exposed for ten seconds only were difficult to identify when reversed from left to right, and almost impossible when inverted (Mooney, 1958).

But also adults may find difficulty in identifying pictures and shapes when they are *orientated at 90°* to their normal position. Rock (1966) found that pictures of real objects, when turned through 90°, with all surroundings obscured, could be identified in only 15 per cent of cases, as compared with 66 per cent when they were upright. Using representations of real objects and shapes which represented the contours of countries and states of the U.S.A., Gibson and Robinson (1935) found that the latter were identified in 43 per cent of cases when they were upright, but hardly at all in any other position. Whether or not the former were identified in positions other than the upright seemed to depend on the frequency with which they had been perceived in varying positions. Thus pictures of an umbrella, a bone, a key and a trumpet were recognized almost equally well in any orientation. But pictures of a cat, a rabbit, a toy cannon and a sunbonnet were identified in only about 30 to 40 per cent of cases when turned through 90°, 180° or 270°.

Rock and Heimer (1957) presented irregular meaningless figures in the upright position, and then subsequently among a number of others either upright or turned through 90°. The latter were much harder to recognize than were the former. Dees and Grindley (1947) found that the time taken to identify simple patterns increased by 83 per cent when they were rotated through 90°. T and L shapes were harder to identify when turned through 45° than through 90° and 180° (Beck, 1966). It would seem that the retention of the horizontal and vertical positions of the lines was the important factor here.

In conclusion, therefore, it would appear that we have little difficulty in perceiving in changing orientation forms and objects which from infancy upwards we have learnt maintain their identity whatever their spatial orientation. Identification is rather more difficult with objects which are habitually perceived in one particular orientation, the upright position. Meaningless shapes are liable to appear different when orientation is varied. And most difficult of all to recognize in abnormal orientations are shapes such as letters which we have learnt very thoroughly to associate with one particular orientation. That learning to acquire this discrimination is particularly difficult when there is reversal from left to right may be due to the fact that children, not surprisingly, take longer to acquire accurate left-right discrimination than up-down discrimination.

(6) The Visual Illusions

There is one type of form which is almost invariably perceived inaccurately, namely that of the visual illusions. But the errors in perception are not random; there is always a distortion of some particular kind which characterizes the illusion. In many cases, these distortions would appear to be related to some kind of interaction between the parts and the whole figure, or between the parts and one another. Some of the principal illusions are discussed below.*

(a) *The Müller-Lyer Illusion.* The effects on perception of the parts by their inclusion in the whole is illustrated in the Müller-Lyer illusion. Here it would seem impossible to segregate the horizontal lines from the whole figures including the arrowheads or fins. One whole figure is larger than the other, therefore the horizontal line is judged to be longer. It might be supposed that this illusion would be stronger in *children* than in adults, since the former appear in many circumstances to be less well able than the latter to discriminate the parts of a figure from the whole. Vurpillot (1963) has indeed found this to be so, and she quotes the results of other experimenters who obtained a similar finding. However, the effects seem to vary somewhat with the particular form of the illusion figure. Vurpillot's own results and those of several other experimenters were obtained with Brentano's figure (see Fig. 16a), in which the central arrowhead is adjusted until the parts on either side of it appear to be equal. Piaget and Stettler-von Albertini (1950) used the form in Fig. 16b, in which each line with arrowheads was equalized to a plain line. Although children of five to nine years showed the illusion rather more strongly than did adults, there was no regular decrease in its magnitude with increasing age. With the form shown in Fig. 16c, adults obtained no illusion because they saw the two lines as parts of the square (Piaget *et al.*, 1954). But children did perceive the top line as being longer than the bottom one, because they did not extract the square from the whole figure. Finally, Fraisse (1960) compared the magnitude of the illusion obtained with Fig. 16a with that of the 'empty' figure (Fig. 16d). At every age from four to ten years the illusion was greater and more variable with the empty version, but it increased somewhat from four to five years and decreased slightly thereafter. The age differences were not, however, statistically significant. But clearly the children found it harder to make accurate judgments with this disjointed empty figure, suggesting again that closure was difficult for them.

* The horizontal-vertical illusion is discussed in Chapter VII.

The magnitude of the Müller-Lyer illusion also differs between children and adults with regard to the effects of varying the *duration of perception*. In general, the magnitude in adults is greatest if the figure is shown for a single short period, and decreases if presented repeatedly for short intervals, or continuously over a longer period. When presented to children for a single short interval, the magnitude of the illusion

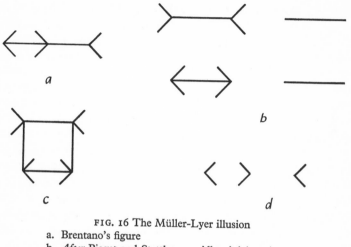

FIG. 16 The Müller-Lyer illusion
a. Brentano's figure
b. *After* Piaget and Stettler-von Albertini (1950) p. 4
c. *After* Piaget et al. (1954) p. 159
d. The empty figure

decreased from four to five years, then rose at six to eight years, and finally decreased again (Hanley and Zerbolio, 1965). When exposed repeatedly, the magnitude increased for children of five to six years up to about the fifth repetition and thereafter remained constant (Noelting, 1960). At seven years there was no such augmentation with repetition; and from eight years the magnitude decreased. It was argued by Noelting and by Vurpillot (1963) that the organization of the figure was not perceived immediately by the younger children, and that a certain period of time was necessary for perception of its structure. This would also explain the results of Hanley and Zerbolio. Once organized, however, the figure exerted its maximum effects, which children could not counteract by analysis and discrimination of the horizontal lines from the whole, as could older children and adults. But the analysis can be manipulated and its effects varied in adults. Brunswik (1935) found that the magnitude of the illusion was significantly reduced when he instructed observers to adopt an *analytical attitude*, asking them to consider the horizontal lines as the important part of the figures. Gardner and Long (1961) obtained a similar result. Day (1962), using the empty figure of Fig. 16d, showed that the magnitude did not decrease with repeated viewing when the figure was fixated, or when instructions were given to match the apparent form of the spaces between the arrowheads. But it did do so when unrestricted viewing was permitted, and instructions given to match physical equality. Thus it would appear again that the illusion depends for its effect at least in part on the extent to which the horizontal lines are analysed out from the whole figure and compared with each other. This type of 'perceptual activity' has been hypothesized by Piaget (1961) to develop only slowly in children. It will be discussed more fully in Chapter V.

But the magnitude of the illusion also seems to depend on the exact physical *dimensions* of the figure and its parts. With a horizontal line of 20 cm., it decreased as the angle between the oblique lines of the arrowheads and the horizontal line increased from 30°-120°, and increased as their lengths increased from 1-4 cm. (Dewar, 1967a). It also decreased more with repeated exposures with relatively small angles between oblique and horizontal lines (Dewar, 1967b). Other variations occurred with the distance of the observer (Hotopf, 1966). On the other hand, the illusion was not destroyed when the arrowheads were replaced by various other shapes (see Figs 17a, 17b and 17c).* But although, as we saw, the illusion might be greater with the empty figure, it reversed in direction with the figure shown in Fig. 17d when the horizontal line was very short by comparison with the total gap (Fellows, 1967). The reversed illusion became maximal when the line was about half the size of the gap, and decreased to zero when it approached the limits of the gap. This effect was attributed by Fellows to the fact that objects in enclosed spaces look larger than those in open spaces; the in-going arrowheads provide an enclosed space, whereas the outgoing do not. Thus with the latter there was no illusion, as shown by comparing it with a line without arrowheads. The effect of enclosure in increasing the apparent length of a line was demonstrated by Fellows (1968b) in a rectangular setting. And Cohen (1967) found that the apparent velocity of a spot of light

* This observation would seem to dispose of the somewhat far-fetched argument of Piaget (1961) that the illusion can be explained by supposing that each part of the traditional Müller-Lyer figure consists of two trapezia, constructed by joining the points of the fins by virtual lines. A further argument accounts for the distorted perception of trapezia. However, it might be supposed that the illusion is due to the inequality of virtual lines joining the points of the fins. Then in the forms in Fig. 17a and 17b such virtual lines would be tangential to the curves.

moving along a path between two inward pointing arrowheads was
greater than that between two outward pointing arrowheads – an effect
also attributed to enclosure.

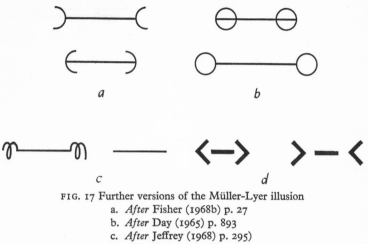

FIG. 17 Further versions of the Müller-Lyer illusion
   a. *After* Fisher (1968b) p. 27
   b. *After* Day (1965) p. 893
   c. *After* Jeffrey (1968) p. 295)
   d. *After* Fellows (1967) p. 209

Interesting experiments were carried out by Boyce and West (1967),
in which eye fixations and eye movements were recorded when observers
successively fixated the ends of the lines in the Müller-Lyer figures.
They were required to look from one end of the line to the other; and it
was found that the movements were longer for the figure with the outward pointing arrowhead than for that with the inward pointing arrowhead. Moreover, the difference of length of movement increased as the
illusion increased in magnitude with decrease in the angles of the arrowheads. If, however, the two figures were exposed independently, when
no illusion occurred, there was no difference in extent of movement.

Now it must not be supposed that the illusion depends on eye movements; rather, they depend on perception of the illusion. There would
appear to be several possible causes for the variations in the illusion.
Attempts have been made to explain them in terms of 'constancy
scaling', a hypothesis which will be discussed in Chapter VIII. But this
hypothesis also fails to account for many of the effects described above.
(b) *The Ponzo Illusion.* This illusion, in which the cross line nearer to
the apex of the two obliques tends to appear longer than the cross line
further from the apex, would also seem to depend upon the relation of
the parts to the whole figure (Fig. 18a). The parts are not integrated
within the whole; the inner lines are contrasted with the outer. Thus the

illusion depends on the discrimination of the parts from the whole. It is therefore not surprising to find that *children* under five years perceived little or no illusion, and that its magnitude increased steadily thereafter

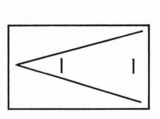 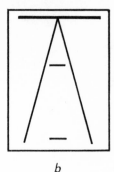

a   b

FIG. 18 The Ponzo illusion
(*After* Hanley and Zerbolio (1965) p. 443)

a   b

FIG. 19 Further versions of the Ponzo illusion
(*After* Fisher (1968a) pp. 212, 215)

(Leibowitz and Judesch, 1967). Presumably the younger children viewed the figure as a whole, without discriminating its parts. However, some doubt is thrown on this hypothesis by the finding of Hanley and Zerbolio (1965) that with a modified version of the figure (Fig. 18b) the illusion decreased with increase in age.

Fisher (1968a) showed that in adults the illusion depended on the varying distances between the oblique lines and the ends of the cross lines. Thus in Fig. 19a there was a gradually increasing under-estimation of the lower cross lines from top to bottom of the figure. But cross lines below the level of the oblique lines were not affected. Furthermore, the illusion could be obtained with a single oblique (Fig. 19b); and the effect of two oblique lines equalled the sum of the effects of two single obliques. Fisher (1968b) also showed that the illusion persisted, though possibly to a slighter extent, in the versions shown in Figs 20a, 20b and

20c.* The magnitudes of the illusion in the different versions are shown below as the adjustments, in mm., necessary to make the lower horizontal line appear equal in length to the upper horizontal, of 100 mm.:

Fig. 18a	Fig. 20a	Fig. 20b	Fig. 20c
13·4	12·6	10·9	8·6

(c) *The Poggendorff Illusion.* This illusion (see Fig. 21a) seems to depend on a capacity, not to analyse the parts within the whole as with the Müller-Lyer illusion, but to integrate the whole figure together in such

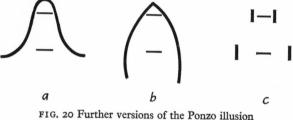

a   *b*   *c*

FIG. 20 Further versions of the Ponzo illusion
(*After* Fisher (1968b) p. 25)

a manner that the two oblique lines appear continuous. Thus it is generally found that the further apart the two vertical lines, the greater the magnitude of the illusion. But although this separation could be responsible for a perceived discontinuity in the obliques, it does not account for the fact that the lower oblique line is almost always perceived as emerging too low from the vertical. Why should the intervening mass shift the lower oblique downwards, as appears also in the version shown in Fig. 21b?

Tausch (1954) related the illusion to the observation that the arms of acute angles tend to be over-estimated in length, whereas those of obtuse angles are under-estimated. This he explained further in terms of the constancy-scaling hypothesis (see p. 154). However, the illusion persists in the version shown in Fig. 21c, although according to this hypothesis it should be reversed. It was reversed in Fig. 21d, and destroyed in Fig. 21e (Jeffrey, 1968), which suggests that the angles between the obliques and the central mass are significant. Lastly, Hotopf (1966) combined this illusion with another illusion, the Hering, in which it was shown that not only did a horizontal block, as well as a vertical, displace the obliques but also that the straight lines might themselves be distorted by cross lines at different angles (Fig. 21f). There are other

---

* The latter has come to resemble the version of the Müller-Lyer illusion shown in Fig. 17d.

variations in the Poggendorff illusion, to which we shall refer in connection with the constancy-scaling hypothesis, in Chapter VIII.

The magnitude of the Poggendorff illusion also shows *age changes*. According to Leibowitz and Gwozdecki (1967), it decreased regularly with increasing age from five to ten years. But Vurpillot (1963) found that it increased from five to seven years and then decreased. Possibly it is

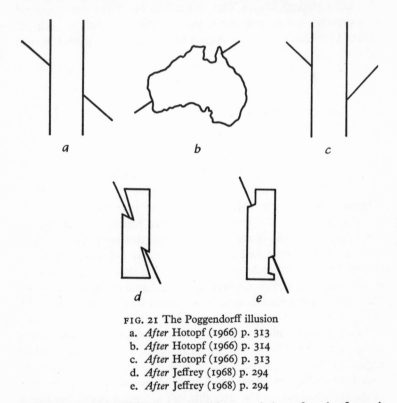

a   b   c

d   e

FIG. 21 The Poggendorff illusion
a. *After* Hotopf (1966) p. 313
b. *After* Hotopf (1966) p. 314
c. *After* Hotopf (1966) p. 313
d. *After* Jeffrey (1968) p. 294
e. *After* Jeffrey (1968) p. 294

labile and variable with younger children, and thereafter the figure is increasingly organized as a single whole.

It has been argued that these illusions appear only in meaningless figures of the type shown above, and therefore are unlikely to produce any inaccuracy of perception in the redundant percepts of ordinary life. Vurpillot (1963) did indeed find that the magnitude of the Poggendorff illusion in the representational picture shown in Fig. 21g, though equal to or even greater than that of the meaningless figure in young children, decreased more rapidly with increase in age. However, the illusion did not altogether disappear; and Fisher and Lucas (1968) have since found that it remains quite markedly in a variety of representational pictures. This does not of course prove that it would appear in real life situations.

It would seem that no one explanation can satisfactorily cover all these illusions, although in many cases they may be related to interactions between the whole figure and the parts of which it is made up. The type of inaccuracy and the nature of the illusion displayed obviously vary

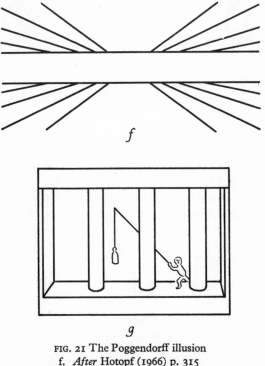

FIG. 21 The Poggendorff illusion
f. *After* Hotopf (1966) p. 315
g. *After* Vurpillot (1963) p. 93

however, from one figure to another in a manner for which there is at present no adequate explanation.

(7) The Effects of Learning on Form Perception

One curious feature observed in perception of the visual illusions is that the illusory error persists, and is not eliminated by prolonged inspection. It is true that with frequent or lengthy inspections the judged amount of the illusion may decrease; but this appears to be the result of a deliberate compensation on the part of the observer, and not of improved accuracy of perception. However, it would seem that in certain other cases we

E

may learn to perceive more accurately and in greater detail, usually through the effects of 'feedback'. The observer finds through further examination of the stimulus pattern or as the result of his responses to an event that his perception was inaccurate or incomplete. He either corrects himself then and there, or does so at a repetition of the event.

FIG. 22 Discrimination learning
(*After* Gibson and Gibson (1955) p. 36)
a. Standard figure
b. Variables

We have noted that a general improvement in accuracy occurs during the perceptual development of children, in part as the result of maturation; but this effect is probably combined with learning and checked by feedback. Gibson and Gibson (1955) considered that such an improvement might occur through learning in adults also, and that sensory

FIG. 23 Identification learning
(*After* Bevan and Zener (1952) p. 436)

discrimination of the objective characteristics of stimuli might become finer and more accurate with repetition of stimulation, as with wine and tea tasters. So also the correspondence between perceived brightness, colour, etc., and the physical characteristics of stimuli might be improved by learning in laboratory experiments.

Gibson and Gibson carried out an experiment in which observers were shown a scribbled pattern (see Fig. 22d) for five seconds, and then series of similar and dissimilar scribbles (Fig. 22a), together with four replicas of the initial pattern. They were required to state which members of the series they had seen before, but were not informed whether they were right or wrong. All the observers learnt to discriminate accurately when the series was repeated several times: for 6·7 trials on the average by children aged six to eight years, 4·7 trials by children aged eight and a half to eleven years, and 3·1 trials by adults. Bevan and Zener (1952) found that the minimum brightness for detection of figures such as those in Fig. 23 and their correct identification decreased with increasing number of repetitions, though the decrease was somewhat irregular. Cappon *et al.* (1968) also obtained an improvement with practice in identification of simple geometrical figures against background visual noise (irregular visual patterns). This improvement was slightly though not significantly greater when feedback was given.

Now E. J. Gibson (1953) pointed out that practice alone without any feedback or correction of errors may stabilize a particular percept, but not necessarily render it more veridical. Presumably in the experiments described above the observer was himself able in most cases to check the correctness of his identifications by re-examination of the original stimuli. In the impoverished conditions of the experiments of Bevan and Zener and Cappon *et al.*, observers may have learnt to identify from reduced cues. In all these experiments, however, observers were learning to identify one or a few particular shapes, rather than to acquire any general improvement in accuracy of perception.

There has indeed been considerable controversy as to whether practice in tachistoscopic perception, even with knowledge of results, can increase the amount that is perceived accurately. Renshaw (1945) claimed that a very great improvement in the correct identification of aircraft could be produced by training in tachistoscopic recognition; but his claims have not been substantiated by other investigators. Thus Gibson (1947) found that proficiency in aircraft recognition was not improved by training in the rapid perception of digits; nor indeed was the general efficiency of perception. On the other hand, Bruce and Low (1951) showed that prolonged training in aircraft recognition improved acuity of perception of the Landolt broken ring when it was presented in central vision, but not when it was shown in peripheral vision. Saugstad and Lie (1964) found that acuity in peripheral perception of the Landolt ring was improved only by training in perception of very small rings, the gaps in which could be perceived correctly in only 50 per cent of cases. With larger rings, the gaps in which could be perceived in 90 per cent of cases, there was no effect. However, Christensen and Crannell (1955) were unable to increase the size of the visual field for form by training in the tachistoscopic perception of digits exposed centrally and peripherally. From these varying results it would seem that any direct increase in the extent and accuracy of form perception through learning is doubtful. Where there is some improvement, it probably results from improvement in the capacity to direct attention towards particular aspects or details of the forms presented which facilitates their discrimination and identification. These effects will be discussed in Chapter V.

It would appear that generalization of learning from one situation to another could occur only in so far as situations or events become organized within the same schemata, in such a manner that present percepts are filled out and extended by memories of relevant past experiences, and that appropriate responses are made available (see for instance Postman, 1955a). That this occurred extensively in the early development of perception in children was shown in Chapter II. The utilization of class categories was a prominent feature of improved identification from the second year. Furthermore, children, and adults also, learn to distinguish the 'invariant' qualities of a class of objects or events, on which identification is based, from chance variations resulting from changes in the background situation. In all these processes, naming, labelling, 'coding' and verbal description play a significant part, as we shall consider in the next chapter. Again, immediate perception is increasingly supplemented and controlled by reasoning processes which, though they may not depend entirely on verbal formulation, are undoubtedly furthered by this. We noted the development in children of 'conservation' (see p. 25), in which the child learns to base his judgments, not on immediate perception of the qualities of objects such as size, etc., but on impressions corrected by reasoning and thought. It is interesting to note that Piaget (1963) is of opinion that perception itself develops little after the early years, and that the improved perception of adults results mainly from 'perceptual activity' (see Chapter V) and from correction through reasoning.

IV

The Perception of Complex
Material

(1) Inference and Naming

It must not be supposed that, even when we perceive with a reasonable degree of veridicality, the forms and contours perceived are exact replicas of the stimulus pattern falling on the eye. We know that light is irregularly refracted and diffracted in passing through the cornea, lens and intraocular fluids. Moreover, it seems probable from the work of Hubel and Wiesel that there are selective responses in the retina, lateral geniculate body and striate cortex to the information conveyed to the retina. Consequently the forms of which we are actually aware may be in some sense reconstructions from the sensory data. It is true that, apart from Gestalt modifications, the contours of simple forms appear to resemble the stimulus forms closely. But there are many aspects of the complex situations provided by the natural environment of which we are by no means accurately aware. Indeed, it may be said that the stimulus pattern in fact gives rise to 'cues' from which we infer the appearances of objects, still more perhaps of their spatial setting.

Thus as a rule perception of form in everyday life does not involve the accurate discrimination of minute detail which was described in the previous chapter. Nevertheless, the capacity is available, and may be utilized for instance in certain scientific activities or in the estimation of precision measurements. In general, however, there is a redundancy of sensory information available, much of it corroborative, and the task of the observer is to select what is relevant to his identification of the objects and events visible, and to react to them appropriately. As we have noted, he makes use of schematized knowledge as to the type of situation and the relevant pattern of response. However, there may be occasions on which information is restricted or conflicting; and perhaps more commonly when it is so abundant that he must select what is relevant and discard what is irrelevant. In such situations he may make *inferences* as to the real nature of the situation or of the objects presented to him, going far beyond what is given by the immediate sensory data. In fact, as Brunswik (1956) pointed out, what is immediately perceived seldom provides a completely veridical impression of the stimulus situation. Thus in making inferences, the observer must extract such information as gives him the truest impression, not of the immediately perceptible aspects of the stimulus but of the fundamental nature of the situation within which the stimulus occurs. This process of inference is clearly demonstrated in the 'constancies' (see Chapter VIII). It was also shown by Craik and Vernon (1942) to occur when silhouette pictures were presented in very dim light. The perception and identification of these depended only in part upon the absolute threshold for vision. If observers could make out the general nature of the pictures, they were able to infer their identity at an intensity of illumination below the cone threshold. Later, Vernon (1947) found that the identification of silhouette pictures, blurred by dazzling light, was related to factors such as intelligence. Again, inference may over-ride the erroneous impressions given by the visual illusions. Thus even if the Poggendorf illusion persists in pictures such as that in Fig. 21g (p. 55), we should be unlikely in real life to suppose that the rope was broken or discontinuous. Identification through inference may remain unchanged even when different perceptual cues are utilized. Thus Brand (1954) exposed some of the Rorschach ink-blots on two successive occasions, a week apart. Though different details of the blots were discriminated on successive occasions, the interpretation in terms of resemblance to real objects varied little if at all.

Nevertheless, there are occasions on which inferences as to the identity of objects and events are erroneous, for instance when they are seen in restricted conditions: in very dim light, at great distances or for very short periods of time. Thus moving shadows at night may seem to jump out at us. A post or a rock on a distant hillside may be seen as a man; and one can verify this impression only by observing that it remains motionless for some time. Judgments of rapidly moving traffic are notably erroneous. Instances of errors such as these may be more frequent than we are inclined to suppose, because they are as a rule quickly suppressed and forgotten. This problem has been discussed at length elsewhere (Vernon, 1957), and we shall note examples in the subsequent chapters of this book. One instance is provided by the observations of Johansen (1954), who presented solid blocks of complex and unfamiliar shape in different orientations in rather dim light. Observers did not realize that they were being shown the same object from different angles, but thought that there were entirely different objects with different identities.

Many experiments have demonstrated the tendency to perceive shapes which are not obviously pictorial as *representations of real objects*, and clearly a considerable degree of inference must be involved here. Thus Bartlett (1932) found that in perceiving somewhat ambiguous materal exposed for short intervals of time, observers characteristically made an '*effort after meaning*'; that is to say, they tried to identify the shapes and patterns shown them as representations of real objects, or, in one case, of a mathematical symbol. Shapes are perceived as representations of real objects more readily and quickly than as meaningless forms. Sleight (1952) found that the forms of a swastika, a crescent and an aeroplane stood out and were quickly selected from a collection of geometrical shapes. Yet pictures differ enormously from the objects they represent as regards their actual perceptual characteristics, and the manner in which they represent objects may be ambiguous (Gibson, 1951).

However, *children* appear to acquire the ability to perceive pictures as representations of real objects at an early age, even as soon as one and a half years. This may occur when they have been in no way taught to recognize pictures (Hochberg and Brooks, 1962). But not unnaturally they are slower to identify pictures than are adults.

Moreover, it is more difficult for young children than for adults to recognize pictures which are in some way distorted, mutilated or incomplete, though they may attempt to identify mutilated meaningless shapes as pictures of real objects (Piaget and Stettler-von Albertini, 1954). Draguns and Multari (1961) showed pictures of real objects in decreasing degrees of blur to children of six to twelve years, and found that ease of identification increased, and number of errors decreased, up to about ten years. Potter (1966) presented coloured photographs of scenes and objects in much the same manner. However, some of the pictures were ambiguous, and were not recognized even at maximum clarity by four-year-old children. The time taken in recognition decreased with increasing age. The four-year-olds identified mainly in terms of single objects, often noting only the salient characteristics of these, and neglecting details of colour and shape. Personal egotistic associations based on their own experiences were frequent. Often there was a wild succession of guesses, quite unrelated to each other; thus successive percepts were restricted and fragmented, and not organized together. The five-year-olds often listed details of shape and colour without trying to identify the objects; or they might identify some objects in complex pictures and neglect others, or ignore incongruities between identifications. It was not until seven years and upwards that the children attempted coherent interpretations which were logically related together.

It was found by Vurpillot and Brault (1959) that the aspects of model objects, shown photographically, which were selected as depicting most satisfactorily the previously exhibited models also varied with age. Children of seven to nine years chose a characteristic photograph which provided the greatest amount of information about the model, for instance the three-quarter face of a house. But younger children of five to six years often selected a photograph showing a characteristic detail, such as the handle of a cup or even the flower on it. Much the same thing occurred when children were asked to say whether a pair of drawings of houses were the same or different (Vurpillot and Zoberman, 1965). Children of four to five years tended to select more or less by chance a single part of each house for comparison in making their judgments. Systematic comparison of all details did not occur until about six years. This suggests that children, making inferences from pictures, may give undue weight to comparatively minor details rather than utilizing a balanced selection which emphasizes the more significant features.

More extensive and more complex inferences are required in understanding pictures of scenes and events; for here it is often necessary to infer additionally what the people in the picture are doing, what are their intentions and emotions. There has been some disagreement as to the exact age at which children are able to do this (see for instance Vernon, 1940); and clearly it depends on the complexity of the picture and the familiarity of the events and activities depicted. Certainly the age is much greater than that at which children can identify objects from pictures; it may be as great as nine to ten years.

This difficulty in understanding complex pictures is also apparent in *uncultured peoples* who have little experience with them and have not been taught to use them (Holmes, 1963). Thus simple representations of familiar objects are understood comparatively readily, though it is important that only as much detail should be included as is necessary to define the object. Irrelevant detail, 'pour faire jolie', is distracting. Colour also must be as realistic as possible. Simplified diagrammatic drawings, like those of 'stick' figures, are understood only when they depict very familiar situations, such as that of a mother lifting a child. Complex pictures are more or less incomprehensible. Symbolic representations, such as that of the skull and crossbones for danger, are seldom understood.

Attempts have been made to quantify the tendency to perceive shapes as representing real objects, in terms of the *number of associations to real objects* to which these give rise. Vanderplas and Garvin (1959a and 1959b) assessed the number of associations to each of a variety of randomly generated shapes, and found that when subsequently these had to be recognized from among a number of similar shapes, those with the greatest number of associations were selected most often, but sometimes erroneously. We shall consider this tendency for representational shapes to be modified in memory again at a later point. Clark (1965) selected shapes which produced either many or few associations, and found that the former were remembered and recognized better than the latter. Now it is interesting to note that Vanderplas and Garvin found associations to be less frequent for complex than for simple shapes; whereas according to Clark simple shapes produced few associations and were usually remembered as shapes and not through their associations. It seems possible that in these experiments 'number of associations' was being equated with 'meaningfulness' or degree of meaning. The undesirability of such an equation is discussed below (p. 67) in connection with the perception of words.

Clark (1965) also asked his observers if they gave *names* or *verbal descriptions* to the shapes, and found that naming occurred most frequently for complex forms with many associations – those that were most often remembered. Ellis and Muller (1964) also showed that naming assisted the remembering of complex forms to a greater extent than that of simple forms. Pfafflin (1960) found that the attribution of a name to a shape by the experimenter was helpful when the resemblance of the shape to the object named was not very strong, that is to say, the shape was somewhat ambiguous. There is little doubt that naming is an important feature in the identification of objects and of shapes which represent them. The name summarizes the characteristics of the object schema and codes it in a simple fashion. But it was more useful when only a general impression needed to be retained than when the exact forms had to be remembered in order that they might be combined in a construction such as a jig-saw pattern; for the latter purpose it was preferable to visualize details (Ranken, 1963).

We noted in Chapter II that naming and verbal description might be of considerable assistance to *children* in the identification of shapes and objects, as soon as they are old enough to use names. In the experiments of Gellerman and Luria (see p. 28) naming was used in connection with the combined visual and tactile identification of objects. Babska also showed that naming was of assistance in purely visual identification (p. 27). Again, Weir and Stevenson (1959) found that children of three to nine years learnt more quickly to make the correct choice between pairs of pictures of animals when they named these than when they did not. Moreover, dissimilar names for different irregular solids, such as 'jod', 'daf' and 'meep', were more effective in producing learning of identification by children of four to five years than were similar names such as 'beam', 'mean' and 'preem' (Dietze, 1955). Even with older children of seven to nine years, Katz (1963) found that pairs of irregularly shaped silhouettes could subsequently be discriminated more correctly when each member of the pair was given a separate name than when the two were given a common name.

Children may also be helped to perceive and identify qualities of objects and aspects of situations by labelling them verbally. Thus Carey and Goss (1957) taught children of four to five years to associate with a series of blocks the names of their characteristics – high-big, high-little, low-big and low-little. Although they did not remember these words subsequently, nevertheless they could sort the blocks into these four categories more correctly than did children who had learnt to associate a nonsense syllable with each of the four categories.

Though naming is a valuable method of simple coding, obviously it may relate to a whole category of objects which differ considerably from each other as to details of appearance. It would seem that there exist schematic '*ideas*' as to the appearance of a class. Indeed, naming a category to which belong common objects shown in pictures was performed more quickly than was giving them individual names (Wingfield, 1967). Again, when an observer is shown a shape which to him represents an object in rather a general way, he may remember that shape subsequently as resembling his 'idea' of the appearance of the object more nearly than the originally present shape (Bartlett, 1932). Indeed the recollection of one and the same shape may diverge in different directions if it is differently named. Thus Carmichael *et al.* (1932) presented a series of shapes to two groups of observers, giving the first group one set of names for these and the second group another set of names. Subsequent reproductions by the two groups diverged from each other to resemble the differently named objects. But Herman *et al.* (1957) compared the effects of naming shapes before and after presentation, and concluded that the effect of previous naming was to make observers pay comparatively little attention to the exact details of the shapes, and to rely on their memories of the names. According to Prentice (1954), naming influenced reproduction rather than actual perceiving and remembering, since there was little tendency to assimilate forms to the names given them if they were recognized rather than reproduced. Nevertheless, it seems likely that in a complex perceptual situation many observers tend to use some type of verbal coding or description to enable them to grasp all the details and their significance;

and it is the verbalized material which is remembered subsequently. Those who are comparatively inept in remembering shape as such may yet utilize the method of verbal description to produce an accurate recall of detailed and complex material (Vernon, 1947).

(2) Perception of Words

The interaction between perception of shape and verbalization is most clearly apparent in *reading*, involving as it does combinations of printed letter shapes into words and sentences. Many years ago Cattell (1886) found that during a tachistoscopic exposure of ·o1 seconds an observer could perceive three to four letters, two disconnected words containing up to twelve letters, and a sentence of four words. Therefore words can be read when the letters composing them are not individually perceived. According to E. J. Gibson *et al.* (1962), what we normally perceive are groups of letters, or graphemes, each of which is associated with a corresponding phoneme, or sound unit. A set of phonemes may form a syllable; and familiar syllables are perceived as easily as are familiar words (Postman and Rosenzweig, 1956). E. J. Gibson *et al.* also found that syllables which could easily be *pronounced* were both perceived and recognized more readily than those which were unpronounceable. The same effect occurred with children of six years for three-letter syllables, and with children of eight years for pronounceable and unpronounceable four- and five-letter pseudo-words such as DINK and NKID, BESKS and SKSEB (E. J. Gibson *et al.*, 1963). Thus they argued that the visual perception of printed material in reading depended primarily on the closeness of its association with spoken language. This they concluded was more important than either frequency of usage or degree of meaningfulness. Nevertheless there are occasions in which interference may occur in the association with speech. Ross *et al.* (1956) presented a set of words, and subsequently exhibited tachistoscopically 'homonyms' of these (words with the same sound but a different meaning, such as 'brake' and 'break'). It was found that the homonyms were less easily perceived than were entirely different words, although it might have been supposed that perception of the former would have been facilitated by the previous perception of the homonyms. But instead the common sound apparently created interference.

However, there can be little doubt that clarity of form or '*graphic structure*' affects the perception of single words. Long words in particular are read more slowly than are shorter ones; and there must also be other features in the appearance of certain words which makes them easy or difficult to perceive. Hoisington and Spencer (1958) found that a word exposed at a distance greater than the normal limit of visibility could nevertheless be selected from a group of words if it had previously been perceived. They concluded that observers were able to match the blurred pattern of the distant word to that of the previously perceived word on the basis of length and of distribution of light and darkness. Again, Foote and Havens (1967) showed that words which have several letters in common with other words, such as 'lint', are perceived less readily than those such as 'drab' which have relatively few and are therefore less easily confused with other words. In normal reading it is probable that important cues for recognition are the 'ascending' letters ('b', 'd', 'h', etc.) and the 'descending' letters ('g', 'y', etc.). But although certain letters are easier to perceive singly than are others (see Vernon, 1931), it is doubtful if these differences are important in the ordinary reading of adults.

It is generally supposed that the most important factor in the reading of words is the *frequency* with which they occur in the English language, and hence their *familiarity*. Even the identification of isolated letters is quicker with the more frequently used than the less frequently used capital letters (Robinson *et al.*, 1964). Again, Miller *et al.* (1954) showed that the more similar a sequence of letters to that of sequences occurring in words, the more easily was it perceived. And Portnoy *et al.* (1964) found that syllables which formed words or were very similar to them were detected most quickly when presented as a target among a large number of other syllables. Moreover, the direct effects of frequency were demonstrated by Soloman and Postman (1952), who found that when seven-letter pronounceable nonsense words were presented with different frequencies among a long list of such words, the more frequently presented were subsequently more frequently recognized in tachistoscopic perception.

With words, frequency of usage in the English language appeared to be the principal factor determining speed of perception (Howes and Solomon, 1951). The frequency with which words occur in the ordinary speech, at least of educated adults, is very highly correlated with their frequency of occurrence in printed texts (Howes, 1954). The effect of frequency may be greater with long than with short words (McGinnies *et al.*, 1952). Indeed, even the naming of objects in pictures is quicker the more frequently used their names (Oldfield and Wingfield, 1964). However, it has been argued that frequency of usage may affect the *responses* made rather than the perceptual processes; that is to say, when an observer is uncertain what word he has been shown, he tends to say a common rather than an uncommon word, which has some resemblance to the shape he has perceived. Goldiamond and Hawkins (1958) required their observers to read lists of nonsense syllables in which certain syllables occurred with frequencies of one to twenty-five. They were then informed that these syllables would be presented to them tachisto-scopically; whereas in fact only vague grey blurs were shown. Neverthe-less, the observers reported that they had perceived the syllables they expected to see, and the frequency of report varied with the frequency of occurrence in the initial list. Thus it was argued that the principal effect of frequency was on response. However, as Neisser (1967) has pointed out, the results of this experiment are not really applicable to the situation in which word stimuli are actually presented. In such a situation perception of common words may be easier in itself. Indeed the findings of Miller *et al.* (1954) suggest that this is so.

But it would appear that familiarity affects the *coding* of printed material in the recognition of letters and words, rather than their imme-diate perception. Hochberg (1968) found that the time taken to discri-minate between two words, two nonsense syllables or two letters, judg-ing if they were the same or different, was unaffected by differences in familiarity, provided that the observer could perceive both in foveal vision. But with two words laterally separated, familiar words were easier to discriminate than unfamiliar because the observer could not make a direct comparison between them, and was obliged to code them. He also had to do this if two letters of different form, capitals and lower-case letters, were presented foveally; and discrimination was then slower with the less familiar. Hochberg also suggested that the great increase in speed of recognition of words which occurs in learning to read is due to improvement in the coding process.

Haslerud and Clark (1957) considered that *understanding of meaning* of words might be more important in their perception than their fre-quency of occurrence. It was found that nine-letter words which observers were subsequently able to define were perceived more correctly when ex-posed tachistoscopically than were words which could not be defined, irrespective of frequency of usage. But according to Noble (1953), both familiarity and meaningfulness are highly correlated with frequency. Kristofferson (1957b) also found that the threshold for perception of words correlated inversely with their meaningfulness. But it should be noted that degree of meaningfulness was defined by Noble (1962) as the number of associations which could be made to a word. It is difficult to comprehend the logic of this definition. The meaning of a word does not lie in its associations, nor can it be more or less meaningful. It is either understood or not understood (as in the experiment of Haslerud and Clark); though there may be a border-line zone in which one is not quite sure what a word means. Again, words such as prepositions and conjunctions are perfectly meaningful, but in all probability have few associations. And although the meanings of common words are usually more likely to be understood than those of uncommon ones, understanding of meaning does not necessarily depend on frequency of usage.

In the reading of a continuous text, the meaning of words is to a considerable extent shown by their *context*. Tulving and Gold (1963) found that the longer the sentence context of words, provided that it was relevant, the more quickly were long words perceived. A similar contextual effect on expectation may have been operating in the experiment in which Taylor (1956a) showed that words were perceived more readily in so far as they associated with a previously presented key word; and there was some tendency for this effect to be stronger, the closer the association.

As we noted, it is rather doubtful whether graphic structure, unless it is extremely unclear, has much effect on the reading of continuous prose. It is true that very small print and a completely unfamiliar type face may retard reading (see Vernon, 1931). But in general frequency and familiarity of *syntactic structure* and comprehensibility of content are the most important factors, and these interact with each other. Absence of normal syntactic structure, for instance in sentences of jumbled words, makes reading very slow indeed. Morton (1964) found that the rate of reading increased regularly with increase in order of approximation to normal syntactic structure, that is to say as connected phrases increased in length. However, there was a further increase with normal prose, the meaning of which could be fully understood. Even when syntactic structure is completely normal and grammatical, reading may be slow and difficult if the contents are not easily comprehensible.

We may conclude therefore that in the reading of literate adults the visual characteristics of the print provide a necessary cue to perception; but perception is regulated by the accompanying thought processes which are to a great extent a function of the syntactic and semantic characteristics of language.

V

The Arousal and Direction
of Attention

(1) Arousal of Attention

For many years, considerable doubt was felt as to whether it was possible to discriminate between attention and perception, since perception implied attention, and it was thought if anyone attended to a stimulus they automatically perceived it. However, recent investigations along separate but converging lines have demonstrated that there may indeed be processes of attending which operate to some extent independently of perceptual processes. The first type of investigation is physiological, involving the discovery of special centres in the brain the functions of which are concerned with attention. The second line is mainly psychological; it relates to the states observed in persons deprived, partly or completely, of the variable sensory stimulation occurring in exposure to the normal environment. These states, which are characterized by a decline in attention and an interference with normal perception, will be considered in Chapter VI. But also additionally there has been a third line of investigation into the manner in which attention may be directed to varying aspects of the environmental field.

It is not possible here to discuss in detail the work of the physiologists, Jasper, Magoun and many others, on the 'reticular formation of the brain'. Full discussions are given by Samuels (1959) and Berlyne (1960). However, to summarize briefly: it has been shown that this cell net-work within the brain stem and thalamic region appears to have two main functions with regard to perception. The brain stem reticular formation sends nerve impulses to the cortex producing general arousal from sleep and passivity to sensory stimulation, and these effects appear in high frequency outbursts ('evoked potentials') in the EEG. The thalamic reticular formation gives rise to a more persistent and localized response, sometimes called the 'orienting reflex', in which attention is directed towards particular types of stimulation. Now clearly the degree of attention to environmental stimulation must depend in the first place on general arousal, according as to whether the individual is alert, quiescent, drowsy or asleep. Direct stimulation of the reticular formation in monkeys produced the same pattern of fast discharge in the cortex, together with arousal and wakefulness, as resulted from afferent stimulation (Segundo *et al.*, 1955). But also perception of particular significant aspects of the environment is quicker and more accurate if the thalamic reticular formation operates to reinforce sensory impulses related to stimulation by these aspects. Thus Fuster (1958) showed that direct electrical stimulation of the reticular formation in monkeys improved their speed and accuracy in discriminating between two shapes. Not only are the principal perceptual responses facilitated and discrimination enhanced; in addition irrelevant impulses may be suppressed. Thus Hernandez-Peon *et al.* (1956) exposed an unaesthetized cat to a regular series of clicks, recording its auditory responses through electrodes inserted in the cochlear nucleus. But these responses ceased altogether when the cat was shown a mouse or could smell fish. Similar inhibitory processes have been demonstrated in man (Jouvet, 1957). Thus it was argued that response to a relatively unimportant type of stimulation was repressed at an early point in the afferent nerve path to the brain by the reticular formation which gave prior entry to the cortex to more significant types of stimulation.

The findings suggest that the reticular formation may operate in man to arouse the cortex and to direct excitation towards it in order to stimulate attention to anything of particular significance. There is much evidence to show that general arousal and activation, as measured by indices such as pulse rate and GSR, increase in motivational states, sometimes to the point of over-arousal, when efficiency may be reduced. Arousal decreases in states of boredom and lack of interest. Moreover, habituation to repeated and unvarying stimulation is accompanied by decrease in arousal. We shall discuss the relation to perception of motivational and monotonous states more fully subsequently. But the direct effect of arousal through the reticular formation on the perceptual functions in man was shown by Lindsley (1957), who found that a shorter time interval was required for discrimination between two successive flashes of light when the reticular formation was directly stimulated. Venables and Warwick-Evans (1967) showed that this accelerated two-flash discrimination was associated with decrease in amplitude of the alpha rhythm of the EEG; that is to say, with increased arousal of the cortex. Alpha blocking has also been found to occur when reaction time to a visual signal is accelerated by alerting the observer through a warning signal (Lansing *et al.*, 1959).

However, the psychological processes demonstrated in the *distribution* of attention are excessively complex, and it is impossible at the moment to assess their physiological basis. Extensive psychological study has been devoted to the types of situation and material to which observers attend, and which they perceive rapidly in order to discover what aspects of the environment are to be examined and explored. Dember and Earl (1957) stated that the events which attract attention are: (1) Temporal change in stimulation – for instance, novel stimulation, especially in so far as what is observed differs from and is discordant with what was expected; (2) spatial change and inhomogeneity of stimulation, as with varying and complex material. However, in the first case the novelty and unexpectedness of the stimulus must not be too great, or the observer may be frightened or repelled by its abnormality, and by his inability to respond to it appropriately. In the second case, the material must not be so complex as to be completely beyond the range of his understanding, or he will reject it because again he is unable to respond to it appropriately. But this rejection may also occur with the excessively novel, especially by young children who, according to Piaget, may ignore novel features of objects and assimilate them to existing schemata.

It would seem that arousal and attention perform two somewhat different functions in these two types of situation. In the first, the individual must be alerted in order to adapt himself speedily to a new and unexpected situation; and we shall consider in some detail how his expectations are created and what their effects are in directing attention. In the second case, he must set himself to acquire information as to the exact nature of the stimulus material, in order to identify its nature.

Extensive investigations have been made on the relation of attention to *novelty* and complexity, especially by Berlyne. With adult observers he used a situation similar to that employed with infants, which we described in Chapter II. That is to say, pairs of stimuli were presented to the observer, and measurement was made of the number of short observations, or the total period of more prolonged observations, given to each of these. We noted that infants tended to look first and longest at novel and unexpected stimuli. So also Berlyne (1957) found that adult observers, presented with incongruous pictures of the head of one animal joined to the body of another, looked longer at these than at ordinary animal pictures. Again, when a series of coloured shapes was presented, with different and unexpected shapes interspersed on two occasions, these were looked at for longer than were those in the regular series (Berlyne, 1951). Incongruous animal pictures produced a greater degree of arousal, as indicated by larger GSR responses (Berlyne *et al.*,

F

1963). But repetition of the same patterns resulted in habituation and decreased GSR response. However, in normal surroundings such habituation is frequently avoided by deliberate changes of view, and by exploration of novel aspects of the environment.

It should be noted that one form of incongruity in stimulation which readily arouses and attracts attention is *intensity*, or strong contrast with the surroundings. Thus bright lights and strong colours tend to produce both general arousal and also specific direction of attention.

With regards to the effects of *complexity*, we noted in Chapter II that infants, as they increased in age, preferred to gaze at patterns of increasing complexity. So also rather older children, aged four to five and a half years, spent longer looking at more complex than at simpler patterns (Cantor *et al.*, 1963). At five years, some children looked a second time at a many-sided irregular figure more often than at a four-sided one; and this preference increased with age (Willis and Dornbush, 1968). The same tendency was exhibited by adults. Berlyne (1958) and Berlyne and Lawrence (1964) found that when simple and complex regular and irregular figures were paired, observers looked first at the complex and irregular. They looked longer at irregular than at regular figures; and at complex rather than at simple figures. When observers were urged to attend carefully, arousal, as measured by GSR responses, was heightened particularly by viewing the irregular patterns (Berlyne *et al.*, 1963).

It is of course likely that more complex patterns, presenting a greater amount of information than do simple patterns, require more prolonged inspection and possibly also greater arousal, for the reduction of uncertainty. Nevertheless, it would seem that there is also a definite preference for a certain degree of complexity, as being more interesting. Thus observers reported that the incongruous pictures and the complex irregular figures were more interesting than the normal animal pictures and the regular figures, but also less pleasing (Berlyne, 1963). However, it is possible that an intermediate degree of complexity may be satisfying on both counts; or one aspect may have more appeal for some people, the other for others. Thus Vitz (1966) found that irregular patterns of medium complexity were liked better on the whole than either simpler or more complex; but there were considerable individual differences. And once the observers had become familiar with the patterns, they tended to like rather more complex patterns than they had liked initially.

Berlyne and Lewis (1963) found an interesting interaction between preference for complexity and general arousal. When aroused by noise or by the threat of electric shock, the observers' period of exploration of both regular and irregular patterns increased, but the preference for irregular to regular patterns decreased. Berlyne argued that a high level of arousal makes it difficult to explore and obtain information; therefore the period of exploration was increased. But also when arousal is high observers do not wish to increase it further by studying more irregular patterns. In other words, there is an optimum level of arousal which produces a maximum degree of attention and investigation, whereas over-arousal may impair it.

(2) The Limits of Attention

Even when attention is concentrated upon a particular point or area of the visual field, the amount that can be perceived is limited. If the material is homogeneous, as for instance in a random distribution of dots, the *number* which can be reported accurately and with certainty is five or six (Kaufman *et al.*, 1949). There appears to be a discontinuity at this point in the process of apprehending number; and with larger numbers, from seven upwards, the observer begins to guess how many there are, and his estimates are uncertain (Minturn and Reese, 1951). If the dots are heterogeneous, in colour for instance, the number which can be correctly estimated is less (Brown, 1929), possibly through distraction by the irrelevant dimension. But there is a strong tendency to group randomly and distributed dots in accordance with the principles of proximity and similarity (see p. 35). In so far as they can be grouped into a pattern or some regular arrangement, larger numbers can be estimated correctly.

If the observer is shown more complex material, and instructed to report on the *identity* as well as the numerousness of the forms presented, the task becomes a different one, for here more than one aspect must be taken into account. Thus Dallenbach (1928) found that, in the tachisti-scopic perception of forms, numbers could be reported correctly for eight to twelve forms; but only four could be reported correctly if additionally their shapes were identified. However, six to eight letters could be identified. There appears to be a strong tendency to recode complex material (Miller, 1956). That is to say, it is organized in 'chunks', and the observer may then perceive almost as many chunks as separate items. A chunk may be an integrated pattern; or in the case of verbal material it may be a word or a sentence. As we noted on p. 65, more letters can be perceived tachistoscopically when they are combined in words and sentences than when they are presented singly. This occurs also if they are combined in nonsense syllables, with which no factor of meaning is operating. Thus in fact we rarely attend to isolated events; in most cases they are organized in some way, and perception, as we have shown, depends on the nature of this organization.

Nevertheless, situations may arise in which what can be perceived depends on the *location* of the forms or objects exposed. In general, as might be expected, forms exposed centrally are perceived more accurately than those exposed peripherally; and the latter may be altogether ignored (Baker, 1958). But attention can be voluntarily directed to different parts of the field, and what is presented there is perceived more accurately than anything presented elsewhere (Meisenheimer, 1929). Though some increase in the amount perceived may be produced by practice (Saltzman and Garner, 1948), it is probable that in many cases these increases result from specific direction of attention towards specific aspects of the material presented, as we shall consider in Section (4) of this chapter.

(3) Scanning and Search

However, we do not commonly depend on what we can perceive at a single glance, in a period of very short duration. More often we are able to search the visual field, scanning and exploring it in order to perceive certain particular aspects. Piaget considered that this active exploration begins in early childhood, at twelve to eighteen months, when the child manipulates objects in order to obtain better results from them, and varies his previous actions to discover what happens then. However, it is not until a later age, of about seven years, that he develops the capacity for '*perceptual activity*', the systematic scanning of complex material, in order to perceive accurately its exact nature (Piaget, 1961). Through this activity immediate perception is corrected and refined by comparing together all the details; this was called 'coupling'.* Before that scanning is irregular and unsystematic. Piaget and Vinh Bang (1961) recorded the eye movements of children and showed that at five to six years the eyes wandered about, sometimes gazing outside the figures presented, and sometimes fixating or oscillating about a point for long periods. Adults fixated accurately on relevant points, for sufficient time to perceive what was necessary, and then moved on to the next point. In comparing different parts of a figure, they moved to and fro syste-

* It should be noted that Piaget attributes the various deformations of shape which occur in the visual illusions to centration and incomplete couplings of 'encounters'. These somewhat hypothetical 'encounters' between the observer and the stimulus object are not to be equated with actual fixation of the eyes. Nor is any particular physiological interpretation hypothesized.

matically; whereas the children tended to remain '*centrated*' on any part of the figure which was larger or more prominent than the remainder, hence frequently over-estimating its size (Piaget, 1961). Even in adults there was a slight tendency to over-estimate the length of the longer side of a rectangle and under-estimate the length of the shorter; but this error was considerably greater in children of five to seven years, because they did not compare the two lines so carefully. So also with the Müller-Lyer illusion; children performed little analysis of the parts of the figure in relation to the whole. In some cases, however, centration produced a reduction of an illusion. Thus the Oppel illusion (see Fig. 24a) decreased with increasing age because the younger children perceived the cross-hatched line as a whole without exploring it. Older children analysed it, and directed successive fixations toward the divided parts; and this had the effect of increasing the magnitude of the illusion (Piaget, 1961; Vurpillot, 1963). The increase was somewhat less when the illusion was shown in a representational picture (Fig. 24b), because here perception of the figures as a whole was induced, rather than analysis (Vurpillot, 1963).

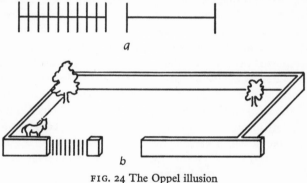

a

b

FIG. 24 The Oppel illusion
a. *After* Vurpillot (1963) p. 170
b. *After* Vurpillot (1963) p. 101

That *systematic scanning* of figures increases with *age* was also shown in an experiment in which children of three and a half to six and a half years were required to match an irregular silhouette shape against a similar shape contained in a row of slightly different shapes (Kerpelman and Pollack, 1964). Accuracy increased up to five years and then decreased. It was suggested that the younger children looked only at the bottom parts of the shapes, whereas the older scanned the whole shapes. This was confirmed in a second experiment in which first the top parts and then the bottom parts of the shapes were shown separately. Again, when a scattered collection of pictures of objects was shown and children were asked to name these, the accuracy of naming increased from five to eight years as systematic scanning increased (Elkind and Weiss, 1967). When the pictures were regularly arranged in a triangular structure, there was no improvement with increase in age, since presumably all the children scanned these regularly. When pictures were arranged in regular rows and columns, there was an increase from three and a half to six years in systematic scanning (Gottschalk *et al.*, 1964). But regular scanning from left to right appeared only among the five- to six-year-olds, who might have had some teaching of reading.

This *habit of left to right scanning* becomes increasingly strong with regularly arranged forms or verbal material in older children and adults. Its effect on peripheral perception in adults was demonstrated in experiments in which figures or letters were briefly exposed to left or right of a central fixation point (Heron, 1957). Letters exposed singly were perceived more accurately on the right than on the left, and so were pictures of familiar objects (Wyke and Ettlinger, 1961); but there was no difference with unfamiliar shapes. It was hypothesized that any material involving verbal responses, including naming, was processed in the left cerebral hemisphere, whereas shapes not involving verbal responses were processed mainly in the right hemisphere. However, if letters were presented simultaneously on the left and the right, more of the former were recognized than of the latter, supposedly as the result of scanning habits acquired by adults in reading (Heron, 1957). In the perception of shapes, scanning may begin at the top of the figure and then proceed through the left and the right sides to the bottom. Thus Mandes and Ghent (1963) presented tachistoscopically series of geometric figures, only one side of which varied. This distinguishing features was most readily perceived when it was at the top of the figure; then on the left side, the right side and the bottom.

If observers were required to detect a particular type of figure from a number of other *figures scattered irregularly* about the field, for instance to locate a single Landolt ring from a collection of circles, the accuracy of performance increased with increase in exposure time, and decreased with the number of circles; but some methods of *search* were more effective than others, for instance in circles or spirals (Erickson, 1964). When a number of target figures was presented for detection, for instance ten triangles among a varying number of squares and diamonds, the time taken to do this increased as the number of background shapes increased (Ericksen, 1955); and also with the number of shapes to be located (Gould and Schaffer, 1965). If time of observation was held constant, the number of target figures detected decreased with the total number of figures exposed, but increased with the duration of observation (Boynton & Bush, 1956). However, some figures were detected more easily than others; thus crosses were more often correctly detected than were triangles, quadrilaterals and pentagons. Gould and Schaffer found similar differences in scanning a regular 6×6 cell matrix containing randomly arranged digits. Although there was a general tendency to scan from left to right and top to bottom, '7s' were detected most quickly, '2s' and '9s' most slowly. But errors were most frequent with '5s' and '9s'. When target forms were made to differ from background shapes in a number of qualities, for instance shape, colour, size and brightness, for a single difference detection was quickest when the differentiated quality was colour; and it was quicker for shape than for brightness or size (Eriksen, 1952a, 1953). But a difference of two qualities, especially colour and shape, produced even quicker detection. A similar effect for colour was obtained by Williams (1967).

Extensive investigations of *search procedures* have been carried out by Neisser (1964). His general technique was to present long columns of rows, each row containing four or six capital letters or words, and to instruct observers to search until they detected a single letter or word. A rounded letter such as 'Q' was detected more quickly if presented with straight-line letters only; and a straight line letter, 'Z', if given with rounded letters only. The search procedure became quicker with practice, until observers achieved a speed of about ten rows per second. However, they took considerably longer to detect a row which did *not* contain a critical letter. Thus it appeared that they achieved the capacity, in the first case, to ignore all irrelevant letters, which were perceived as a blur or 'ground' from which the 'figure' emerged. In the second case, they had to read all the letters. Searching for a single word in a series of different words was more rapid than searching for a single letter in a series of letters; so also was searching for a word of a given meaning, for instance the name of an animal. Again it would seem that the irrelevant words were not completely read, since they could not be recognized afterwards; but were processed at a low level of attention. Thus people may be able to process material without becoming fully aware of it, and this procedure is accelerated by practice. It may also be improved by special instructions such as we shall describe in the next section.

It was noted that Piaget (1961) considered that systematic scanning by *eye movement* and *successive fixations* of important aspects of the figure was an essential feature of perceptual activity. Somewhat the same theory had been put forward by Hebb (1949), who postulated that in viewing a triangle, the three corners were successively fixated. Now it may be true that children need to fixate with the eyes every part of a figure before they can analyse it adequately. Thus we noted that children did not match figures correctly as long as they looked only at the bottom parts of these. But it may be that such scanning is unnecessary in adults. Thus Mooney (1960) showed that learning to recognize forms of varying complexity was as rapid when they were exposed tachistoscopically, thus eliminating eye movements, as when they were shown for periods of five seconds, allowing inspection and scanning. Fraisse *et al.* (1956) suggested that centration and movement of attention could occur in comparing parts of a figure without any eye movement and fixation on different parts of the figure being necessary. A line divided into two equal parts was presented tachistoscopically, one end of the line being at the fixation point. Thus one half of the line was more central in vision, the other more peripheral. If the observers were informed beforehand which side of the fixation point the line would appear, they tended to under-estimate the length of the more peripheral part, presumably because attention was centred on the more central part. But when they were not so informed, attention was equally distributed about the field, and no such effect was obtained. Gould and Schaffer (1965), in their experiments on scanning a matrix to detect a single digit, recorded the eye movements of their observers while carrying out this task. Observers did not fixate centrally all the cells in the matrix; about half of the fixations fell in peripheral vision. Although fixations on or near the target digits were longer than others, even these were not always centrally fixated, especially the '7s' which were easily perceived. But less easily perceived digits often received two central fixations. Thus it would appear that adults possess the capacity to attend to and assimilate material which is not clearly perceived because it falls on the periphery of the retina. This capacity may have been acquired through experience in rapid reading, in which only a few words in the line are centrally fixated.

(4) Set and Expectancy

On very many occasions attention is not aroused simply in response to stimulation from the immediate situation, but is directed in a particular manner by previously existing intentions or expectations. In such cases, the observer may be 'set' to perceive particular aspects of the situation, because he wants to perceive them or expects to perceive them, perhaps because he has previously been informed that they may be presented to him. And it may then be found that he is more ready to perceive these particular aspects than he would otherwise have been. In a well-known article, 'On Perceptual Readiness', Bruner (1957) pointed out that stimulus patterns were identified by classifying them within particular categories of objects or events (as we noted on p. 22); and that this classification depended not only on the similarity between the particular stimulus qualities and those characteristic of the category, but also on the relative accessibility of different categories. Moreover, accessibility was a function of the probability which we have learnt to expect for the occurrence of instances of that category. Thus we are more ready to perceive objects or events of a type which we have frequently experienced in the past, and to formulate hypotheses as to the identity of objects in accordance with this experience. However, in particular states of motivation and need, we may deliberately search for relevant objects and events, without taking into account any probabilities; and in such circumstances, perception may be non-veridical (See Chapter XI). Expectations may also be aroused by the course of events in which we are currently participating, or from information or instructions given by the experimenter. In so far as attention is directed towards expected events, it may be directed away from unexpected and unimportant events. Indeed, the effects of these may actually be prevented from reaching the cortex, as in the experiments of Hernandez-Peon *et al.* (1956). However, it may be noted from the experiments on novelty described above that new and unexpected events may in certain circumstances produce arousal and hence gain prior entry into consciousness.

Usually, frequency of past experience is equated with *familiarity*, on the argument that the more often an event has occurred, the more familiar with it we are likely to be. But as we have noted, the effects of frequency and familiarity may depend not so much on mere knowledge as on the expectation that in familiar circumstances a familiar event is likely to recur. Thus we considered the manner in which experience in reading leads to expectations of the more frequently used words, and of the normal syntactic structure of the English language, both of which facilitate rapid identification of words from partial cues. But also familiarity with particular types of material and context gives rise to yet more facilitation, and more rapid reading. On the other hand, an unfamiliar type face may retard reading, because its perceptual characteristics are unexpected. Long *et al.* (1960) presented letters which had been distorted by the removal or addition of certain parts. The greater the degree of distortion, the harder they were to identify. But in some cases, distortions may be altogether overlooked, as when a reader fails to notice misprints. Set to perceive certain types of words may also facilitate perception, but Freeman and Engler (1955) showed that such a set affected the perception only of rather infrequent words. The narrower the range of the set, the greater the effect; if for instance observers were told to expect some words related to colour, it was stronger than if the instructions were to expect words related to colour or food. There are many other instances of the manner in which familiar objects are readily recognized. As we noted on p. 61, shapes which appeared to represent real objects were more readily perceived than shapes which did not. Bruner and Postman (1949) presented tachistoscopically playing cards with the colours reversed – red spades and clubs, black hearts and diamonds. These were perceived with considerable difficulty, and sometimes could not be identified at all. In some cases the colours reported were those normally expected; in others, there was a compromise, red being reported as purple. Similar instances are shown in the effects of learning on perception in the education of children. Thus Vernon (1946) found that children and even adults could not recognize and understand graphs and charts unless they had previously been taught to do so. Johnson (1953) showed that medical and biology students were frequently unable to perceive radiographs and biological specimens correctly. There was a tendency to confuse what was really there with what they thought ought to be there, often in terms of text book diagrams. They also made incorrect inferences from what they saw, based on false hypotheses as to the nature and identity of the specimens. Thus expectations do not necessarily ensure greater correctness in perception; and training must emphasize essential features if it is to produce improvement. 'Invariants' must be distinguished from irrelevant variations (Gibson, 1966).

We have already noted (p. 57) that *training* often failed to produce any general improvement in range and accuracy of perception. Another instance of this was given by Goins (1958), who trained children in the tachistoscopic perception of digits, over a considerable period of time. Although their perception of digits improved, there was no transfer to the perception of letters. Thus the effect was entirely specific to the material used. But a greater effect may result if observers learn to look for particular aspects which can be perceived in a number of different settings. This may occur especially if the significant aspects can be classified in an effective manner, as Gibson (1947) found in training for aircraft recognition. Again, Turnure and Wallach (1965) showed that observers were more able to recognize a particular part of an unfamiliar irregular shape if it had been presented as a part of a number of different shapes than if it had been shown only in a single shape. And Bevan *et al.* (1966) found that memory for a class or type of object was better when different examples of the same type had been presented initially than when only the same examples had been shown. It would appear therefore that for general improvement of perception through training, expectations should be created through the formation of the general schemata relating to the situation which covers a variety of specific instances. But an even more general expectation of a type of situation may facilitate perception. Thus Luchins and Luchins (1955) found that ambiguous pictures were perceived more correctly when preceded by other ambiguous pictures than after presentation of clear and unambiguous pictures.

However, it has been found that *expectations may be created in the course of an experiment* such that observers tend to perceive forms which are similar to those which have previously been perceived. These expectations may be more specific than those in the experiment of Luchins

a　　　　　　　　　*b*

FIG. 25 Ambiguous forms

and Luchins. Bruner and Minturn (1955) found that an ambiguous figure (Fig. 25a) was perceived as a B by observers who had previously been shown four capital letters; and as a 13 by those who had just seen four digits. Ex and De Bruijn (1956) showed that observers may develop their own expectations. Those who saw a form such as that in Fig. 25b simply as a shape, for instance of two tops, immediately noticed the difference when this form was replaced by a W. But those who saw the original figure as derived from a letter, for instance as a W plus a line, did not in most cases notice any change when the W was presented.

This formation of set to expect a particular figure apparently does not occur to the same extent in children. Thus adults saw the ambiguous figure in Fig. 26 as a rat after perceiving an animal picture, but as a face after being shown the picture of another face (Bugelski and Alampay, 1961). But when children of four to eight years were shown this ambiguous figure preceded by six drawings of animals or of human faces, only those of seven to eight years showed the effects of set in subsequent judgments (Reese, 1963).

It must seem that this result was obtained because the younger children did not relate the previously shown series of pictures to the ambiguous figure. Yet experiments have been carried out on adults which suggest that a tendency to select particular perceptual aspects may be created without any awareness on the part of the observer. Thus Walters (1958) gave observers preliminary problem tasks, with guidance as to the correct direction in which to proceed being shown on green or blue cards; whereas incorrect directions were shown on red and yellow cards. Subsequently the observers were required to extract simple from complex Gottschaldt figures, the complex figures being printed in different colours, red, green, blue and yellow. The simple figures in blue and green areas were detected significantly more often that those in the red and yellow areas, although none of the observers was aware of the relationship.

FIG. 26 The rat and profile
(*After* Bugelski and Alampay (1961) p. 206)

There has been some controversy as to the effect on expectation and subsequent perception of previous *partial and incorrect perceptions*. This matter was first raised by Wyatt and Campbell (1951), who found that blurred pictures were perceived less readily when they had been preceded by much more blurred presentations of the same pictures than when they followed only slightly more blurred pictures. It was suggested the observers made incorrect guesses as to the identity of the highly blurred pictures which became stereotyped, and impaired accurate perception of the less blurred pictures. A repetition of this experiment by Bruner and Potter (1964) produced similar results. Observers who began a series with very blurred pictures finally recognized only 23 per cent; those who began with medium blur, 45 per cent; and those with light blur, 60 per cent. Those who began with the very blurred pictures formed incorrect hypotheses and retained them for too long.

On the other hand, Bricker and Chapanis (1953) considered that in the tachistoscopic perception of nonsense syllables, guesses, even when incorrect, afforded some information which assisted the observer to perceive the syllables correctly at subsequent presentations. However, it is not very easy to see from their experimental findings why they reached this conclusion. Hodge (1959) studied similar effects in a rather different type of experiment, in which observers had to judge which dimensions (form, size, colour, brightness, internal markings, etc.) of a large set of complex figures were relevant to the classification of these shapes. In fact, the dimensions of form and size were always relevant; the others only occasionally. The greater the number of irrelevant dimensions, the slower were observers to make their judgments. Thus it was concluded that irrelevant information retarded perception and judgment. Clearly the experiments described do not cover all the possible ways in which expectations may be affected by additional information. It would seem, however, that it assists creation of expectations which facilitate perception only when it can be utilized appropriately, and not when it produces conflicts of expectation.

Now there may be some doubt, in the experiment of Walters (1958) and in other similar experiments, whether the observer developed expectations, conscious or not, as to what he should attend to; or whether he acquired some kind of cue as to how he should *respond*. Thus Lawrence and Coles (1954) presented pictures of familiar objects, each of which was immediately preceded or followed by a set of names, one of which was the name of the object. Accuracy of naming was similar in the two conditions, and greater than if no name were given. Thus it was argued that the memory trace was modified selectively in both cases to produce a specific choice of response. Reid *et al.* (1960) presented words out of focus, for identification, either preceded or followed by words of a similar category. The category varied from a general one, 'sport' for instance, to a highly restricted one, for instance the names of players in baseball teams. Identification was superior when it related to the more restricted categories. But the effect was much the same whether the category was named before or after presentation of the word. Thus it was concluded that the restricted category directed the responses rather than the perceptual expectations.

But in an experiment by Long *et al.* (1960), observers were presented with distorted letters, some parts of which had been added or removed. Some observers were shown previously lists of letters containing the letter subsequently presented in distorted form; others saw the list afterwards. The number of alternative letters in the lists varied. Identifications of distorted letters were most frequent when lists were presented beforehand, and contained few alternatives. Here then it might be supposed that a definite set was created to perceive one of a small group of letters. A similar result was obtained by Egerth and Smith (1967), who found that perception of pictures was facilitated by previous presentation of similar pictures, but not of dissimilar pictures. Again, Neisser (1954) claimed to have demonstrated a facilitation of perception rather than direction of response in an experiment in which observers were shown tachistoscopically words from a longer list of words already seen; or from a list of homonymous words. In the first case there was a definite increase in accuracy of tachistoscopic perception of the words; but in the second, accuracy was not greater than if observers were previously shown a list of completely different words. Thus there was no facilitation of response by the homonymous words.

There has been a large number of experiments in which set has been deliberately created by the experimenter through his *instructions* to his observers. Again there has been some disagreement as to whether perceptual expectation or response tendency was involved – or indeed both. One well-known example of these was the experiment by Gottschaldt (1926), using embedded figures, as we have already described. He first exposed the simple figures each for a second, a large number of times in succession. Subsequently he presented the complex figures and asked his observers to describe them. They scarcely ever noticed the simple figures embedded in the complex. But when the observers were instructed beforehand to look for the simple figures, they detected these in about 30 per cent of cases. Now here it would appear that a completely specific expectation was created of particular forms which were then more readily perceived.

In a rather different type of experiment observers are presented with complex material and instructed by the experimenter to report certain aspects of this before others, or rather than others. In the prototype experiment by Külpe (1904), four nonsense syllables were presented, printed in different colours and arranged in different groupings. Observers were instructed to observe and if possible reproduce these afterwards; but also on different occasions special instructions were given to report the number of letters, the colours and their positions, the form and arrangement of the syllables, or the identity and positions of the letters. In general, these special tasks were performed most accurately whereas other aspects not emphasized in the instructions were often not reported. A number of similar experiments (described fully in Vernon, 1952) produced similar results; namely, that observers were apparently set by the preliminary instructions to perceive particular aspects or attributes which they subsequently reported more correctly and fully than other aspects. Moreover, the greater the number of features which observers were required to report, the less accurate their reports of any of these (Dallenbach, 1928). But if instructions were not given until afterwards, accuracy of report was less because the observers had to retain memory imagery of all the material until they were told which aspects to select (Chapman, 1932).

These observations suggest that instructions may affect what is retained in the *immediate memory span*, rather than the initial percept. Thus Sperling (1960) presented rows of letters for an exposure of 50 msec., and found that observers could report four to five of these correctly. However, when the observer had to read one row only, the row being signalled at the time of exposure, Sperling calculated from the proportion of letters perceived in that row that the total amount which could be perceived initially was much greater than that which could be reported from the immediate memory span. Again, Lawrence and Laberge (1956) presented varying numbers of different shapes in different colours, with different sets of instructions to each of four groups of observers. These instructions were: (1) To pay equal attention to all the attributes; (2) to pay primary attention to one attribute (number, form or colour), but to report all three; (3) to pay primary attention to one attribute, reporting only that; (4) to pay equal attention to all attributes, the experimenter specifying after presentation which attribute was to be reported. It was found that the accuracy of report of the single attribute in (3) was similar to that of the first reported attribute in (2). Therefore, keeping the other attributes in mind did not interfere with reporting the principal attribute. The main effect of instructions was to specify the order of report, which order determined its accuracy. Again, the effect of reporting the principal attribute was much the same in (4), when instructions were given afterwards, as in (2) when they were given before. Thus it was concluded that observers retained in the memory image information about all the attributes of the stimulus material, which could then be reported in accordance with the instructions. But since the memory image decayed rapidly, the attribute first reported was most correctly reported. However, Egerth (1967) considered that the emphasis given by the instructions might have had some additional effect on initial perception.

In a rather similar experiment, Brown (1960) presented tachistoscopically to his observers cards each with two rows of four coloured letters or digits on it. There were two sets of instructions: neutral instructions telling the observer where to record his report; and critical instructions, on what aspect of the stimulus to report. One set of instructions was given two seconds before presentation, the other at the same moment; sometimes critical instructions preceded neutral, sometimes *vice versa*. Report was more accurate with the critical instructions given first when the class of stimulus (letters or digits) was specified, but not when they related to position or colour. Brown concluded that the main effect was on selection from the primary memory image, though it would appear that there was some additional effect when attention was directed to the perception of a particular class of stimuli (letters or digits). However, it must be realized that attention to all aspects of the primary memory image is enhanced when the observer expects from the instructions that he will subsequently be required to select and report on one part of it.

In ordinary everyday life conditions, the distinction between set to perceive in accordance with expectations and direction of response is perhaps somewhat academic. Schemata laid down by prolonged experience both produce greater expectations as to the kind of object or event likely to be encountered in particular situations, and also direct the individual towards reactions appropriate to the situation. Moreover, it may be supposed that schemata related to particular classes of event include also a variety of related behaviour tendencies such that in any one case the appropriate form of behaviour is rapidly engendered. On the other hand, it would happen only rarely that observers would expect to utilize the primary memory image independently of the original percept, or to select certain parts of it without any foreknowledge as to which would be relevant to behaviour.

That in many of the experiments described familiarity and expectation lead to more rapid and extensive, and sometimes more accurate, responses, has been associated with direction of attention in an appropriate manner. Now these results might seem to conflict with the observations described in Section (1) of this chapter, that arousal and attention are greater with novel and unexpected stimulation. It would seem that the novel and unexpected do indeed arouse attention and direct it towards the investigation and exploration of the cause of stimulation. Nevertheless, these stimuli may not be identified until after such an investigation has been concluded. Hence there may be a retardation of identification, and even non-veridical perception, if investigation cannot be adequately performed. On the other hand, any such delay is eliminated by expectation. But it may also occur that when repetition of a familiar situation is excessive, habituation sets in, with consequent decline in arousal and a failure of focal attention, until some change in the situation takes place.

(5) Division and Fluctuation of Attention

It is clear that there are numerous situations in which it is difficult to ascertain the direction of attention, and that the focus of attention may vary from time to time, according to circumstances. Thus stimulation which is irrelevant to the main task may produce *distraction* which interferes with the concentration of attention upon this task. Such distraction may be set up by a sudden interruption from a novel, unusual or intense stimulus which, as we noted, tends to attract an observer's attention, and he is liable to abandon the task in hand until he has investigated the cause of interruption. Again, a succession of irrelevant stimuli occurring at unexpected intervals is likely to cause distraction and impair performance on the main task. It would seem probable that this is most likely to occur when the main task possesses little intrinsic interest. Yet in some circumstances, when the observer has come to expect irrelevant stimulation to occur, arousal may be increased and the main task performed as well or even better. Vogel-Sprott (1963) found this to happen in prolonged tasks with extraverted observers.

On the other hand, in situations of *stress* it would appear that there may be both a funnelling of attention and also an increased effect of distraction. Thus Bartlett (1943) described experiments on aircraft pilots in an experimental cockpit, which showed that towards the end of a two-hour period attention became concentrated mainly on the dials of the instrument panel to which response was most frequent, and other dials used less frequently, for instance the petrol gauge, were often ignored. But also irrelevant lights flashing up at intervals, which were ignored during the early part of the experiment, became increasingly distracting. Additionally, pilots became more aware of their own feelings of discomfort and fatigue, and often reacted emotionally to these. Again, Easterbrook (1959) found that in situations of emotional stress there was a narrowing in the range of cue utilization such that observers tended to ignore certain aspects of the situation to which they would otherwise have attended.

If an observer is required to perform two tasks simultaneously, performance of whichever is considered to be the main task is less likely to be impaired by *division of attention* than is that of the minor task. Thus Webster and Haslerud (1964) presented as the main task counting the appearances of a flashing light seen in foveal vision; and as the subsidiary task, responding to lights appearing for two seconds in peripheral vision. As compared with the performance of either task singly, in the dual task a smaller percentage of the peripheral lights was responded to,

G

and reaction times were slower; but the main task was not impaired. With two tasks of unequal difficulty, the easier may be more affected than the harder. Mowbray (1952) compared the successive with the simultaneous performance of two tasks, to detect omissions in series of letters or of numbers. The former task is the harder, because there are more letters to choose from than numbers. The increase in omissions from the successive to the simultaneous condition was less for the letters than for the numbers.

But in some cases discrimination in the main task may be considerably

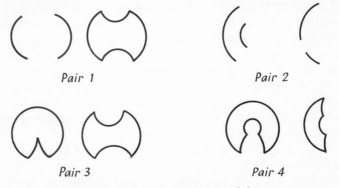

Pair 1   Pair 2

Pair 3   Pair 4

FIG. 27 Assimilation between pairs of shapes
(*After* Gardner and Lohrenz (1961) p. 608)

affected by simultaneous performance of a subsidiary one. Thus Gardner and Lohrenz (1961) presented pairs of diagrams to observers who at the same time counted backwards by twos (see Fig. 27). In reproducing them subsequently there was a tendency to assimilate the diagrams to each other, transposing elements from one to the other. Again, Kahnemann *et al.* (1967) required observers to detect particular letters from among groups of five letters flashed at successive seconds, while simultaneously carrying out an adding task. Arousal was raised, as indicated by increased pupil dilatation. Performances of both tasks was impaired, but more in the detection task than in the adding task; attention to the former appeared to be fragmented. Memory of the material was also affected, suggesting that it may be difficult to store material presented visually under distraction. Mackworth (1965) found that the matching of a letter presented tachistoscopically in foveal vision to one or other of two letters presented peripherally was considerably impaired when other letters were shown in the field. Perception was interfered with when only two extra letters were added if these were just outside the peripheral signal letters. When the whole field was covered with additional letters, perception was confined to a central tunnel.

It seems clear, as we noted in Section (2) of this chapter, that there are necessarily *limitations on the amount of information* which can be simultaneously attended to and perceived; though it is possible that, while some information is attended to centrally and processed immediately, other information may be temporarily stored for subsequent processing (Broadbent, 1958). But it would seem that limitations of the total amount which can be perceived simultaneously necessitate selection, hence interaction between different percepts. Observers will tend

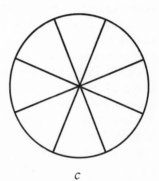

FIG. 28 Alternating figure and ground
a. *After* Rubin (1921)
b. *After* Rock and Kremer (1957) p. 25
c. Sector figure

to select and to process information which they regard as important and interesting – or to which their attention has been specifically drawn, as shown in Section (4); and to disregard the less significant. But the balance of selection may in some cases be upset by distraction.

But also there are situations in which attention seems to *fluctuate* between two aspects of the stimulus material which cannot be perceived simultaneously. In *figure-ground alternation*, sometimes one part of a pattern appears figural, the remainder constituting the ground, and sometimes the other. Rubin (1921) found that with figures such as that in Fig. 28a, some observers spontaneously saw the black part as figural, others the white. On subsequent presentation, there was in general a tendency to recognize the same part as figural. Rock and Kremer (1957) modified Rubin's procedure by presenting the black or white parts alone of figures such as Fig. 28b. The complete double figures were later presented with other new figures, and the observers were required to say whether the black or white part appeared figural. In this case, there was no significant tendency to report as figural the part previously seen alone. Subsequently Cornwell (1963), using figures in which the figural part was exaggerated in size, did demonstrate a tendency to see as figural the part previously presented. Nevertheless, it was clear also that observers were in fact aware of both parts of the complete figure. Thus Epstein and Rock (1960) and Epstein and De Shazo (1961) found, using a figure such as Fig. 39c (p. 206), that the expectation of one aspect was less effective in producing subsequent perception of this as figural than was the frequency and recency of its exposure. However, even in these cases there was some oscillation. If a GSR response was conditioned to the non-favoured aspect, it was found to occur in presentations of the complete figure.

If certain figures are steadily fixated for a period of time, 'figure' and 'ground' *alternate* spontaneously. With even so simple a figure as that in Fig. 28c alternation takes place during prolonged fixation between the horizontal-vertical and oblique (Maltese) cross. In general, the horizontal-vertical cross tended to predominate over the oblique; and if the sectors of one cross were narrower than those of the other, the former cross was more figural and was perceived to a greater extent (Oyama, 1960). The same effect was observed with a brighter or more highly coloured cross. Directing the observer to attend specifically to one cross rather than the other prolonged its appearance; but the other could not be altogether suppressed. Similar alternations have been demonstrated with meaningful figures such as the 'wife and mother-in-law' (Fig. 29); (Boring, 1930), and others used by Fisher (1967). But one aspect may be more persistent than the other, either through spontaneous selection or through the previous establishment of set. Thus Bugelski and Alampay (1961) found that the face or the rat (see Fig. 26, p. 82) tended to predominate when preceded by pictures of faces or animals; and Leeper (1935) obtained the same effect with the 'wife and mother-in-law'.

Similar alternations occur with *reversible perspective figures*, in which an ambiguous figure appears to be sometimes protruding and sometimes receding. Several of these were discussed by Vernon (1952); and it was noted that again one aspect could be emphasized and prolonged by enhancing figural characteristics, and also that attention could be to some extent controlled voluntarily. Donahue and Griffiths (1931) found that alternation was less with more complex figures; but was greatest when the two aspects possessed similar amounts of complexity and meaningfulness.

A number of more recent experiments have studied the alternation between the two aspects of the *Necker cube*, the left face appearing in front of or behind the right face. Now it has been suggested that these and other forms of alternation are due to '*satiation*'; that is to say, that some process in the central nervous system, possibly in the reticular formation, becomes satiated by one part or one aspect of an ambiguous figure which is then replaced by the other. This form of satiation could be related to the type which Köhler and Wallach (1964) claimed to occur

FIG. 29 'My wife and my mother-in-law'
(*After* Boring (1930) p. 444)

in the 'figural after effect', in which previous inspection of a figure causes the subsequent perception of a test figure to recede from the position of the inspection figure. However, experiments with the Necker cube suggest that any satiation which does occur is of a different type, if indeed satiation there be. Thus Kolers (1964) found that reversals occurred more frequently when the Necker cube was displayed intermittently or moved about, when little satiation would be expected, than when it was observed continuously in a stationary position. Previous inspection of another Necker cube did increase reversal. But this inspection figure could be a black on white Necker cube preceding a white on black, or a cube of another size (Cohen, 1959). However, there was no effect from another figure in the same position. A general enhancement of depth cues was found by Howard (1961) to decrease reversal. He measured the period of time until the first reversal occurred, and showed that it increased from a flat cube drawing to a stationary solid cube; to a rotating cube seen in monocular vision, and then to one seen in binocular vision (the rotating movement increases the depth effect, see p. 132). The effect of satiation on reversal was highly specific, and occurred only with previous exposure of an identical object in exactly the same position. Thus it would seem from these and from other observations on alternation that enhancement of the ambiguity of these figures makes it difficult to preserve a particular aspect in central attention; and it is liable to be replaced by an alternative aspect.

A similar phenomenon appears when two different figures are presented one to one eye and one to the other, so that they are projected on corresponding retinal positions. Three different types of *binocular interaction* may occur. One percept may completely suppress the other; this usually occurs if a figured field is presented to one eye and a plain unfigured one to the other. If the two percepts are fairly similar, they may fuse together. A particular case is the partial fusion of images obtained of solid objects by the two eyes from their differing viewpoints. This produces the stereoscopic perception of depth and distance (see Chapter VII). But two dissimilar figures, with approximately equal degrees of figural quality, tend to alternate with each other in *binocular rivalry*. The rate of alternation is to some extent under voluntary control, and observers given suitable instructions can make alternation quicker or slower, for instance between sets of horizontal and vertical bars (Meredith and Meredith, 1962). Rivalry may be related to meaningful factors. Thus Ono *et al.* (1966) found that photographs of men showing strongly contrasted emotions, such as rage and glee, produced more binocular rivalry than when the emotions were less obviously different from each other. But if one figure is more impressive or more meaningful than the other, it tends to dominate over and even suppress the other. Thus Engel (1956) found that if the photograph of a face was presented to one eye, and the same photograph upside down to the other, the former predominated. Hastorf and Mayo (1959) found a similar predominance of an upright postage stamp over an inverted one. Engel (1956) also presented a picture of a face to one eye, and of the male genitals to the other. All observers saw the face first, and nearly half continued to do so throughout the period of exposure; the remainder saw the genitals after a few seconds. Bagby (1957) showed a Mexican scene to one eye and an American scene to the other. The former tended to dominate the perception of Mexican observers, the latter of American.

These phenomena, although they may be due basically to interaction of the formal properties of stimulation, clearly are influenced by attention based upon the cognitive factors of meaning and interest. It is more difficult to attribute to any effect of attention the phenomena which occur when one stimulus immediately succeeds another, though even here they may be some interaction with attentional processes. It has been found that perception, especially of low intensity stimulation, takes time to develop fully. Thus awareness of near threshold stimulation is not complete until about 200 msec. after its onset (Crawford, 1947). Hence there may be interference between two rapidly succeeding stimuli, or even inhibition of one by the other. Alpern (1953) demonstrated this phenomenon, which he called '*metacontrast*' (often since termed '*masking*'), showing that the apparent brightness of a test patch, exposed for 5 msec., was reduced by exposing brighter contrast patches at a time interval of 100 msec. before or after it. The effect was increased by increasing the brightness of the contrast patches or increasing their duration, but decreased by prolonging the exposure of the test patch. The effect was reduced if the two stimuli were spatially separated from each other. If figures were employed as test stimuli, they might be masked and altogether obscured. Cheatham (1952) presented various shapes for 100 msec., followed in each case at intervals of 0-100 msec. by a larger and brighter field. With short intervals, the figures were obscured by the bright field; as the time intervals lengthened, the figures gradually broke through, more and more of the contour appearing. The brighter the figures, the sooner this occurred. Humphrey *et al.* (1955) showed that the partial or total suppression, by the subsequently exposed bright field, of perception of a black cross on a white ground varied with the duration of exposure of both stimuli. But the interposition of a short dark period of 20-65 msec. between the two stimuli prevented suppression, although often the darkness was not perceived. Weinstein and Haber (1965) found that masking was greatest at an interval of about 30 msec. between the initial and the subsequent masking stimulus. This they demonstrated by presenting a capital O or D, followed by a ring which surrounded its position. Correct recognition of the letter was ncreasingly prevented as the time interval increased to 30 msec., and improved thereafter. Schiller and Wiener (1963) studied the masking of capital letters by presenting homogeneous and patterned fields for 100 msec. at an interval of 40 msec. afterwards. Here the effect was greater when the homogeneous field was less bright, but was greater still when it was patterned. Moreover, when the patterned field was presented to one eye and the capital letter to the other, the latter was masked by the former; but this effect did not occur with the homogeneous field. But a masking dichoptic effect was demonstrated by Wagman and Battersby (1959) with plain unfigured fields.

Thus although the simpler phenomena of masking might be attributed to interference at retinal level, the dichoptic masking would appear to result from some process in the central nervous system. Sperling (1960) found that the visual memory image of complex figures was affected by the post-exposure field. Thus the memory span for a series of capital letters was greatly reduced if the post-exposure field was bright instead of dark, through destruction of the after image.

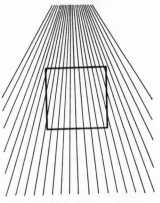

FIG. 30 Metacontrast figures
(*After* Smith and Henriksson (1955) p. 347)

In these cases, the observers were usually aware of an interfering stimulus. But other cases have been reported in which perception of figures is *distorted* by previous or subsequent presentation of other figures, although the observer is unaware of these. Smith and Henriksson (1955) demonstrated this effect with two figures which, when presented simultaneously, produced an illusory effect (see Fig. 30). The square appears trapezoidal through distortion by the radiating lines. If these lines were presented for a period of 3 msec. immediately before presentation of the square, the lines were not perceived but the square appeared distorted, the distortion increasing when the time of exposure of the lines was increased. A somewhat similar effect was demonstrated by Goldstein (1960), with illusions in which the distorting background was exposed simultaneously with the figures, but below the threshold of intensity of vision. However, this phenomenon should perhaps be more properly classed as an instance of 'subliminal perception' (see p. 96).

More curious effects were obtained using meaningful figures. Thus

Smith and Klein (see Smith and Henriksson, 1955) showed the drawing of a face, preceded by a face with a happy expression exposed for a period of 10 msec. The latter was not perceived by the observers; nevertheless, the second face was said to have a happy expression, not apparent when it was shown alone. In a second experiment (Klein *et al.*, 1958), drawings of nude figures of neutral sex were preceded by drawings of the male or female genitals, for periods of 20-35 msec. There was a tendency in some observers to perceive the neutral figure as male when preceded by male genitals, and as female when preceded by female genitals. But other observers perceived a contrast effect. Klein *et al.* attempted to relate these individual differences to personality differences in masculinity and femininity of the observers, who were all males.

Eagle (1959) presented the drawing of a youth standing alone, preceded by one or other of two pictures; the first showed the same youth stabbing a man, and the second, the youth presenting the man with a drink. These initial stimuli were masked by the following one. Nevertheless, it appeared that the youth in the second picture was rated as more unpleasant and aggressive when preceded by the aggressive scene than by the non-aggressive scene. Guthrie and Wiener (1966) attempted to explain these effects in terms of the greater angularity of the figures in the aggressive than in the non-aggressive scene. This angularity could be perceived even when the scenes were masked. They also produced evidence to show that angularity may be associated with aggression, and curved contours with non-aggression. But these effects were not very convincing.

Neisser (1967) has attributed many of these effects of masking, and particularly those of Sperling, to the persistence of the immediate stimulation in an 'immediate memory image'; or, as he calls it, '*iconic memory*', to differentiate it from other forms of imagery. When complex material is presented, it cannot be fully identified during the period of exposure, though the perceptual processes may begin then. But for full identification, the observer needs to process the iconic memory, which persists for periods of a second and over if the post-exposure field is dark, but for less than a second if it is bright. A second, masking, stimulus interferes with the process of identification of the iconic memory, and may either modify it or suppress it altogether. However, in experiments such as that of Eagle some part of the iconic memory would appear to persist and to affect subsequent perception, although the observer is not conscious of the iconic memory. These phenomena again suggest that the interaction between direction of attention and what is perceived and remembered subsequently is exceedingly complex.

(6) Subliminal Perception

In the previous section we have considered some of the masking effects attributed to partial perception of stimuli of which observers are not really aware. But it has been claimed that such partial perception may occur also in 'subliminal perception', with stimuli which are presented *below the normal threshold of visibility*; that is to say, when intensity is so low or duration so brief that normally nothing would be perceived. In the most characteristic type of subliminal perception, though the observer is not consciously aware of the stimulus, nevertheless he is able to guess with greater than chance accuracy what it might have been, or to say what kind of stimulus it was.

The forerunner of investigations into subliminal perception was a curious experiment carried out many years ago by Perky (1910). He presented coloured shapes, such as those of a tomato, orange, banana, etc., in illuminations of about threshold intensity, instructing the observers to fixate the point where they appeared and imagine each of the objects in turn. In general, the observers did not realize that they were perceiving actual shapes, but believed that they had imaged them. But observers instructed that they would be shown these shapes had little difficulty in perceiving them. Thus the phenomena experienced depended upon the observer's expectations.

Miller (1939) created expectations that some type of ESP* phenomenon might be experienced. He presented five shapes such as a circle, square, star, etc., at below threshold intensity, and instructed his observers that every time a bell rang they should try to guess which of the five shapes had been turned up by the experimenter in a pack of ESP cards. At very low illuminations, judgments showed no greater than chance accuracy. When illumination was increased to just below the threshold intensity, accuracy improved considerably, although the observers were quite sure that they had actually seen nothing. Observers told the true purpose of the experiment were able to guess correctly at lower intensities of illumination. King *et al.* (1944), however, found that accuracy of guessing three shapes at below threshold intensity was unrelated to the absolute brightness, which varied from five f.c.s. to sixty f.c.s. below threshold. But there were considerable individual variations, some observers achieving only chance accuracy.

* At the time at which this experiment was carried out, there was a general interest in the phenomena of ESP – extrasensory perception – in which it was claimed that people could guess the nature of figures on cards which were being viewed by someone else.

Investigations have also been carried out into the subliminal perception of *words*. Thus Edwards (1960) found that when words were presented below the threshold at which they could be recognized correctly, observers could nevertheless make several correct guesses, especially if they were asked to choose the word from among five others. Kolers (1957) presented rows of figures tachistoscopically, asking the observer to name the figure that appeared in all three rows. For half the observers this figure was flashed for an exposure of 3 msec. immediately beforehand. These observers were significantly more accurate in identifying the common figures than were observers who had not received the preliminary signal. However, it is possible that it may have been partially perceived, and was not wholly subliminal. Thus Wiener and Schiller (1960) found that observers, asked to choose between a pair of names attached to a diagram, one of which was ringed by a circle exposed at threshold intensity, selected the ringed name only when they could see some part of the circle.

However, Dixon considered that in his extensive investigations of these phenomena he was able to demonstrate the occurrence of true subliminal perception. In one experiment (1958a), he presented ten words singly, four of them with sexual meanings, below the absolute threshold of intensity. At the signal given when a word was presented, the observer had to say the first word that came into his head; and also his GSR was recorded. The GSR and the delay in responding verbally were significantly greater for the sexual than for the neutral words. Even when the words guessed were incorrect, they were frequently associated to the stimulus words in meaning. Moreover, the observers were sometimes able to associate from their responses to the stimulus words. Thus it was concluded that the observer became aware of the type of word exposed, and especially of its emotional significance, in conditions in which he could not identify it completely. This result is related to the findings on 'subception' which we shall discuss in Chapter XI. However, later experiments of the same type by Fuhrer and Eriksen (1961) produced entirely negative results.

Dixon (1955) also found that observers could guess with greater than chance accuracy the numbers 1, 2 and 6, and their printed names, when they were presented below threshold intensity. In order to compensate for temporary fluctuations in threshold, and prevent the stimulus from rising above the threshold, he then required the observer to maintain a spot of light, viewed with the left eye, just below the threshold of visibility, while viewing with the right eye numbers exposed at a constant intensity below the threshold value. Those who had been instructed beforehand that numbers would be projected to the right eye identified the 1 and 2 with above chance accuracy, though not the 6. This effect did not occur with observers who had not been so instructed. It would therefore seem that a slight amount of subliminal perception may occur even with unemotional stimuli if there is appropriate direction of attention. Again Fiss (1966) found that observers instructed to adopt an alert expectant attitude reported imagery relevant to a complex meaningful figure exposed subliminally, whereas those told to take a passive non-expectant attitude did not do this. Yet neither set of observers could report any actual perception of the stimulus.

Considerable doubts were cast on the existence of genuine subliminal perception by Goldiamond (1958). He discussed at some length the problem of obtaining consistent and reliable *measures of the threshold* of vision, and quoted Blackwell as finding that it depended on the manner in which it was estimated. The most common method is to require the observer to view a stimulus in gradually increasing intensity of illumination or duration of stimulation, and to state whether or not he perceives it. Different observers respond differently, some saying 'Yes' when they are very uncertain, others refraining from saying 'Yes' until they are absolutely certain. Moreover, the criteria may vary even during the experiment. Blackwell found that thresholds determined in this manner were both higher and more variable than those assessed by the 'forced-choice' method, when the observer is required to state the position of the stimulus in the field as soon as he can. This ensures that he is actually perceiving it.

The relevance of these observations to subliminal perception is that with a rather high threshold determination obtained by the 'Yes-No' method, what is supposed to be subliminal is not in fact below the threshold of vision. Even when observers are unable to identify what they have seen, they may have observed fragments of it sufficient to give some clue as to its identity, or to its emotional significance. Thus Eriksen *et al.* (1959) found that when words were presented tachistoscopically, round about the threshold point, some could be judged as pleasant or unpleasant even when they were incorrectly identified. However, the threshold for correct affective judgment was not on the average lower than that for correct identification. Thus they concluded that emotional classification and identification take place independently, on the basis of fragmentary perception; and sometimes one, sometimes the other, is first made correctly.

Now it is true that threshold variation can hardly account for Dixon's results using the two eyes independently. However, it is still possible that the numbers were not so far below threshold as to provide no information, even of a fragmentary character. It must be remembered also that observers are very prone to make inferences from such fragments which, as we noted in section (4), are much influenced by what the observer expects to perceive. Thus the existence of truly subliminal perception is still a matter of doubt. But it is not impossible that the focusing of attention on particular aspects of the stimulus, and the expectation that certain types of stimulation may occur, give rise to the identification of stimuli which in other circumstances would be completely ignored.

VI

The Restriction and Failure of Attention

(1) Vigilance

In recent years there has been much investigation into the effects on arousal and attention which occur when stimulation is homogeneous rather than variable, or is excessively limited. As we noted on p. 71, Dember and Earl (1957) stated that the conditions in which attention was maximally aroused were either temporal change, as in novel situations, or spatial changes with inhomogeneous stimulation. Many experiments have been carried out in relation to absence of temporal change, when the same type of stimulation is repeated monotonously over a considerable period of time. The usual effect is a decline in 'vigilance', that is to say of attention to and perception of the stimuli.

It has for long been known that in industry tasks involving the prolonged *repetition* of a single short operation throughout the day tend to lead first of all to an increased variation in the time taken to perform the task, and later to a general decrease in rate of work (Wyatt and Fraser, 1929, 1937). The rate tends to be lowest at the middle of the working spell, and to increase towards the end. Feelings of boredom are often experienced. But these effects could be due to the monotony of the actions performed, rather than to perceptual repetition (see McGrath, 1963b). The effects of repetition on perception were first investigated experimentally by Mackworth (1950). He presented to his observers, for a period of two hours, a type of clock face with a pointer moving round it in small regular jumps. At fairly infrequent and irregular intervals, the pointer made a double jump; and the observer was required to signal each occurrence of a double jump by pressing a key. After about half-an-hour observers began to miss the double jumps; and the number of omissions increased throughout the two-hour period. Several varieties of task produced similar results: observing a regular series of flashes of light, with an occasional brighter flash (Bakan, 1955);

detecting signals lit up by a sweeping line of light on a simulated radar screen (Mackworth, 1950; Baker, 1956); reporting the appearance of a circle of unusual size among a number of other circles (Fraser, 1957).

The decrease in efficiency in performing these tasks was attributed to a decline in the observer's *vigilance* or *attention* to the task. Though it occurred in several different tasks, decline in efficiency varied considerably with the *nature of the task*. In general, it was less when discrimination between signals and non-signals was easy, perhaps because arousal is greater when there is a strong contrast with surroundings. Thus using his type of radar task, Mackworth (1950) found little decline in performance with relatively bright signals. Fraser (1957) obtained a similar result when there was a large difference in size between signal and non-signal circles. Fraser also found that there was no decline in performance when the exposure of the signals was increased from one to two seconds.

Variable effects were produced by varying the *difficulty* of the task. Jerison (1963) found that making the task more complex by requiring the observer to respond to signals on three clock faces instead of one produced a very rapid initial decline in performance, followed by no further decrement over a two-hour period. But here the initial effect could have been produced by the difficulty of scanning, which then maintained arousal throughout the period. Buckner (1963) found that performance was better initially and also declined less in a complex task involving monitoring both visual and auditory signals, than with either singly. But Broadbent (1963) considered that decline was less with tasks of moderate difficulty than with either very difficult or very easy tasks. And indeed it has been postulated that arousal is greatest in tasks of medium difficulty. The very easy do not stimulate effort. The very difficult may produce over-arousal, with perhaps a tendency to over-speediness and hence inaccurate response, or even anxiety. Again, a variable irrelevant auditory stimulus (music, etc.) prevented decline in a visual vigilance task to a greater extent than did a steady irrelevant stimulus, provided that the visual signals were not too rapid (McGrath, 1963a). But with rapid signals, the effects were reversed. Presumably in the first case arousal was increased by the auditory stimulus; but in the second, there was over-arousal. The presence of the experimenter in the room with the observer also prevented decline, possibly also through increased arousal (Fraser, 1953). Decline in arousal may also be demonstrated in an increasing failure to perceive signals which are actually being fixated by the eyes; Mackworth *et al.* (1964) showed this to be a common cause of omissions. Haider (1967) found that amplitude of evoked responses in the EEG was less with missed signals than with those perceived.

But another important factor may be the observer's *expectations* as to the appearance of signals. If these are presented at even intervals of time, the observer comes to expect their appearance and hence does not overlook them (Baker, 1956). On the other hand, if one signal appears shortly after another, it is often missed because it is unexpected (Mackworth, 1950). A relatively high rate of presentation, with short intervening intervals and a knowledge of where the signal will appear, increases expectancy and improves performance (Baker, 1963). Again, it was found that when the frequency of all signals was high, including the frequency of those to which a response was to be made (high probability), performance was better and decline less than with low rate and high probability; while the results were poorest with high rate and low probability (Colquhoun, 1961). This result might also be related to the increased caution in responding shown to occur during the later stages of an auditory vigilance task (Broadbent, 1963).

Most experimenters have found considerable *individual differences* in vigilance tasks, and individuals may differ even in the performance of different types of task (Buckner, 1963). However, there seemed to be a tendency for those originally more alert to show less decline than did the originally more sluggish. Vogel-Sprott (1963) presented a dual vigilance task in which observers had firstly to report whenever rotating pointers reached a certain position on a dial, and secondly whenever an irregularly flashing light appeared. In addition, for some observers distracting picture slides were exposed from time to time at one side. The reaction times to the dial signals were unaffected by the distracting pictures, but those to the flashing lights were usually increased, especially for introverted observers. The extraverted did relatively worse when there were no distracting pictures; it is possible that distraction increased their arousal. Davies and Hockey (1966) found that in a task of very rapid cancellation of digits, which did not correspond with digits exposed for two-thirds of a second each, extraverts showed decrease in accuracy over a half-hour period, whereas introverts did not.

It is likely that vigilance performance is affected by *motivation*, which also could lead to individual differences. This problem has not been fully explored. But motivation may have caused the effect obtained by Mackworth (1950) of giving observers some knowledge of their results. Thus there was little or no decline in performance when they were informed after every signal whether they had responded to it correctly or had missed it. It is possible also that the presence of the experimenter in the room may have had a motivating effect.

It will have appeared from the preceding discussion that the main factor involved in decrease of vigilance in tasks of this kind is a *decline of arousal*. The cause seems to be habituation to a relatively unchanging situation which has little natural interest. It is possible even that some degree of inhibition arises from the frustrating effects of a task that leads to no particular goal and gives little intrinsic satisfaction. However, increase in motivation may heighten interest; and the existence of strong achievement motivation could provide the observer with a built-in incentive to persist. On the other hand, it is probable that vigilance is maximal with moderate degrees of arousal; and that anxiety and excessive desire to succeed could lead to over-arousal, especially in difficult tasks, and hence a decline in performance. Again, observers who tend to restlessness, possibly indicating over-arousal, performed less well than did the less active (Baker, 1959).

It would seem that the effects of expectation may interact with those of arousal, and that in so far as the former are linked to the functions of the thalamic reticular formation, they may also deteriorate with habituation to repeated unvarying stimulation. Broadbent (1958) considered that as the effects of novelty wore off, increasing blockage of perception by irrelevant stimulation, including that from the observer's own fantasies and emotions, might interfere with the concentration of attention on the signals. It would seem that such a blockage might also be related to failure in functioning of the specific reticular formation; or indeed to blockages similar to those observed by Hernandez-Peon *et al.* (1956).

A somewhat different explanation, of the vigilance phenomena is suggested by the more recent experiments of Broadbent and Gregory (1963, 1965). They presented a regular series of flashes to their observers, the signals being irregularly occurring slightly brighter flashes. To every flash the observer had to respond by pressing one of three buttons which signalled 'Sure Yes', 'Unsure' and 'Sure No' respectively. Thus it was possible to calculate both the certainty with which observers detected signals and also the number of 'false positives', that is to say, sure and unsure judgments that the flash was a signal when in fact it was not. From these data it could be shown that the number of signals detected did not decrease during a watch period of seventy minutes, but that the *certainty of response* did decrease. Thus capacity to attend to and detect signals did not decline, but observers' disposition to report them did decline. This occurred to a greater extent when signal rate was low than when it was high. Now it must be noted, firstly, that this

H

effect did not appear at a second watch, suggesting that it disappeared after greater experience of the situation. And secondly, J. F. Mackworth and Taylor (1963) carried out experiments using as signals short pauses in the motion of the hand of a clock, in which they found a genuine decrement in ability to detect these signals which was independent of degree of response suppression (disposition to report). Broadbent and Gregory suggested that in these experiments it was more difficult to detect signals than in their own. But Mackworth and Taylor stated that the effect was not limited to near-threshold discrimination. The results of Broadbent and Gregory suggest that there must be some hesitation in attributing the findings of vigilance experiments to decrease in perceptual arousal, rather than to changes in judgment and response. But it is difficult to explain why response tendencies should have been limited in this manner. If the limitation was due to increasing caution in reporting signals of which the observer was uncertain, why should caution increase during the course of prolonged monotonous tasks? Is it possible that on the other hand a decline in physiological arousal and activation caused observers to be unwilling to make the effort to discriminate between signals and non-signals and to respond appropriately? There seems at present to be no answer to these questions.

(2) The *Ganzfeld* and the Stabilized Retinal Image

We must now consider what occurs when information is restricted by lack of spatial variation in the field. The effects on perception of presenting a completely homogeneous field have been investigated in two slightly different types of experiment, on the *Ganzfeld* and the stabilized retinal image. Now Metzger (1930) found that if an observer looked at an extensive white wall in dim light, it appeared as a grey fog, without spatial localization. When the intensity of illumination was increased, the observer was able to see the grain or 'microstructure' of the wall's surface, and it then appeared as a flat surface. From this Koffka (1935) concluded that for any normal perception of surfaces, some degree of inhomogeneity in the stimulus pattern is necessary. Again, Katz (1935) showed that if a homogeneous coloured surface was viewed through a small hole in a screen, it lost all detail and appeared not as a surface but as a film, vague, soft and unlocalized in space. If the size of the aperture was increased, the surface then lost the appearance of a film and was perceived as a hard textured surface (Gibson and Dibble, 1952). Hochberg *et al.* (1951) produced an even greater homogeneity of stimulation, termed the *Ganzfeld*, by covering the observer's eyes with two halves of a ping-pong ball and directing on to these a uniform coloured light. After a few minutes the colour faded completely and was replaced by a grey or black fog or cloud. If then the eyes were moved briskly to and fro, half the observers perceived a brief flash of the colour of the incident light, sometimes preceded by a flash of the complementary colour. Gibson and Waddell (1952), using a similar technique, also found that observers perceived a cloud or fog; although there was some suggestion of distance within it, this was very indefinite.

In the experiments of Cohen (1957, 1958, 1960) the observer gazed into a uniformly illuminated white sphere which fitted closely to the face; thus he was presented with a completely homogeneous bright surface. He perceived at first a kind of diffuse impenetrable fog, beginning close to his eyes and extending for an indefinite distance. It was succeeded by a 'blank-out' of the whole field of view, which thereafter alternated with the fog. Bursts of alpha rhythm in the EEG, indicating decrease in arousal, accompanied blank-out; these were intermediate in amount between those occurring when the eyes were closed and when they were open (Tepas, 1962). Periods of blank-out increased with exposure to the *Ganzfeld*, and then became stabilized at about 10-15 per cent of exposure time. Saccadic eye movements were reduced or absent. After prolonged exposure to the *Ganzfeld*, some observers felt that they could no longer see (Cohen, 1960). They did not know if their eyes were open or closed, and sometimes felt disturbed and dizzy. Though the earlier blank-out could be removed by extensive blinking, this later condition was very resistant to blinking. It might be terminated by presenting forms in the field, but observers were extremely slow to perceive these. Even quite early in the period of exposure to the *Ganzfeld* there might be difficulty in recognizing forms. Contours might be blurred and shapes transformed. Movement was perceived with difficulty. The time taken to locate forms was greatly increased, and sometimes observers were unaware where they were searching or where they had previously searched (Miller and Ludvigh, 1960). However, any inhomogeneity in the field, such as a spot of light of different intensity, did produce a separation between figure and ground. Moreover, a movement of a figure in the field seemed to give rise to regeneration of normal perception through varying stimulation.

In normal circumstances, perception is maintained even during apparent fixation, by constant *eye movement*, such that there is always some movement of the image across the retina. Ditchburn and Ginsborg (1953), using a system called the 'optical lever' by which light is reflected from a small mirror attached to the cornea and recorded, demonstrated three types of eye movement during fixation: (1) A continuous small rapid tremor; (2) a gradual slow drift across the field; (3) rapid flicks which corrected the drift. It was later shown by Boyce (1967) that the drift was related to instability in the maintenance of fixation by the extra-ocular muscles; the flicks brought the image back to the point of fixation, and in some cases shifted the image to prevent it from falling for too long on the same area of the retina. The slight tremor also assisted this function.

However, it was found possible to eliminate these effects of eye movement, and to project the image of a figure continuously on to the same area of the retina. Ditchburn and Ginsborg (1962) and Riggs *et al.* (1953) independently designed a technique in which the stimulus pattern was directed on to the retina by a mirror attached to a contact lens fitted to the cornea. In this way, the retinal image was *stabilized*; it moved as the eye moved, and thus maintained a constant position on the retina. In another technique, designed by Ditchburn and Pritchard (1956), a minute telescopic system containing the stimulus and a lens system was attached to the contact lens; and this system focused the stimulus figure on the retina. Ditchburn and Ginsborg (1952) used a half-black half-white target, and found that the line of demarcation between the two halves disappeared from view for two to three seconds at intervals of about a minute. In a similar experiment with a black line target, the stabilized image was regenerated after disappearance by projecting a flickering light (Ditchburn and Fender, 1955). It could also be regenerated if sharp flicks were imparted to the image; and a rapid imposed tremor largely prevented disappearance (Ditchburn *et al.*, 1959). Riggs *et al.* (1953) also found that the disappearance of a black line, which occurred more quickly if the line was narrow than if it was thicker, was prevented by eye movement. Using the technique of Ditchburn and Pritchard, Pritchard *et al.* (1960) and Evans (1964, 1965) found that, for a variety of *figures*, there was after a short time a softening of the contrast between figure and ground, and then a fading and disappearance of the whole figure, or parts of it, the field then appearing homogeneous. The figure reappeared within a few seconds, and then fading and reappearance alternated, at random intervals. But the amount and type of fading varied with the nature of the figure.

Pritchard *et al.* (1960) were struck by the fact that the target figures they presented seemed to break up into their natural parts; some of these disappeared while others remained. Thus with triangles and squares as targets, one or two sides might disappear as wholes, leaving the remainder. Figures with continuous curved contours were more stable than jagged irregular figures. So also were *meaningful figures*; a profile disappeared less than did a meaningless curved line, and the former tended to fragment in such a way that recognizable facial features remained. A letter B superimposed on jagged lines disappeared less readily than did the lines (Eagle and Klein, 1962). The word PET was more stable than the nonsense syllable TEP. Low frequency words were less stable than high frequency. Words also fragmented in a meaningful manner; thus BEER broke up to give PEER, PEEP BEE or BE, but seldom EER (Pritchard, 1961).

Pritchard *et al.* (1960) also found that in certain complex meaningless figures, fragmentary disappearance was in accordance with the *Gestalt principles*. Thus with columns and rows of small squares, one or more whole rows could disappear at a time. Evans (1964) was able to demonstrate other similar effects. Thus with randomly distributed red and green dots, those of similar colour tended to disappear together. A similar effect occurred with dots in close proximity; and with dots making up a straight line or a circle. With a trapezium overlapping a circle, one or other figure (more commonly the trapezium) disappeared, leaving the other intact. With a figure similar to that of the Poggendorff illusion, either the oblique line disappeared as a whole, or the column of two parallel lines (Evans and Piggins, 1963).

The resistance of contours to disappearance was also demonstrated in experiments by Beeler *et al.* (1963), with the Ishihara plates. When prints were made of these and viewed as stabilized images, in the miniature telescopic system, the colours desaturated until the number patterns were no longer visible. But the contours of the dots did not disappear entirely, although the dots were coloured a neutral grey or brown.

Now the results of Evans described above, and those of Pritchard *et al.*, were based on reports of the occurrence of these phenomena, without any assessment of their *frequency of occurrence*. Since they were rather striking in nature, it would seem possible that their frequency was over-estimated. Evans (1964, 1965) carried out more systematic quantitative studies, both of the relative frequencies of disappearance of different figures and also of the manner of disappearance, whether as a whole, a random disappearance of different parts, or a structured disappearance as in the observations described above. Observers were required to signal whenever these effects occurred; thus their duration could be measured. Evans then found that the total time of disappearance did vary greatly with the type of figure. A circle was more stable than an ellipse, and also than a circle containing crossed diagonals. Rounded and curved figures disappeared less than did jagged or spiky figures with acute angles. Breaking up and random disappearance of parts was the most frequent type of disappearance for all figures. But with the circle, and to a rather less degree with the ellipse, disappearance of the figure as a whole was almost as frequent. With other figures there was some structured disappearance; thus for the circle with crossed diagonals, halves or quadrants might disappear, or one or both diagonals, or the circumference of the circle. Reappearance was often fragmented in the same manner. But total reappearance might be produced by blinking or eye movement.

Effects similar to these were obtained when the *after image* of a brightly illuminated figure was viewed in a dark room or with eyes closed. Figures such as a square with crossed diagonals and a N faded in the same way as did stabilized images, through fragmentation; straight lines disappeared as wholes (Bennett-Clark and Evans, 1963). With a circle containing crossed diagonals, the proportions of unitary (whole), random and structured disappearance were similar to those obtained with a stabilized image (Evans, 1964). After images of whole words persisted for longer than did meaningless structures resembling words (Arnold *et al.*, 1968).

Non-quantitative studies have also been carried out with *steady fixation* of a bright figure in a dimly illuminated or dark room. Evans and Piggins (1963) found that in these conditions there was rapid partial fading, but little or no total disappearance; and fragmentation of figures occurred in a manner similar to that of stabilized images. McKinney (1963) also observed fragmentation during steady fixation, with the figure HB giving H, B, 3 or 13. Another experiment by McKinney (1966) showed that with steady fixation fragmentation occurred less readily with capital letters that had been named as such than when the letters L, T and V were not named and were presented in a group with other meaningless figures. Here the fragmentation was related to verbal identification rather than to figural qualities. On the other hand, Eagle *et al.* (1966) found that there were no significant differences in the number and duration of disappearances between P E T and T E P. Thus there was no effect of meaning, but structural factors did seem to affect the fragmentation of letters, which was more frequent than the disappearance of whole words or letters. However, there were considerable individual differences in what was perceived.

Now it was suggested that the effects of stabilization might be due to *retinal adaptation* produced by continuous stimulation of the same retinal cells. This indeed may have occurred with the simple figures of Ditchburn and Ginsborg and of Riggs *et al.*, and even perhaps with some of the simpler figures of Evans. Again, Hunt (1964) and Schuck *et al.* (1964) found that in the steady fixation of luminous figures there was a tendency for the part of the figure at the point of fixation to disappear more readily than other parts, suggesting retinal adaptation at that point. However, the simple figure of the circle, which might have been expected to produce adaptation, faded and disappeared less readily than did complex forms (Evans, 1964).

Again, the differential amounts of disappearance in stabilization of different figures, and the disappearance of figures in parts, especially in structured parts, all suggest that, even if some retinal adaptation is involved, central mechanisms are also operative, producing habituation. Thus Evans and Smith (1964) found that during the viewing of a bright after image, alpha rhythm disappeared, and reappeared when the after image faded. Evans (1964) has suggested that the fragmentation of stabilized images may take place in relation to the visual units of lines and curves such as were demonstrated by Hubel and Wiesel to exist in the visual cortex of the cat and the monkey (1962, 1968). Thus Evans showed that lines of more than a certain length were more likely to fragment than were shorter lines, which disappeared as wholes possibly because they corresponded to such units. However, some of the structural disappearances and the reduced tendency to disappear of meaningful stimuli would suggest more complex forms of organization, including the effects of attentional processes.

(3) Sensory and Perceptual Deprivation*

The effects on perception, and indeed on behaviour generally, may be severe when the whole environmental field is homogeneous, and continues to lack variation over a long period of time. Such situations were first investigated by Bexton *et al.* (1954) and Heron *et al.* (1956) in a very well known series of experiments, carried out at McGill University, of what has been termed 'sensory deprivation'; though as we shall see the deprivation may be perceptual rather than sensory. In the initial experiment (Bexton *et al.*, 1954), twenty-two male students, well paid for their participation, were each isolated in a cubicle in the following conditions: They lay flat on a bed; they wore translucent goggles which

---

* The literature on this subject is very extensive. In a recent bibliography by Weinstein *et al.* (1968), over a thousand titles were cited. In general, only those articles related to laboratory experiments on sensory and perceptual deprivation are discussed here.

transmitted only a vague blue of light, and gloves and cardboard cuffs which prevented tactile stimulation (except when eating and going to the toilet); and they heard only a continuous hum of sound, except when the experimenter communicated with them. Thus they were exposed to prolonged homogeneous stimulation, over a continuous period of up to six days. At first they slept a great deal, but later sleep became intermittent, and they were excessively bored and restless. They were unable to concentrate or think clearly, and lapsed into day-dreaming. Performance of simple mental tasks, such as mental arithmetic, was impaired. They also frequently experienced hallucinations: simple colour phenomena, patterns of dots or geometrical shapes, even complex meaningful pictures. There was considerable emotional lability and increased irritability towards the end of the period. Some refused to stay in the situation for more than two to three days, and others gave up even sooner. On emerging, they felt dazed and confused, sometimes for as much as twenty-four hours afterwards.

Observations on *perceptual changes* during the period of isolation (Heron *et al.*, 1956) indicated that the visual field soon lost any surface qualities. Immediately after termination of isolation, the whole visual field appeared unsteady and tended to drift. When the observer moved his head or eyes, objects in the field seemed to move; when he approached or withdrew from them, they appeared to move towards or away from him. There was also some distortion of shape, straight edges appearing curved and flat surfaces bulging inwards or outwards. The perceptual effects were studied further in an experiment by Doane *et al.* (1959). Observers were given tests after four days in diffuse visual stimulation, and a decrease in size and shape constancy was found, together with an increase in certain after effects such as that of perceived movement. Again on emergence there were gross visual disturbances, which disappeared in about half-an-hour, similar to those which occurred in the earlier experiment. Grunebaum *et al.* (1960) reported changes in apparent size and shape, and movement of figures, after only eight hours in conditions of deprivation. Held and White (1959) showed that after a similar period the speed of movement of a rotating bar was considerably under-estimated. Zubek (1964) found that perception of auto-kinetic movement was also impaired.

More immediately striking than these perceptual effects are the general *changes in thought and feeling* which have been reported in experiments on deprivation. Thus Wexler *et al.* (1958) required each of their observers to lie prone and rigidly confined in a tank-type respirator, such as is used for polio patients, with only a small patch of ceiling visible. In addition to lack of concentration and hallucinations such as those in the McGill experiments, many observers felt anxious, and four retired in panic before the end of the thirty-six-hour period. Goldberger and Holt (1958) found that their observers became distressed and experienced feelings of depersonalization even before the end of an eight-hour period. The experiment of Smith and Lewty (1959) was carried out in a sound-proof cubicle, but there was homogeneous visual stimulation. All their twenty observers became anxious and agitated before the end of the ninety-two-hour period; feelings of depersonalization were experienced, and in some cases mental disorganization producing complete panic which caused them to give up the experiment. Zuckerman *et al.* (1962) reported similar experiences in observers exposed to continuous white noise but total darkness, for seven hours. These observers experienced hallucinations during the early part of the experiment, which later disappeared.

Some experiments were carried out in *sensory deprivation*, complete darkness and silence; and curiously enough the effects of this were often less severe than were those of homogeneous light and sound. Thus the observers of Vernon and Hoffman (1956) experienced little or no hallu-cination or thought disorders during a forty-eight-hour period in dark-ness and silence. However, some observers panicked and had to give up during a seventy-two-hour period (Vernon and McGill, 1960). Dur-ing a seven-day period of darkness and silence, the observers of Zubek *et al.* (1960) experienced some impairment of recognition and recall at the third or fourth day, but there was little general deterioration of thinking ability. Some rather vague hallucinations were reported from the third day on (Zubek *et al.*, 1961); and one observer who stayed in isolation for ten days experienced particularly vivid and prolonged hallu-cinations of flashing lights which persisted for about a day after the end of isolation. From about the eighth day there was pronounced euphoria, accompanied by day-dreaming and lack of intellectual activity. It is notable that although some irritability and depression were felt in the middle of the period, the distressing experiences occurring during ex-posure to homogeneous light and sound have not been reported with exposure to darkness and silence. Some loss of motivation was felt after emergence.

Some perceptual changes occured as the result of sensory deprivation, though these were not marked. An extensive study was made by Zubek *et al.* (1961). Observers were tested before and after completion of two days in darkness and silence. There were slight but insignificant decreases in accuracy of depth perception and of constancy. But there was a marked deterioration in performance on the Mackworth clock test. No gross perceptual experiences, of dizziness or nausea, were reported after emergence, but slight curvature of the vertical and horizontal lines of the wall was perceived for a short period by those isolated for seven days. The observer who remained in isolation for ten days, however, perceived the environment as two-dimensional, and people as somewhat unreal. In fact, he felt so detached from the environment that he wanted to return to isolation.

The general effects of homogeneous perceptual stimulation appear to have been greater than those of deprivation of sensory stimulation. It would seem that it was the lack of *patterned vision* which was the operative factor. Thus Davis *et al.* (1960) found that when observers, confined in a tank-type respirator with constant homogeneous noise for ten and a half hours, were exposed to flashes of light appearing at random, the effects were similar to those produced by homogeneous light stimulation. There were frequent hallucinations and feelings of mental clouding. Only five of the ten observers remained for the whole period; and one screamed to be let out after thirty-eight minutes. Again the apparent speed of a rotating line, estimated at intervals during a three-hour period of exposure to randomly flashing light, decreased to a greater extent than during a similar period of homogeneous light (Freedman and Held, 1960). Thus it would appear that it is the deprivation of form perception which produces the greatest effect.

Nevertheless, the condition of darkness and silence did increase the *desire for stimulation*. Jones *et al.* (1961) found that when observers confined in darkness and silence were allowed to press a button in order to view various light stimulus patterns, the number of these responses was greater for purely random arrangements of red and green lights than for lights all of the same colour, or colours arranged in patterns. Jones *et al.* concluded that a high degree of uncertainty was therefore preferred to a lower degree. In a later experiment, Jones (1964) showed that complexity of pattern was relatively unimportant. Vernon and McGill (1960) found that those who were able to survive a seventy-two-hour period of darkness and silence availed themselves less frequently of the opportunity to view a simple configuration than did those who gave up sooner.

Now it might be supposed that changes in *arousal* occurring in sensory and perceptual deprivation might be indicated by changes in the EEG. Heron *et al.* (1956) noted that changes in EEG rhythm took place both during and after a period of homogeneous perceptual stimulation. There was an increase in alpha rhythm, and even the slow delta rhythm occurred in some cases. Zubek *et al.* (1961) found abnormal changes in alpha rhythm during confinement in darkness and silence, and in some cases theta rhythm appeared. With exposure to homogeneous perceptual stimulation over a period of two weeks, Zubek *et al.* (1963) showed that there was a progressive decrease in rhythm frequencies, especially during the second week. After release the frequency increased, but did not return to normal even in a week. The decrease in frequency was greater for perceptual than for sensory deprivation, although the incidence of theta waves was similar (Zubek and Welch, 1963). Hallucinations and disorganized thought processes occurred during periods of low arousal, as measured by the EEG, during darkness and white noise (Rossi *et al.*, 1964). From these observations it would appear that the phenomena of perceptual deprivation are associated with decreased arousal as mediated by the reticular formation (Schultz, 1965). However, it would seem that there may be reactions of over-arousal in those who become anxious and panic-striken. Such over-arousal is indicated by an increase in the GSR. Berlyne (1960) considered that over-arousal, with desynchronization of the EEG, occurred during periods of restlessness and irritability also.

But some of the effects observed in perceptual deprivation could have been caused by *restriction of movement*. The most severe effects occurred when there was complete restriction of movement in the tank-type respirator. Doane *et al.* (1959) found that fewer hallucinations were experienced by observers exposed to diffuse illumination when they could walk about and touch things. There was rather less visual distortion when observers were required at intervals to sit up on the bed on which they had been lying and touch something (Courtney *et al.*, 1961). Observers who simply remained recumbent for a period of a week but were not exposed to homogeneous stimulation experienced no hallucinations, disorientation or depersonalization (Zubek and MacNeill, 1967). Nor were there any changes in EEG rhythm. But when observers in perceptual deprivation conditions were permitted to take some exercise at intervals, the decrease in EEG frequency was less than when there was no such exercise, and there were fewer reports of hallucinations (Zubek, 1963). Performance on perceptuo-motor tasks was impaired to the same extent in both conditions. However, when observers were completely immobilized by being strapped down in a coffin-like box for twenty-four hours, although they could see and hear normally, pattern perception was impaired, and observers became restless, irritable and anxious (Zubek *et al.*, 1963). They reported feelings of depersonalization to a far greater extent than did those who were merely recumbent.

When the period was prolonged to seven days, the hallucinations, anxiety and loss of contact with reality were greater for both immobilized and recumbent observers than for those who were permitted to walk about (Zubek and MacNeill, 1966). But performance on certain perceptual tests was impaired to a greater extent in the immobilized and there was a greater decrease in EEG frequency. Finally, Zuckerman *et al.* (1968) made a direct comparison between the effects of immobilization and of total darkness and silence, over an eight-hour period. The former condition produced more bodily discomfort and more effects on autonomic functions, heart rate, breathing rate and GSR. The latter gave rise to more hallucinations and impaired thought processes. But visual performance was not greatly affected.

A further factor appears to be the *expectations* of the observer as to what he may experience. In the early McGill experiments, observers had to undergo conditions entirely different from anything they had previously experienced, and the nature of the effects was completely unknown to them. Thus they may well have felt that fear of the highly incongruous and unknown which we noted on p. 71. In later experiments, observers had some idea what to expect, and were therefore able in most cases to meet it with fortitude Thus there were fewer reports of hallucinations, anxiety, etc., in a second exposure to sensory deprivation than on the first occasion (Jackson and Pollard, 1962). But expectations of unpleasant experiences, hallucinations, etc. could be created by providing previous information on these, and the expectations affected observers even after one hour's confinement (Jackson and Kelley 1962). Requiring observers to predict whether or not they would experience irrational fears and hallucinations had a similar effect (Jackson and Pollard, 1962); and so did requiring them to give a continuous account of their experiences. Again, those who knew that they would be confined for two hours only experienced less severe emotional effects than did those who thought their confinement might last for an indefinite period (Zuckerman *et al.*, 1962). But it was the subjective effects of anxiety and hallucinations which were affected by experience and expectations. Pollard *et al.* (1963) found that responses to behavioural tests were similar during a second period of perceptual deprivation to those during the first; therefore presumably these responses were unaffected.

In many experiments considerable *individual differences* have appeared in reactions to deprivation, which seem to be fairly consistent. Thus Pollard *et al.* (1963) found that those who tolerated perceptual deprivation at one test did the same at another; whereas some observers gave up on both occasions. These results suggest that *personality character-istics* may be involved; but there has been some disagreement as to the nature of these. Wexler *et al.* (1958) found that relatively sociable and placid individuals were best able to survive the effects of confinement in the tank-type respirator. Smith and Lewty (1959) also showed that calm, placid and somewhat unintelligent persons were least affected, whereas the two observers who gave up after five hours were prone to anxiety. Zuckerman *et al.* (1962), however, found that although there were considerable differences in increase in anxiety in observers confined in total darkness but with white noise, these did not correlate with the results of personality tests. But Hull and Zubek (1962) showed that observers who could survive seven days in either constant light and noise or darkness and silence were more passive and dependent than those who did not. The former had less need for change, were less impulsive and had good imaginations. Wright and Abbey (1965) found that those who survived a week of unpatterned light and white noise subsequently gave Rorschach responses which indicated more control of drive-dominated behaviour than did those who gave up after three days. But it was possible that these observers' Rorschach responses were to some extent affected by failure to survive (the Rorschach test should have been administered before deprivation). In contradiction to these findings, Wright and Zubek (1966) found that observers who were able to survive a week's perceptual deprivation were less rational, more neurotic and immature and more socially dependent than were those who terminated isolation within three days. According to Berlyne (1960), relaxed observers were those with low arousal, while anxious and irritable observers showed over-arousal. On the other hand, Rossi and Solomon (1965) found that introverts experienced more discomfort than did extraverts, and were more prone to interrupt a period of sensory deprivation when they were permitted to do so. And Suedfeld (1964) showed that observers more capable of abstract reasoning experienced a greater degree of stress from twenty-four hours in darkness, silence and restricted movement than did those who tended to employ simpler, more concrete thought processes.

Clearly therefore the relation of these effects to cognitive and personality characteristics is by no means simple. Schultz (1965) has discussed the discrepancies between results. Some of the variations in effects might be attributed to differential effects of *social isolation*. Davis *et al.* (1961) did indeed find that the effects of social isolation enhanced those of perceptual deprivation in some cases, though the results of this experiment are difficult to interpret. However, they are not due to social isolation alone; nor, as we saw, to restricted movement alone. Therefore it seems justifiable to conclude that prolonged deprivation of sensory stimulation, and perhaps even more of perceptual stimulation, may have far-reaching effects on the normal functioning of the cognitive processes even if these effects are more severe in some persons than in others.

These findings suggest that indefinite prolongation of exposure to perceptual deprivation might result in *long-term impairment* of cognitive ability and emotional stability. Furthermore, the effects might be even more severe with young children, who are not only more sensitive to such factors but also lack any knowledge or foresight as to the possibility of their termination. There is indeed evidence that perceptual restriction may have far-reaching effects on young organisms, including children. It is of course easier to apply such restrictions to *non-human animals*; and Hebb (1958), for instance, described the deterioration in perceptual and cognitive ability produced in young chimpanzees by restricting visual and tactile stimulation. Again Fantz (1961) found that monkeys reared in darkness for a week or two after birth showed good spatial orientation and normal interest in patterned stimuli after a few hours' exposure to daylight. But if kept in darkness for eleven weeks, they were almost completely disoriented when brought into daylight, and showed little interest in patterned stimuli. It took them some weeks to learn to perceive normally. Deprivation of patterned stimulation, rather than complete darkness, may also produce considerable effects. Infant monkeys exposed to unpatterned light from the first month of life were allowed, during a period of one hour per day, to press a lever which lit up their surroundings (Wendt *et al.*, 1963). The rate of lever pressing rose to as much as 3,000 pressures per hour and remained at this figure over a five-month period without decline. But monkeys which had been brought up normally in early life and then confined to diffuse light pressed the lever only about one hundred times per hour.

A significant study on *human infants* was carried out by Schaffer (1958), which suggested that certain conditions might produce perceptual deprivation in them. He found that infants of two to seven months of age, hospitalized for periods of one to two weeks, did not show the distress exhibited by older infants resulting from separation from their mothers. They were not restless and unhappy during hospitalization. But when they returned home they seemed excessively preoccupied with their environment, scanning their surroundings, sometimes with blank and bewildered expressions. They made little response to people, even to the mother. This behaviour continued for periods of half an hour to four days, and was unrelated to visiting by the mother during hospitalization. It was attributed by Schaffer to the perceptual deprivation experienced during hospitalization, infants being confined to cots from which they could see little, and rarely taken up and handled. It would appear that their relation to and understanding of the normal variable environment had not been sufficiently well established at this age to persist during deprivation; and that they had to relearn this when they emerged, and to re-establish their reactions to the normal perceptual field.

Studies such as those of White *et al.* (1964) and White and Castle (1964) suggested that visual attention and the capacity to explore and manipulate objects might develop more slowly in infants brought up in *institutions* than in those brought up in more varied environments. Goldfarb (1945a and 1945b) compared the perceptual and intellectual development of children aged about three and a half years brought up in institutions until three years with that of children brought up in foster homes. The institutional children not only showed poorer linguistic development but also more primitive responses in the identification of pictures of objects; space concepts used in finding their way about were also inferior. No doubt this was due in part to their lack of affectionate relations with a mother or mother substitute; but also they had suffered from a more restricted environment and a relative lack of varied perceptual experience.

VII

The Spatial Framework and
Perception of Distance

(1) The Organization of Factors related to Spatial Perception

We have so far considered the perception of objects as if they were entirely distinct from the surroundings in which they are situated. Indeed, we noted on p. 21 that it was essential for the young child to learn that an object retained its identity unchanged, despite the surroundings in which it was encountered. Thus in identification it was necessary to disregard the manner in which the visually perceived shape and size of an object varied with its position in space. Nevertheless, we are continuously aware of the complex inter-relations of objects with their environmental setting. Indeed, the perceptual field is spaced out by means of a continuous sequence of objects from near to far in three-dimensional space, and this constitutes the stable environment within which we habitually perceive objects. They themselves are observed to possess solidity or three-dimensional depth within their spatial setting. Furthermore, we perceive, often with considerable accuracy, the spatial location of objects and hence their distance from us and from one another. But we shall see presently that in some situations spontaneous impressions of three-dimensionality, in depth and distance, may occur although the observer is unable to assess the exact nature of these; that is to say, judgments of depth and distance depending on inferences from immediate impressions are variable and inaccurate. Sometimes also it is possible to say that two objects are not equidistant, but not which is the nearer and which the farther.

Adults perceive their surroundings as a continuous spatial whole, from near to far distance, which includes those parts to the side and behind them and not immediately visible, as well as those parts at which they are looking. But a *great variety of information* is included in the *schemata* on which perception of and reaction to the total spatial framework is based. Many different processes may come into play in perceiving and assessing the various aspects of these. Thus the disparate images of the two eyes are involved in perceiving the location and three-dimensional solidity of near objects, together with shadows on their sides and the shadows they cast. The continuous perspective changes in size, brightness and surface texture which Gibson (1950a) termed 'gradients' are the principal aspects contributing to perception of the 'ground' on which objects are situated; but also they enable the location of these objects to be made, and hence judgments as to their distance. Normally all these and other percepts corroborate each other and provide redundant information as to the appearance and lay-out of the surroundings; and the more information available, the more accurately can judgments of the distances of objects be made. Thus Luria and Kinney (1968) found that whereas absolute distances of objects up to fifteen feet could be made accurately when the full surroundings were visible, distances were increasingly over-estimated when targets were viewed in a large empty room; and still more when they were seen monocularly through a circular opening in a screen, with walls and floor draped in black. Again, Gruber and Dinnerstein (1965) showed that absolute, though not relative, judgments of distance over about forty-eight feet were more accurate both when observers could actually perceive the lighted corridor in which the objects were situated, and also when they were given previous knowledge of its dimensions, than when this information was not available.

However, when observers are asked to make judgments of distance, they may select certain features of the environment as affording clearer or more reliable information than others. Or the experimenter may so arrange the conditions of experiment that only certain features are available as a basis for judgment. But it must be realized that in ordinary circumstances the observer may incorporate all the various types of information he can obtain, sampling those which are appropriate to any judgments of spatial relations, absolute or relative distance, which he needs to make.

However, the operation of an inclusive schema in which are integrated all percepts, concepts and reactions to three-dimensional space develops only gradually in *children*. Piaget (1955) considered that in the first three or four months of life the infant perceived various aspects of space as they were related to his own activities, and without relation to each other. Thus the 'month space' developed first, in relation to sucking; then tactile space, primarily through touching his own body; and visual space, in following moving objects with his eyes. These various spaces were integrated together when from about four months of age he began to touch and mouth the objects at which he also looked. Cruikshank

(1941) showed that at about six months an infant could discriminate between a rattle close to him, and another at three times the distance. Piaget (1955) considered that assessment of distance developed through the reaching movements made by the infant in order to obtain objects that he wanted. Thus during the latter part of the first year a firm distinction was established between near objects which could be obtained by reaching, and far objects which could not. Fairly accurate judgments could be made of the distance of the former, but little attention was given to the latter.

However, it became apparent from the experiments of Walk and E. J. Gibson (1961) on the *'visual cliff'* that infants of eight months were in fact aware of the existence of intervening spaces, greater than the reaching distance, between themselves and objects. Infants were placed on a centre board between two horizontal sheets of glass, one with a checkered surface immediately beneath it, and the other with a checkered surface four feet below it. As soon as the infant began to crawl, at six to eight months, he crossed the shallow side to his mother when she beckoned to him. But only one or two of the younger infants crossed the deep side. Thus by the age of eight months there was some understanding of the spatial drop threatened by the visual cliff on the deep side.

Experiments by Bower (1965) indicated that there was some awareness of the relative distances of objects as early as six to eight weeks of age. He was able to train infants of this age to reach for the nearer of two solid cubes, even when they projected the same sized retinal images; thus judgment was not based on relative size of the image. Relative size was also inoperative in the judgments of absolute distance studied by Cruikshank; the distant rattle was three times the size of the near one. Bower (1965) considered that judgments of relative distance were based on *motion parallax* – the relative magnitude of apparent movement of objects at different distances. Thus no judgment could be made with flat projections of objects, when motion parallax could not be used, although other cues to distance were the same. Again, Walk and Gibson (1961) concluded from their experiments on infants, and also on young animals, that motion parallax was the operative factor, and not difference in relative size of the checkered pattern on the two sides, or binocular disparity. Walk and Dodge (1962) found that an infant of ten and a half months, blind in one eye from an early age, refused to cross the deep side. Thus he could perceive depth without binocular vision. However, it is not perfectly clear whether in these experiments the infants could not perceive the receding sides of the framework which contained the lower checkered surface. It would appear that binocular judgment of distance is well developed by two years (Johnson and Beck, 1941); and Smith and Smith (1966) showed that by five years distances of up to twenty feet could be accurately matched in both monocular and binocular vision.

Whatever the processes involved, it seems clear that in his early years the child develops the capacity for making fairly accurate judgments of distance of comparatively near objects, in relation to himself. Furthermore, during the second year he acquires some understanding of the spatial relations of objects to their surroundings, irrespective of the position of his body. Thus Piaget (1955) found that by the age of about one and a half years his children could point correctly, though sometimes after hesitation, to the position of people in a distant chalet who were not themselves visible. Moreover, they could make detours to reach a particular point, again without being able to see the point at that moment. But a more complete and *systematic understanding of the spatial relations of objects*, in which all information, both perceptual and conceptual, is coordinated together, does not develop until much later. Children begin to employ and to name concepts of space at about two and a half to three years, as shown by their understanding and use of words such as 'above', 'below', 'in' and 'out' (Ames and Learned, 1948). But these are rather vague and general. Piaget and Inhelder (1956) found that a real grasp of perspective, as shown by its reproduction in drawings, was not complete until about eight years. Nor did children realize until this age that objects seen from different view points have different appearances, though related to each other. Thus younger children, shown a solid model of mountains, could not select the photograph which represented their appearance as seen from the other side. Finally, when they were shown models of houses, trees, etc., placed on a large board, they could not until ten to eleven years of age place similar models in exactly the same positions on another board. At about seven years the models were not even correctly situated to left or right, or nearer or further, than one another. Later, when the relative positions were roughly correct, the distances between them were incorrect.

Thus it would appear that finally there develops in older children a *concept of total Euclidean space*, with objects located in a landscape which recedes gradually into the distance. As Teuber (1966) has pointed out, this operates at three levels: (1) the immediate direct perception of visible spatial relations; (2) the compensation for change in spatial relations produced by movement of the body in space; and (3) the representation of spatial relations not immediately apparent, such that we know where objects are situated in the total environment and can find the way to them. The first type of information is processed in the occipital lobes of the cerebral cortex, and may be impaired by injuries to that area of the brain. In such cases, distortions of shape and distance may be perceived in the region of the injury. Processes occurring at the second level are associated with the functions of the frontal lobe, in relation to movement; we shall consider them more fully in section (2) of this chapter. But parietal lobe functions are involved in all activities dependent on representation of space and spatial concepts.

However, even if simple information as to distance and spatial relations of objects is primarily processed in the occipital lobes, it is probable that normally these are integrated together and co-ordinated with spatial concepts, through parietal lobe functions. For as we noted above, we commonly utilize a variety of perceptual data for making inferential judgments of distance. An important constituent would appear to be the *disparate* projections of objects perceived in *binocular vision*. Although distance can usually be assessed with fair accuracy in normal surroundings in monocular vision, Barrett and Williamson (1966) found that binocularly perceived scenes had a greater 'depth quality' than monocularly perceived scenes. Moreover, it is possible to perceive a 'depth quality' on the basis of binocular disparity alone, in the absence of other data, as is apparent in *stereoscopic* viewing, when diagrams or photographs of objects taken from the viewpoints of the left and right eye are fused together in a stereoscope. Julesz (1964) presented stereoscopically two sets of randomly arranged dots; in one, a central group of dots was shifted slightly to one side of the position of the dots in the other. This central group then appeared to stand out from the background. The depth impression was produced by this slight degree of disparity irrespective of any other data related to three-dimensional vision, or any expectations in the observer, in as short a period of exposure as one msec,; though there was some prolongation of the impression in an after image.

Thus it seems that the appearance of depth and non-equidistance of different parts of the field may be created solely by the disparity between the retinal projections of those parts of the field equidistant with the fixation point and those non-equidistant, at least within a short range of distance from the eyes. In everyday life, disparity is used for judging equidistance in tasks such as threading a needle, which is extremely difficult to perform with one eye closed. With objects at a considerable distance, disparity disappears. Moreover, it is doubtful if disparity can be employed either for judging which of two objects is in front of the other, or for assessing their absolute distances from the eye, since the evidence goes to show that degree of disparity does not vary exactly with distance (for discussion of this evidence, see Vernon, 1952). However, for stereoscopic fusion to occur, it is necessary that the two eyes should *converge* and be focused on the point of fixation. Parts of the field which are indicated by their disparity to be at different distances may be focused successively by adjusting convergence. Thus there is a change in the tensions of the extra-ocular muscles as the eyes converge and diverge to fixate points at different distances. That some information is obtained from these changing tensions is indicated by the comparatively correct judgments of equidistance between the edge of two black screens which can be made in binocular, but not in monocular, vision (Vernon, 1952). Again, Teichner *et al.* (1955) showed that in normal terrain distances up to two hundred feet were judged considerably more accurately in binocular than in monocular vision. In these situations, disparity would be weak or non-existent. It is not possible to say whether the information is provided by changing sensations of tension from the extra-ocular muscles; or by means of the motor impulses to these which produce the changes in contraction and relaxation necessary for convergence and divergence. However, accurate impressions of absolute distance cannot be obtained in this manner, since degree of convergence does not vary exactly with distance. Thus Gogel (1960) found that the distance apart of two objects was increasingly under-estimated the greater their absolute distance from the eyes.

It has been supposed that similar information, related to changes in tension of the ciliary muscle occurring in the *accommodation* of the lens to focus objects at different distances, may be utilized in monocular assessments of distance. It is now considered a more probable explanation that as the distance between two objects increases, the image of the object which is not fixated, and for which the lens is not accommodated, becomes increasingly blurred. Thus two objects may be placed at the same distance by minimizing blur. However, this cannot be done with any great accuracy.

In recent years, study has been increasingly directed to those aspects of our surroundings perception of which is modified regularly and gradually as distance increases, in what Gibson (1950a) termed '*gradients*'. Thus as we perceive a landscape receding into the distance, we observe a *linear perspective* effect. Receding parallel lines converge as the retinal projections of objects become increasingly small with increasing distance, and surface texture becomes condensed. Clarity of outline and detail, and brightness, decrease; and colour becomes less saturated, changing finally to blue grey. These changes, in so-called '*aerial perspective*', are attributed to the dampness of the interposed atmosphere. Other features of the perceived surroundings which are related to the gradients of linear and aerial perspective are interposition, the covering of further objects by nearer ones, and height in relation to the level of the eyes – more distant objects appear higher up than nearer ones.

In normal perceptions of the spatial dimensions and judgments of the distances of objects, information from these gradients and from the gradient of decreasing disparity and convergence is redundant. The different types of information corroborate each other, hence enabling us to make judgments as to the absolute distances of objects. It seems probable that the various cues contributing to perspective are the most important in correct spatial location of objects. But it is possible to carry out experiments in which one or other of these types of information is studied singly, and its relation to distance judgments investigated more or less in isolation from others. It then appears that change in *size* of the image projected on the retina can be a very compelling cue – according to Ittelson (1960), the most effective cue in monocular vision with surroundings concealed. This change is often not perceived as such; an object appears to maintain its size while increasing its distance (we shall discuss this phenomenon more fully in connection with size constancy, in Chapter VIII). In certain circumstances, actual difference of size may be perceived as difference of distance. Thus Ittelson (1951) found that, in monocular vision with surroundings concealed, a half-sized playing card was perceived to be twice as far away as a normal-sized playing card. However, this phenomenon does not depend on assumed knowledge of size. Gogel (1954) showed that smaller shapes of unknown size appeared further away than larger shapes even when viewed binocularly, if they were laterally separated from one another and viewed with surroundings concealed. But an object viewed monocularly tended to appear to be at the same distance as an object viewed binocularly, no matter what their sizes (Gogel, 1956). If there were two binocularly viewed objects, the monocularly viewed object appeared to be at the same distance as that to which it was closest laterally. In binocular vision the perceived distance of an object might vary with its apparent size, though disparity was kept constant (Gogel, 1964). And Ittelson and Ames (1950) found that both convergence and accommodation adjusted to the apparent distance of an object as indicated by its apparent size.

A very strong effect of change in distance may be produced if a shape is made to expand or contract regularly in the absence of other cues to distance. Thus rhesus monkeys started and jumped back in fright when the shadow of a ball on a screen was magnified and produced a 'looming' effect (Schiff *et al.*, 1962). If it was reduced in size, interest, curiosity and exploratory responses occurred. If the sides of a rectangular patch of light were increased equally and regularly, three-dimensional movement was always perceived (Johansson, 1964). But if the rate of expansion of the horizontal and vertical sides of the rectangle was uneven or out of phase, some rotation or change of shape was perceived additionally. Johansson considered that the three-dimensional movement was a primary percept and was not merely inferred from the changes in size of the rectangle. The effect can vary, however, if the location of fixation is varied. Sayons (1964) presented a rectangular frame which expanded and contracted regularly. There was a horizontal line in the middle of the frame, and the majority of observers, when they fixated the line, perceived it as moving to and fro, in and out of the frame, while the latter remained stationary. But if the frame was fixated, it moved backwards and forwards while the line appeared stationary.

Gibson (1950a) attached particular importance to the *'texture gradient'* of a receding surface in producing three-dimensional impressions; that is to say, the perception of regularly increasing density of texture and small detail. These he illustrated convincingly in diagrams and photographs of natural scenes. Whether in ordinary surroundings texture is important and affords reliable information as to distance is more doubtful. Thus Teichner *et al.* (1955) found that neither binocular nor monocular judgments of long distances, from 200 to 3000 feet, varied with the structure of the terrain, its roughness or smoothness. Using a tunnel-like structure, Gibson *et al.* (1955) found that in monocular vision absense of surface texture did not produce a completely flat impression, though increased surface texture gave rise to a stronger impression of receding depth. The surface texture of randomly distributed dots was found by MacKay (1965) to produce an impression of depth in monocular vision, though flattened and reduced in amount.

In making judgments of the angle of *slant* of a surface with photographs from different angles of textured surfaces projected at right angles to the line of sight and viewed monocularly, the slant of these surfaces was greatly under-estimated (Gibson, 1950b). But the slant of a regularly textured brick-like surface was judged more accurately, presumably from the apparent trapezoidal shape of the bricks. Indeed, such a modification of apparent shape can act alone as a cue to slant, though not a completely accurate one (Clark *et al.*, 1956a). Tilted luminous outlines of rectangles and ellipses were better cues to degree of tilt than was surface texture (Clark *et al.*, 1956b). Perceived slant also varied with type of texture gradient, and was maximal with a medium density of texture (Gruber and Clark, 1956). Thus in general texture gradient produces a cue to distance, but does not constitute a basis for accurate judgment.

We have already mentioned that the apparent *brightness* of an object may be related to its apparent distance. A steady decrease in illumination might produce an impression of recession in distance (Carr, 1935). It also gave rise to the 'looming' effect with rhesus monkeys (Schiff *et al.*, 1962). Coules (1955) found that in restricted viewing conditions, the brighter of two objects tended to appear nearer. However, there was no consistent relationship between differences of brightness and of distance. In general, brightly *coloured* objects tended to stand out from the background, and appeared to be relatively nearer than when there was little colour contrast between them and their background (Mount *et al.*, 1956). Coloured objects were also judged to be nearer than grey ones of equal intrinsic brightness. A somewhat similar though less compelling effect occurred with black, grey and white objects having different degrees of contrast with the background (Luria and Kinney, 1968). We noted that at far distances brightness, colours and their contrasts faded in aerial perspective. However, these effects may produce erroneous impressions of distance in an unusually clear atmosphere.

Differences in brightness between different parts of an object may contribute, as *shadows*, to the impression of three-dimensionality. The receding sides of a solid object, and any part of its surface in relief, tend to be shadowed on the side away from the direction of illumination. By changing this direction it is possible to produce a change in the appearance of relief into that of protrusion. Objects equally illuminated from all sides may lose their three-dimensional appearance and be perceived as flat (Wagner, 1941).

It seems reasonable to suppose that, even if perception of distance through motion parallax (to be discussed more fully in the next section) and binocular disparity is innate, appearing in infancy and early childhood, the ability to judge distances accurately is greatly improved through *experience*. The child learns that he must make longer or shorter movements of the body in space to reach objects the distances of which are indicated visually by their position in relation to the various gradients. He finally incorporates all this variety of information into a spatial schema which includes also the various spatial concepts described on p. 121. In adult life, the conceptual aspects of distance estimation may be further refined by *special training*, though it is doubtful if much change can be made in the perception of location and of the relative distances of objects. But the trained observer may learn to make better use of the perceptual information available to him. Thus E. J. Gibson *et al.* (1955) trained observers to make absolute judgments of long distances in normal outdoor surroundings by employing a 'fractionation' procedure of dividing them up into smaller units of twenty-five yards. The correctness of and the errors made in these short distance estimates were demonstrated to the observers. Thereafter they were able to employ this fractionation procedure in a variety of different settings, and their distance judgments were considerably improved. However, judgments of the relative distances of two distant objects were not improved. Presumably these could be made more easily by means of the perceptual gradients with the use of which they were already familiar.

Again, in restricted conditions of viewing, observers may be trained to utilize particular cues more effectively. Thus Freeman (1966) showed that observers could be trained to discriminate between the degree of tilt of two rectangular surfaces on the basis of perspective cues, or relation of height to width.

It would seem then that the normal individual in normal surroundings utilizes a redundancy of perceptual cues associated with a knowledge of spatial relations, in a well-established spatial schema which enables him to judge the nature of his surroundings and to move about them efficiently. Nevertheless, experiments have been carried out in which perceptual data have been made to *conflict* with each other, with resultant breakdown in correct judgment of spatial relations. Of these perhaps the best known is the 'distorted room' of Ames (1946) – sometimes known as the 'equivalent room' – which, viewed monocularly, appeared as an ordinary rectilinear room, although in reality its ceiling, floor and back wall sloped away from the observer. In fact these projected images to the eye identical to those projected by a rectilinear room; and the observer was said to perceive the latter rather than the former because of his familiarity with rectilinear rooms. However, it is difficult to reconcile with this explanation the exaggerated apparent size of a man in the nearer corner facing the observer, where the ceiling was lower, as contrasted with the diminished size of a man in the further corner, where the ceiling was higher. The illusion is destroyed by using binocular vision, when cues from disparity come into operation. However, binocular rooms have been designed which are binocularly equivalent and produce the same phenomenon (see Forgus, 1966). Weiner (1956) showed that the monocular rectilinear effect was extremely stable and resistant to replacement by veridical perception of the real structure of the room. Only after repeated exposures did it begin to lose its appearance of definiteness and solidity. Active comparison of the shape and size of different parts of the room assisted adjustment, but it was not complete until after twenty-five to forty hours of exposure, the period differing for different observers. At first a cigarette packet moved across the back wall appeared to change in size, but after a time an active attitude towards the phenomenon transformed this to a change in distance. However, in experiments by Kilpatrick (1954), in which observers were given specific cues to the true dimensions of the room, adjustment took place more quickly. They were allowed either to throw a ball at the back wall or trace it with a stick; or to observe the experimenter do this. After two learning sessions, all observers perceived the true shape of the back wall. Moreover, they did the same for another room with the back wall sloped in the other direction. The effect was slightly more rapid for the active observers. Kilpatrick attributed the adjustment to a definite re-learning of the significance of the stimulus pattern.

The size differences of objects in the distorted room could show a certain lability, however, according to Wittreich (1952). He required observers to report changes in apparent size of a stranger walking across the end of the room, or of the married partner. The stranger appeared to change size, just as did the cigarette packet in the experiment of Weiner. But in several cases, especially with couples who had been married some considerable time, the married partner retained his (or her) normal size throughout, or varied very little. In these cases the room was seen to be distorted.

Among the conceptual skills related to spatial perception which we acquire as we grow up is the understanding of *pictorial representation* of three-dimensionality in objects and perspective recession in space. We noted that, according to Piaget and Inhelder (1956), the latter was not fully developed until about eight years of age. *Cross-cultural studies* have also shown that less educated and sophisticated individuals may have difficulty in perceiving distance effects in pictures. Thus Hudson (1960) found that adult white labourers and black mine labourers in Africa tended to see as flat drawings and photographs which were intended to show distance effects. Better educated individuals could perceive these correctly at the age of twelve years, though six-year-old children did not do so. In a later study, Hudson (1967) showed that white adults perceived three-dimensional effects better than did Bantus and Indians. The latter did not understand the reproduction of perspective by converging lines. Dawson (1967) found more three-dimensional perception among the more educated adults in Sierra Leone; and Kilbride and Robbins (1968) showed that pictorial representation of perspective (in the converging lines of a receding road) was better understood by more educated Bagunda children and adults than by less educated. That lack of three-dimensional perception was due to failure in comprehending its pictorial representation was indicated by the results of Deregowski (1968). He found that many African school boys and men servants, who had all received about three years' schooling, and who failed to perceive three-dimensionality in Hudson's pictures, could nevertheless construct three-dimensional structures correctly from perspective drawings. Thus it would seem that people acquire during the course of their education the concepts related to current conventions as to two-dimensional representation of space and distance. These conventions developed in European painting at the time of the Renaissance, and were not observed in earlier European painting; nor in primitive art.

A visual illusion known as the '*horizontal-vertical*' illusion has been associated with perspective effects, and the apparent differences in magnitude of different parts of the visual field. In general there is a tendency to over-estimate vertical by contrast with horizontal dimensions, which has usually been attributed to the greater length of the horizontal field of view than of the vertical field. Some evidence for this explanation was obtained by Künnapas (1957), who found that the magnitude of the illusion was decreased by 30 per cent when it was presented as a horizontal and vertical luminous line in an otherwise dark room. The illusion reversed when it was viewed with the head inclined through 90° (Künnapas, 1958). Chapanis and Mankin (1967) found that the illusion also operated in a real life setting. They required observers to view a variety of objects, such as a parking meter, a tree, the chimney of a house, and estimate where the tops of these would lie if they were tipped over into the horizontal position. In general, the vertical dimensions were overestimated, especially those of very tall objects. It might be hypothesized that these most nearly approached the limits of the horizontal and vertical fields of view.

The magnitude of the illusion varied with different forms of the illusory figure. It was greater with Fig. 31a than with Fig. 31b. This difference was attributed by Künnapas (1955) to the effect of an additional factor in Fig. 31a, namely the intersection of the two lines, the divided line appearing as shorter than the divider. The magnitude also varied with *age*. Fraisse and Vautrey (1956) found that, when viewing time was unlimited, the magnitude of the illusion in Fig. 31c increased with age up to nine to ten years and then remained constant. But with Fig. 31a there was no such change. They considered that the younger children did not relate the two parts of Fig. 31c together, and were therefore not susceptible to the illusion. But in tachistoscopic exposure, the magnitude of the illusion in Fig. 31a increased up to adult age. However, observers with scientific training showed only a small illusion, presumably because they employed an analytical procedure, comparing the parts with each other even during a short exposure. Other adults tended to view the illusion synthetically in the restricted time; and they were more capable than were children of perceiving the whole structure of the figure which produced the illusion. This effect was therefore similar to that which occurs with the Oppel illusion (see p. 75).

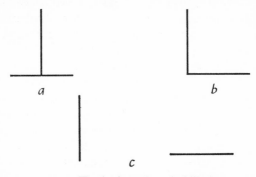

FIG. 31 The horizontal-vertical illusion

Piaget (1961) described somewhat different results, obtained by himself and his colleagues. He considered that the illusion was not due to inequality of perceived space in the horizontal and vertical dimensions. It was found that the magnitude of the illusion was greater in adults than children with Fig. 31b, as well as with Fig. 31c. It was also greater when the vertical line was fixated than when the horizontal line was fixated; indeed, in the latter case, children of five to seven years showed a negative error (reversal of the illusion). And when eye movements were recorded, there were more fixations on the upper end of the vertical line than on the ends of the horizontal line. Thus Piaget attributed the illusion to the tendency to centre on the summit of the vertical line rather than on the ends of the horizontal line, producing a corresponding over-estimation of the former. Other experiments with different figures had also shown great centration on the upper elements of figures. This tendency was fully operative in adults; but children possessed little capacity for perceptual activity, and therefore explored the extremes of the horizontal-vertical figure to a less extent. It is not always easy to follow Piaget's argument, however; nor is it immediately apparent why there should be more fixations in the upper part of the field, since in general the eyes would seem to move less readily in the upward than in the horizontal dimension.

The horizontal-vertical illusion seems also to exhibit cross-cultural differences, which will be discussed in the next chapter. But there are other even more curious types of illusion involving three-dimensional

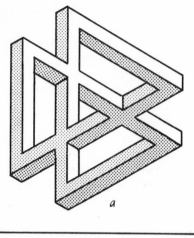

a

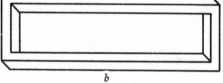

b

FIG. 32 Impossible objects
a. *After* Penrose and Penrose (1958) p. 32
b. *After* Hochberg (1968) p. 314

effects – the so-called '*impossible figures*' (Penrose and Penrose, 1958, see Fig. 32a), in which different parts of the figure suggest alternative perspective aspects. Yet the impression of three-dimensionality may be retained, especially if the conflicting cues to distance are well separated from each other, as in Fig. 32b (Hochberg, 1968). Hochberg considered that the cues to distance, given for instance by the corners, are intergrated in normal three-dimensional figures into a consistent three-dimensional impression. With impossible figures, such integration cannot take place. But the three-dimensional convention is not destroyed if the conflicting cues are not viewed simultaneously.

We noted earlier the hypothesis of Teuber that concepts relating to spatial relations operated through functioning of the parietal lobe of the minor hemisphere. There is indeed evidence to show that such concepts may be impaired by *injury to the parietal lobe of the right hemisphere*. Patients with such injuries could usually make direct estimates of perceived distance in the normal manner, but might have lost the capacity to utilize spatial concepts. Thus McFie *et al.* (1950) found in such cases characteristic losses of topographical orientation and memory. The patients were usually able to find their way about. But they could not draw ground plans of their own houses, but proceeded piecemeal from one feature to another without relating them together. Yet verbal accounts might be substantially correct. Descriptions of street routes were however markedly erroneous. Attempts to draw simple outline maps of the British Isles showed a complete disorganization of the topographical relations between different parts of the country; thus Brighton was situated at the top, Land's End at the bottom, Glasgow and Manchester in between. In an experiment by Semmes *et al.* (1955), patients with parietal lobe injuries were found to be particularly deficient in following a simple map which directed them how to proceed from one point to another marked on the floor. They were completely confused in translating the map directions into actual movements. Ettlinger *et al.* (1957), who obtained results similar to those of McFie *et al.*, considered that patients of this type tended to perceive in a piecemeal and fragmented manner, and to be incapable of integrating together the parts of a situation within a single comprehensive configuration such as a complex drawing or a map.

(2) Movement in Relation to Spatial Perception

We must now consider the somewhat surprising relationship between the perception of three-dimensionality and location of objects, and of their movements: the actual movements of objects or of their shadows, or the apparent movement imparted to them by movement of the body in space. It should be noted first that the appearance of three-dimensionality may be perceived in a two-dimensional shape in movement. Wallach and O'Connell (1953) projected the shadow of a solid object on to a translucent screen. The shadow appeared to be that of a flat shape as long as the object was motionless; but when it was rotated, the shadow was perceived as that of a solid, and the observer could frequently identify its shape. This 'kinetic depth effect' was produced by the progressive modification in shape of the shadow, changing in a systematic fashion as the object rotated. A mere expansion and contraction of the shadow in a single dimension, for instance that of a rod rotating about its centre, did not produce any three-dimensional impression; it was necessary for contours to show characteristic changes in length and direction. Moreover, Wallach *et al.* (1953) found that once observers had perceived the kinetic depth effect, they also saw shadows of the same objects while stationary as cast by three-dimensional objects. Later experiments by Wallach *et al.* (1963a) and Wallach and Karsh (1963a and 1963b) indicated that observers could be trained in various ways to perceive accurately the depth of objects when disparity was artificially distorted, by observing their shadows while the objects were rotating. And Green (1961) found that impressions of depth and solidity could be obtained from films, the successive frames of which showed dots and lines which were differently related to the surfaces of three-dimensional rotating objects. That is to say, not even a complete changing outline was necessary, but merely some indication of the surface of an object in successive spatial positions; though the impression was stronger the greater the number of dots and lines.

However, the most curious and striking phenomena of this kind, *continuous perspective transformations*, were demonstrated by Gibson and his colleagues. Gibson and Cornsweet (1952) found that observers could judge with fair accuracy when a textured surface, viewed in monocular vision and rotated about an axis, had reached an angle of 45° to the line of sight. Judgments were more accurate with a regular plaid pattern than with an irregularly mottled surface. Gibson and Gibson (1957) then projected a scattered group of irregularly shaped patterns as shadows on to a translucent screen, and rotated these patterns about a vertical axis. The observers perceived this continuous perspective transformation as a set of rigid shapes rotating and thus changing in slant – a phenomenon similar to that of the kinetic depth effect. The angle of slant could be estimated at any one moment with fair accuracy. If squares were presented instead of irregular shapes, the impression was less compelling. Further experiments relating to the perception of separation and recession respectively were carried out by E. J. Gibson *et al.* (1959). In the first, they projected on to a translucent screen two dark spots, located on surfaces at different distances from the observer. When motionless, a single undifferentiated surface was perceived; but when the two surfaces were set in motion laterally (at right angles to the line of sight), the spots usually appeared to lie in different planes. The effect was enhanced when the surfaces were 'textured' by sprinkling them with talcum powder. But estimates of distance apart of the two surfaces were quite uncertain and inaccurate. In the second experiment, the slant of a textured surface, similarly projected, was not perceived when it was stationary, but was apparent when it was set in motion, although the angle of slant was usually underestimated. Finally, Fieandt and Gibson (1959) contrasted the rigid transformations, in which the shape or pattern projected maintained the relationship of its parts unchanged, with a *non-perspective transformation*, in which a projected pattern made by an irregular network of dark lines was compressed and decompressed laterally. It was perceived as the elastic movement in depth of a non-rigid surface, with topological transformation of shape characteristics, similar to the movements of a living organism.*

Now it must be concluded that these movements, usually observed in monocular vision with disparity factors absent, produced a three-dimensional impression without any definite localization of the objects in space. Thus it would seem probable that perception of inequality of relative distance was derived from them, as from disparity, but that they gave no accurate information as to the actual distance apart, or the absolute distance. The related phenomenon of *'motion parallax'* between two actually moving objects would seem to have a similar function. Thus Graham (1951) found that observers could perceive with a high degree of acuity whether two needles, moving at the same rate one behind the other, were non-equidistant. This was because the angle subtended at the eye by the two movements was different when they were not equidistant; hence the motion parallax. But the observers did not estimate the distance between the needles; and indeed they were not always certain which was in front of the other. However, Epstein (1967) found that observers could be trained to judge, with fair accuracy in monocular vision, the distance of a luminous rod of unknown length in otherwise dark surroundings, by moving the rod to and fro. Information during learning as to the position of the rod was provided by a series of light boxes set at one-foot intervals along the track.

But in general judging the actual distances of objects seems to require that motion parallax be associated with other data, as in normal surroundings. Thus Gibson (1947, 1950b) and Gibson *et al.* (1955a) pointed out that, as an observer moves through the surroundings, the projected images of objects move towards him and expand as he approaches, are progressively and regularly deformed as they pass on either side of him, and contract behind him. The rate of flow and of change in shape of the projected images varies with the distances of the objects, increasing as he approaches them, while at the horizon motion is zero. If the observer looks at right angles to his direction of movement, again apparent move-

* Other instances of the inter-relation between perceived shape and movement will be discussed in Chapter VIII, Section (3), and in Chapter X, Section (5).

ment is most rapid for near objects and vanishes at the horizon. If he is flying above a surface, the rate of apparent movement is greatest immediately below him. However, all these movements and deformations of shape are seldom perceived as such, but as changes in distance resulting from the observer's movements. Thus a gradient of motion parallax may be associated with other gradients, such as those described in the last section. Gibson suggested that the ability to estimate distance from these phenomena could be of considerable use to aircraft pilots in judging their distance above the ground when landing.

Wallach and his colleagues carried out experiments to examine the effects of a *conflict* between disparity and the kinetic depth effect. Thus Wallach *et al.* (1963a) presented a rotating wire cube to binocular vision in which the effective distance apart of the two eyes was increased by a mirror arrangement, the 'telereoscope'. This produced an increase of disparity and hence of the apparent depth of the cube. The kinetic depth effect of the cube in rotation, from which a veridical impression of depth could be derived, in part compensated for and reduced the effect of increased disparity produced by the telereoscope. It was decreased further by prolonging the period of exposure to the rotating cube, especially when its perspective was strengthened by viewing it against a checkered background. When the rotating cube was viewed subsequently without the telereoscope, it appeared distorted in depth, the distortion gradually disappearing. If the period of viewing through the telereoscope was preceded by viewing a rotating pyramid in normal vision, the subsequent effect of the telereoscope was less (Wallach and Karsh, 1963a). The interaction between stereoscopic perception of depth, through disparity, and the kinetic depth effect was further demonstrated by comparing what occurred when two wire shapes were rotated, one with vertical prongs and the other with oblique prongs (Wallach and Karsh, 1963b). Rotation of the former produced only an increase and decrease of apparent length of the prongs; but with the latter there was additionally a deformation of shape. Judgments of depth through the telereoscope were considerably less affected by viewing the former rotation than by the latter. From these experiments, Wallach and Karsh concluded that the stereoscopic effect of disparity was relatively unstable, and could be modified by interaction with the kinetic depth effect.

(3) The Position of the Body in Space

Of equal importance in the appropriate regulation of behaviour with the perception of the spatial dimensions and relations of the surround-

K

ings is constant awareness of the position of the body in space, and adaptation to any change in its spatial orientation. For this purpose, the integration of a variety of information is performed: visual perceptions of the spatial aspects of the environment; proprioceptive and kinaesthetic sensory data from the muscles, indicating their tension in maintaining the body upright, and changes of tension in movement,* and data from sense organs in the joints signalling the position of the body and limbs in relation to gravity; and sensory data from the labyrinth, which also indicates static posture and changes in bodily orientation with movement. Normally we are not fully aware of this integrated information; it constitutes the 'ground' of our experience rather than the 'figure', and we react to it automatically, rapidly and appropriately. But if some of the essential information is inadequate or distorted, or if there is any discordance between information from different sources, then we may experience disorientation and even vertigo, and be unable to act effectively. Deliberation as to the nature of the situation may appear, with conscious attempts to reconcile conflicting sensory impressions, and voluntary direction of appropriate action.

The visually perceived surroundings form a kind of *framework* to which the position of the body and of other objects is related; and the main coordinates of this framework are the *horizontal and vertical dimensions of space* as perceived from the horizon and from vertical objects such as buildings. The vertical visual coordinate is linked with the *gravitational vertical,* and the perception of these together enables observers not only to keep the body upright but also to make accurate judgments as to whether objects are vertical or not. However, in darkness, when the visual vertical is not apparent, an object such as a luminous rod may take on the function of a coordinate, and appear vertical or almost vertical when it is slightly tilted (Radner and Gibson, 1935). But even in darkness observers are able to adjust and maintain the vertical position of the body by means of the gravitational forces acting on it which are registered by the proprioceptive senses (Gibson and Mowrer, 1938). Thus judgments of the visually perceived vertical are seldom more than slightly inaccurate because the observer can coordinate them with the gravitational vertical. If, however, the observer's head or body is slanted at an angle with the vertical, his judgments may become more uncertain and less accurate (Mann *et al.,* 1949). Thus

* Gibson (1966) considers that muscular sensory data do not contribute to awareness of movement, since muscle tension is not accurately related to extent of movement. However, they might contribute to awareness of static bodily position.

when the head was tilted through 30° from the vertical, a luminous bar in a darkened room was judged vertical when it was in fact tilted in the opposite direction; and the effect was greater the longer the head was tilted (Wade and Day, 1968). Blind observers were less affected in their estimates of the vertical by tilting of the body than were sighted observers blindfolded, presumably because the former must always depend on the gravitational senses alone for estimating the vertical (Bitterman and Worchel, 1953).

However, Asch and Witkin (1948) and Witkin and Asch (1948) showed that estimation of the vertical when the normal visual framework was concealed varied with the nature of the visually perceived objects and the position of the body. As in the experiments just described, Witkin and Asch found that observers could accurately adjust a luminous rod in a dark room to the vertical as long as they were upright, but became less accurate if the head or body was tilted. When instead of the rod a tilted square luminous frame was presented, there was a tendency to tilt the estimated vertical parallel to the frame, which was increased when the body was tilted. An even greater tilting of the vertical occurred when a 'stronger' visual framework was viewed, the interior of a tilted 'room', with all other surroundings concealed. The effect could also be enhanced by further weakening the postural senses – placing the observer in a small enclosed room which was driven round a circular track, thus subjecting him to a combination of gravitational and centrifugal forces (Witkin, 1950).

But throughout these experiments, consistent *individual differences* were obtained. Some observers were able to make fairly accurate estimates of the true vertical, by relying on their gravitational senses. Others not only set their estimates of the vertical parallel to the main coordinate of the tilted framework but also perceived the latter to revert gradually to an apparently vertical position. Moreover, when they were asked to put their own bodies in a vertical position, they set them parallel to the edge of the framework (Witkin, 1949a). They often had great difficulty in making their judgments, became confused and emotionally blocked, and even experienced vertigo. Children were more liable to do this than were adults (Witkin, 1949b). Witkin *et al.* (1954) also related these characteristics to differences in personality qualities, as we shall consider in Chapter XII.

These findings have been contraverted by those of other experimenters. Thus Passey (1950) found that his observers were able to set the position of their bodies to the vertical with fair accuracy when they viewed a tilted room from a chair tilted through 45°. There was no tendency to set their position in alignment with the tilted room. However, only five observers were studied, and it is possible that they all fell into the first category described by Witkin and Asch. Gibson (1952) considered that observers might have perceived two types of apparent vertical, one corresponding to the visual framework and the other to the postural vertical; and that some selected one type in making their judgments, and others the other. Gruen (1957) stated that this behaviour was very variable, and observers were not consistent, but shifted their judgments during the experiment, as they became adapted to the situation. Weiner (1955) also found that many observers improved the accuracy and stability of their judgments as to the verticality of a luminous rod, surrounded by a luminous tilted frame, when they were instructed how to judge the position of the body and adjust the luminous rod accordingly. Again there were considerable individual differences, and one observer became even more inaccurate. However, these observations do suggest that Witkin's visual-postural dichonotomy may not correspond to any consistent perceptual difference between individuals. This conclusion is supported by the findings of Gross (1959), who showed that judgments could be considerably affected, especially in some persons, by suggestions of an actually non-existent distortion of orientation.

These errors would seem to occur to a greater or less extent when the *horizontal co-ordinate* is functioning. Thus Rock (1954) required observers to lie prone, and presented a luminous horizontal bar immediately above their heads. They were then able to set it with considerable accuracy to the co-ordinates of the face, left-right and top-bottom. Thus judgments in relation to the position of the body which are independent of gravity can be made with fair but not complete accuracy. However, if the frame of reference of the bar was concealed by surrounding it with a screen, observers tended to set the bar parallel to the edges of this. Again, observers could judge with considerable accuracy when a rotating luminous dot was in the twelve o'clock position if they inclined their heads into a horizontal plane and viewed the dot on the floor beneath them (Rock, 1966). Judgments were less accurate when this was done in a vertical plane. Rock concluded that when gravitational forces were not operating, judgments of position were related to the visual framework and its relation to the horizontal orientation of the body.

A curious illustration of what appears to have been a form of dependence on the visual framework was reported by Dixon and Dixon (1966). They were in a yacht which grounded on the receding tide, and gradually listed over. The conflict between visual and gravitational cues had the effect of causing hanging objects to appear out of the vertical; and the surface of water which had seeped into the cabin, to seem inclined to the horizontal. Yet the observers' impression of the list was noticeably less than the actual list; and it decreased progressively when the yacht reached a state of equilibrium.

A large number of experiments has been carried out to discover whether it is possible to *adjust to a new spatial framework* which conflicts with the habitual framework. In the earliest of these, Stratton (1896, 1897) himself wore continuously over a period of two weeks prismatic spectacles which both *inverted and reversed* the field of view. At first he experienced great disorientation of both perception and movement; after a time he was able to adjust his movements, but continued to perceive the abnormal visual field. The best known experiments are, however, those of Erismann and Kohler, carried out at the University of Innsbruck.* In the main experiments, two observers wore continuously over a long period of time, for twenty-four and thirty-seven days respectively, prismatic spectacles which either inverted the visual field or *reversed* it from left to right. The main observations were recorded in the latter situation; they were obtained in the course of normal everyday life, and no controlled experimental observations were made. At first movements guided by vision, such as bicycling and walking along a path, were grossly disturbed, but were gradually corrected by deliberate thought, and by planned manipulation of objects. Finally adjustment was more or less automatic. After about two weeks, some parts of the visual field began to appear in normal left-right orientation, though others, such as unfamiliar writing, remained reversed for much longer. The reversing lenses also had the effect of reversing depth cues; and this effect apparently was not overcome. On removal of the lenses, left-right reversal of the field reappeared, and lasted for some hours. From these observations, Harris (1965) argued that a radical adaptation could take place in kinaesthetic and postural data, whereby they become adjusted to the reversed direction of movement, and that this is independent of the visual perception of the field of view.

The effects of long-term *inversion* of the field (without reversal) by viewing continuously through mirrors was also studied. These effects were at first more severe; disorientation and vertigo were experienced and movement was exceedingly difficult. However, there was a fairly rapid adaptation especially of voluntary movement, followed by a slower perceptual adaptation which was nevertheless quicker than with the

* Descriptions of this work appear mainly in rather obscure journals; but good accounts and discussions are given by Smith and Smith (1962) and Rock (1966).

reversing spectacles, and in one case became complete in nine days. Kottenhoff (1957) considered that an active endeavour to restructure the perceived inverted field was necessary to restore its normal appearance; without this the field, or certain parts of it, might continue indefinitely to appear inverted.

Somewhat similar observations were made by Taylor (1962). He argued that if adaptation became complete, an observer should be able to alternate between wearing reversing spectacles and not wearing them without loss of adjustment. An observer tested this by wearing the spectacles in the morning but not in the afternoon, over a period of time. Through learning to perform specific tasks, such as reaching for objects under verbal direction, adaptation was more rapid than in the Innsbruck experiments, such that the observer could put on and take off the spectacles without loss of adjustment. Taylor himself wore intermittently prismatic spectacles which had the effect of making surfaces appear to slope downwards from right to left. Walking became difficult, but after two weeks he perceived a level path in front of him along which he could walk normally, the ground sloping on either side. He always walked with a stick and with close attention to the path in front of him, which may have facilitated this type of adaptation. His working table also ceased to appear curved and unstable, but it continued to slope obliquely, and surrounding objects were unstable in shape and position. Taylor therefore argued that it was possible to adapt movement and to perceive normally those parts of the field which were deliberately subjected to exploration and manipulation, whereas other parts of the field and other movements remained unaffected.

Many observations have also been made in which the field was *tilted laterally* or *displaced to one side*, rather than completely reversed or inverted. Kohler (see Smith and Smith, 1962) studied the behaviour and experiences of several observers who wore, over varying periods of time, prismatic spectacles which displaced the field through varying angles, from 5° to 30°. They perceived a variety of distortions in the field of view: bent lines, distorted angles, slanting of the floor, etc. With angles of displacement of less than 20°, there was gradual adaptation, varying considerably for different observers; but with larger angles, disoriented perception and disordered movement persisted. After effects were variable, greatest when adaptation was slowest; sometimes periods of distortion alternated with periods of normal perception. Pick and Hay (1964) also showed that when prismatic lenses producing a displacement of 11° and curvature of the field were worn continuously for forty-two days, there was considerable adaptation in the ability to touch a target with the hand concealed, and errors were largely eliminated after three days. The perception of curvature was considerably reduced after forty-two days. But differential distortion of the field when the hand moved was unaffected. In another experiment, Hay and Pick (1966) found that eye-hand co-ordination, in reaching for a target, adapted to a considerable extent during the first day, and was almost complete in ten days. There was little visual adaptation when the observer was required to walk towards a target with his body concealed from his view, but a good deal more when he looked at his body and legs moving along a path on the floor. Thus Hay and Pick concluded that visual perceptual change was slower than proprioceptive adaptation, and depended on the possibility of perceiving the conflict between visually perceived and kinaesthetically felt movement. That this adaptation occurred cortically was demonstrated by an experiment by Pick *et al.* (1966) which showed that, if only one eye was covered by a prismatic distorting lens, there was considerable perceptual adaptation in the other, occluded, eye, though not as much as in the viewing eye.

Numerous experiments have shown that some degree of *compensation for displacement*, curvature and tilting of the visual field may be made during comparatively *short periods of exposure*. According to Held and his colleagues, this occurs only when the observer undertakes *active movement*, and not when he is moved passively. But other experimenters believe that compensation is due, as Hay and Pick hypothesized, to some kind of active perception of the effects of displacement. Held and Bossom (1961) required an observer to turn his body, while sitting on a rotating chair, until he faced a vertical line straight ahead of him, displaced through 11° by prismatic spectacles. A slight compensation for this displacement was produced if he had previously walked along a path out-of-doors, but none if he had been wheeled along the path in a chair. Observers who had been exposed intermittently to these conditions over a period of four days showed almost complete compensation in 50 per cent of cases after active walking, though it was somewhat fluctuating and variable; but there was no compensation after being wheeled in the chair. A period of fifty minutes walking along a passage produced much greater compensation for displacement than did a similar period in which the observer wheeled himself along it in a chair, although in the latter condition he had to take some account of errors in direction of movement (Held and Mikaelian, 1964). After walking or being wheeled along the passage for one hour, there was a slight compensation in the passive condition for tilting and displacement of the field, though far more after the active condition (Mikaelian and Held,

1964). There was less compensation after the active condition if the well-lit passage was replaced by a very dimly lit passage in which no straight lines were visible; and no compensation at all after the passive condition. Some degree of compensation for and reduction in apparent curvature occurred when an observer walked for half an hour round the inside of a large drum with an irregular pattern of dots on its surface; but none when the observer was wheeled passively (Held and Rekosh, 1963). Active pointing with the hand in view over a period of three minutes produced some compensation for the error in pointing, with hand hidden, to a target displaced through about 11° (Harris, 1963). This compensation occurred with a variety of targets as long as the adapted hand was used, but not in pointing with the other hand. In a similar experiment, Held and Freedman (1963) showed that there was less compensation if the hand was concealed during the practice period; and none if the pointing movement was passive, the arm being moved by the experimenter. Thus Held and his colleagues concluded that adaptation took place by virtue of the feedback from active movements which the observer corrected when they were perceived to produce erroneous localization of the displaced, curved or tilted perceived patterns.

This conclusion was contraverted by other experimenters, who hypothesized that adaptation would take place irrespective of active movement provided that the observer could perceive the incorrectness of his localization. Thus Wallach *et al.* (1963b) found that compensation occurred for lateral displacement through prismatic spectacles if the observer tilted his head forward and looked down at his legs for ten minutes. At first his legs appeared slanted and displaced, but this effect disappeared through the comparison of the visual appearance with the felt position of the legs and feet. Thereafter observers were able to point accurately at a target. Howard *et al.* (1965) moved a rod towards an observer until it touched his lips; but since its image was displaced by viewing it through mirrors, it appeared to the observer as if it would touch his face 2° to the left of his mouth. This produced compensation in pointing to an equally displaced target, though clearly no movement of the observer was involved. It was also shown by Foley and Abel (1967) that in certain cases compensation may occur only when there is continuous information. They required observers to propel a ball to reach a target when the field size was reduced to a third by viewing it through binoculars, and found that improvement in localization occurred only when the observers were informed throughout of their errors, and not when training in the distorted depth conditions alternated with performance of localization. However, it is possible that the effects may be somewhat different in three-dimensional localization.

Weinstein *et al.* (1964) performed an experiment similar to that of Held and Bossom (1961), in that observers had to rotate their bodies to face a displaced target. But compensation in directing the body occurred after they had been wheeled to and fro along a corridor, either completely passively, or pushing with their feet, or both directing the chair and pushing. There was also compensation when the observer was informed of his errors in rotating to face a displaced target, without the previous movement. Again, Mack (1967) found that compensation for tilting of the field through 40° by prismatic spectacles occurred both when the observer walked up and down a corridor for thirty minutes and also when he was moved in a cart. But it was only slight when he sat viewing the corridor without moving. Mack concluded from these observations, which appeared directly to contradict those of Held, that provided the observer knew that the field which appeared tilted was in fact a familiar upright scene, he could learn to compensate for the tilt. But if he was unfamiliar with it, he was forced to move in order to obtain information as to its actual nature. However, Morant and Beller (1965) found that although some compensation for tilt occurred while viewing passively for fifteen minutes a familiar room (but no compensation if he merely looked at a luminous vertical line), the compensation was greater when the observer walked about. Thus in some cases more information may be obtained through such movement even in familiar surroundings. But Rock (1966) considered that visual adaptation was also occurring in this case. The observer must develop some association between the immediately perceived stimulus, and information signifying its actual form or position. This association develops gradually, but probably more rapidly if the observer consciously corrects the normal relationship between the two forms of information.

Now it would appear that in short-term experiments, in which compensation for displacement is measured by the performance of activities such as pointing at a target, the observer may well deliberately correct his erroneous localizations in the light of the information he has obtained as to the discrepancy between what he perceives visually, and the kinaesthetic data as to the location of the hand. That is to say, he may say to himself that in order to point his hand towards a point X, he must direct the hand kinaesthetically to one side of its normal direction. This correction he may be able to make in the light of information he has previously received through viewing the discrepancy in position between the field he perceives visually and the 'real' field in which he moves

He may obtain more accurate and extensive information through actual movement; but movement would not appear to be essential provided that he carefully observes and estimates the discrepancy.

However, this type of intentional correction would occur principally in comparatively simple voluntarily controlled and directed movement, and might cease to operate in complex habitual patterns of movement which are normally performed automatically. It is the gradual adjustment of these, which were studied in the long-term experiments of Kohler, Taylor, and Pick and Hay, to which the term 'adaptation' should more properly be applied. In all probability this adaptation developed through intentional correction of voluntary movement over a period of time; just as in the normal acquisition of skills voluntarily controlled movements are ultimately superseded by automatic habitual movement patterns. Clearly in the adaptation experiments these movements were 'cued off' by the visual perception of the field, but were independent of perception of a normally oriented field. Adjustment of perception such that the field was actually seen as normal usually did not occur until later, and sometimes not at all. Thus the establishment of stable spatial schemata in which visual and kinaesthetic data are effectively integrated is probably a long and gradual process; and such schemata are resistant to alteration through environmental change.

VIII

The Constancies

(1) Introduction

A form of interaction between 'figure' and 'ground' in perception which has given rise to continued speculation and an enormous amount of experimental investigation is that which occurs in the so-called 'constancies'. It appears that an object may retain the shape, size and colour which are characteristically associated with its identity although the information as to these qualities which is projected to the eye varies with variation in the relation of the object to its surroundings. We noted in Chapter II that infants learnt to identify objects and to disregard changes in the sensory data related to shape which occur when the objects are tilted or rotated; and changes in projected size which are produced by varying the distance of the object from the eye. So also it is found that from an early age children and adults may seem actually to perceive a rotated shape as having the same form as that of the unrotated shape; or perceive a form part-way between that of the unrotated shape and that of the actually projected shape. And they may perceive the size of a distant object to approximate to the size of the same object when it is close to them. Finally, they may perceive the brightness and colour to vary less than do the brightness and colour of the projected image. But the preservation of perceived constancy in spite of variation in the projected sensory data depends to a large extent on the ability of the observer to differentiate the inherent qualities of the object from those aspects which vary with changes in the environmental setting. Thus in general it is necessary for the observer to perceive the characteristics of the environmental setting or 'ground' clearly and unambiguously.

These phenomena were first described independently by Thouless (1931a and 1931b) and by the Gestalt psychologists, notably Koffka (1935). The former termed them *'phenomenal regression to the real object'*, and the latter, the *'constancies'*. Koffka considered that the different types of constancy described above could be explained in terms of certain general laws relating perception to processes in the central nervous system associated with the theory of isomorphism. These were discussed in some detail by Vernon (1937, 1952). However, it appeared from subsequent experiment that the constancies of size, shape and colour did not necessarily operate in the same manner, and that they were affected by a number of varying factors including the nature of the surroundings and individual characteristics of the observer. In the following discussion, additional evidence will be considered as to the nature and conditions of appearance of these phenomena.

It has been customary to assess the *degree of constancy* by matching an object in altered orientation, or at varying distances, against variables in normal orientation, or close to the observer. From these matches, the perceived shape, size, etc., can be measured and compared with the 'real' shape, size, etc., and those of the projected image, calculated geometrically. The comparison is then expressed quantitatively by means of a formula. Thouless used an *index of phenomenal regression* which equalled

$$\frac{\log P - \log S}{\log R - \log S}$$

where $P =$ perceived size or shape, $R =$ the real or objective size or shape and $S =$ the projected size or shape. However, Brunswik's index (1928) is now more commonly used:

$$\frac{P - R}{C - R}$$

C being the objective size or shape and R the projected size or shape. In either case, the magnitude of the index varies between 1·0 for complete constancy, and zero for judgments of projected size or shape. It must be pointed out, however, that all these data on the degree of constancy are based upon judgments which are inferred usually from prolonged inspection of the objects. We cannot be certain as to the nature of immediate perceptions of size, shape, etc. such as people make in everyday life circumstances.

(2) Size Constancy

The experimental evidence on the extent of size constancy is more extensive than that relating to the other types of constancy, and therefore it will be considered first. Now it was noted in the previous chapter that judgments of distance and apparent change in distance were often related to the sizes of the projected images of objects, which decreased regularly as distance increased. It seems, however, that if the observer is able to perceive the distance of an object, by means for instance of gradients in surrounding space, he tends to ignore the reduction and to perceive the object to be of the same size as it would have were it close to him. Thus he will match the size of a distant object to that of an equal-sized object near to him, rather than to that of an object having the same size as the projected image. This match is said to accord with the 'real' or 'objective' size rather than with the projected or 'visual angle' size, that is to say the size as indicated by the angle subtended by the object at the eye. The index is of the order of 1·0, and a compensation would appear to be made for the reduction in visual angle size by means of the perceived distance. Brunswik (1944) found that in viewing objects of varying sizes *in natural surroundings* at distances of up to 10 km. an observer could make accurate judgments of size, though there tended to be some under-estimation at far distances. Gibson (1947) required observers to match a stake, of unknown height and placed at a considerable distance in natural surroundings, against one of a series of stakes of variable height, close to him. Constancy was found to be complete up to a distance of about half-a-mile. Gilinsky (1951) showed that constancy began to break down at about the maximum limit of perceived distance, that is to say, the point at which the distance of the object could no longer be estimated. In several of these experiments some degree of *over-constancy* appeared; the further object was matched with a near object larger than itself. In some experiments this effect may have been due to what Piaget and Lambercier (1943) called the '*error of the standard*'; namely, that because there are more centrations on the standard stimulus than on the variables, the magnitude of the former tends to be over-estimated by comparison with that of the latter. In many experiments the further object is the standard throughout, since this is more convenient. However, it cannot be concluded that all over-constancy is due to this cause and, indeed, Piaget and Lambercier showed that adults tended to over-estimate the size of the more distant object, whether standard or variable, presumably because they were over-compensating for distance.

Over-constancy is more likely to occur with comparatively near objects. It decreases with increase in distance, as Brunswik showed; and at great distances, especially when there is intervening space as in looking down into a valley from the side of a mountain, constancy is greatly reduced. Objects such as people and vehicles appear so minute that they are difficult even to identify. Nevertheless, some degree of constancy is maintained even at great distances, for instance in viewing distant mountains, which appear higher than they do in photographs which show the projected size.

If, however, the observer is unable to perceive the *surroundings*, as in so-called *'reduction conditions'*, constancy tends to diminish and even disappear. Holway and Boring (1941) studied the ability of observers to match the size of a circle of light subtending a constant visual angle at distances of ten to 120 feet, by adjusting the size of another circle of light at ten feet. It was found that there was over-constancy (index 1·09) when the observer could perceive the surroundings of the objects clearly in binocular vision. Constancy was still of the order of 1·0 when monocular vision was used, but was reduced to 0·44 when the observer wore an artificial pupil that restricted his field of vision; and to 0·22 when in addition the distant stimulus was placed in a long dark tunnel. Even in this condition constancy was not completely eliminated, possibly because there was some reflected light in the tunnel. Hastorf and Way (1952) were able to reduce it to zero by presenting the distant stimulus as a circular area of light seen through a hole in a 'reduction screen' in a totally dark room. Further evidence as to the effect of perceived surroundings was obtained by Lambercier (1946), who showed that constancy in equating the height of a wooden strip at a distance to one close to the observer was increased by placing strips of equal height between the near and the distant strips.

A particular instance of the relation between perceived size and surroundings which has received considerable attention is the phenomenon of the *'horizontal moon'*; the moon appears much larger when it is close to the horizon than when it is at the zenith. Taylor and Boring (1942) suggested that in the former condition but not in the latter the moon was seen in the frame of reference of terrestial objects which afforded clues to distance. Rock and Kaufman (1962) projected bright discs reflected by a half-silvered mirror through which the observer also saw directly either the sky or the receding landscape. In the latter case, but not in the former, constancy was complete. Orbach and Solhkhah (1968) obtained somewhat different results when observers viewed, in reclining position, a disc attached at one side of a tall chimney above their heads. Two out of six observers made estimates showing complete constancy, but for the remaining four the suspended disc appeared diminished in size. However, it seems possible that, although their vision was restricted, the two observers did obtain some view of the receding chimney. When no such information as to distance was available, constancy was reduced.

It might be supposed that if the observer was compensating for the decrease in visual angle size with increase in distance, there would be a constant or *invariant relationship* between estimates of perceived size and distance, as indeed Koffka hypothesized. Yet Gruber (1954) found little or no correlation between estimated size and distance. Smith and Smith (1966), using a variety of familiar and unfamiliar objects in restricted and unrestricted vision, also obtained no significant correlation between size and distance in adults or children. Piaget (1961), however, found that size and distance estimates did correlate in children, though not in adults, and considered that children were more directly aware of the visual angle size. But in adults apparent size and distance were too closely associated together in 'global' perception for it to be possible to estimate either independently of the other. Isolated judgments of distance were made in a different manner. Gruber and Smith and Smith argued that essentially different types of cue were used in making size and distance judgments respectively. Nevertheless Hartman (1964) found that the ratios of perceived size to distance were invariant whatever the magnitude of size constancy in varying degrees of restriction of surroundings. According to Baird (1963), size and distance judgments were positively correlated when objective instructions were given, that is to say, to compare the objective sizes of near and distant objects; but not when the emphasis was on attempting to make visual angle judgments. Epstein (1963b) obtained a correlation when spontaneous judgments were made, unaided by cognitive deliberation.

Some experimenters have claimed that perception of constancy may also be affected by *knowledge of the objective size* of the object, especially when the surroundings are concealed, and cues to distance are weak. Indeed, in some conditions perceived size and distance are largely determined by what the observer assumes, on the basis of previous knowledge, to be the objective size. Hochberg and Hochberg (1952) found that a screen on which was depicted a small picture of a boy was judged in monocular vision to be further than one on which was a large picture of the same boy. Ittelson (1951), as we noted, showed that a half-sized playing card, viewed monocularly, was perceived to be double the distance of a playing card of normal size, whereas a double-sized playing card was judged to be at half the distance. These effects were less with objects the size of which was less familiar. Gogel *et al.* (1957) found that they did not occur in absolute judgments of distance, but only when there was a comparison between the differences of distance of playing cards of different sizes – as in the experiment of Ittelson. However, Epstein (1963a) showed that when photographs of a 'quarter', a dime enlarged to the size of a quarter, and a half-dollar reduced to the size of a quarter, were presented at equal distances in totally reduced conditions and monocular vision, the dime was perceived as the smallest and nearest, the half-dollar as largest and furthest, and the quarter intermediate.

There were correlations of 0·6 to 0·7 between apparent size and distance, though with some difference between individuals. Nevertheless, apparent distance varied with apparent size, which corresponded to the assumed identity of the objects. But in binocular vision, sizes and distances appeared equal. This equation of apparent with assumed size is perhaps not surprising in view of the findings of Bolles and Bailey (1956) and McKennell (1960) that estimation of sizes of familiar-sized objects can be made almost as accurately from memory as in direct perception.

But such effects do not occur when surroundings can be normally perceived. Slack (1956) found only a slight tendency to approximate the size of over- and under-sized chairs to that of a normal-sized chair, as compared with objects of unknown sizes. Fillenbaum *et al.* (1965) obtained even slighter effects, and judged that there was little or no regression of this kind in normal surroundings. This judgment was confirmed by Schiffman (1967), who found that known size was effective in determining the apparent sizes of objects such as half- and double-sized playing cards only with far-distant objects in reduced-cue conditions. When the objects could be seen clearly, size judgments were determined by the visual cues to distance.

However, judgments of size constancy have been found to vary considerably between different individuals and to relate to varying individual characteristics. There has been some disagreement as to the effects of increasing *age*. As we noted on p. 19, quite young children were able to perceive the identity between an object close to them and one beyond their reach. Thus it appeared that for relatively near objects constancy was complete within the first year. Moreover, Bower (1966a) found that infants as young as six to eight weeks, when trained to respond to a cube of a particular size, transferred this response to a cube of the same size at a greater distance, rather than to a larger cube; that is to say, they responded to objective size and not to visual angle size. On the other hand, several experimenters have found that in the experimental matching of size of near and fairly distant objects, constancy was lower for younger than for older children and adults (for discussion of the earlier work, see Vernon, (1952)). Moreover, Piaget and Lambercier (1951) showed that children of six to eight years could judge visual angle sizes more accurately than could older children and adults. It thus appeared that there was a stronger tendency in younger children making judgments of this kind to notice visual angle size. However, Cohen *et al.* (1958) found size constancy to be high in children of five to twelve years for objects at eight metres, though it increased somewhat between twelve and seventeen years, when judgments became more consistent. Zeigler and Leibowitz (1957) showed that size constancy for an object of unfamiliar size was approximately complete at seven to nine years with objects at ten feet, but that it decreased steadily with increasing distance, up to a hundred feet. The Brunswik ratio was then 0·35, as compared with 0·86 for adults. Smith and Smith (1966) found that in viewing an object of familiar size in reduction conditions, only a small number of five-year-old children made visual angle matches. No adults made such judgments, and only 23 per cent of children aged six to twelve years. In unrestricted conditions, scarcely any children made visual angle matches; and in the remainder size constancy was complete. Smith and Smith also stated that when individual results were considered in the data of Zeigler and Leibowitz, it was found that some children made visual angle matches and others objective size matches. Thus it would seem that the apparently lower mean size constancy of children may be simply the average of different individual estimates; and it is possible that these differences relate to different attitudes to or interpretations of instructions, which, as we shall see, can also occur in adults.

It does seem possible, however, that young children are less well able than older ones to utilize cues given by the surroundings, when these are somewhat limited. Thus Lambercier (1946) found that children showed a lower degree of constancy than did adults when, in restricted conditions, some information was provided by strips of wood placed between the near and far strips. Again, Leibowitz *et al.* (1967) found that, whereas for adults there was no difference between binocular and monocular size matches for objects up to two hundred feet away in natural surroundings, smaller size matches were made by the children in monocular than in binocular vision, especially of the more distant objects. Thus apparently the children were less well able to utilize monocular cues to distance. Children also tended, by comparison with adults, to under-estimate differences in empty space between two objects suspended in the air; that is to say, when relations to surroundings were not clearly visible (Costa, 1949). But also Denis-Prinzhorn (1960) found that children of five to seven years tended to under-estimate distance between further objects, as compared with that between nearer ones; whereas adults over-estimated the further distances. Wohlwill (1963) obtained much the same results when he required adult and child observers to estimate distances along a receding textured surface.

The relationship between constancy and *intelligence* also appears to be somewhat ambiguous. Jenkin and Feallock (1960) found that in

L

unrestricted conditions of viewing, children of fifteen years with low intelligence showed a significantly greater degree of constancy than did younger children of the same mental age (eight years), and much the same degree of constancy as did normal children of fifteen years. Thus they concluded that constancy increased with age and maturation, and not with intelligence. Hamilton (1966a), however, found that twelve-year-old children of low intelligence (average I.Q. 74) showed some over-constancy in unrestricted vision, but less than did children of normal intelligence, especially with complex objects. Over-constancy increased and under-constancy decreased with increase both in age and in intelligence, but to a great extent with the latter. Nevertheless, the fact remains that, according to Hamilton's findings, some children of low intelligence were apparently capable of making the type of over-compensation on which over-constancy is thought to depend. This fact is difficult to explain.

Numerous experimenters have discovered that there are considerable *individual differences* in adult judgments of size constancy; and in particular that it is greater if the observer judges that the further object has the same 'real' or objective size as the nearer than if he judges that the further object looks as if it would project the same size as the nearer (Tolman, 1935). In the former case there is 'thing constancy', generated by a *'synthetic'* or *'object attitude'*; in the latter, the *'sensory'* or *'analytic attitude'*, immediate perception is corrected by means of thought processes (Tolman and Brunswik, 1935). It is possible to determine to a considerable extent which 'attitude' or procedure will be adopted through the wording of the experimental instructions: in the one case, to judge the real size of the object; in the other, the angular section of the field cut off by the object. Gilinsky (1955) termed the latter 'retinal matching', instructing observers to equalize the images of objects as they would appear in a photograph. She obtained two quite independent estimates using these and 'real' size instructions. With the latter there was over-constancy, but with the former estimates increasingly approached visual angle size as distance increased up to 4,000 feet. Jenkin and Hyman (1959) obtained similar results, and concluded that the two types of judgment were quite independent of each other. But if there is nothing in the experimental instructions to suggest that one or the other of these procedures is to be adopted, then, according to Joynson (1958), some observers may spontaneously utilize one and others the other. He found that if the near and distant objects were presented one vertically above the other, there was a tendency to match visual angle size directly. As the lateral separation between the two objects increased, objective size judgments became relatively easier to make, and indeed about three-quarters of his observers made these throughout. But some continued to attempt visual angle judgments, though with great difficulty. However, all observers realized that the two types of judgment were possible; and if they had made one initially, they were able to made the other subsequently. Joynson considered that results obtained in other experiments which showed apparent size as a compromise between objective and visual angle size were in fact averages of judgments of objective size made by some observers and of visual angle size made by others.

However, other experiments seem to suggest that judgments of apparent size may be made specifically and independently of those of objective or visual angle size. Carlson (1962) found that in unrestricted viewing conditions there was slight over-constancy with objective size instructions, under-constancy with projective (visual angle) size instructions, and somewhat variable intermediate constancy judgments when observers were asked to match objects as 'looking equal'. Leibowitz and Harvey (1967) required observers to match the heights of human beings at distances of 340 to 1680 feet, in natural surroundings, against a rod close to them. Again with objective instructions there was slight over-constancy. With instructions to report 'apparent size', 36 to 20 per cent of matches were of test object size, the number decreasing with distance; and with 'retinal' (visual angle) instructions, only 18 to 9 per cent of matches were of test object size. There was no overlap between these ranges of judgment. These findings therefore seem to contradict Joynson's argument that apparent size was merely a compromise between objective and visual angle size.

There is also some evidence that *personality characteristics* may induce observers to choose spontaneously to make either objective or visual angle judgments. Carlson (1960) found that more intelligent observers tended to under-estimate in making apparent size judgments, whereas more suggestible observers tended to over-estimate. He considered that the latter, trying to conform to the experimenter's instructions in making objective size judgments, were liable to over-compensate for distance and hence to over-estimate. The more intelligent observers may have applied their reasoning capacities in making analytic visual angle judgments. Singer (1952) found that extraverts more easily adopted the synthetic attitude and achieved a high degree of constancy; whereas introverts, adopting an analytic attitude, showed lower constancy. The former also were more affected when the meaningfulness of the stimulus, a square, was increased by drawing a face on it. Jenkin (1958) showed that with analytic instructions, neuroti individuals tended to give more visual angle judgments than did normals; and this tendency was stronger in introverted than in extraverted neurotics. Normal extraverts tended to over-constancy, as compared with normal introverts. But with objective instructions there were no significant differences. It is possible that relatively naive and unsophisticated observers also tend to give more objective size judgments than do educated European adults. Hence the findings of Thouless (1933) and Beveridge (1935) that Indian and African students had larger size constancy indices than did European students.

It must be realized, as we noted above, that in experiments in size constancy the data obtained relate to judgments about percepts, and do not necessarily indicate what the observer initially perceives. It may be that in fact he perceives 'objective size at a distance', something which differs from objective size, apparent size and visual angle size, estimates of which are formulated by reasoning about the initial percept. In his reasoning, he may over-compensate for the distance effect, and produce objective size judgments showing over-constancy. In making a visual angle judgment, he may even neglect his initial perception altogether, and deliberately judge the angular segment subtended by the object. The apparent size judgment, if indeed it exists independently, might depend on the perception of the surrounding field as a sequence of concentric rings at increasing distances, with the observer in the centre. The distant object might then be fitted to its appropriate ring, the 'apparent size' then constituting the correct angular segment of that ring. It would seem that this type of judgment is more labile and variable than the others. What is perhaps most surprising is that in normal unrestricted conditions of viewing, the visual angle judgment, though fairly consistent, never completely conforms to the actual visual angle.

(3) Constancy Scaling and Visual Illusions

The theory was advanced by Thiéry (1896) that certain visual illusions were the result of the correction of apparent size, in size constancy, in relation to the three-dimensional perspective impression created by the illusion figures. This theory was revived by Tausch (1954) and Von Holst (1957), and extensively promulgated by Gregory. It has given rise to a great deal of discussion and experiment by other experimenters.

Whereas, according to Gregory (1963), size constancy in normal surroundings is set by '*secondary constancy scaling*', it can also operate, in '*primary*' or '*inappropriate constancy scaling*', with actually flat figures that might suggest three-dimensional perspective, although the observer may not be consciously aware of any three-dimensional effect. Nevertheless, parts of a figure which might be more distant tend to appear larger, whereas parts which might be nearer appear smaller. These effects are said to be demonstrated in the *Müller-Lyer illusion*. The expanding arrow head or fins and the shaft between them correspond to the corner of a cubical structure seen from within, and the shaft therefore appears longer than that of the figure with the contracting arrow head, which corresponds to the external view of a cube. Prolonged previous experience of real perspective perceptions of this kind has created a tendency to perceive three-dimensionality in reproductions of perspective views, as we noted on p. 129; though these actually retain their two-dimensionality because they are located in the plane of the paper. If the Müller-Lyer illusion is presented as a luminous wire model, or on a transparent surface illuminated from behind, it appears three-dimensional, provided that the angles between the fins are not marked exaggerations of perspective. In Gregory's Müller-Lyer figures, the angles between the fins were considerably larger than those normally used, and therefore exaggerated perspective less. Gregory (1966a) presented a Müller-Lyer figure on a transparent surface illuminated from behind to one eye; and at the same time a movable spot of light was reflected to both eyes from a half-silvered mirror. Observers were then able to set the distance of the spot of light to the same apparent distance as the shaft of the Müller-Lyer figure. The magnitude of the illusion, as found in separate experiments with the figure shown on a non-transparent textured background, varied with the angle between the fins and the shaft, over a range of angle from 70° to 150°. The distance indicated by setting the spot of light varied in the same manner. Therefore it was concluded that the primary constancy scaling of the illusion (on the textured background) was determined by the degree of apparent distance measured when the figure was illuminated from behind.

However, Gregory (1966b) considered that any actual perception of distance associated with the Müller-Lyer illusion was irrelevant to primary constancy scaling and the appearance of the illusion. Thus he dismissed as irrelevant Hamilton's finding (1966b) that there was no correlation between the magnitudes of size constancy judgments of different observers, viewing real objects at different distances, and those of their independent estimates of the Müller-Lyer illusion. Presumably the same criticism could apply to the arguments of Fisher (1968b); and to the experiment of Brown and Houssiadas (1965), who required observers to estimate the magnitude of the inverted *Ponzo* figure, and other illusions, and then to say which part of the field looked further away. Though the Ponzo illusion was seen in the normal way by some observers, others perceived no illusion; and still others perceived the divergent upper parts of the oblique lines as further away. Now although the primary constancy scaling hypothesis might predict that no differences in apparent distance would be perceived, it is difficult to understand how it can be reconciled with this variation in the perceived illusion.

We noted Gregory's statement that the Müller-Lyer illusion operated only over a limited range of angles between the fins, such as were not marked exaggerations of normal perspective views of rectangular structures. Yet other experimenters have found that the illusion increased as the angle decreased, to an amount which is far smaller than can ever be perceived in real perspective views of such structures. Dewar (1967a), for instance, found the magnitude of the illusion to increase with decrease in angle between fin and shaft from 60° to 15°. It is difficult to see how primary constancy scaling could apply to the version of the illusion shown in Fig. 16a with the central arrow head; or to the versions in Figs 17a to 17d (see p. 51) which do not represent any real three-dimensional views of normal objects. With the *Ponzo illusion*, also attributed by Gregory to primary constancy scaling, the versions shown in Figs 20a to 20c (see p. 52) do not correspond with any normally experienced three-dimensional effects.

The *Poggendorff illusion* was also attributed by Tausch (1954) to a form of primary constancy scaling. Green and Hoyle (1963) presented the illusion in a representation of one end of a room seen in perspective (Fig. 33). It is difficult to understand why anyone should tend to see the picture rail as continuous with the skirting board, as they suggested. However, they stated that the illusion was reduced when parts of their drawing were deleted, making it look less like a room; and it was also reduced when the oblique lines were viewed in a horizontal position. Again it is difficult to understand how the primary constancy scaling hypothesis could account for all the variations in the illusion described on p. 53, and particularly for the appearance of the illusion in Fig. 21b.

Evidence for the inappropriate constancy scaling hypothesis has also been claimed to appear in observations which have been made as to the magnitude of the illusions perceived by *uncultured peoples*, as contrasted with people living in civilized countries. The former are said to have had less experience than the latter in perceiving the strongly emphasized three-dimensional appearance of the '*carpentered*' world containing rectangular buildings, furniture, etc. Many years ago Rivers (1905) found that Europeans showed a greater magnitude of the Müller-Lyer illusion than did primitive peoples such as the Todas; but the latter showed a greater horizontal-vertical illusion. Segall *et al.* (1963) confirmed this result, and also found that the *Sander illusion* was greater for

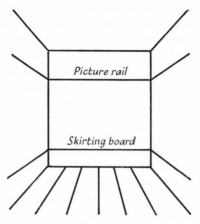

FIG. 33 The Poggendorff illusion
(*After* Green and Hoyle (1963) p. 612)

Europeans. In this figure (Fig. 34) the line 'a' tends to look longer than 'b', the effect being attributed to primary constancy scaling. However, Segall *et al.* (1966) did not find any systematic differences between Europeans and non-Europeans in the magnitude of the Poggendorff illusion.

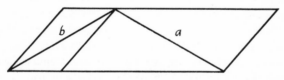

FIG. 34 The Sander illusion

These authors considered that the *horizontal-vertical* illusion was the result of foreshortening of the vertical line, which represented the perspective view of a horizontal line receding into the distance. They found that the magnitude of the illusion was greater in rural dwellers in the plains than in urban dwellers, who were less accustomed to view long distances in perspective. The illusion should have been least in dwellers in equatorial forests, with their very restricted view of distances; but the differences between different societies were not consistent. Jahoda (1966), comparing the magnitude of illusions in different Ghanaian tribes, found no relationship of this kind. Europeans were intermediate between different Ghanaians in the horizontal-vertical illusion. The Müller-Lyer illusion was greater for Europeans than for Ghanaians; but there was no difference among the latter corresponding to life in 'carpentered' and 'non-carpentered' environments. He considered that the difference between Europeans and non-Europeans might be due to lack of ability in the latter to perceive three-dimensionality in perspective drawings, such as we noted on p. 128. Finally, Berry (1968), testing Eskimos and the Terure of Sierra Leone, differentiated the relationship between the Müller-Lyer illusion and two sets of characteristics: rural *v* urban living environment, and degree of cultural development, through age, education and amount of contact with Western civilization. The illusion was found to be greater for urban than for rural dwellers; and also for those with less cultural development than for those with more. The latter result agrees with the data on p. 151 showing the decrease in magnitude of the illusion with increase in age in European children. The former seems to confirm the effect of the 'carpentered' environment, as independent of the capacity to perceive the perspective effects in two-dimensional drawings.

A final piece of evidence adduced by Gregory for the primary constancy scaling explanation of the illusions was the finding obtained by himself and Wallace (1963) as to the experiences of a man who had had no useful vision from an early age, as the result of corneal opacity, until, at the age of fifty-two years, he received corneal grafts which enabled him to see. But shortly after the operation he was unable to perceive the Poggendorff and other illusions, and the Müller-Lyer illusion was unusually small. He perceived no depth effects in the Necker cube and staircase figures, nor in landscape views. Gregory inferred that failure to perceive the illusions was due to lack of primary constancy scaling. However, it could also be the case that this man's undeveloped visual form perception prevented the normal perception of both these somewhat complex types of pattern; there was no proof that they interacted.

In spite of the evidence as to the relationships between the perception of visual illusions and prolonged exposure to three-dimensional objects in the environment, there must be great doubt as to the general application of the primary constancy scaling hypothesis. It is quite uncertain that two-dimensional representations of depth and distance can be considered to be in any sense primary, since as we noted on p. 129; they are based on particular conventions of pictorial representation, which are learnt. Size constancy itself is an extremely labile effect, varying in different settings; and its relation to perspective drawing requires further elucidation.

(4) Shape Constancy

It might be supposed that shape and size constancy constituted two aspects of the same general situation, namely the correction applied to information projected to the retina which varies in accordance with the spatial setting. In the first case, the variation of the information is produced by the recession in depth of parts of the surfaces of near objects; in the second, the variation arises from the intervention of empty space. Though many of the same factors influence judgments in the two cases, there does appear to be a fundamental difference between them. Thus Sheehan (1938) found that the correlation between the indices of different observers for size constancy assessed in different settings was high; but that between shape constancy in different situations was low. And correlation between size and shape indices was negligible.

Numerous experiments have suggested that judgments made by matching tilted shapes such as circles, squares and rectangles, against ellipses and trapezia situated in a plane at right angles to the line of sight, seldom give rise to constancy judgments as complete as those normally obtained in apparent size constancy judgments. Thus Thouless (1931a) obtained indices for shape of the order of 0·6 to 0·8. Brunswik (1956) quoted findings which gave indices of only about 0·5. However, the index varied considerably with the *angle of tilt*; in general it decreased as the angle increased (Eissler, 1933; Leibowitz *et al.*, 1959). Sheehan (1938) and Lichte (1952) also found an average decrease with increasing angle of tilt, but there was great individual variability in judgment (hence the low correlation Sheehan obtained). However, as we shall discuss later, constancy may be complete in some circumstances, especially if observers know the shape of the stimulus object and make judgments of objective shape.

Shape constancy depends primarily upon a *view of the surroundings* which enables the observer to perceive that the object is tilted and not at right angles to the line of sight. Thus Beck and Gibson (1955) found that a plain white triangle presented at an angle of 45° to a vertical black board in an otherwise dark room was perceived monocularly as flat; and its shape was equated with its projected shape, that is to say, constancy was zero. In binocular vision, slant was perceived, and constancy was high. Nelson and Bartley (1956) also obtained approximately zero constancy in judgments of luminously outlined circles and ellipses viewed at varying angles in a dark room. Nevertheless, as we noted on p. 125, slant may be perceived on the basis of the distortion imparted to shapes such as squares and circles by tilting them, in the absence of other cues to surroundings. This indicates that there is an association between *perceived shape and orientation*. But the ratio between these is not necessarily invariant; according to Stavrianos (1945) and Kaiser (1967), invariance occurred only in monocular vision. It also varied with conditions of viewing (Epstein *et al.*, 1962).

That shape constancy is dependent on viewing conditions was shown in the experiment of Leibowitz and Bourne (1956), who found that it increased both with increase in *intensity of illumination* and also with *length of viewing time*. Constancy was almost zero in very dim light, whatever the duration of exposure. It was greater at higher illuminations, and increased with increase of exposure time from 0·1 to 1·0 seconds, approaching a maximum at about 1·0 second. Curiously enough, size constancy was unrelated to changes in duration of exposure (Leibowitz *et al.*, 1956).

It might be hypothesized that shape constancy judgments would be affected to some extent by *previous knowledge* as to the real shape of the object. Many values for shape constancy, from those of Thouless (1931a) onwards, might have been affected by the knowledge of the observer that he was looking at a tilted circle. However, Nelson and Bartley (1956), who presented both ellipses and circles in darkness, found that their observers' judgments were unaffected by the information as to whether they were looking at ellipses or circles. Again, Epstein (1962) showed that constancy was equally low when a slanted playing card, a rectangle with irregular internal detail and a plain white rectangle, were matched against a series of trapezoidally shaped patches of light, both in monocular and in binocular vision; though degree of slant was judged with fair accuracy. It was possible that this effect was due to some extent to the instructions which suggested that judgments of projected shape should be made. A somewhat different result was obtained by Borresen and Lichte (1962), who used totally irregular and unfamiliar shapes. The observers were required to match, when tilted, what they supposed to be the 'real' shapes of these against shadows of these shapes projected at varying angles on to a screen. Previous to this they were given varying numbers of trials to familiarize them with the appearance of the shapes from different angles. Whereas without this preliminary viewing the Brunswik index of shape constancy was only 0·5, it rose to 0·7 after fifteen familiarity trials.

As with size constancy, shape constancy varies with individual characteristics and with instructions suggesting the adoption of particular 'attitudes' or procedures. As regards the effects of *age*, we noted on p. 19 that infants learnt during the first year of life to identify objects in different spatial orientations, since although the visually perceived shape varied with orientation, it did so in a regular manner which could be related to the constant tactile impressions obtained from it. Bower (1966b) found that infants as young as seven to nine weeks, trained to respond to a rectangular board slanted at 45°, subsequently responded almost as frequently to the board when it was an upright rectangle as when it was in a slanted position; whereas responses were much fewer to an upright trapezium having the same projected shape as the slanted rectangular board. Thus he concluded that they learnt to recognize the 'real' rather than the projected shape. Meneghini and Leibowitz (1967) carried out an experiment in which children aged four and a half to nineteen and a half years were required to match a tilted circle, at distances of three feet and fifteen feet, against one of a series of ellipses. At three feet, the youngest children showed complete constancy, which decreased somewhat with age, adults making a compromise between real and projected shape. However, at fifteen feet matches at all ages corresponded to projected shape, presumably because cues to slant were imperceptible at that distance.

These data conflict with those quoted by Brunswik (1956) which demonstrated a low degree of shape constancy in early childhood, which increased up to the age of about ten years. It seems possible that these differences may be explained in part by the variation between synthetic and analytic procedures. In the experiment of Meneghini and Leibowitz, the well-known shape of the circle was used, and it would seem natural that the younger children should make a 'real' shape judgment of this as long as they could see clearly what it was. The older children may have adopted an analytic procedure, at least in some cases, giving rise to projected shape judgments. The experiments of Vurpillot (1964) throw a clearer light on the age changes. She presented both unfamiliar irregular shapes and a square, inclined at varying angles, to children aged five to twelve years, who were required to match them against a series of corresponding shapes laying flat on the table. She used two sets of instructions. In the first, children were asked to choose the variable which was most like the standard as perceived at that moment; in the second, to choose the variable which would be most like the standard if it were laid flat on the table. These would seem to correspond to 'apparent' and 'objective' instructions. She found that the youngest children were unable to differentiate between these two conditions; whatever the instructions, some chose the objective and some the projected shape, while others oscillated between the two types of judgment. At seven years, there was some differentiation between the two conditions, but they were still confused; there was no realization of the successive modifications of form at different angles of tilt. The older children differentiated more clearly between 'apparent' judgments, which approached nearly the projected shape, varying regularly with the angle of tilt; and the objective judgments, in which shape constancy was considerably greater. These were consistently judged by twelve years, and it was clear that these children, unlike the younger ones, could differentiate between the permanent intrinsic characteristics of the shapes and their momentary appearance in a particular setting. There was no significant difference between familiar and unfamiliar shapes. But these observations demonstrate the characteristics of perception in young children which were noted in Chapter II: lack of accurate differentiation, and of ability to discriminate, between permanent inherent qualities and those imposed by the situation of the moment.

With adult observers, different degrees of shape constancy were shown according as to whether the observer concentrated on the real shape (*synthetic judgment*) or the projected shape, as seen in a photograph (*analytic judgment*). Brunswik (1956) presented data obtained by Klimpfinger which showed that high degrees of constancy, with the modal index of 0·8 to 0·9, were obtained with the former type of judgment; low degrees, with the mode at about 0·2 with the latter. Ardis and Fraser (1957) found a lower degree of constancy in *introverted* than in *extraverted* observers; though it is not clear if this difference was due to a difference in selective attitude. However, such a difference may account for the finding of Leibowitz *et al.* (1959) that constancy decreased with increase of *intelligence*, in adult observers. The instructions were to some extent analytic: to choose an ellipse which looked most like the shape of the tilted disc. Mental defective observers, like the children, were probably unable to discriminate between projective and objective judgments, and gave mainly the latter.

But again it would appear that with shape constancy, as with size constancy, if no *specific instructions* are provided as to the type of judgment to be made, the observer may vary these. Joynson and Newson (1962) presented a triangle of unknown elevation to a hundred naive observers, each of whom made only one judgment; the observations of different groups of observers were made with differing degrees of inclination. Vision was binocular, and there was an unrestricted view of the surroundings. The observers were instructed to choose one of a series of triangles, at right angles to the line of sight, which most 'looked like' the tilted triangle. It was found that 62 per cent of the observers were aware of the possibility of only one type of judgment, the objective.

Among the remainder, there was some realization that another type of judgment was possible, the apparent shape as given by a direct and instantaneous impression. The majority of these observers actually made the objective judgment, though there were some 'apparent' judgments which became more frequent at greater angles of tilt; here presumably it was more difficult to perceive what the real shape was. But no one was aware only of the possibility of 'apparent' judgments. When special instructions were given to make 'apparent' judgments, some observers were able to do this, but not all. As expected, objective judgments produced approximately complete constancy; 'apparent' judgments, a much lower value. However, judgments seldom conformed completely to projected shape.

These results conflict to some extent with those of Landauer (1964), who found that with instructions to judge apparent shape, which did not specifically direct towards either objective or projected shape, observers were able to make quite stable judgments of 'apparent' shape, intermediate in constancy between objective and projected shape judgments. But the more restricted the conditions of viewing, the nearer they approximated to projected shape judgments. They were not, however, an average of objective judgments made by some observers and projective judgments made by others. But it is possible that some training is necessary to make 'apparent' judgments which are independent of objective and projective judgments. Epstein *et al.* (1962) also found that differences in magnitude of shape constancy were produced by objective, phenomenal ('apparent') and analytical (projective) instructions in binocular vision with somewhat restricted surroundings. These differences did not occur in monocular vision, when judgments were uncertain and irregular. The results of Lichte and Borresen (1967) were different. They used the same unfamiliar irregular shapes as in their previous experiment (p. 160), but gave the observers some familiarity with these. They then presented them in binocular vision and relatively unrestricted viewing conditions, with lengthy explanatory instructions requiring objective, 'apparent' or projective judgments from different groups of observers. The apparent shape judgments showed a bimodal distribution of constancy, the peaks of the two modes lying near to the modes for objective and projective judgments respectively. Thus it appeared that, as in the experiments of Joynson and Newson, observers given instructions for apparent judgments made objective judgments in some cases and projective judgments in others.

We noted that although there was a tendency to relate perceived shape to perceived tilt, the relationship between them was not necessarily exact or invariant. But it appears that judgments of shape may be made more readily if the observer is able to perceive the manner in which apparent shape changes regularly in *movement* with change in angle of tilt. Thus Langdon (1953) presented, in restricted conditions of viewing, a series of ellipses and a rotating circular disc. Observers were required to stop the rotation at the point at which the shape of the rotating circle appeared most similar to each of the ellipses in turn. The experiment was repeated with wire outlines of a circle and ellipses. In binocular vision, constancy was high when the ellipses were narrow, corresponding to a view of the circle almost parallel to the line of sight, but it decreased to a low value with almost circular ellipses. Thus apparently constancy was lower with a circle almost at right angles to the line of sight, a result directly contrary to that obtained by Eissler (1933), with stationary objects. It is difficult to account for Langdon's finding. Constancy was considerably lower in monocular vision, though there was a similar relationship to angle of tilt. It was lower still when the observers saw the circle in a succession of stationary positions. In the early part of the experiment, all observers reported that they perceived a rotating circular disc or wire outline; but later they perceived a circle being squeezed in and out. However, this variation in experience did not affect the judgments made.

Now we noted in Chapter VII, Section (2), that the appearance of three-dimensionality could arise as the result of movement, and particularly the continuous rotation in space of a shape which appeared flat when stationary. It may be that in Langdon's experiments shape constancy, which is related to recession in depth, was enhanced by this continuous rotation. Yensen (1957), who used only a brief period of rotation, obtained lower values of shape constancy than did Langdon. However, although in the experiments of the latter judgments of constancy were stable and fairly high, the actual appearance of the rotating circle was labile, and subject to the kind of satiation which occurred in alternating perspective (see p. 90).

If more complex objects are employed, a variety of curious movement phenomena may appear, as was demonstrated by the *Ames oscillating window* (Ames, 1951). This type of window frame, though trapezoidal not rectangular in shape, was rotated about a vertical axis in an otherwise dark room; and sometimes a tube was inserted through the apertures corresponding to the windows. In general, this apparatus was perceived as a rectangular window which oscillated to and fro, reversing its direction of movement, rather than rotating continuously; and as it did so, the tube seemed to bend to and fro. This illusion was attributed by

Ames to the effects of *familiarity* on shape constancy; that is to say, the trapezoidal shape appeared as the familiar rectangular shape of a tilted window frame. The oscillatory movement of a rectangular shape would produce the same series of projected images as would a rotating trapezium. However, Mulholland (1956) found that there was considerable variation in what was perceived. He rotated both trapezoidal and rectangular window frames at varying speeds. At slow speeds, the rectangular frame was seen predominantly as rotating, and the trapezoidal as oscillating; but sometimes the rectangular frame appeared to oscillate also, or to expand and contract in a plane at right angles to the line of sight (like Langdon's rotating circle). At higher speeds, the latter type of movement was more frequent; and sometimes the trapezoid also appeared to rotate or to expand and contract. Thus a variety of configurational associations between apparent movements and shapes seemed to be possible which were unrelated to any special familiarity with particular shapes. It would seem again that the relationship between shape constancy and changing orientation was labile.

Further evidence for the generality of these effects was given in experiments which showed that they might occur with a variety of different shaped objects. Thus Pastore (1952) found that oscillatory movement was perceived with rotating circles, ellipses, diamonds and irregular figures. A rectangle might appear first as rotating and later as oscillating, as in Mulholland's experiments. Day and Power (1963) compared the movements perceived in monocular vision of three rotating trapezoids, one made to look like a window frame, one with vertical bars and one with a plain surface; and of three rectangles with similar markings. Observers were required to signal whenever the direction of rotation reversed. Reversals were more frequent with trapezoids than with rectangles, but were unaffected by the various markings. A rotating ellipse also frequently appeared to reverse. Shapes with irregular edges reversed more readily than did those with straight edges perpendicular to the axis of rotation (Power, 1967). Day and Power (1963, 1965) argued that clearly any experience of perceiving rectangular windows was irrelevant to these movement effects. The shrinkage, first of one vertical edge and then of the other as the shape rotated, was ambiguous with regard to the direction of rotation; that is to say, the changes in shape of the projected shapes related equally to approach or recession, but the difference was more obvious with the rectangles than with the trapezia or irregular figures. Thus movement tended to alternate from one direction to the other, in a manner similar to the alternations of the Necker cube (see p. 91). Epstein *et al.* (1968) showed that both the perception of oscillation and the perceived angle of oscillation depended on the height-width ratio of shapes and the changes in this.

Presumably because these effects are ambiguous, there are considerable *individual differences* in perceiving them. McGhee (1963) found that reversals of the Ames trapezoidal window could be increased in frequency by instructing observers to concentrate and perceive more carefully. This effect was greater for adults than for children. Allport and Pettigrew (1957) showed that urban European and African boys perceived the oscillating effect to a significantly greater extent than did rural African boys, in binocular though not in monocular vision. They argued that the experience of the former of 'carpentered' houses with rectangular doors and windows produced an illusory effect in marginal conditions, that is to say, in binocular vision at short distances where other depth cues were available. But rural African boys, accustomed to living in rounded huts, were less affected. However, in the more restricted conditions of monocular vision and at a greater distance, all observers perceived the illusion. We may perhaps conclude that differences in expectancy may affect this labile relationship between perceived shape and changing orientation, though the nature of the expectancy is ill-defined.

We noted that with the Ames window some conflict might occur between the percept of a rectangular window and the bending this imposed on a tube inserted between the bars. Michotte (1955) noted that such conflicts might occur in a number of experimental demonstrations. He presented a large disc in rotation, on which two interlacing circles were drawn. These then appeared to rotate eccentrically. If they were coloured in different but related colours, two uniformly coloured transparent circles were seen, turning over one another. But if strongly contrasted colours were used, for instance red, yellow or blue, at first unstable displacements and colour changes occurred. But after a time a multicoloured three-dimensional cylinder appeared, which effected some reconciliation of the dissonant phenomena.

An extremely complex set of observations was made by Mefford and his colleagues (summarized in Mefford, 1968a) of the apparent shape, slant and three-dimensionality of objects in rotation. These they demonstrated by rotating asymmetric objects, such as ellipses, in restricted viewing conditions, in a plane at right angles to the line of sight. The observers could see nothing but the ellipse, cut out of cardboard, sometimes in outlined (skeletal) shape and covered with fluorescent paint. At first they perceived a flat rotating ellipse, but this percept was soon replaced by a series of phenomena: (1) a kind of plastic or amoeboid movement with deformation of shape; (2) shapes, sometimes circular, sometimes elliptical, slanted and oscillating as in perspective reversal; (3) a wobbling, rolling or tumbling movement as of a flat plate; (4) a rotating ellipse which appeared like a cigar. Pairs of overlapping skeletal ellipses were then rotated in the same manner, which appeared in the following succession of stages: (1) two rings; (2) a cylinder slanting in depth; (3) a thick (three-dimensional) wobbling or rocking plate. Again there were frequent alternations between these phenomena, with reversals of perspective; and three-dimensionality was apparent, which was not seen in the same way with the single ellipses. The phenomena could be perceived in both monocular and binocular vision, and were unaffected by previous knowledge as to the actual shapes which were being presented. Thus Mefford concluded that a large number of different configurations of shape, slant, depth and movement could be perceived, which alternated and replaced each other, possibly each in turn being satiated and giving place to another. But fluctuation rates were also affected by other factors, brightness, symmetry, speed of movement, etc. (Mefford, 1968b). However, the phenomena were stabilized by anything which increased apparent depth.

(5) Brightness and Colour Constancy

These two phenomena, though at first sight differing considerably from each other, may in fact be considered in conjunction; since it is found that what is often termed 'brightness constancy' is in fact the comparatively constant appearance, during changes in intensity of illumination, of the '*whiteness*' or 'lightness' of a neutral coloured surface (white or grey). 'Whiteness' is a function of the *reflectance* or reflecting power of a surface; the greater the proportion of incident light reflected, the 'whiter' the surface. The phenomenon of whiteness constancy then depends on the ability of the observer to distinguish between this property of the surface, and brightness imparted by the light falling on it. As an illustration, we can usually see that an object casts a dark shadow on an adjacent surface or on the side of it opposite to the direction of the illumination; and we can discriminate between this shadow and a dark patch on the surface with low reflectance.*

In general, it has been found that if the observer is unable to perceive the manner in which illumination falls on a surface, whiteness constancy disappears, and the perceived surface brightness is a compound of the

* Early work on neutral and chromatic colour constancy was discussed by Vernon (1937, 1952), and the former has also been discussed by Forgus (1966).

M

illumination intensity and the reflectance of the surface. This may appear in the case of shadows. Thus Fieandt (1936) projected a shadow on to a disc which was viewed through a circular aperture in a screen in such a manner that the casting of the shadow could not be perceived, and the disc appeared dark grey. But if part of the shadow fell on the screen also, the disc appeared as light grey in shadow.

However, there may be complex relationships between the constancy of the surface viewed and the *reflectances of surrounding objects*, as was indicated in the experiment of Gelb (1929). The principal finding in this experiment was that if a bright spot of light was directed on to a black rotating disc in such a manner that the light fell on and covered the disc only, and not on the dark surroundings, constancy was zero and the disc appeared whiteish-grey. If, however, a piece of white paper was held near the disc so that the light fell on its also, constancy was restored and the disc appeared dark grey or black, but brightly lit. This phenomenon was further explored by Stewart (1959), who presented small white discs of various sizes, one at a time, in front of a large black disc at varying distances from its centre to just outside its margin. The larger the sizes of the small white discs, the greater the darkening of the large disc; but as the small disc was moved away from the centre, the effect decreased.

Newson (1958) carried his investigation further. He presented as his test object a square grey surface illuminated by a beam of light, and suspended by an invisible thread. It then appeared white, but became grey when another '*inducing*' surface was introduced into the field. The closer the two surfaces together, and the higher the reflectance of the inducing surface, the greater the darkening of the test surface. The perceived whiteness of the test surface was largely controlled by that of the inducing surface when they touched each other. But if the inducing surface possessed a higher reflectance than any other surface in the field of view, it then controlled the appearance of the test surface even if it was not in contact with it. Thus it seemed that, in these restricted conditions of viewing, apparent whiteness was largely determined by contrast with adjacent surfaces of higher reflectance.

A somewhat similar conclusion was reached by Wallach (1948, 1963). He found that in reduction conditions (restricted viewing), it was the ratio of brightness between a surface and its surroundings which determined how the former appeared. A disc and a ring round it were separately projected on to an otherwise dark background. When the intensity of the former was greater than that of the latter, it appeared white; when less, it appeared grey, the grey becoming darker until it was completely black as the difference in intensity increased. However, it was also possible to discriminate surface whiteness from brightness or luminance. When the intensity ratio was greater than 4 : 1, the more intensely illuminated surface appeared luminous as well as white. Of two contiguous surfaces, the larger appeared luminous. When a series of alternate light grey and dark grey bars was projected on to a screen, the outer ones tended to appear luminous but the inner did not. Wallach considered that this luminosity appears mainly when surfaces are not in close contact with one another; and it is determined wholly by intensity of illumination. But with surfaces in close contact, only degrees of surface whiteness and greyness are apparent; and these, as was stated, result from the contrast effects between adjacent surfaces.

There is other evidence as to the association between whiteness constancy and the *spatial setting* of the objects viewed. Beck (1965) presented a surface divided vertically into two halves, with different degrees of tilt, in such a manner that one half was partly shaded, the other fully lit. In monocular vision, the surface appeared flat, with the shaded half darker, that is to say with less whiteness. But in binocular vision, when half of the surface was seen to be tilted, there was a tendency to perceive a single continuous surface possessing the same whiteness throughout, but shadowed in one half. Beck concluded that the degree of whiteness constancy was a function of the manner in which *the field was organized*, as determined by cues relating to stimulus pattern, to the apparent spatial position of the surface and to direction of illumination. Thus he had found earlier (1961) that if he varied the appearance of the test surface by using a variety of textures, whiteness was a function of the reflectances of these, and was unaffected by varying the intensity of illumination. He concluded that organization took place in such a manner as to produce the maximum degree of congruence between cues.

In general, the *magnitude* of whiteness constancy is considerably less than that of size and shape constancy, Brunswik (1956) quoted results obtained earlier by himself which gave an index of only about 0·45 Sheehan (1938) found one of 0·6. However, as we have noted, the magnitude varies greatly with the experimental conditions; nevertheless, the index rarely approaches complete constancy. Brunswik also found a slight but not very marked increase between the *ages* of four to ten years. But experiments by Burzlaff (1931) suggested that there was little difference between the whiteness constancy of children and adults.

Forgus (1966) considered that whiteness constancy, depending entirely on the reflectances of objects, was a phenomenon of a more primitive type than were size and shape constancy. It was affected but little by learning during childhood or by different attitudes in the observer set up by instructions. Now it is true that, in restricted vision, the apparent brightness of objects, as determined by the amount of incident light reflected by them and by surrounding objects, may be a simple and primitive phenomenon. But in unrestricted vision the observer is able to discriminate between the whiteness dependent on reflectance from the brightness resulting from illumination intensity, a discrimination which depends on relating the object to certain aspects of the environment. Important here is the perception of the general over-all brightness of the surroundings. The observer must have acquired schemata relating such over-all brightness to the spatial organization, and differentiating from it that part of the surface brightness which is due to its intrinsic whiteness or reflectance. That whiteness constancy is not in general as great as size and shape constancy may be due to the fact that we are not able to remember very accurately absolute degrees of 'whiteness' – or rather, different shades of grey.

We noted that in size constancy, and to some extent in shape constancy, observers were often aware that two types of judgment could be made from their perceptual impressions, objective and projective size and shape judgments. Forgus queried the possibility of making a similar choice between different types of whiteness judgment. Observers were generally aware of only one possible judgment which usually was found to be a compromise between judgment based on reflectance only and judgment based on total brightness. Yet according to Landauer and Rodger (1964) observers could modify their judgments in accordance with *instructions* to judge in relation to reflectance only (objective judgment); in relation to luminance, meaning the total brightness of the object (projective judgment); and by making snap judgments of apparent equality with the matching series (apparent judgment). The mean setting for the third type was mid-way between the first and second. Some observers in this condition made objective judgments, some projective, and some oscillated between the two. But there were also some who made a genuine compromise between objective and projective judgment. It would appear therefore that even if it is harder with whiteness than with size and shape constancy to manipulate judgments in accordance with instructions, yet it can be done. Thus we are not justified in considering whiteness constancy as a phenomenon different in kind from size and shape constancy. It would seem more correct to conclude that the psychological tendency to preserve the constant appearance of objects ('thing constancy') operates in whiteness constancy also, but less effectively because we have a less efficient capacity to remember exact degrees of whiteness.

The same also appears to be true of *chromatic colour constancy*. It is extremely difficult to remember hues exactly, except perhaps those of the primary colours; and there is no doubt that they do change in appearance with the colour of the incident illumination. But this change is less than that of the total illumination reflected to the eye. Surfaces obviously possess intrinsic colours, dependent on their differential reflection of different wave lengths of light; and we possess some capacity to differentiate these from the colour imparted to them and to their surroundings by coloured incident illumination. Thus, as with whiteness constancy, concealing the *surroundings* from view reduces and even destroys colour constancy. However, Wallach and Galloway (1946) considered that chromatic colour constancy was due to contrast, as was whiteness constancy. Coloured light reflected from a differently coloured surface was of a hue intermediate between the two colours; but the contrast between this intermediate hue and the colour of the incident illumination tended to enhance their difference, hence to make the object appear in its intrinsic colour. Wallach and Galloway were able to arrange contrast colours which appeared in every way similar to those of colour constant objects. But again these contrast effects are more likely to appear in restricted vision than in the unrestricted vision of the normal surroundings.

It would also seem that in some circumstances the perceived colour of objects of familiar colour may approximate to the latter, the so-called '*memory colour*'. Some early but rather unsystematic observations of Adams (1923) indicated that the colours of natural objects, such as grass, snow, etc., did achieve considerable constancy in memory, and influence current perception. An experiment by Duncker (1939) showed that when pieces of green paper shaped like a leaf and a donkey respectively were exposed in red light, observers perceived the leaf shape to be greener than the donkey shape. However, Bruner *et al.* (1951) considered that memory colour was a relatively unstable phenomenon, operating only when the stimulus conditions were weak. They presented pieces of orange-coloured paper shaped as red objects, such as a tomato and a lobster claw, and found that they appeared redder than pieces shaped as yellow objects such as a banana and a lemon. But this phenomenon occurred only when the orange colour of the paper was produced by colour contrast; the paper was grey, on a blue-green background. More recent experiments, however, have given different findings. Harper (1953) found that pieces of orange paper shaped like a heart, an apple and a lobster stood out more readily than did meaningless shapes from a background which could be varied from orange to red. Fisher *et al.* (1956) confirmed these results for apple and lobster shapes, but not for the heart shape. But Delk and Fillenbaum (1965) found that orange-red shapes of a heart, an apple and a pair of lips matched a redder background than did shapes of non-red objects.

However, none of these findings except those of Adams and Duncker demonstrate colour constancy effects; and in general they relate to highly artificial conditions. It is unfortunate that Adams' experiments on memory colour of real objects have never been followed up. It seems probable that, from her comments on her findings and also from general experience, judgments of apparent colour in ordinary unrestricted viewing conditions are comparatively unaffected by memory colour; and if they are, only by the easily remembered primary colours. As with whiteness constancy, a more important factor in chromatic colour constancy is the differentiation between *intrinsic surface colour* and the colour imparted to the general surroundings by coloured illumination. According to Katz (1935), we possess schemata relating apparent colour, surface colour and illumination colour, the operation of which enables us to discriminate the effects of surface and illumination colour. They would appear to be of the same type as, though probably more complex than, those associated with whiteness constancy.

IX

The Perception of Movement

(1) Real movement

We have considered a number of phenomena in which the perception of form and of spatial location is modified when objects are set in motion. Indeed, it seems that a series of schemata may have been established relating particular types of form and movement. However, it is important to consider the perception of movement itself, since it seems to constitute a phenomenon *sui generis*; though it may be related to particular objects in movement, and affected by the surroundings, the environmental framework in which it occurs. Also we shall discuss certain characteristic types of movement pattern.

We noted in Chapter II that the investigations of Hubel and Wiesel of the visual mechanisms in some animals demonstrated the special sensitivity of certain cortical cells to movement. It seems probable that human beings also from *infancy* upwards rapidly become aware of any movement in their surroundings, before they identify the object in movement. Also there is an immediate response to movement perception, of turning the head and eyes and directing them towards the moving object, fixating it and viewing it attentively in order to discover what it is and what is its direction of movement. Though perception of form in *peripheral vision* is blurred, any movement is quickly perceived there. However, Cohen (1965) found that peripheral perception of moving objects rapidly habituated; a continuous sequence of dots moving vertically appeared to slow down and stop within fifteen to a hundred seconds. Larger objects continued to appear in movement for a longer period, and horizontal bands, though they slowed down, did not stop altogether. The further out in the periphery the moving objects were presented, the sooner the movement ceased to be perceived. On the other hand, there was no such cessation of movement perception in foveal vision. Cohen hypothesized that in the periphery there was an immediate sensory response such as that discovered by Hubel and Wiesel, which rapidly habituated. But in the fovea there was additionally a clear perception of forms changing position in relation to the spatial framework, which persisted indefinitely. Therefore in normal circumstances the immediate response to movement as such is extended and modified by the perception of particular objects moving in various ways; and it is this latter form of perception which is often affected by relation to the environmental setting, and indeed in some cases to the nature of the objects in movement.

It has been a matter of some debate as to how we distinguish the movement of objects themselves from the *apparent movement imparted to them by the movement of the body in space*. In normal surroundings, objects in movement change position in relation to the spatial framework. But if the framework and the objects within it all change position in a congruent manner, this phenomenon is usually attributed to a movement of the body. It is true that confusion sometimes occurs. Thus if, when one is sitting in a railway train, another train moves along side it, one may believe that one's own train is moving. This is because the actually moving train fills the whole visual field, and therefore appears as a moving framework imparting a sense of movement to the body.

Similar phenomena occur more readily when *normal surroundings are concealed*. Thus in complete darkness a small stationary point of light may appear to move. The *autokinetic movement* would seem to be linked to some form of imbalance of tension in the extra-ocular muscles, there being no steady framework to which the eyes can be anchored. However, its origin is still obscure. Even a rudimentary framework, such as a surrounding luminous semi-circle, suppresses the autokinetic movement.

However, it should be noted that whenever *the eyes move* to and fro, in discontinuous jerky *saccadic* movements, the image of the surrounding framework and the objects within it moves across the retina, yet the surroundings do not appear to move. Nor do they do so if an object moves its position in the field of view, and saccadic movements occur in order to refixate it. Yet if the eyes follow a moving object, in smooth pursuit movements, some movement of the surroundings may be perceived. Gregory (1958) postulated, in accordance with a hypothesis advanced by Von Holst, that with voluntary saccadic movements there is a cancellation of the sensory data relating to movement of the image across the retina through impressions associated with the motor impulses from the cortex to the extra-ocular muscles which produce eye movement. But pursuit movements are involuntary, and therefore this cancellation does not occur. MacKay (1958), however, believed that no such cancellation is necessary, and postulated that the perceptual organization is relatively insensitive to changes in position of retinal images, and remains unaltered as long as all the information from successive samplings of the external environment indicates its stability. In involuntary eye movement, the absence of expected retinal change evokes an impression of environmental movement.

Perception of movement is related to perception of the *surrounding field*. Movement is more readily perceived, and the threshold is lower, when there is a clearly visible frame of reference. Thus Brown and Conklin (1954) found that the least perceptible movement of a spot of light in a dark room was at a speed of nine minutes of angle per second. But they quoted a rate of one to two minutes of angle per second obtained by Aubert for a black line exposed in daylight on a rotating drum. Brown (1931b) found that with black squares on a moving white belt, perception of movement rather than of mere displacement of position (as with the hands of a clock) occurred at a rate of two to three minutes of angle per second. There was also an upper limit to the rate at which movement could be perceived; at twelve to thirty-two minutes per second, the squares fused to form a greyish streak. But the threshold was decreased by inhomogeneity of the surrounding field; that is to say, it was easier to perceive movement across an inhomogeneous than a homogeneous field.

But also the *apparent speed* of objects is affected by the nature of the surrounding field. Brown (1931a) required observers, in a dark room, to adjust the velocity of a moving band of white paper with black squares on it to that of a similar band with squares which could be varied in size and shape, and the surrounding field manipulated also. He found that apparent velocity was greater in an inhomogeneous than in a homogeneous field. If the dimensions of the squares and of the field were all increased, the actual velocity of the moving objects had to be increased by a like amount for apparent velocity to remain constant. Thus if the dimensions of the squares and field were doubled, velocity appeared the same when it was almost doubled. With unrestricted view of the surroundings the effect was somewhat less, though still considerable. However, when Cohen (1964) repeated these experiments, using a single square, he found that the velocity ratio was only 1:1·25, instead of 1:2. Moreover, most of the effect was produced by varying the length of the field in the direction of movement, and comparatively little by varying the height from top to bottom. Brown had hypothesized that these effects were due to variation in the apparent time taken by the object to move across the field; but it would seem more probable, from Cohen's findings, that the length of the path of movement was the effective factor. This seems to be supported by the finding that apparent velocity remains approximately constant at different distances from the eye, because there is apparent constancy of the length of the path of movement. However, constancy of velocity was less than constancy of size (Brown, 1931a).

But apparent velocity is also affected by the *form of the moving objects*. Brown (1931a) found that larger objects appeared to move more slowly than smaller ones, and that rectangles moving parallel to their longer sides appeared to move more quickly than did rectangles moving at right angles to their longer sides. Similar effects may be produced by variation in *direction of movement*. Gemelli (1958) found that black discs appeared to move more rapidly from left to right than from right to left; and when moving vertically downwards than vertically upwards, horizontally or obliquely. These effects he attributed to habit and to past experience. Eye movement habits in reading make left to right movement easier than right to left. Falling objects are perceived more frequently than are rising ones.

So also numerous experimenters have found that perceived rate of movement may vary with the *nature of the object* in movement. Comalli (1960) showed that moving pictures of running children and running horses appeared to move more quickly than did pictures of motionless children and horses. He reported Werner and Wapner as finding these differences to be greater with children of six to seven years than with adults.

Indeed, it has been shown by Piaget (1946) that *children* below the age of six to seven years were unable to make any accurate comparisons between the velocity of movement of different objects other than in the very simple case in which two objects began to move side by side and one passed the other. That is to say, they could make only a simple direct perceptual comparison, and not one which involved reasoning about the conditions in which movement was taking place. They could not take into account the relative positions of the starting and finishing points of the movements, nor that one object travelled by a longer path than did the other. Neither could they understand the relative movement of a moving object on a moving background, but took into account the movement of the object alone. The over-estimation of speed of a downward moving object by comparison with that of an object moving upwards was exaggerated.

The normal response to continuous movement is *involuntary pursuit movement of the eyes*. Thus when an object began to move, the eyes started to pursue it after about 100 msec., soon caught it up and followed the movement smoothly and regularly with a fair degree of accuracy provided that the velocity was less than about 30° per second (Miller, 1959). With higher speeds, the eyes could not maintain accurate fixation on the object, and fell behind, making jerky saccadic movements to catch it up. Johansson (1968) found that pursuit could follow not only a clearly defined object but also streaks of slightly brighter and dimmer light shading into each other with no sharp edges between them. These moved at a speed of 0·75 cm. per second. Some observers could follow these when the total path of movement subtended only seven minutes of angle. Others, however, were unable to do so; and pursuit movements were sometimes replaced by saccadic movements. Johansson argued that there was a summation of signals from the succession of receptors excited along the path of the movement. It would seem that these signals may be employed also as a basis for the estimation of velocity, which has generally been found to appear less when the eyes followed a moving object than when they fixated a stationary point (Cohen, 1964).

(2) Apparent Movement

It had for long been known that stationary forms exposed successively in a series of adjacent spatial positions gave rise to the impression that these forms were moving – as in the apparent movement of the cinema film. But Wertheimer (1912) demonstrated that if two very simple stimuli, such as dots or lines, were exposed in different positions, one after the other at a short interval of time, observers frequently perceived a single dot or line moving from the position exposed first to the position exposed second. This observation, and the many similar observations that succeeded it, were crucially important to the Gestalt theory, in that they demonstrated the apparence of a movement phenomenon *sui generis*, termed by Wertheimer the *phi phenomenon*, when no objective movement was taking place. Furthermore, Wertheimer and Korte (1915) went on to show that the perception of apparent movement was in every way similar to the perception of real movement; and that it was deter- mined by specific conditions of intensity of stimulation and distance and time interval between stimuli, but was independent of subjective factors such as the attitude and previous knowledge of the observer.

A very large number of experiments was subsequently carried out to test the accuracy of these statements, and many of these were discussed by Vernon (1937, 1952). It was found that apparent movement, though often extremely compelling, was not subject to the rigidly limited physical conditions defined by Korte's laws, but could occur with a wide variety of shapes, distances apart and time relations. Moreover, there were considerable individual differences in the onset and disappearance of apparent movement as the time interval varied; and also differences in the appearance of the more complex movement phenomena.

The simple phi phenomenon, however, seems to be an immediate primary percept, similar to that of real movement. Thus Tauber and Koffler (1966) found that the majority of a group of newborn *infants* followed with their eyes the apparent movement resulting from the stroboscopic illumination of a stationary pattern of black lines (the stroboscope produces a rapid alternation between bright light and darkness). Meili and Tobler (1931) showed that continuous alternation of exposure of two bright lines produced the perception of apparent movement on the whole more readily in *children* than in adults. But some children tended to see two stationary stimuli succeeding each other, while others perceived sometimes movement and sometimes succession. Gantenbein (1952), however, found that the younger the child, down to the age of five years, the more easily he saw apparent movement rather than succession with short time intervals; and with longer time intervals, simultaneity rather than apparent movement. Brenner (1957) showed that there was a gradual decrease, with increase in age from three to fourteen years, of the time interval between stimuli for which apparent movement was perceived. She considered that the younger children were less able to discriminate the phenomenon accurately. Or it may be that adults are more apt than are children to reason about the phenomenon and its basis. According to Hamilton (1960), failure to perceive apparent movement is related to 'intolerance of perceptual ambiguity', an aspect of perception we shall consider in Chapter XII. This failure is more frequent in neurotic than in normal observers, and in older observers, aged about forty years, than in younger ones, aged about thirty years.

One of the experiments frequently cited to demonstrate the *similarity between real and apparent movement*, and the conditions in which they occur, was performed by Brown and Voth (1937). They exposed in succession four lights in the positions of the corners of a diamond. The times of exposure were equal to the times between successive exposures; and when these were of the order of 150 msec., apparent movement of a single light was observed. Moreover, its path of movement was circular, the circumference of the circle lying within the outline of the diamond, as if it had been contracted centripetally by the rapid circular movement. A light really moving along a circular path at 450° per second appeared to follow an identical contracted circular path. But Sylvester (1960) repeated the experiment, using a larger number of observers, with time intervals of 50 to 300 msec. At the longer intervals, circular movement was occasionally reported, though it was seldom at all clear; and the circular path never lay within the positions of the lights. Sometimes also a single light was perceived to move round the four sides of the diamond but more commonly to and fro movements appeared along the sides of the diamond, or along the diagonals between its opposite points. Sylvester pointed out that his findings contraverted not only those of Brown and Voth but also Korte's law stating that for any particular time interval between stimuli apparent movement would occur at only one single distance. For, in Sylvester's experiment, movement could be perceived equally clearly between lights succeeding one another immediately and lights the exposure of which was separated by a considerable time interval. Thus if lights A, B, C and D were exposed in succession, movement between A and D was as clearly perceived as movement between A and B. Indeed, some observers reported that the former looked like a ball bouncing up and down. In fact, therefore, it would seem that conditions for the perception of apparent movement can vary more widely than the conditions for the perception of real movement.

Wertheimer postulated that apparent movement was similar to real movement in that it involved the stimulation of adjacent points in the occipital lobe of the same hemisphere, at specific intervals of time. However, experiments by Shipley *et al.* (1945) and Gengerelli (1948) demonstrated that apparent movement could be perceived when the two stimuli excited different eyes, or the opposite cerebral hemispheres, although the phenomenon was less readily apparent than when a single hemisphere was excited by both stimuli. More recently, Rock and Ebenholtz (1962) demonstrated, in a complicated experiment, that apparent movement was perceived when stimuli at two points located at different positions in external space were presented successively, even if they stimulated the same retinal location. On the other hand, if separate retinal points were excited successively by stimuli situated at the same point in space, no apparent movement was perceived. Thus the cortical basis of the phenomenon is clearly not simple and direct. It must be supposed that complex processes are involved at the higher cortical levels.

Another obvious difference between real and apparent movement would seem to be that in the latter there is presumably no stimulation of the points on the retina between those excited by the two stationary stimuli. This was demonstrated directly by Humphrey and Springbett (1946), who found that if bright stimuli were used in a dark room, an after image could be obtained in which only these were perceived, but no after image of moving stimulation across the intervening space.

Again, Kolers (1963) showed that the threshold for perception of a stationary luminous line was higher if it was exposed in the path of a moving luminous line. But no such effect occurred when the stationary line was presented in the path of an apparent movement; indeed, the path was seen to curve in depth round the stationary stimulus.

Nevertheless, Bender and Teuber (1946) showed that *injuries to the occipital lobe of the cortex* produced impairment in perception of both real and apparent movement. For perception of real movement in the injured area, a longer distance or a greater speed was required than normally; otherwise a succession of stationary stimuli might be perceived. Succession was also more likely to be perceived instead of apparent movement, unless the rate of alternation of the stimuli was increased. Similar effects were noted by Werner and Thuma (1942) in children who suffered from brain injury. However, Teuber (1960) argued that these phenomena parallel the impairment of pattern perception which results from occipital injuries, and are not caused by interference with the simple responses to movement such as occur in the mechanisms described by Hubel and Wiesel.

More complex and elaborate apparent movement patterns occur when *complex forms* are employed rather than simple lines or dots. Orlansky (1940) showed that apparent movement could be perceived when two stimuli of different shapes were presented in succession, but it became less readily apparent as the difference of shape increased. Squires (1959) found that movement could be perceived between stimuli of unlike shape if there was the possibility of a topological transformation of form; for instance, with a diamond which could be stretched out, as if on a rubber sheet, to form a circle. But when such a transformation was impossible, as with a diamond and a cross, complete apparent movement was not perceived, but an incomplete movement disappearing in the middle of its path.

The readiness with which apparent movement is perceived can also be manipulated by presenting stimuli with different types of *representational meaning*. Thus Jones and Bruner (1954) showed two series each of three pictures, the first of which depicted a car in three successive positions crossing a bridge; while the second showed an elliptical shape in similar positions relative to the arc of a circle. Repeated presentations were given, and at intervals the middle phase of the sequence was omitted. With the meaningful sequence, fewer changes in the character of the perceived movement were reported when the middle phase was omitted than with the meaningless shapes. Meaningful content also affected the perceived path of ambiguous movements. Thus a picture was first presented of two men throwing baseballs towards each other. In a second picture, the baseballs were touching each other between the two men; and in a third, they were situated above the men. When these were presented in quick succession, the majority of observers perceived each ball as crossing over from one man to the other, rather than colliding in the middle and bouncing back. But with similar pictures of men playing billiards, collision and rebound were reported more frequently than was crossing over. Again, Toch and Ittelson (1956) presented vertical series of three pictures of bombs and three of aeroplanes flying vertically upwards. If the middle one was shown first, and after an interval of time the other two, the bomb appeared to move downwards and the aeroplane upwards. However, Brenner (1956) found that although meaningfulness, for instance in representations of a moving clock pendulum, facilitated the rather uncertain appearance of movement given in a single presentation, it had no effect on the much more striking movement phenomenon obtained by continuous alternation of the stimuli. The former seemed to be an inference; the latter, an immediate primary percept.

Thus it would seem that the phenomenon of apparent movement may be readily perceived in a variety of conditions whenever a stimulus in one position is rapidly succeeded by a similar stimulus in another position, their common identity being schematized to produce the impression of a single stimulus in movement. This occurs most strongly with repeated alternation of the stimuli, and the phenomenon is unlearnt. But more complex instances of the phenomenon depend on the expectations of the observer, acquired from previous experience, and are affected also by his inferences as to the nature and relationships of the stimuli presented to him.

Meaningful factors also operate in another form of apparent movement, '*induced movement*'. Now Duncker (1929) found that if two moving luminous shapes were presented in an otherwise dark room, the perceived relative movement was attributed solely to one of them, the 'figure', while the other, the framework or 'ground', appeared to remain stationary. If a stationary point of light was enclosed by a moving rectangle, the point appeared to move and the rectangle to remain stationary. Jensen (1960) presented a stationary luminous silhouette of an aircraft, and to one side of it a luminous bar, moving either to left or to right, in an otherwise dark room. Induced movement was imparted to the aircraft, but this occurred more readily if it appeared to move in a forward direction than in a backward direction. Again, the stationary silhouette of a ship was shown, and beneath it a silhouette of waves which were moved either to left or to right. Induced movement of the ship in a forward direction was more easily perceived than induced movement in a backward direction.

(3) After Effects of Perceived Movement

Another instance of the perception of induced movement in objects which are actually stationary results from the after effect of perceiving really moving objects. In the '*waterfall*' effect, an observer after fixating for a period of time a continuous movement such as that of a stream or waterfall, and then turning to fixate the stationary ground, perceives the latter to move in the opposite direction. In the *spiral after effect*, a disc with a spiral is rotated in front of the observer. During rotation, the spiral appears to expand; when it is stopped, it seems to contract. A very simple example of this phenomenon is obtained from the rotation of a disc with a single radial line on it. Half-a-second's rotation produced subsequently an apparent backward movement of the line (Johansson, 1954).

Unlike the phi phenomenon, this effect is not immediately apparent in *children*. Harding *et al.* (1957) found that children below four and a half years of age did not report it, whereas all those of six and a half years and over did so. However, it is possible that the younger children did not fixate the moving spiral steadily enough. There has been considerable discussion as to whether the phenomenon is due to *retinal satiation and adaptation*, or whether cortical processes are involved. Freud (1964) found that if the movement was projected on to one half of one retina, the after effect occurred in the corresponding half of the other retina, but not on the other half of either retina, suggesting that cortical interaction was involved. However, the after effect lasted rather longer in the half-retina directly stimulated, indicating that there was a retinal contribution also. Anstis and Gregory (1965) claimed to have proved that the effect was entirely retinal. With a field of horizontally moving stripes, exposed for forty-five seconds, observers either followed the movement with their eyes, or fixated a stationary point in the field. In the first case they perceived the original movement but no after effect; in the second, they did see the after effect. If the lines were stationary but the fixation point moved smoothly across them, the after effect was perceived. It appeared then that the after effect was a reaction to the movement of the image across the retina, rather than resulting from real spatial movement. Thus it seemed directly opposite in nature to the phi phenomenon as investigated by Rock and Ebenholtz (see p. 179).

However, it is possible that the rotating spiral involves some degree of pattern perception, in addition to the simple passage of an image of stripes across the retina. Thus cortical processes may be functioning. This would also appear to be the case if more complex stimuli are used. Thus Dixon and Meisels (1966) presented two rotating discs, one with a regular black and white checker board pattern on it, and the other with randomly distributed black and white squares. The after effect produced by the latter persisted for longer than did the after effect of the former, and indeed was, they considered, more striking than any other type of visual after effect. Its velocity appeared to be greater than that of the actually moving pattern. Thus they concluded that its lack of redundancy and high rate of presentation of information necessitated complex recoding at the cortical level, resembling that which occurs with novel and unpredictable events. This maximised the after effect.

(4) The Perception of Causality

There have been numerous studies of a wide variety of movement patterns which have suggested that particular patterns of movement are perceived to result from particular types of event in the external field. Of these the best known is the phenomenon of *mechanical causality*, investigated extensively by Michotte and his colleagues. Michotte (1946, 1963) demonstrated that observers perceived that if an object in movement impinged on another object, it might cause it to move in turn even when no impact of solid objects was involved. Thus, he exposed a

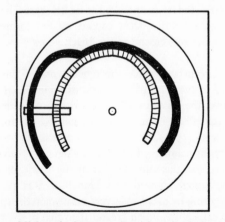

FIG. 35 Michotte's demonstration of mechanical causality
(*After* Michotte (1946) p. 28)

N

rotating disc with coloured tracks on it (see Fig. 35), and squares cut off from these appeared through a slot in a screen. The observer then perceived a black square moving horizontally along the slot until it came in contact with a motionless red square. At impact, the red square began to move. In one case, the black square remained motionless, and in the other it continued to move behind the red square. In the first case, the black square seemed to 'propel' or 'launch' the movement of the red square (*'l'effect lancement'*). In the second case, the black square appeared to 'entrain' or carry the red square along with it (*'l'effet entraînement'*). In these demonstrations there was a spontaneous appearance of causality independent of the nature of the stimuli, provided that they could be clearly differentiated from each other. (In other demonstrations, Michotte employed the projection of moving stimuli which could be varied in shape; the effects were the same.)

In an extensive series of experiments, Michotte showed that the occurrence of these phenomena depended upon certain *objective relationships* between the speed of movement of the stimuli, the time interval between the impact of the black square on the red and the moment at which the latter began to move, the directions of movement and the distance moved by the squares. The impression of causality broke down if the red square moved too far – outside the *'radius of action'* of the black square – or if its direction of movement was greatly different. These conditions therefore appeared to resemble those in which the movement of a real object would cause another to move on impact. In particular, it seemed that causality was perceived only when the speed of movement of the red square did not greatly exceed that of the black squares; for if it did, the latter appeared to be 'triggered' or 'touched off' (*'l'effet déclenchement'*) rather than caused by the former, and some cause other than the movement of the black square was necessary to account for it.

Now it might seem that since the movements of the two squares resembled those of two real objects, one of which hit the other and caused it to move, the causality effect was the result of long *experience* in perceiving such effects occurring in the natural environment. However, Michotte *et al.* (1957) subsequently demonstrated that entraining was perceived by the majority of observers when the speed of movement of the red square was the same as that of the black, or even slightly greater. Crabbé (1967) showed that launching was perceived more readily than triggering by naive observers even when the speed of movement of the red square was much greater than that of the black. Clearly such effects would never occur in the impact of real objects. Crabbé indeed found that entraining and launching constituted simple spontaneous impressions, readily visible by untrained observers; whereas triggering was seen only by observers who had considerable experience with the Michotte demonstrations. Thus it seemed to depend on a more careful analysis of the stimulus situation.

A variety of other movement patterns was demonstrated by Michotte (1946) using stimuli of this type. Thus '*transportation*' was demonstrated by projecting on a screen the movements of two rectangular patches, the longer immediately below the shorter. The shorter then appeared to be transported by the longer, but its movement did not seem to belong to it, as in entraining, but to the longer transporting object. Again, in the launching demonstration, if the speeds of movement of the two squares were high, the black square might appear to *tunnel under* the red square and to pass along the slit in a continuous movement, changing colour as it did so. The phenomenon was similar to the 'tunnel effect' which appeared when a single moving object reached a stationary one, disappeared and then reappeared on the further side. A similar tunnelling or screening effect occurred if a rectangle moved towards a vertical edge and shortened in length when it touched this until it disappeared (Sampaio, 1962).

Kanizsa and Metelli (1961) carried out a variety of experiments similar to those of Michotte, from the results of which they concluded that the physical conditions postulated by Michotte were not essential for the perception of causality. The one indispensable condition, they considered, was that the first stimulus must be in movement before it impinged on the second. However, their observers seem to have been well practised in the perception of the causal phenomena, which may have enabled them to perceive causality more readily than would someone unaccustomed to this type of demonstration. This fact may also have been instrumental in producing another type of causal effect, that of *attraction at a distance* without physical contact between the two stimuli. In one experiment they presented a large circle and a small square moving in the general direction of the circle, though not directly towards it. However, when the square was close to the circle, it sharply altered its direction and proceeded directly towards it. The impression was that the square was attracted by the circle. Michotte (1963) was somewhat sceptical of this finding.

In view of these and other results which appeared to contravert those of Michotte, there has been considerable discussion as to whether, as Michotte supposed, causality is a universally experienced phenomenon which we have an innate disposition to perceive as we perceive movement. It seems an unlikely supposition, firstly because there would not appear to exist any physiological mechanism on which perception of causality could be based; and secondly, as Piaget showed (1955), perception of causality appears to develop gradually during the first and second years of life. Thus in infants the intention to make movements of the body was succeeded by the intention to make inanimate objects move, but with little understanding at first how this was done. Still later to appear was the understanding of how one object caused another to move. Experiments by Piaget and Lambercier (1958) showed that even in older children causality might be less readily perceived than by adults, in some circumstances. Thus whereas Yela (1952) found that adults frequently perceived launching even when the two stimuli did not come completely into contact with each other, children of six to eight years saw this phenomenon less easily. Piaget (1961) attributed this difficulty to the fact, which he himself had demonstrated (1955), that children learnt only gradually that in normal circumstances one moving object must come into contact with the other before it causes it to move. The effect of this knowledge might inhibit the perception of causality at a distance.

Gruber *et al.* (1957) and Powesland (1959) showed that the opposite effect, facilitation of the perception of causality, might be produced by *experience*. Here the stimuli were more realistic in nature. A horizontal bar appeared to rest on the tops of two vertical posts, one of which could be made to move away. The bar, which was actually suspended magnetically, could be dropped at any interval of time after the post was moved. Although this arrangement had been demonstrated to the observers, they received a strong impression that the bar was caused to drop by the removal of support when the post was moved, even when there was a delay between the movement of the post and of the bar. This delay could be lengthened, and a causal relationship still perceived, by presenting a series of these demonstrations with long delays. Such practice effects were found by Houssiadas (1964) only with relatively intelligent observers. Without any preliminary preparation, mental defectives perceived entrainment as readily as did university students. But if a demonstration was first given in which no causal effect could be perceived – the two stimuli simply moved side by side across the screen – the students subsequently perceived causality much less frequently in the original presentation, but the mental defectives were unaffected by this.

Olum (1956) found that in circumstances in which adults perceived launching, children of seven years often reported other phenomena; in particular, that one stimulus passed over the other and went ahead of it, changing colour as it did so. This was never reported by adults in this setting. Another phenomenon perceived by the children resembled the apparent movement phenomenon; the real movement of the black square towards the red was accompanied by apparent movement of the red towards the black. Gemelli and Cappellini (1958) also found considerable differences between adults in reports of launching. Some observers, with synthetic tendencies, perceived this effect readily, whereas others, with analytic tendencies, described the demonstration objectively in terms of its physical characteristics.

It could of course be argued that there is an innate tendency to perceive causality which does not come into operation in early infancy, but appears when the young child has had the opportunity to observe the circumstances in which objects can be caused to move, both by himself and by the movement of other objects. In this respect, the phenomenon would resemble the perception of form and distance. Whether or not there is some innate tendency, it is clear that the impression of causality becomes spontaneous and even compulsive by adult life, though seemingly it can be overcome by deliberate analytical observation. Clearly also the exact circumstances in which the various causal phenomena appear, and especially the more complex conditions, are considerably affected by experience and training.

X

The Perception of Persons

(1) Introduction

There is one perceptual schema, or more probably a set of related schemata, which differs very considerably from those which we have already discussed, related to form, inanimate objects, verbal material, space and movement: the schemata which are associated with the perception of people, their emotions and their actions. It seems clear that from their earliest years children perceive other people, their faces and their behaviour, in a manner peculiar to this category of percepts, and that special schemata are evolved within which these percepts are integrated. The main peculiarity of these is that observers are usually aware only to a minor extent of the details of physical characteristics presented by the appearance and behaviour of other people, and are concerned mainly with their intentions, their emotions and their personality characteristics. Such inferences appear so early in life that certain psychologists, such as Werner (1948), suppose that there is an innate tendency for what has been called '*physiognomic*' perception; that is to say, to perceive the dynamic properties of objects, as well as of people, as characterized by a special type of causality, such as that which is involved in human motivation. Indeed, we may note that children tend to classify all moving objects as living, and as having intentions to perform specific actions. Heider (1958b) also pointed out that the stimulus patterns involved in the perception of persons were more complex and extensive than those on which perception of objects was based; the former gave rise to actions embedded in a whole sequence of events (though of course this may occur with inanimate objects also). From early infancy, previous knowledge and expectations as to the actions and motives of people are obviously highly significant to us. Other psychologists consider that children from their earliest years learn to make inferences from their perceptions of physical properties as to the significant characteristics of people and of their behaviour, and perhaps to a lesser extent of all living organisms. But attribution of physiognomic qualities to inanimate objects declines as age increases.

(2) The Development in Children of Perception of Persons

In Chapter II we considered the manner in which in the early months of life infants looked longer at faces, and even pictures of faces, than at other forms and patterns; and that they were able to discriminate pictures of normal faces from those with the features 'scrambled'. Moreover, at about three months faces, more than any other object, gave rise to the response of smiling. Towards the end of the first year, the infant developed the capacity to discriminate between *familiar* and *unfamiliar faces*. These observations do indeed indicate that infants either possess an innate capacity to schematize perceptions of faces into a single general category which is soon differentiated according to familiarity; and also, as we shall consider in the next section, according to emotional expression. Or else they acquire this capacity at an early age. Three-year-old children were able to identify 70 per cent of the photographs of their class-mates, and six-year-olds, 90 per cent (Brooks and Goldstein, 1963). But few were able to identify these photographs in the inverted position until ten years and over. Half of a group of children of four and a half years could identify photographs of their class-mates when only halves of the photographs were presented; but all the children of ten and a half years could do so (Goldstein and MacKenberg, 1966). Faces were always easier to identify from the upper parts of the face than from the lower. This appears to reinforce conclusions based on other observations that infants and children look predominantly at the eyes and upper parts of the faces of people.

(3) The Perception of Emotional Expressions

Now it must be noted that in the perception of persons, some differentiation is commonly made between perception of facial expressions related to relatively temporary emotions; and perception of more enduring characteristics on which is based both the identification of familiar people and also impressions as to personality characteristics. Of course we may fail to make this differentiation accurately; there is a tendency to suppose that an angry face belongs to a naturally irritable and aggressive person, and a smiling face to a happy and cheerful person. However, it is true also that emotions which are frequently felt and expressed may give rise to permanent facial characteristics such as wrinkles in the brow or round the eyes. We shall consider these characteristics in the next section.

There has been considerable controversy as to the accuracy with which people's *emotions* can be judged from their *facial expressions* as shown in *photographs*. Woodworth (1938) assessed a number of early experiments in which were employed photographs in the main of actors who posed to express a variety of emotions. On the whole, identification of these was variable and frequently incorrect. Nevertheless, Woodworth deduced from data obtained by Feleky (1924) that emotional expressions could in fact be classified into the following six groups, which are usually differentiated from each other, though expressions within the groups might be confused: (1) love, happiness, mirth; (2) surprise; (3) fear, suffering; (4) anger, determination; (5) disgust; (6) contempt. Later, Schlosberg (1941), using photographs of more natural poses, obtained results which suggested that these groups could be classified along two major dimensions: pleasant – unpleasant, and attention (as in fear and surprise) – rejection (as in contempt and disgust). But although this classification may be interesting from a theoretical point of view, it would not appear at first sight to be particularly apposite to actual perception of emotional states. However, it does suggest that emotional expressions are easier to differentiate if they correspond to the extremes of pleasant – unpleasant, or attention – rejection.

It has been claimed that *infants* are able to perceive and respond to the emotions of adults at an early age. Thus Bühler and Hetzer (1928) found that 90 per cent of a group of five-month infants responded to an angry face. However, it is doubtful if infants normally respond to the face alone; nor if they really understand the nature of the emotion. Recognition of emotional expression in pictures of faces is naturally more difficult. However, Gates (1923) found that some expressions, laughter for instance, were identified in photographs prepared by Ruckmick (1921) as early as three years. Thereafter recognition improved steadily. The order of appearance of identification was: pain, anger, fear and horror, surprise, contempt.

Honkavaara (1961) discussed at length earlier experiments on the perception of emotional expression, and concluded that it did not develop as early in life as had previously been supposed. She postulated that development occurred in four successive stages: (1) the dynamic-affective, in which perception is related closely to personal desires and feelings; (2) the matter-of-fact and objective; (3) the physiognomic, in which the emotional expressions of others are perceived independently of personal feelings and desires; (4) the intuitive, the making of inferences about objects and people. Honkavaara presented pictures, cut out of periodicals, of people whose faces showed marked emotional expression, to children aged five years and upwards to adults. When asked what the pictures showed, the youngest children gave matter-of-fact answers, such as 'man'. Physiognomic perceptions began to appear at about seven to eight years, and by fifteen years they were more frequent than others, though there was considerable variation in the emotions attributed to the faces shown. When presented with another set of pictures of people and asked to say if they were 'happy' or 'sad', 'friendly' or 'hostile', the youngest children gave few correct answers; but these increased rapidly with increasing age. There was a tendency, also found in uneducated adults, to be confused by other features of the pictures; thus a frowning girl wearing a red dress was sometimes said to be 'happy'. This would seem to be an example of physiognomic perception in the sense used by Werner (1948): the appearance of emotional characteristics in inanimate objects. Honkavaara obtained other examples of such physiognomic perception, for instance in the attribution of emotional moods to landscape pictures.

But it should not be concluded that because difficulty is experienced in perceiving and understanding emotional expressions presented in pictures and photographs, there is equal difficulty in perceiving them in every-day life experience with real people. In such circumstances, facial expression is dynamic and constantly changing, and is accompanied by actions, expressive gestures and changes in the intonation of the voice. Thus it is comprehensible that even infants may understand the emotions of others, especially the simpler and more forceful emotions of fear and anger. This would of course depend on the existence of a consistent relationship between felt emotion and its outward expression. That at least with some emotions there is an innate relationship of this kind is indicated by observations on blind children, which show that they express the simpler emotions in much the same manner as do sighted children, though perhaps rather less clearly (Thompson, 1941).

But it is also probable that in different societies children learn from others as they grow up to express their emotions, and to control this expression, in somewhat different ways. However, a recent investigation by Ekman et al. (1969) indicated that recognition of emotional expression was more universal than was previously supposed. Natives of the U.S.A., Brazil, Japan, New Guinea and Borneo, shown photographs of white men expressing the emotions distinguished by Woodworth (see p. 190), agreed widely as to the nature of these. Happiness, anger and fear were well recognized by all people, and the majority were able to recognize the other emotions, though there was more agreement among the literate than the non-literate observers. Among the latter confusion occurred in some cases; thus a considerable number of the New Guinea observers mistook sadness for anger. When these people were re-tested with photographs of New Guineans, similar results were obtained.

(4) Perceived Characteristics of Faces and Bodies

These observations suggest that the perceptual data on which are based our assessments of the emotions of others are exceedingly complex, and that it is difficult if not impossible to isolate any *particular characteristics of the facial features*, or any combination of these, which can consistently be associated with particular emotional expressions. Undoubtedly there are certain features the significance of which is readily recognized: the upturned mouth of mirth and pleasure, the down-turned mouth and frowning forehead of displeasure. Thus it is not surprising that these two general classes of emotion are readily distinguished. But numerous attempts have been made to discover which features, and what modifications of these, are most significant. Thus Boring and Titchener (1923) prepared sets of interchangeable features which could be inserted in a profile shape. Observers were able to recognize particular combinations of brows, eyes, noses and mouths as corresponding to recognizable emotional expressions. However, later experimenters found that observers differed considerably as to the emotions they assigned to particular combinations.

Other experimenters were more concerned to discover the appearances and modifications of features which were associated with particular *personality characteristics*. Thus Brunswik and Reiter (1938) used a schematized drawing of a face with features which could be modified independently to produce expressions thought to be related to personality characteristics (see Fig. 36). The width of the face, the height of the forehead, the width and distance apart of the eyes, the length of the nose and the position of the mouth could be independently varied; and 'representative sampling' combining all these various dimensions produced in all 189 different faces. These were then ranked by observers for the degree which they exhibited of age, intelligence and various moods and personality qualities such as gaiety of mood, likeability, good or bad character, energy, etc. A variety of associations resulted, with considerable consistency between different observers, but with some features being more indicative than others, Thus: high chin and broad face appeared as gay and young; low chin and narrow face as sad, old or bad; long nose as unfavourable throughout; low forehead as low in intelligence. Samuels (1939) selected the faces associated with the extreme values of favourableness and unfavourableness of the characteristics listed above, and presented them to a much larger group of observers (247 students). The agreement between observers as to the applicability of these characteristics was very high. Kremenak (1950) studied the effects of varying the width of the eyes and the position and shape of the eyebrows, and found that the latter characteristic had a considerable effect on the assessment of personality qualities. Thus a face with eyebrows close to the eyes and slanting upwards to the sides

FIG. 36 Schematized face
(*After* Brunswik (1956) p. 101)

of the face was most often judged as bad and introverted; a face with arched eyebrows and a wide distance between them and the eyes was seen as unintelligent and extraverted. Winkler (1951) studied the effects of varying the shape, height and inclination of the mouth. The shape of the mouth was found to be important. Thus a wide mouth slit with downward sloping corners was perceived as malicious; a narrow mouth slit as introverted. However, as Brunswik pointed out, we probably do not as a rule make judgments of this kind from variations in the appearance of single facial features, but from the almost infinitely variable configurations in which they are all combined and integrated. But Goodnow (1954) found that there was a tendency to select certain characteristics, such as height of brow, as being more indicative of personality qualities than was justified by their actual importance; whereas others, such as length of nose, were correspondingly underrated in importance.

In other experiments cited by Brunswik (1956), facial characteristics appeared to be more influential in judgment of personality qualities than did bodily characteristics such as height and breadth. Nevertheless, it seems possible to infer personality qualities from *bodily poses*. Thus

Sarbin and Hardyck (1955) presented forty-four 'stick' figures, such as those shown in Fig. 37, together with a list of adjectives relating to personality qualities which were to be matched to the figures. They found a high degree of agreement between different observers; though those of poorer social adjustment showed less agreement. However, when the observer is given a list of personality qualities, this may affect their attribution to figures through suggestion. Wallach and Kogan (1965) showed some of these stick figures to children aged ten to eleven years, asking them to give free descriptions of the figures. It was then

a b c d

FIG. 37 Stick figures
(*After* Wallach and Kogan (1965) p. 156)

found that about one third of the children spontaneously produced descriptions of emotional and personality characteristics, whereas the remainder described the shape characteristics of the figures. Responses from two of the former described A (Fig. 37) as cheerful and happy; B as showing dislike and avoidance; C and D as angry and aggressive. On the whole, children with greater intelligence and creative imagination produced more responses of this kind than either the less intelligent or the less creative. Thus it would appear that these attributions are not related to any primitive tendency, but to a highly developed form of inference, perhaps the same as Honkavaara's stage (4). It is not clear if there was any consensus of opinion as to the emotions attributed by different children to the figures; but these responses did not correlate highly with the results obtained when the experimenters provided a list of descriptive adjectives. However, Forrest and Lee (1962) found that pairs of stick figures could be used successfully to depict actions relevant to contrasting needs (see p. 218). But Holmes (1963) showed that uncultured people had some difficulty in understanding the actions represented by stick figures, unless they were very simple (p. 62).

A long series of experiments was carried out by Secord and his colleagues on the assessment of *personality qualities* from randomly selected *photographs* of male faces, not markedly emotional in expression (Secord *et al.*, 1954). These photographs were first rated as to the magnitude of certain facial characteristics, width, depth and distance apart of the eyes, fullness of lips, width of face; and on the appearance of other characteristics including mouth turned up or down, facial wrinkles, type of skin texture. The faces were then rated on a variety of personality qualities. There was a marked agreement between different judges on the facial and personality characteristics attributed to the faces, though there was disagreement on some photographs; and agreement was greater for some facial and personality characteristics than for others. Again, the listing of personality qualities may have exerted some effects of suggestion on the judges.

The facial characteristics which most affected assessments of personality were: coarse or smooth skin texture, fullness of lips, facial tension (wrinkled brow), depth of eyes. Though some relationships were noted between single facial characteristics and personality qualities, for instance mouth curvature and facial tension with pleasantness and unpleasantness, more important relationships were demonstrated between clusters of characteristics. In the first place, there were clusters of associated personality qualities: warmth and tolerance, morality and social respectability, annoyance and intolerance, etc. Some examples of associated clusters of facial and personality characteristics were: (1) Older face, thin lips, wrinkles at eye corners, level gaze, eyes of medium depth, associated with intelligence, distinction, refinement, responsibility and determination; (2) coarse skin, dark complexion, dull eyes, facial tension, heavy eye-brows, associated with boorishness, slyness, quick temper and hostility.

Later, Secord and Bevan (1956) obtained similar ratings on facial and personality characteristics from American and Norwegian students which on the whole closely resembled each other, though there were wide differences on certain photographs. Secord and Bevan suggested that the latter represented the 'American ideal' to the American students, who therefore rated them very highly on desirable personality qualities, whereas the Norwegians rated them much lower. When the experiment was repeated with female faces (Secord and Muthard, 1955a), the results were somewhat similar, but different personality clusters appeared: moral character (good moral character was associated with bright and wide eyes, absence of bow-shaped lips), social acceptability, sexuality. Other important facial characteristics were skin texture and fullness of lips. On the whole, however, the female faces seemed to possess less individuality of personality than the male, and assessments were more stereotyped. Differences in rating also occurred between different judges, male and female, older and younger (Secord and Muthard, 1955b). Older men rated the female faces less favourably than did younger men; and there were also significant differences between men and women judges.

In another experiment, Stritch and Secord (1956) selected photographs in which facial characteristics such as the above were varied systematically. They then found that change in one characteristic seemed to affect the appearance of other, unchanged, characteristics. Thus wrinkles in one part of the face suggested the occurrence of wrinkles in other parts. There were some corresponding alterations of personality qualities; for instance, facial tension, related to anxiety, decreased when wrinkles at the corners of the eyes, associated with good humour, were introduced. But these alterations were not marked.

Cline (1956) also showed that there might be interaction between faces. He presented pairs of three-quarter faces which appeared to be looking at each other. Some characteristics remained consistent throughout; smiling faces appeared pleased, frowning faces, angry. But some characteristics varied according to the relationship between members of the pair. Thus a smiling face paired with a glum face looked domineering and gloating, but with a frowning face, friendly and peaceful. A glum face paired with a smiling face looked defeated and discouraged, but with a frowning face, aloof and independent.

Now in all these experiments there is of course no evidence that the people whose faces were viewed in fact possessed the personality qualities attributed to them; but merely that the observers showed some agreement in thinking that they did. However, as we noted, there was some disagreement, for instance between male and female observers. There may also be differences in the extent to which different observers associate personality qualities with facial characteristics, as Shrauger and Altrochi (1964) suggested.

It is also possible that the association between facial and personality characteristics may result from *social stereotypes*. Thus it is a common belief that a smiling face, with upcurved mouth, belongs to a good-tempered person, and that wide open eyes characterize an innocent and ingenuous individual (Secord, 1958). Thick lips and a relaxed mouth are thought to indicate sexuality, and high foreheads, intelligence. Indeed, Heaton (1968) cited a whole list of such associations. But no evidence was given as to whether they were anything more than conventional stereotypes. Stereotyped associations may vary in different societies, and in different groups within these societies. They are particularly likely to be attributed to strangers and foreigners. In so far as the latter resemble familiar persons, the stereotypes tend to be favourable; the greater the dissimilarity, the less favourable they are. This occurs particularly in cases of *prejudice*. This stereotyping tendency was demonstrated by Secord *et al.* (1956) by presenting photographs of Negro and white faces to groups of observers known to be high and low in prejudice against Negroes; and requiring them to rate the faces on certain facial characteristics associated with Negroes such as width of nose and fullness of lips. Prejudiced observers showed a tendency to exaggerate these characteristics in the Negro photographs; and, unlike the unprejudiced, they did not vary their ratings as between the Negro faces darkest and lightest in colour. However, some degree of stereotyping appeared even in the unprejudiced.

A somewhat similar effect of prejudice was demonstrated by Pettigrew *et al.* (1958). They presented in a binocular stereoscope pairs of photographs of people of unlike race, white, Indian, African and Coloured (mixed white and African). These were viewed by English-speaking and Afrikaans-speaking South Africans, Indians, Africans and Coloured. There was no binocular rivalry; each observer perceived a single face, which might be a composite of two very different races, or of two more similar to each other. In the first case, the composite was usually judged to be of a group intermediate in colour between the extremes, Indians or Coloured. But the racially prejudiced Afrikaans-speaking South Africans tended to perceive either white or black faces, all non-Europeans being judged as black. Thus perception of colour, the main focus of racial prejudice, may be distorted by the influence of this prejudice, as were the other characteristics studied in the experiment of Secord *et al.* (1956). Indeed, even Negroes themselves tended to associate lightness of colour with attractiveness, a medium degree of lightness being considered the most attractive (Marks, 1943). Also many observers tended to rate their own colour as nearer to this desired hue than they actually were.

(5) Perception of Movement of Living Organisms

It seems possible that the attribution of physiognomic qualities to inanimate objects and shapes may be associated with their movements. We noted that children tended to think of objects in movement as alive. Several experiments have demonstrated that certain types of movement may be associated with the characteristics of living organisms. Thus Michotte (1946) showed observers a black rectangle which moved horizontally while at the same time contracting and expanding regularly in length. With suitable speeds of movement and of contraction and expansion, these movements appeared to be linked together, and the object seemed to move laterally by means of the expansion and contraction of its body, like a worm or a tadpole. Johansson (1950) presented complex movement patterns of bright circles on a dark ground, and found that the perceived movements formed configurations which did not correspond with the actual physical movements. In particular,

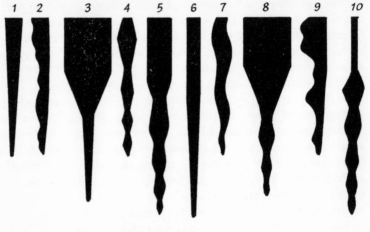

(a)   1, 3, 6
(b)   4, 5, 8, 10
(c)   2, 7, 9

FIG. 38 Movement patterns
(*After* Defares and De Haan (1962) p. 218)

elements which moved in phase were grouped together, and differentiated from those in a different phase of movement. Thus with four elements moving to and fro along different sections of a horizontal path, the two in phase seemed to approach and recede from the two in another phase. If the phase difference was maximal, the phenomenon appeared to be caused mechanically. But if there was only a small phase difference, the same kind of wriggling movement, as of a living creature, appeared as in Michotte's demonstration. Defares and De Haan (1962) presented a series of black strips which moved vertically downwards behind a horizontal slit, in such a way as to show characteristic changes of form with movement. Those in group (a) (Fig. 38), which changed regularly, gave the appearance of mechanically caused movement; and those in group (c), the impression of intentionally caused human movement. But those in the intermediate group (b) showed systematic movement either physically caused, like waves on a beach, or living in origin, like the flapping of a bird's wings.

But some complex patterns of movement may be specifically associated with *human actions*. Michotte (1963) demonstrated that the perception of *intentionality* in action could occur. He presented two black squares which moved towards a red rectangle. When they were close to it, one square disappeared and re-appeared on its farther side. The two black squares then closed in on the rectangle, and all three together moved back in a direction opposite to that of the original movement of the black squares. The impression created was that the two black squares were intentionally pouncing on the red rectangle and carrying it off.

Heider and Simmel (1944) found that observers spontaneously described the filmed movements of a large and a small black triangle and a small black circle in terms of human intentions. Thus the large triangle appeared to be chasing and hitting the small triangle and the circle, which tried to hide (in a stationary open-sided rectangle) and escape. Shor (1957) found that there was a general tendency to view the large triangle in an unfavourable light, by contrast with the small triangle and circle. This tendency was intensified when the observers were told that the large triangle represented an unpleasant aggressive person; but was lessened in those who were told that it was a fair-minded person. Marek (1963) presented twelve short films each of which showed the movements of geometrical figures which varied in complexity of form, direction and speed of movement. The observers, who were boys of ten to eleven years, in general perceived a greater degree of animation the greater the complexity. But again movements which sharply changed direction sometimes suggested relationships of mechanical causality. Continuity of movement and direction, associated with smooth changes and variations, facilitated the perception of animation, and the inference that the moving objects were anticipating and even planning their movements.

Now clearly these descriptions represent inferences from perceptions, rather than immediate percepts. Heider (1958a) considered that patterns of movement in the Heider and Simmel film were organized in terms of the *motivated acts* of persons, which gave them coherence and meaning. Michotte found the perception of intentionality to be less direct and spontaneous and more labile than were the mechanical causality phenomena of his original experiments. They were more liable to show *individual differences*, in that some observers did not report intentionality at all. Marek also found that some boys were more sensitive to animation than were others. The latter, curiously enough, were boys who had

o

experienced the exercise by their parents of considerable social restriction. But clearly certain types of movement do in themselves appear more readily than others to resemble the movements of living creatures; those characterized by smooth continuous relations between successive movements. According to Heider (1958b), movements and actions provide better evidence as to the nature of personality than do the physiognomic properties of motionless figures, because they are dynamic, as emotional changes of expression are dynamic. Nevertheless, there is no universal association between movement in itself and motivation or emotion. As the experiment by Shor (1957) indicated, predisposition and even prejudice may be highly influential. We must conclude that the schemata within which are organized perceptions of the formal characteristics of movement, as of faces and of bodies, are exceedingly complex and as yet little understood.

XI

The Effect of Motivation
on Perception

(1) Introduction

The type of motivation to which perception is most directly related is
the necessity of maintaining contact with the environment and adapting
behaviour to environmental change. We noted that the perceptual capacities seem to function in such a manner as to produce rapid reaction
to change, whereas in an unchanging environment they may cease to
operate effectively. Nevertheless, it would appear that in special states
of need and desire, perception may be facilitated and directed towards
particular aspects of or objects in the environment which may satisfy
these needs. It has even been supposed that need may give rise to
exaggerated and non-veridical perception. But as we shall see this occurs
mainly in conditions of ambiguous stimulation. In normal circumstances,
erroneous perception would have little value to adaptation, and would
fail to ensure the most rapid and efficient satisfaction of need. But the
observations described in Chapter V suggested that perception might
be improved through the establishment of set and expectation, which
are geared to motivation, and especially to well-established long-term
motives such as interests.

Great concern with the relation of perception to motivation arose
during the 1940's, leading to a wide range of experiment. Unfortunately
perhaps the principal type of motivation studied was that of short-term
needs, such as hunger, thirst and the avoidance of pain, and there was
comparatively little investigation of the effects of more permanent and
indeed more important types of motivation. The number of experiments
of this kind has decreased in recent years, but continuing attention has
been directed to the complex results of anxiety.

It would seem that there is a number of ways in which perception
may be facilitated and guided by motivation, as Henle (1955) noted.
In the first place, motivational drive increases arousal, and stimulates
attention and effort to perceive and explore the perceptual field. But

particular needs may also increase particular expectancies, directing attention narrowly to relevant aspects of the field, and causing these to be selected and emphasized as 'figural' while the remainder of the field sinks into the 'ground'. 'Physiognomic' properties may be emphasized, for instance the agreeableness of desired people or objects; but this may lead to overemphasis and perception of exaggerated size, brightness, etc. Relevant past experiences are also aroused, and the perceived field is órganized in such a manner that, for instance, similarities are observed which hitherto were not apparent. Events and symbols not previously recognized as relevant may now be perceived as important. Unfortunately all these processes tend to be inextricably mingled with each other, and comparatively little experimental work has been devoted to the isolation of each and the assessment of the part played by each in facilitating perception. Thus the effects studied tend to be relatively crude and undifferentiated.

(2) The Effects of Hunger and Thirst

The early experiments of Levine *et al.* (1942) and of McClelland and Atkinson (1948) suggested that observers who were required to identify and name vague blots or blurred pictures, exposed tachistoscopically, gave more responses related to *food* after a period of food deprivation than when they were not hungry. However, this tendency operated over a limited period of food deprivation only; and thereafter observers increasingly failed to name the pictures. Similarly, Lazarus *et al.* (1953) found that the intensity of illumination necessary to perceive photographs of food decreased up to three to four hours of food deprivation, and then increased up to six hours. But hungry observers made no more incorrect guesses as to the identity of the photographs than did non-hungry observers. Food deprivation had no effect on the perception of *words* which were names of food objects; a result also obtained by Taylor (1956b). On the other hand, Wispé and Drambarean (1953) found that words related to food, as contrasted with neutral words, were perceived more readily up to ten hours of food deprivation, but thereafter, at twenty-four hours, more slowly. Perception of both common and uncommon words was affected in the same way. However, the effect of frequency was greater than that of food deprivation. A similar result was obtained by Postman and Crutchfield (1952), who found that the perception of 'skeleton' food-related words, such as LUN-H, was facilitated to a greater extent by a previously established set – exposure of similar skeleton words – than by food deprivation. However, the latter did have a slight effect.

But it would seem that in some cases hunger and thirst may actually modify the appearance of objects relevant to these needs. Thus Gilchrist and Nesberg (1952) found that the estimates of apparent brightness of pictures of food made by observers deprived of food increased steadily up to twenty hours' deprivation. Brightness of pictures of *drink* increased up to eight hours' water deprivation. And if these observers were then allowed to drink as much as they wanted, estimated brightness immediately decreased to its initial value. These changes did not operate in the perception of neutral objects. But as Saugstad (1966) pointed out, these estimates were made from memory and not by direct matching. Therefore apparent brightness may have increased in memory rather than in immediate perception. Another experiment, by Beams (1954), indicated that variation might occur in immediate perception, but with children of ten to twelve years as observers. They were shown pictures of liked and disliked foods and asked to set them at the distance at which they appeared to be the same size as an actual piece of food. The liked objects were set nearer than the disliked. Beams concluded that the apparent sizes of the former were greater than those of the latter; but it is possible that the children placed the former nearer to themselves than the latter because they liked them better.

A series of experiments carried out by Klein (1954) on thirsty observers indicated that the effects of *thirst* on perception varied with differences in the ability to control direction of attention and to ignore distraction. Thirst was aroused, not by water deprivation but by giving the observers a thirst-producing meal, of hot salty substances. They were then shown tachistoscopically a picture of an ice-cream soda surrounded by letters and numbers which they were required to identify. Some observers, who were well able to control their direction of attention, perceived more of the surrounding letters and numbers than did others who tended to centre on the ice-cream soda. The observers were then shown words related to thirst and neutral words printed in various colours. They had to report the colours and not the words, but subsequently to recall the words. All observers tended to recall more thirst-related words than neutral words, but those with less control of direction of attention did so to a greater extent than did the others. The former invented more thirst words, and thus their accuracy of recall was impaired. But in the latter, accuracy was increased. Now these results show that different effects occur when there is a conflict in perception and memory; nevertheless, it is possible that distortion of perception in states of need may affect some observers more than others.

(3) The Effects of Reward, Success and Failure

A simple type of motivation may be produced by *rewarding* observers for good performance on a task. This would seem to have the effect of increasing arousal, and with it speed and accuracy of perception. Laberge *et al.* (1967) found that observers who were told they would gain twenty points for pressing a button as soon as they perceived a particular colour did so more quickly than when they were told they would receive only a single point. The experiment was so arranged as to eliminate effects on response alone. Smock and Rubin (1964) showed that children of nine to twelve years, promised the gift of a toy as an incentive, were more accurate in perceiving and matching pictures of animals and irregular shapes than when there was no incentive. However, decision time was not affected, presumably because speed was not directly rewarded. Rewarding accuracy may be more effective. Smith *et al.* (1951) required observers to estimate the number of dots in groups of dots presented tachistoscopically. One set of observers was rewarded for every correct response; the reward of the other set increased with the number of dots in every correct response. The observers of the second set tended at first to make over-estimates of the number of dots, but by the twentieth trial they ceased to do this, and eventually made more correct responses than did the first set of observers.

In some circumstances, reward appears to *narrow the span of attention,* improving the accuracy of central perception only. Bahrick *et al.* (1952) presented a tracking task in central vision, at the same time exposing lights at irregular intervals in the periphery. When rewards were given for good performance early in the task, the tracking performance improved considerably. But there was no improvement in the detection of the light signals, although observers were informed that their scores on this would count towards their total reward. Indeed sometimes there was a deterioration; or observers did not even notice the light signals until their attention was drawn to them. However, such a centralization of attention need not occur. Fisch and McNamara (1963) found that the matching of the distances of irregular shapes was improved in accuracy to a greater extent the greater the monetary reward attached. They concluded that the attentional activity of scanning or 'decentration' was increased. However, this activity would not seem to depend so greatly on 'decentration' as did the detection of the peripheral light signals in the experiment of Bahrick *et al.*

Rewarding particular responses may sometimes affect tasks even when the observers are not directly aware of the connection between response and reward. Rigby and Rigby (1956) rewarded children when particular letters were turned up in a game of tossing cubes; tokens were given which could subsequently be exchanged for sweets. When the letters were then exposed tachistoscopically, the rewarded ones were perceived more rapidly than were the unrewarded. Here the reward may have directly speeded up perception, and also established a set to perceive particular letters. In the experiment of Fisch and McNamara (1963), it was found that adult observers responded in a similar manner when the only reward they obtained was that the experimenter made the comment 'good' whenever they gave certain responses. Observers were required to judge the mid-point of various distances. In general, they showed a tendency to set the mid-point too far away, but there was considerable variation. Whenever a judgment was made in accordance with this natural tendency, the experimenter commented 'incorrect'; when the judgment went contrary to the natural tendency, he commented 'good'. After a considerable period of practice, more and more judgments were made contrary to the natural tendency. With control observers who had received no such comments, the natural tendency became stronger. Thus it appeared that the reward of 'good' had a directional effect on perception.

However, it could be argued that these responses were judgments rather than immediate perceptions. A rather similar effect on judgment was obtained by Tajfel (1957). He found that when observers were required to judge the heaviness of ten weights according to a scale of seven categories, rewarding the heaviest judgments produced a tendency to give more 'heavy' judgments. Rewarding the lightest judgments resulted in more 'light' judgments being given. The rewards were paper tokens which could subsequently be exchanged for book tokens. When in another experiment the paper tokens were made valueless, the above effect did not occur.

A number of experiments has been carried out in which both *reward and punishment* have been used. Now it has sometimes been assumed uncritically that reward and punishment are equal and opposite in their effects; where reward stimulates, punishment deters. In fact, the situation is more complex. As we have seen reward may increase arousal and facilitate action, and may also direct perception towards certain specific aspects of the situation. Punishment may or may not increase arousal; that is to say, it may increase arousal towards avoiding action if such action is possible, but if not it may produce inhibition of action. It may also give rise to withdrawal from some specific aspect of the perceived situation, and hence the perception of alternative aspects, especially if avoidance of the one automatically leads to selection of the others. Nevertheless, situations sometimes occur in which the punished aspect is emphasized.

One of the earliest experiments on the effects of reward and punishment on selection was carried out by Schafer and Murphy (1943). They presented separately the two halves or faces (Fig. 39a and 39b) of each of two ambiguous contour figures such as that of Fig. 39c. For each of the faces, the observer had to learn a name. Two faces were 'rewarded' by giving the observer money whenever they were shown; the other two

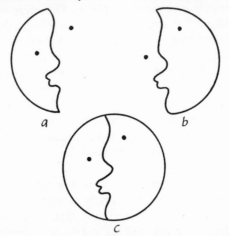

FIG. 39 Ambiguous figures
(*After* Schafer and Murphy (1943) pp. 336, 337)

were 'punished' by taking money away. Finally, the complete figures were presented, together with other similar but unambiguous figures. It was found that in the majority of cases the complete figures were given the names of the rewarded faces rather than the punished, although, it was claimed, the observers were unaware of the connection of these and reward or punishment.

This experiment has been repeated several times, with varying results. Rock and Fleck (1950) found that with one ambiguous figure there was a tendency to perceive the rewarded face; with the other, the punished. They considered that learning the names for the faces caused considerable difficulty, and that in so doing one aspect might in itself appear easier to perceive and recognize subsequently than the other. Jackson (1954) obtained a result similar to that of Schafer and Murphy. But some observers, who were less interested in the money rewards and punishments, chose the punished faces. In a second experiment, Jackson presented four new pairs of faces, which were apparently harder to discriminate, since the observers reported that some of them looked different when they were combined in the ambiguous figure. The reactions to reward and punishment were more variable; and there was a tendency to select mainly the leftward pointing face. Sommer (1957) compared the effects of rewarded and neutral, unrewarded, faces, and also those of punished and neutral faces. The rewarded face was perceived more readily than the neutral; but the punished face, though less readily perceived than the rewarded, was perceived more readily than the neutral. Thus when reward and punishment were divorced from each other, the latter appeared to have the effect of emphasizing the punished aspect. This result was confirmed by a further experiment by Messick *et al.* (cited by Solley and Murphy, 1960), in which the three conditions of rewarded-neutral, punished-neutral and rewarded-punished were employed. Punishment had a slightly greater effect than reward when each was paired with neutral. When reward and punishment were paired together, results were about equally divided.

In an experiment by Beatty *et al.* (1959), four profiles were presented, all facing in the same direction. After the observers had learnt to identify these by name, they were shown them again, twelve times over, two being accompanied by reward and two by punishment. When finally the threshold of illumination for identification was measured for each profile separately, it was found that there were no differences in threshold for rewarded and punished faces, even by observers who reported that they felt 'involved' in the task; that is to say, they minded how well they performed. These observers had lower thresholds for all profiles than did the uninvolved. However, this experiment relates to ease of perception rather than to direction of attention.

Finally, in an experiment by Smith and Hochberg (1954), there was no reward, but two faces were accompanied by the punishment of an electric shock, while others were neutral. There was a slightly greater tendency to choose the neutral, unshocked faces; but one face was chosen significantly more often than the others, whether shocked or not. However, punishment by electric shock raises several important problems which will be considered more fully in Section (5) of this chapter. In a comparable experiment, Hochberg and Brooks (1958) presented four of the Gottschaldt simple figures, two of them accompanied by an unpleasant loud screeching noise. When the complex figures were presented subsequently, detection in them of the simple figures previously accompanied by noise was more difficult than detection of the other simple figures.

It seems possible that the reception of reward and punishment may produce feelings of success and failure respectively, and these experiences may affect subsequent perception. We have seen that the results of punishment may be ambiguous, and the same is true of the experience of *failure*. Several experiments have been carried out to discover the effect on perception of words previously given as anagrams, which the observers failed to solve. Postman and Solomon (1950) found that some observers perceived these more quickly than words which they had succeeded in solving as anagrams; other observers more slowly. Keehn (1959) found no difference in mean time for perception, possibly because the results of the quicker and slower observers cancelled each other out. Spence (1957) praised observers when they solved anagrams and shamed them when they failed. But in general the failure words were subsequently perceived more readily, especially by those whose *anxiety*, as assessed on a questionnaire*, had been increased by failure. The same result was obtained by Eriksen and Browne (1956) for observers who scored high on the Psychasthenia scale of the MMPI and who were of a generally anxious disposition. They were ready to admit failure, whereas low scorers were not and their perceptions of the failed anagrams were to some extent inhibited by previous failure. Caron and Wallach (1959), however, could not discover any relationship between assessments on an anxiety scale and rise in threshold for words which had previously been incorporated in a scrambled sentences test, half the items of which were insoluble. But they did find that those in whom the threshold was lowered showed a high degree of perseverance in the achievement of goals towards which they were oriented. Those with raised thresholds showed little such motivation.

There may be a general effect of failure on performance in some tasks, however. Smock (1955) presented a series of pictures varying successively from being completely blurred to completely clear. For one group of observers, failure was enhanced by stressing it; for another group, reassurance was given by the experimenter. The former began somewhat earlier than the latter to guess what the pictures represented, and were later in attaining a correct response. Smock considered that anxiety was aroused by aggravating the sense of failure, and thus impaired recognition.

It would appear also that what is actually perceived may be influenced differentially by success and failure. Thus Postman and Brown (1952)

---

* However, there is some doubt as to the accuracy with which a disposition to be affected by anxiety in perceptual experiments is in fact assessed by means of these questionnaires. This problem will be discussed again on p. 225.

first presented a preliminary perceptual task. It was made to seem to some observers that they had succeeded on this by surpassing their own estimates as to how well they would perform; whereas others were made to appear to have failed, by falling short of their estimates. Subsequently all observers were shown tachistoscopically a series of words, four of which related to success – excellent, succeed, perfection, winner – and four related to failure – failure, unable, obstacle, defeat. The successful observers perceived the success words more readily than the failure words, whereas the failing observers perceived the failure words more readily. A similar result was obtained by McClelland and Liberman (1949) with observers who had been judged, on the basis of T.A.T. performance, to possess varying degrees of need for *achievement* and *security*. Those with strong need for achievement perceived most readily words related to achievement, those with anxiety tendencies perceived words related to security. But Wall and Guthrie (1959) found that among a group of students who were in some danger of failing in examinations and being dismissed from the University, those with the poorest academic achievement had a high perceptual threshold for words related to failure, whereas words related to success were unaffected.

Again it would appear that the hope of success and fear of failure may affect perception differentially in those with different degrees of *self-esteem*. Boys of ten to thirteen years were rated, by themselves and by others, for their degree of self-esteem as shown by their answers to a questionnaire (Coopersmith, 1964). They were then required to make shape constancy matches for tilted squares, in stress and in non-stress conditions. In the former, they were informed that performance was related to academic success. When they hoped for success, in the stress conditions, those high in self-esteem tended to adopt the analytic procedure and constancy was low. It was suggested that boys with a high degree of confidence in succeeding were able to break with their immediate perceptions of real shape, and analyse the perceptual situation carefully. This did not occur in non-stress conditions, or in those with low self-esteem.

(4) The Effects of Monetary Value

A number of experiments has been performed which indicate that the manner in which objects are perceived may be affected by the value attached to them, even when the observers are in no way rewarded. The most widely known experiment demonstrating this effect was an early one by Bruner and Goodman (1947), which showed that adults

and ten-year-old children overestimated the sizes of coins, by comparison
with cardboard discs, in proportion to the monetary value of the former.
Moreover, poorer children over-estimated to a greater extent than did
richer children. There were however certain faults in the method of
this experiment, and other experimenters have claimed that these effects
operate only when observers have to remember the sizes of the coins in
order to match them with the discs (Carter and Schooler, 1949; Pastore,
1949). But Landis *et al.* (1966) found that when six coins, from a dime
to a dollar, and six discs of similar size, were assessed for size, each by
a different group of adults, there was a steadily increasing over-estimation with increase in size for both coins and discs. For the three larger
sizes, the over-estimation for coins was greater than for the discs. Tajfel
(1957) suggested that these effects were due to over-accentuation of the
differences in size between coins of different denominations, a useful
type of judgment which enables us to discriminate more accurately
between them. Tajfel and Cawasjee (1959) obtained such an over-
accentuation of the difference in size between a florin and a half-crown.
Again, Bruner and Rodrigues (1953) found that the differences were
even more over-estimated by observers given a set to perceive accurately
than when the values of the coins were emphasized, presumably because
in the former case attention was specifically directed towards the differences. In a useful discussion of experiments on the effects of value,
Tajfel (1957) pointed out that size estimation was affected by value only
when size and value were directly related; that is to say, with coins which
increase in size as they increase in value. Thus Klein *et al.* (1951) found
no tendency to over-estimate the size of discs on which a dollar sign
was printed.

(5) The Effects of Pain and Fear

There have been many experiments in which electric shock has been
introduced to investigate the effects on perception of pain, fear of pain
and perhaps fear of crying out with pain. There are several different
types of behaviour to which painful stimulation may give rise. It increases arousal, and may make the sufferer more alert, especially to avoid
or withdraw from the situation. Or it may startle him and distract his
attention from the perceived situation. If there is no obvious means of
escape, or if the pain is severe, over-arousal may occur and behaviour
become disorganized and disrupted. In some cases, a general state of
inhibition may result, or repression of certain aspects of the situation.
But also the association of pain with a stimulus may have the effect of
emphasizing it, so that it is readily remembered afterwards.

However, in this work a particular methodological difficulty has arisen. When it appears that perception of painful and fear-arousing stimuli is retarded, inhibited or distorted, by comparison with neutral stimuli arousing no particular emotion, the questions then arise: Is perception itself affected, and if so, how can an observer perceive the fear-arousing characteristics of a stimulus before he in fact appears to identify it – that is to say, when perception is retarded? Or does he perceive it and then repress it or retard his reaction to it including the report of what he perceived? Thus much discussion has ensued, to which we shall return in Section (7) of this chapter, as to whether motivation affects perception itself or merely the reactions to that perception including verbal report. It is indeed possible that fragments of a word are perceived, and full identification repressed. Or Hochberg (1968) has suggested that the visual memory image, normally utilized in tachistoscopic identification, is inhibited.

One effect of painful shock was demonstrated by Hatfield (1959), who found that if a list of nonsense syllables was repeatedly presented, some of which were accompanied by electric shock, these were subsequently perceived more readily than those which had not been associated with electric shock. However, in an experiment in which syllables were learnt by the paired associate method, and some of the responses coupled with shock, the corresponding stimulus syllables were less accurately perceived subsequently, and it was concluded that some repression had occurred (Lowenfeld, 1961). Lysak (1954) not only accompanied with shock some of the syllables in a preliminary list learnt by the observer, but also informed him that he would receive a more severe shock whenever he recognized and reported one of these, presented tachistoscopically. Not surprisingly, these syllables were reported more slowly than the others, and Lysak considered that in all probability the observer was witholding his response. When there was no such threat of shock during perception, the previously shocked syllables were recognized more quickly than those not shocked; in other words, perception was sensitized, presumably through the initial emphasis created by the shock.

But other experiments indicated that perception might be delayed or disrupted by shock. Jones (1959) presented blurred figures which gradually became clearer, and found that a greater degree of clarity was necessary to perceive those accompanied by shock at irregular intervals than those unaccompanied by shock. With severe shock, considerable disruption occurred, and some responses were perseverative and grossly inaccurate. A similar effect was obtained by Hochberg *et al.* (1955) on the perception of nonsense syllables. With one set of these, a buzzer signal was presented just before exposure and a shock during it; with a second, the signal and the shock occurred after presentation; and with a third, there was a signal alone and no shock. More letters were perceived in the third set than in the first or second. It was hypothesized that the signal accompanied by the shock produced a startle response, immediately before or after presentation, which prevented the development of the perceptual responses.

If, however, there is some possibility of *escape from shock*, as the result of rapid perception, the perception may be facilitated. Rosen (1954) presented nonsense syllables to one group of observers who received a shock for every incorrect perception, which was terminated as soon as the correct response was given; and to another group who were shocked at random. Perception became more rapid with the first group; but that of the second was slower than with a control group who received no shock. Thus in the first case observers were alerted to avoid painful stimulation; in the second, perception was disrupted. A similar result was obtained by Phares (1962), who found that when observers could terminate the shock by learning to press the correct button in response to nonsense syllables, these syllables were perceived more quickly than when learning was impossible because there was no connection between any particular syllable and the button. However, the former performed no better than did a control group who received no shock. Therefore it was concluded that any incentive provided by escape from the shock was cancelled out by its disruptive effects.

In a more elaborate experiment by Reece (1954), certain nonsense syllables in a list learnt first were for some observers accompanied consistently by shock; whereas for others shock was given at random. These two groups were each subdivided into those who could escape from the shock by giving the correct response, and those who could not. Furthermore, the shock was adjusted, by means of a preliminary test, to give strong pain. The differences of time required for perception between the predictable and non-predictable shock groups were insignificant; but perception was more rapid when it was possible to escape from the shock than when it was not. Thus the effect of escape was facilitating, by comparison with the situation in which escape was impossible and in which there was some disruption of perception. Nevertheless, as in the experiment of Phares, the control group receiving no shock performed as well as the escape group, presumably for the same reason.

However, in spite of these frequent inhibitory effects, it would appear that in some cases shock may have a *directive effect* on perception, particularly if the non-shocked aspect is a simple alternative to the shocked. Thus we noted that Smith and Hochberg (1954) found a tendency to choose the non-shocked face in the Schafer and Murphy figure. A rather similar result was obtained by Mangan (1959), who presented a series of drawings, designed by Luchins (1945), which changed gradually from the representation of a face to that of a bottle. Observers were previously shown pictures of faces and bottles; for one group of observers the faces were accompanied by shock, for another, the bottles. If the shock was a mild one, they perceived respectively the shocked face or bottle more readily than when there had been no shock. But if the shock was severe, they perceived the shocked face or bottle less readily. Thus the mild shock had a facilitating effect, the severe shock a disrupting effect.

In another experiment, observers had to report the position of what appeared to them to be the clearest shape among four shapes arranged circularly (Dulany, 1957). If a shock was given whenever this shape was presented, they soon ceased to report it. If the other shapes were shocked, they tended to report the non-shocked shape more frequently. In a rather similar experiment by Pustell (1957), observers again had to state which of four shapes seemed to stand out most clearly. They were given a training series in which one of the shapes was black, the other grey, and were shocked just before the response was made to the black shape. In a subsequent test in which all the shapes stood out equally clearly, 63 per cent of the observers reported that the previously shocked shape appeared clearest, whereas 37 per cent avoided the previously shocked shape. The former were mainly men and the latter, women. It was concluded that the women tended to be frightened and inhibited by the shock, whereas the men were agitated and alerted by it. Such individual differences are frequent in experiments in which fear is aroused; we shall return to this in Section (7) of this chapter.

A remarkable finding as to the effects of shock is that not only do stimuli previously associated with shock produce a heightened *GSR response*, but that this response may occur before the stimuli are fully perceived, and even when they are not correctly perceived. The best known experiment on this effect was carried out by Lazarus and Mc-Cleary (1951). They first presented nonsense syllables, some of which were accompanied by shock, and continued to do so until a heightened GSR response to these was firmly established. They then presented the syllables for tachistoscopic perception, and found that a heightened GSR response occurred to the previously shocked syllables even when they were incorrectly perceived. Voor (1956) obtained the same effect, but it was greatest when the syllables were presented at an illumination only just below that at which full correct identification was possible. Thus he concluded that there was a partial recognition of the syllables which gave rise to GSR responses even when they were not fully and correctly perceived. Moreover, more unshocked than shocked syllables were correctly perceived, indicating again that some recognition must have occurred. Murdock (1954) found that observers who were unable to perceive the nonsense syllables employed by Lazarus and McCleary correctly at the first presentation nevertheless gained some impression as to what they were, and perceived them correctly at the second presentation. Again, Wiener and Schiller (1960) showed that a GSR response, associated with shocked words presented in very brief exposures so that they were scarcely visible, generalized to other words of similar structure, presumably because fragments alone of the former were perceived. With full visibility, generalization takes place to words of similar meaning rather than of similar form.

Finally, it should be noted that experiments such as those of Lazarus and McCleary do not demonstrate the occurrence of 'subception' (subthreshold perception) with the GSR arising as the natural consequence of shock, but only in connection with GSR responses established through previous conditioning. However, in the next section we shall consider the appearance of heightened GSR responses induced directly by the emotional effects of perceiving particular types of stimulus.

Anxiety aroused by conditions other than electric shock may also affect perception. The most frequent finding is some impairment in accuracy of discrimination. Thus Goldstone (1955) showed that clinic patients with a high degree of anxiety had a lower sensitivity to flicker and a stronger tendency to perceive fusion of flickering light than did patients low in anxiety. Moreover, the sensitivity of the former decreased during testing and their variability increased. Korchin *et al.* (1957) found that anxiety patients, given a stressful interview which tended to increase their anxiety, were less accurate in their estimates of the areas of squares when they experienced a considerable increase in emotional disturbance. Over-arousal may have given rise to these effects.

Some interference with accuracy of perception may occur in normal persons exposed to conditions arousing anxiety. Korchin and Basowitz (1954) found that men on a training course for parachute jumping scored consistently less well just before and after jumping than at other times, on a test of perceiving whether circles exposed tachistoscopically were open or closed. But the discrimination was poorest after jumping, suggesting that anxiety was greatest when defences against stress were relaxed. Moffitt and Stagner (1956) and Kidd (1965) showed the same tendency towards closure of incomplete figures in observers who scored highly on the Taylor Manifest Anxiety scale, and were threatened that their test performance might indicate neurotic tendencies. They also showed a high degree of intolerance of perceptual ambiguity, and rapid adaptation to the Ames distorted room. Moffit and Stagner concluded that in a stress situation such individuals tried to maximise the constancy of the environment and to rely on memories of past experience rather than on their immediate perceptions of the situation. However, Binder (1958) found that anxious observers were slower than others to identify shapes from gradually more detailed cues; and Rockett (1956) showed that as the complexity of line figures increased, so the more anxious observers became progressively slower in recognizing them. Thus there seems to have been a widespread decrease in the power of discrimination.

Longenecker (1962) found that performance could be either impaired or facilitated according to the degree of anxiety experienced. Observers, assessed as high in anxiety and exposed to stress conditions in which they were informed that the test they were taking was related to their academic performance, took longer to recognize the embedded figures in the Witkin version of the Gottschaldt test. But without the stress condition, and in observers low in anxiety, a slight degree of anxiety facilitated performance. Longenecker also found that a moderate degree of achievement motivation operated in the same manner; and concluded that the important factor was the degree of arousal produced. Moderate arousal was more effective than high or low arousal.

But also the stimulus material itself may be manipulated to show the effects of anxiety. Greenbaum (1956) found that observers, rated high in anxiety on the Taylor Manifest Anxiety scale and shown pictures of friendly and hostile faces, had no more difficulty in perceiving hostile as compared with friendly faces than did observers with a low degree of anxiety. But when they were informed that their leadership ability was being assessed from their performance on the perceptual test, the observers high in anxiety tended to see the hostile faces more readily than the friendly faces.

(6) The Effects of Other Types of Motivation

Other types of motivation which seem to be related to ease of perception are those associated with *interests*. Thus Postman *et al.* (1948) assessed the major interests of observers by means of the Study of Values test (Allport *et al.*, 1951), and found that observers subsequently perceived

P

words related to their major values or interests more readily than other words. This result was criticized by Solomon and Howes (1951) on the grounds that the words were not equated for frequency; and, as we have seen, frequency and familiarity are important determinants of differences in perceptibility of words. However, Postman and Schneider (1951) showed later that though there was little difference in speed of perception between words associated with different interests if they were common words, yet there was considerable difference if they were infrequent words. But it seems likely that people would acquire a more extensive vocabulary in relation to their major interests than on other topics. Nevertheless, Haigh and Fiske (1952) found that not only were words related to the more salient interests, as measured by the Study of Values test, more easily perceived; but also the same result was obtained when the observers were asked to rank these words in the order in which they valued them. A slightly different variant of somewhat the same technique has been used in relation to *personality* traits. Postman and Leytham (1961) presented the names of twelve different personality traits for tachistoscopic perception. There was no relation between speed of perception and desirability of the trait in the mean results. But in cases in which the observers thought that their friends would rate them higher or lower than they rated themselves as to the degree of a trait they possessed, perception was slower. This result might have been due to the conflict arising from the rating differences.

A different approach to the relation between perception and motivation was adopted by Eriksen (1951a). He presented words related to the motives of *aggression, succorance* (demand for protection and maintenance) and *homosexuality* to psychiatric patients, and assessed the degree of repression of these needs by means of a free association technique.* Subsequently he presented pictures relating to these needs, and found some correlation between general difficulty in free association and slow recognition of the pictures. But there was little relationship between specific needs and perception of corresponding pictures. However, in another experiment (1951b), patients who produced exaggeratedly aggressive stories on the T.A.T. took less time to recognize aggressive

---

* The use of the free association technique will be mentioned frequently in the succeeding discussion. It has been demonstrated that when an observer is required to produce free associations to words, the time taken to associate with highly emotional words tends to be long, the implication being that some avoidance or repression of the emotional situation is taking place. Additionally, if the GSR is measured, it is commonly heightened in response to emotional words. Thus these techniques afford a means of selecting words with emotional implications for particular observers.

pictures than did patients who did not produce aggressive T.A.T. stories even when the test suggested them. Lindner (1953) obtained similar results with *sexual* and non-sexual delinquents. The former were quicker than the latter to perceive the sexual aspects of drawings of the sex organs as these were increased in clarity of representation. Sexual avoidance in normal individuals, as indicated by lack of sexual responses in the Rorschach test, was associated with delay in recognition of a picture of a female torso (Silverman and Luborsky, 1965). Carpenter *et al.* (1956) employed a sentence completion test to estimate whether observers were *'sensitizers'* or *'repressers'* with regard to sex and aggression. The sensitizers were quicker than the repressers to perceive words related to sex and aggression. Zuckerman (1955) found that aggressive words were perceived more slowly than were neutral words. He attempted to relate this result to natural tendency to aggression, as assessed by the Rosenzweig Picture Frustration Test; and to aggression experimentally aroused by a frustrating experience. No differences in delay of recognition between aggressive and neutral words were associated with the assessments. But the frustrated observers perceived all words more slowly, both neutral and aggressive, possibly as the result of the anticipation of further damage to their self-esteem. Nevertheless, there were individual differences in reaction to frustration, and in the perception of aggressive words. Rosenstock (1951) presented sentences the second clauses of which were sexual or aggressive in meaning. These sentences were perceived more slowly than those with neutral meanings; in particular, the aggressive ones by female observers and the sexual ones by male observers. It was concluded that women tended to repress aggression, and men, sex. Neel (1954) differentiated the effects on perception of pictures of people engaged in aggressive activities, in women with conflicts over aggression and in those without. The former showed avoidance of the aggressive pictures.

Van de Castle (1960) employed a different technique for investigating these effects. He presented pairs of words, an aggressive and a neutral one, to the two fields in a binocular stereoscope. Observers were grouped by means of the MMPI Anxiety scale and the Edwards Personal Preference scale, into high and low aggressive sensitizers and high and low aggressive defenders (repressers). When binocular rivalry occurred between the aggressive and neutral words, sensitizers reported significantly more appearances of the aggressive words than did defenders. But no differences in perception appeared between the high and low aggressors.

Forrest and Lee (1962) carried out an extensive study of the relation to perception of ten of the major *needs* postulated by Murray (1938). These included aggression and sex. The strength of the need states of observers was assessed by means of a questionnaire and a projection test, and it was hypothesized that a need was repressed when it appeared clearly in the projection test but not, in overt form, in the questionnaire. Pictures of 'stick' human figures in activities related to these needs were presented for perception and for subsequent recall. Those related to overt needs were perceived more quickly and correctly than those not so related; but there was no relation between repressed needs and delay in perception. There was, however, some tendency for difficulty in recall of pictures related to repressed needs. But also it was observed that verbal response was clearer and more emphatic, both in perception and recall, for pictures related to high degrees of overt need. Thus Forrest and Lee concluded that need states might have more effect on responses to perceived material than on initial perception.

(7) The Effects of Emotion on Perception

We have already noted that the perception of material associated with pain and fear may be facilitated in some circumstances and inhibited in others. It has been claimed that the perception of material arousing other emotions may be affected in a similar manner; and indeed certain experiments have indicated that even the simple affects of *pleasure* and *unpleasure* may have some influence. Thus Gilchrist *et al.* (1954) found that both pleasant words, such as 'able', 'brave', 'honest', and unpleasant words, such as 'cheap', 'dirty', 'vulgar', were more difficult to recognize than were neutral words. On the other hand, Aronfreed *et al.* (1953) showed that unpleasant words were perceived more slowly, pleasant and neutral words equally easily. Newton (1955) found a greater number of errors in perceiving unpleasant than pleasant words. These had been equated for frequency of usage.

In later experiments, Newbigging (1961) showed that response time and minimum time for recognition were shorter for pleasant words such as 'graceful', 'lovable', etc., than for unpleasant words such as 'putrid', 'sickness', etc. It is possible that some of these words may have been less common and familiar than others. However, Johnson *et al.* (1961) controlled for frequency of usage, and obtained similar results for pleasant and unpleasant words. Moreover, recognition times were not related to the frequency of the words they used. On the other hand, Doehring (1962) found a variation with frequency, but none with pleasantness and unpleasantness.

Further evidence as to the effects of unpleasant stimuli was given by measurement of the *GSR*. Aronfreed *et al.* (1953) found that GSR responses were greater to unpleasant than to pleasant and neutral words. These did not occur, as in responses to pain, before the words were perceived, but when they had been perceived. Again, it would seem that even delayed full recognition does not preclude recognition of parts of words. Fuhrer and Eriksen (1961) found that words presented below threshold could be matched to words of similar structural characteristics, but not to those of similar emotional connotations. Thus structure had been partially perceived without the full recognition necessary for understanding of meaning.

It would seem therefore that the effects of pleasantness and unpleasantness may be variable and not very extensive. But some of these words may have given rise to actual emotion, in which case the effect on perception might have been greater. In fact, a large number of experiments has been carried out, again with somewhat variable results, to study the effects of *unpleasant emotions* on perception. The first experiment of this kind was performed by Bruner and Postman (1947), using the free association technique. For each observer, the six words with the fastest reaction time, the six with the slowest and six with intermediate reaction times, were selected and presented a fortnight later for tachistoscopic perception. It was found that with some observers there was a steady increase in the time necessary for perception as the emotionality of the words, measured by the reaction times, increased. With other observers, perception time increased up to a certain point and then decreased. Thus it appeared that some observers showed selective '*vigilance*' or 'sensitization' to highly emotional words; others perceptual '*defence*' or avoidance. Now in this experiment there was no control for frequency of usage of the more and less emotional words. But De Lucia and Stagner (1954) obtained a similar curvilinear relationship between perception time and reaction time in free association – an increase of the former as reaction time increased, followed by a decrease – even when word frequency was controlled. It was hypothesized that perception of mildly unpleasant words, which could be safely ignored, was inhibited, whereas there was sensitization to words which might arouse ego defence. It must be noted, however, that this curvilinear relationship was established only for the whole group of twenty observers; no evidence was cited that it held in individual cases. Thus it seems possible that some observers were predominantly vigilant and others mainly defensive in their perceptions.

The same criticism applies to the support given subsequently by

Brown (1961) to the existence of the curvilinear relationship, and to the experiment he carried out himself. He found that this relationship between perception time and emotionality as measured by reaction time in free association held for a group of well-adjusted women; but not for poorly adjusted women, in whom there was no significant relationship. Male observers showed a steady rise of perception time throughout. Brown therefore concluded that the words were less emotional for the men than for the women, who showed vigilance at the highest levels of emotionality. But again results from single individuals are necessary to establish that one and the same person is first of all defensive and then vigilant. There is one piece of evidence for this hypothesis, provided by Neel (1954), who showed that observers presented with pictures of people engaged in aggressive activities exhibited avoidance to mildly aggressive pictures, but increased sensitivity to pictures openly showing hostile situations. However, the opposite effect occurred with pictures of sexual activities; there was sensitivity to mild sexuality, and increased avoidance of directly sexual situations. Other evidence has suggested that certain personalities tend to be uniformly vigilant, others defensive and repressive. Thus Chodorkoff (1956) found that the amount of effect exerted on perception time was related to the degree of emotional threat, but this effect might be either positive or negative. Those shown by the Rorschach test to be relatively well adjusted showed sensitization; those less well adjusted, defence.

Now some of the words utilized by Bruner and Postman and by De Lucia and Stagner were words with sexual meanings, termed '*taboo*' words, in that observers might experience a conflict when they read them between sexual arousal and repression of words not normally uttered in polite society. A very large number of experiments carried out since has employed such taboo words, which have been supposed by the experimenters to have highly emotional effects, though these have not in fact been measured by the free association technique. Some experiments have demonstrated sensitization, others defence. Thus McGinnies (1949) found that taboo words such as 'raped', 'belly', 'whore', 'penis', were perceived more slowly by all observers than were neutral words; and GSR responses arising before the words were recognized were greater for the taboo than for the neutral words. The guesses made before recognition as to what the taboo words were indicated resistance to recognizing them. Thus autonomic reactions to the anxiety-arousing words occurred before they were fully recognized, a 'subception' effect similar to that which appeared in the experiment of Lazarus and McCleary (see p. 213).

We have noted that, according to De Lucia and Stagner, the relationship between emotionality and perception time was independent of frequency of usage. However, Fulkerson (1957) found that low frequency taboo words were perceived more readily than neutral words of similar frequency; whereas there was little difference between high frequency taboo and neutral words. However, he pointed out that frequency as measured by the Thorndike-Lorge word count is really no guarantee of their actual familiarity for any particular observer. He considered that the low frequency taboo words might be more familiar than the neutral ones; and this might indeed be true for young male observers, as the findings of Postman *et al.* (1953) suggested. But some of the sexual slang words might be unknown to young women. They would, however, be familiar with words such as 'rape' and 'whore'. Yet a later experiment by Dixon (1958b) showed that women were relatively slower than men to perceive the latter word.

Another explanation for these effects would be that observers would hardly expect to be shown taboo words in the setting of a university psychological laboratory! Several experiments were therefore performed to discover the effect of giving observers some forewarning. Postman *et al.* (1953) found that observers who were told that they would be shown some taboo words subsequently perceived them more quickly than neutral words, perhaps because they were *set* to perceive this type of word. Cowen and Beier (1950) showed that observers who had previously been read a list containing the taboo words subsequently were no slower on the average in perceiving blurred representations of these, though responses were variable and erratic. Without the preliminary alerting, the taboo words were perceived more slowly. But in later experiments (Beier and Cowen, 1953; Cowen and Beier, 1954), the taboo words were perceived more slowly by almost all observers. In another experiment (Cowen and Obrist, 1958), some observers were first read lists of neutral words, others lists of mixed taboo and neutral words and others taboo words only. They were told to expect to perceive similar words, but none of those presented for perception was the same as those read previously. Taboo words were perceived more slowly by the first two groups of observers, but there was no significant difference for the third group. It is possible that a stronger set to perceive taboo words was established here, which neutralized the defence effect that apparently occurred with the other observers.

Further light on the effects of expectation was thrown by an experiment by Lacy *et al.* (1953), who found that the first taboo word shown was perceived more slowly when taboo words were not expected, but not subsequent taboo words. Freeman (1954) also found that the effect of a previously established set to expect taboo words increased the speed with which they were perceived, provided that it was confirmed early in the series, but not otherwise. Finally, Wiener (1955) showed that words of ambiguous meaning, 'fairy', 'pussy', 'balls', 'screw', were perceived more readily when embedded in a context of taboo words than when presented in a context of neutral words. Here then the taboo effect facilitated perception.

However, a further objection was raised to the perceptual defence hypothesis similar to that described on p. 211 in connection with painful stimuli, namely that observers were delaying their *responses* rather than their perceptions of the taboo words. They were afraid to utter aloud words which were socially tabooed. In certain experiments, observers admitted this; thus Siegman (1956) noted that 77 per cent of his observers said that they had witheld their responses. In other cases observers may have delayed their responses without being fully aware that they were doing so. Postman *et al.* (1953) found that observers who were instructed to write down what they had perceived instead of saying it aloud reported taboo words more readily than neutral words. McGinnies and Sherman (1952) attempted to overcome dislike of saying taboo words by presenting a series of paired taboo and neutral words. The neutral word appeared just after the taboo word, and observers were required to report only the latter. These were still found to be perceived more slowly than were words preceded by other neutral words, suggesting that in the first case a defence effect had generalized from the taboo word to the associated neutral word. However, Forrest *et al.* (1965) explained this effect as resulting from a disruption of set; that is to say, observers expected to perceive a second taboo word and not a neutral one. When they presented nonsense words before neutral words, the same type of disruption occurred, and the neutral words were read more slowly. In another experiment (Taylor and Forrest, 1966), in which observers were first given lists of taboo or neutral words to read, the retardation of perception of a neutral word associated with a taboo word appeared after the previous reading of a neutral word list, but not after the reading of a taboo word list – an effect similar to those previously described in the reading of single words.

To return to the effects of *response bias*: Boardman (1957) claimed that early discrimination between taboo and neutral words occurred when observers were able to perceive fragments of the words without being able to perceive them completely. These fragments appeared in the guesses made before the whole words were reported, though the observers did not attach any meaning or emotional significance to them. But when the words were fully perceived, verbal report of the taboo words was inhibited. Kempler and Wiener (1963) also considered that when an observer was aware of partial cues only to the identity of a word, the response to these might be modified by the threat to social approval it constituted.

Another experiment suggesting that perceptual sensitization and defence do not occur in the absence of response bias with words which provoke anxiety but are not tabooed was performed by Goldstein *et al.* (1962). Observers were presented with cards on which, typed side by side, were a neutral word and a word giving rise to anxiety as judged from a previous free association test. In the perceptual test, observers had merely to say whether the anxiety provoking word or the neutral word was on the right or the left. The locations of anxiety and neutral words were reported equally accurately. Thus it appeared that there was neither sensitization to nor defence against the perception of anxiety words. But a contrary result was obtained by Minard (1965). Anxiety words were selected, on the basis of a free association test, and observers were informed that they would be shown these tachistoscopically, together with neutral words which they had also seen. In fact, half of these words were not presented, whereas in some cases only blurs were shown. Nevertheless, the observers often guessed that they had perceived the words not given them; but there was no response bias in their guesses towards emotional or neutral words. There was, however, some tendency to perceptual defence in male observers against the words actually perceived, and for sensitization in female observers.

Further evidence as to the effects of different types of response bias operating with taboo words was provided by an experiment by Barthel and Crowne (1962). They considered that there were individual differences in both perception and response which corresponded with the observer's goal and intentions in performing the task. In answer to the question, 'What was the experiment about?' some observers showed that they thought its performance related to social disapproval; others, to their keen-ness and ability to carry it out successfully. The former, if they possessed a strong need for social approval (as indicated by a questionnaire) took longer to report taboo words than neutral words; the latter did not. Moreover, the former admitted to witholding some taboo word responses, and to a fear of reporting these words until they were quite certain as to the experimenter's purpose. But Barthel and Crowne considered that some of the delay may have been due to shock, the effect of which decreased after a time.

It cannot be supposed, however, that voluntary response bias was operating in situations such as that in the experiment of McGinnies (1949), in which increased GSR responses occurred on presentation of taboo words before they were consciously perceived. As we noted, it has sometimes been supposed that perceptual defence operates through '*subception*', in that the observer perceives the taboo words subliminally and then inhibits their full perception. There is experimental evidence which seems to support the occurrence of such processes. Walters *et al.* (1959) found that neutral words which were preceded by the presentation of taboo words below the threshold of awareness were identified less correctly than neutral words preceded by sub-threshold neutral words.

We have noted the argument of Goldiamond (1958; see p. 98) that in experiments claimed to demonstrate the effects of subliminal perception and subception, the thresholds of vision have not been accurately measured, and that in fact the stimuli, or at least some fragments of them, have been perceived although the observers were unable to report the identity of the words exposed. However, this explanation does not seem valid in all cases. Thus Worthington (1964) presented taboo and neutral words at gradually increasing intensities of illumination to previously dark-adapted observers, and required them to report, firstly, when they were vaguely aware that a stimulus might be present; and secondly, when they were certain it was there, though not what it was. Although the taboo words were presented upside down, a substantially higher level of illumination was required to report the two stages for these than for neutral words. Moreover, with the taboo words there was a longer delay between the first and second stages.

A series of experiments by Dixon indicated similar subliminal effects. We noted on p. 97 that he found that the GSR and the delay in responding were greater for sexual words presented subliminally than for neutral words (1958a). However, Fuhrer and Eriksen (1961) were unable to obtain these effects. But Dixon (1958b), in order to prevent any possibility of conscious perception, carried out a further experiment in which he required his observers to view with one eye a light which they continuously adjusted to the threshold point. To the other eye, he presented taboo ('penis', 'whore') or neutral words at an illumination sufficiently far below threshold to be invisible. Nevertheless, the observers set the threshold for light at a higher intensity when taboo words were presented than with neutral words. Finally, Dixon and Haider (1961) found that the word 'cancer' produced an effect similar to that of the taboo words, and observers subsequently reported that this word did give rise to disturbing effects when consciously perceived. Thus it was concluded that certain words possess inhibitory qualities which affect the functioning of the reticular formation; and this may take place below the level of consciousness.

If indeed some inhibitory process is aroused by taboo or other anxiety-provoking words, its occurrence might be expected to vary in different individuals according as to whether they are prone to exercise such inhibition. *Individual differences* in the characteristics of inhibition and constrictedness of personality were assessed by Kissin *et al.* (1957) from responses to the Rorschach test. It was found that they correlated with a coefficient of 0·64 with the delay in recognition of taboo words by comparison with neutral words. But some highly inhibited observers showed very small delays. There was some response suppression, but the authors claimed that they corrected the times for perception accordingly. Eriksen (1952b) showed that observers who exhibited perceptual defence against highly emotional words, as estimated by the free association test, were also liable to forget their failures in performing tasks; that is to say, they were consistently inhibited.

Inhibition may of course be related to anxiety; and a number of experiments has been carried out to investigate the relation between *anxiety* and perceptual sensitization and defence. Unfortunately, measures of general disposition to feel anxiety are not very satisfactory, nor can one be certain that such a disposition necessarily operates in these experimental situations. Thus Bitterman and Kniffin (1953) found that observers rated on the MMPI as possessing a high degree of anxiety showed no greater delay in reporting taboo words, except the first, than did those rated low in anxiety. It was considered that response delay occurred with the first word. Siegman (1956), however, showed that observers assessed by means of the Taylor Manifest Anxiety test as liable to avoid and suppress anxiety did perceive taboo words more slowly than neutral words, although they had previously been shown the taboo words and indicated that they understood their meanings and regarded them as unpleasant. Therefore there was no unexpectedness, but there may have been some response suppression. However, this could not account for the fact that observers low in anxiety perceived taboo words more quickly than neutral ones. Smock (1956) found that observers rated high in anxiety on the Sarason and Gordon Test Anxiety scale were slower to perceive threat words, such as 'cheat' and 'guilt', than were observers rated low in anxiety. But this difference was eliminated when the threat words were shown before the perceptual task was carried out. This suggests that the anxiety of the high anxiety observers was removed by expectations as to what they would be shown.

However, it hardly explains the effect obtained by Osler and Lewinsohn (1954), that observers rated high in anxiety on the Taylor Scale perceived anxiety words more readily than neutral words matched for frequency, as contrasted with low anxiety observers who showed no differential effect. But as we noted above, scales such as the Taylor may not differentiate adequately between those who tend to react repressively to anxiety and those who react sensitively.

Matthews and Wertheimer (1958) found that observers who scored highly on the Hysteria scale of the MMPI, which may be related repression, were slower to perceive words which produced slow reaction times on the free association test. But those who scored high on the MMPI Psychasthenia scale, who might be expected to be alert to threat, showed no sensitization effect in perception of emotional words. A similar experiment by Bootzin and Natsoulas (1965) minimized the effects of response suppression by requiring observers to match each word perceived against one of a pair of words shown in a booklet. Observers high in anxiety were unaffected by the anxiety words. Those assessed as low in anxiety were less accurate at first in recognizing the anxiety words, but the effect decreased with repeated trials.

Thus it appears from many of the above experiments that observers who did not expect to be shown taboo words were slow to attribute such an identity to their fragmentary percepts, consisting of only a few letters; although the shock caused by even the possibility of such an identity might produce heightened GSR responses. If they had been alerted to the possible occurrence of such words, they might perceive them more quickly, unless they hesitated to say them openly. However, the subliminal effects described above, if indeed they were genuine, could not be attributed to the operation of a conscious set or repression. The effects of non-taboo emotional words can hardly be explained in terms of response bias. We must still be cautious in postulating the existence of an inhibitory process functioning below the level of consciousness; though Brown (1961) was convinced that autonomic processes aroused at a sub-cortical level could produce a feedback, *via* the reticular formation, affecting cortical identification. He further believed that this could be either inhibitory or facilitating; but, as we noted, the evidence for the occurrence of both these effects in one and the same person was weak. It seems more probable that facilitation occurs in some individuals and inhibition in others, according as to whether or not they are prone to inhibit anything which constitutes a threat to social security and acceptance.

However, it must again be emphasized that, as we noted on p. 6, study of individual differences in motivational effects has often failed to take into account the real nature of individual motivation as reported by the observers themselves. Thus lack of agreement between the findings of different experimenters may have been due to the fact that the motivation of their observers was not that which the experimenters sought to establish by their experimental design and instructions. A good illustration of such a variation is given by the experiment of Barthel and Crowne (p. 223), who by their enquiries established an explanation for it.

XII

The Effect on Perception of
Personality Characteristics

(1) Consistency in Modes of Perceiving

We have seen that perception may be facilitated or inhibited, and directed towards particular features of the environment, in accordance with knowledge, experience, interests and motives of particular persons. But it would seem that it may also be related to other aspects of the personality; to modes of perceiving which are based on general characteristics of the personality not specifically related to particular experiences, interests or motives.

If indeed perception is related to type of personality, it would be expected that there are *consistent modes of perception*, and that individual differences in the manner of perceiving would appear regularly in a number of different settings. Unfortunately relevant studies have been few. Moreover, there has been a tendency to group modes of perceiving into two contrasting types, such as the *synthetic* and *analytic*. These we noted especially in connection with the constancies; but they have also been postulated to function in perceiving visual illusions, apparent movement and causality. However, no evidence has been adduced as to whether particular individuals spontaneously adopt consistent synthetic or analytic procedures in perceptual experiments generally, still less in perceiving in normal everyday life. It seems quite possible that many if not most people vary their procedure according to the circumstances and to the nature of the task they think they are expected to perform.

However, Thurstone (1944) did carry out a very extensive investigation of differences in modes of perceiving in a large number of different perceptual situations. He administered to 170 students forty tests which included the perception of visual illusions, closure of Gestalt figures, alternating perspective, embedded and hidden figures, apparent movement, constancy, etc. The quantitative results of the observers on these tests were correlated and the correlations submitted to factorial analysis.

The *two main factors* extracted corresponded, firstly, to the ability to perceive closure rapidly and strongly and to maintain it during distraction; and secondly, to the ability to manipulate configurations flexibly and to pass easily from one configuration to another. However, it was not clear whether these differences were related to differences in intelligence, education or personality qualities.

The author found (1947) that certain characteristic *differences of ability* appeared in the tachistoscopic perception of simple and complex figures, letters, digits and pictures. The first was the ability to discriminate and perceive simple shapes and patterns; it may have corresponded to Thurstone's 'strength of closure'. The second type of ability, which functioned in the perception of representational and symbolic material such as pictures and letters, was the capacity to make inferences as to the identity and meaning of these. But it also varied considerably with different types of material, indicating that it was affected by different schemata established through experience, education and training, which varied in different observers. Some evidence of the effects of these factors was obtained in a subsequent experiment (Vernon, 1961) in which some of the vague blurred pictures of Phillipson's Object Relations Test (1955) were exposed tachistoscopically for successive short intervals of time. Now Kragh (1955) had found that when this technique was employed with somewhat different material, there was a tendency for observers to produce sequences of elaborate and varying inferences as to the contents of the material which were related to incidents in their past experience. But this rarely occurred in the author's experiment; the majority of observers reported either meaningless shapes or simple objects. Nevertheless, there were some cases in which more elaborate inferences were made, which were related to prevailing interests. Moreover, even the simpler identifications, in terms of patterns and objects, appeared to be affected to some extent by such factors. For instance, there were characteristic differences between the reports of Fine Art and Science students. The latter tended to report small details with objective accuracy; the former included comments on general formal properties, shading and contrast. It is possible, however, that response bias may have affected these reports.

(2) Relationship of Modes of Perceiving to Personality Qualities

These findings, although they suggest that there may be consistent modes of perceiving different types of material in experimental conditions, give little evidence as to the existence of any relationship between them and enduring personality qualities. Extensive work has in fact been carried out to investigate such relationships. But much of it is of doubtful value because of the tendency to group the personalities of those whose percepts are being studied into two contrasted '*types*', regarded as opposites; and to compare the differences in perception of these as they appear in a single experiment. The best-known dichotomy is the '*introvert-extravert*', and we have noted on p. 153 experiments in which introverts were claimed to perceive in one manner and extraverts in the opposite manner. We might of course argue that extraverts would be relatively more interested in the external environment, whereas introverts are concerned mainly with their own ideas about it; or that extraverts take a rather superficial global view of the surroundings, whereas introverts inspect them carefully and methodically. There does indeed seem to be some correspondence between introvert personality and analytic procedure on the one hand, and extravert personality and synthetic procedure on the other. However, it seems possible that extraverts are less able than introverts to conform to instructions requiring analytic procedures (Singer, 1952; Jenkin, 1958).

Investigations have also been made to relate perceptual *sensitization* and *defence* to introversion and extraversion. Brown (1961) summarized these as indicating that in the curvilinear relationship he postulated between emotionality and perception time, extraverts reached the peak of the curve sooner than did introverts; that is to say, the latter were slower to show the perceptual sensitization effect. But in these experiments neither emotionality nor introversion-extraversion were continuously graded; thus intermediate reactions were not studied. In his own experiment, well-adjusted extraverted female observers did reach the peak perception time at lower emotionality levels than did introverts, but no such relationship appeared in male observers.

It seems probable, however, that relationships between personality qualities and modes of perceiving are more subtle and varied than can be defined by a single dichotomous typology. Thus Pemberton (1952), for instance, related Thurstone's two main types of ability to personality qualities, and found that observers who showed a strong tendency to closure on a Gestalt completion test were on the whole outwardly and socially oriented, uninterested in analysing situations or theorizing about them. But those who showed considerable flexibility in manipulating configurations, in the Gottschaldt embedded figures test, were detached from the environment and lacking in sociability, possessing a tendency towards abstract analysis, with marked theoretical and scientific interests.

(3) The Studies of Witkin and his Colleagues

In the studies of Witkin and his colleagues, there has been an attempt to relate certain general modes of perceiving, not to single personality qualities but to general types of personality covering a number of different characteristics of these, and the various modes of perceiving have been investigated extensively. We noted on p. 137 that Witkin and Asch discovered characteristic differences in the manner in which tilted frameworks were perceived in otherwise dark rooms. Witkin *et al.* (1954) devised three tests based on these situations, the Rod and Frame test, the Tilted Room-Tilted Chair test and the Rotating Room test. In all these, observers were required to give estimates of the true vertical; and it was found that some observers located it as parallel to the visual framework, and others in accordance with their gravitational sensations of the vertical. Witkin (1949b) had also found that the latter type of observer was better able than the former to extract the embedded simple figures from the complex figures in a modification of the Gottschaldt test; and an Embedded Figures test was included in the 1954 study. Witkin *et al.* hypothesized that those who relied on the visual framework, whom they called '*field dependent*', were people greatly affected by standards derived from environmental pressures; whereas those who utilized their postural senses, termed '*field independent*', were people who relied on their own internal feelings and convictions. Observers were also given projection tests of personality, the Rorschach, T.A.T. and Figure-Drawing tests. The field dependent were said to be relatively passive, low in self-esteem and self-reliance, and ready to submit to external authority. They were lacking in awareness, understanding and acceptance of themselves, and anxious and fearful of their aggressive and sexual impules. By contrast, the field independent were active, socially independent, ready to struggle for mastery, able to come to terms with themselves and to analyse their perceptual performance.

These findings have met with some criticism. Postman (1955b) noted that the hypothesized types of perception and personality tended to be vague and metaphorical. There was no reason to suppose that the visually related judgments were more passive than those related to postural senses. Moreover, there were numerous individuals who were intermediate in their judgments. The reliability and validity of the projection test results were somewhat dubious. However, Young (1959) obtained substantial agreement with Witkin *et al.*, in that scores on the Rod and Frame and the Embedded Figures tests showed considerable intercorrelation. Also the field dependent, as assessed on the Rorschach and other personality tests, were relatively passive, self-distrusting and in-effectual in dealing with external demands. But Young pointed out that these characteristics were demonstrated only in tests such as the Rorschach which tapped unconscious tendencies, and not in tests of self-evaluation which operated at the conscious level.

Elliott (1961), however, obtained a correlation of only 0·4 between the results of the Rod and Frame test and the Embedded Figures test. Those assessed as highly field dependent on the Rod and Frame test did not appear to be more passive and helpless than others on a difficult puzzle test; nor did they show any inferiority in discriminating the personality characteristics of themselves and others. But they did seem to be more dependent on social approval, whereas the field independent were socially aloof and independent. On the other hand, Shrauger and Altrochi (1964) found that the field dependent were more likely than the independent to characterize other people in terms of external physical characteristics than of internal psychological characteristics. Though Elliott considered that the deficit in the field dependent was mainly intellectual, in the ability to cope with new and incongruous situations, he admitted that it might result from a failure in personality develop-ment. There would appear also to be some relation between field de-pendence and independence, and synthetic and analytic tendencies in perceiving. Thus Perez (1955, cited by Witkin *et al.*, 1962) found that the field independent were able to adopt either the analytic or the synthetic procedure in size constancy experiments, whereas the field dependent generally employed the synthetic procedure. Pressey (1967) showed that the field dependent were more susceptible to the Poggen-dorff illusion than were the field independent.

Witkin *et al.* (1954) also studied the development of field indepen-dence in children, and this study was extended in a later book (1962). They considered that field independence was related to *psychological differentiation* and the ability to segregate the self from the not-self. Field independence increased sharply between ten and thirteen years of age, but decreased somewhat between seventeen and twenty years. It was related to intelligence, but to non-verbal rather than to verbal performance on the WISC test; and also to a high level of structuring in the Rorschach test. But there were considerable differences in field independence not related to intelligence which persisted as the children grew older. The field independent perceived the environment, and also other persons, with greater clarity, objectivity and flexibility; were more competent and self-reliant and less socially conforming; and showed a greater capacity for directed action. Field dependence and independence were considered to be partly constitutional in origin, but also to be related to parental attitudes, especially to the mother's encouragement of freedom and independence.

¦ Throughout, boys were slightly more field independent than girls. But the field dependence of the latter increased sharply between seventeen and twenty years, and adult women were significantly more dependent than adult men. Corresponding differences appeared in the projection tests. Iscoe and Carden (1961) noted parallel differences in boys and girls of eleven years. Field independent boys were less anxious and more socially popular than were field dependent, but the reverse was true for girls. Thus it would appear that these characteristics are modified by social conventions, which favour independence in boys and dependence in girls.

(4) The Findings and Theories of Gardner, Klein and Others

The field independence-field dependence relationship would again appear to endeavour to incorporate too wide a range of perceptual characteristics and personality qualities within a single dichotomous classification. It would seem wiser to consider field dependence and independence merely as one aspect of the manner in which people perceive and react to the environment. In fact it has been included as one dimension in a much broader and more varied classification of the principles of '*cognitive control*', designed by Gardner and his colleagues at the Menninger Clinic. They termed it '*field articulation*', and hypothesized that it appeared as selectiveness of attention, the capacity to direct attention appropriately to the significant features of the field, and to disregard irrelevant aspects. It was also related to Thurstone's flexibility of closure. Gardner (1961) assessed field articulation by means of the Rod and Frame and Embedded Figures tests, and found it was also related to the magnitude of the Müller-Lyer illusion.

Another important type of cognitive control, independent of field articulation, was *extensiveness of scanning*; that is to say, the tendency to deploy attention broadly over a wide field, or to concentrate it narrowly on a small area. The latter behaviour was of the same nature as Piaget's centration (1961). It could be measured directly from the number of eye fixations made in regarding the field (Gardner and Long, 1962a). It was also demonstrated in the estimation of size of circles containing drawings of faces, etc. (Schlesinger, 1954). These were over-estimated to a greater extent by narrow than by wide scanners. The horizontal-vertical illusion was greater for narrow than for wide scanners, who presumably compared the horizontal and vertical lines more carefully (Gardner, 1961). A further test, the Stroop Color Word test (Stroop 1935), was also used at one time to investigate scanning. The essential feature of this test is that the observer is given a list of colour names printed in colours which differ from the name, and is required to name the colours, not read the colour names. It is hypothesized that this task necessitates the inhibition of immediate response; and it was found that the capacity to perform it rapidly correlated with width of scanning (Gardner and Long, 1962b). However, in later enquiries (Gardner and Moriarty, 1968) performance on this test was said to relate to another type of cognitive control, the *constricted-flexible*, operating in the inhibition of irrelevant motor responses.

An earlier suggestion by Klein (1951) was that two types of perception could be differentiated in some situations, '*sharpening*' and '*levelling*'. These terms were perhaps derived from the opposed tendencies demonstrated by Wulf (1922) to operate in the recall of certain complex shapes. In successive reproductions of these, there was a consistent tendency to diverge from the originals either by accentuating certain peculiarities, or by reducing them, towards symmetry. However, no connection with these results was implied by Klein, who found that some observers showed a characteristic tendency towards sharpening, others towards levelling, in several experimental settings. In the first experiment, observers were presented with a series of squares of gradually decreasing size, one at a time, and required to judge the size of each one. After five squares had been presented, the smallest was removed, unknown to the observer, and a larger one was added. In this way the observer judged successive series gradually increasing in magnitude. It was found that some observers, the sharpeners, kept pace with the changes and judged the sizes of the squares accurately. Others, the levellers, responded slowly to the changes, lagged behind and progressively under-estimated. It would seem that they developed a stable preconceived notion of the range of sizes, and assimilated their subsequent percepts to this, rather than considering each stimulus on its merit. Levellers also perceived less clearly than sharpeners the contrast between grey squares, surrounded by contour lines, placed on a background of a different grey. Again, the comparison between one brightness and another was more affected by an interpolated brightness with levellers than with sharpeners (Holzman, 1954). And levellers showed a stronger tendency than sharpeners to assimilate together two rather similar figures presented successively, under distraction (see Fig. 27, p. 88; Gardner and Lohrenz, 1961).

It seems possible that this type of behaviour is related to that demonstrated by Bruner and Tajfel (1961), who exhibited clusters of dots to their observers and required them to say whether a cluster did or did not contain twenty dots. When the numbers in the clusters varied, some observers, termed 'narrow categorizers', shifted their estimates appropriately. Others, 'broad categorizers', tended to maintain their estimates in spite of changes in the stimulus conditions. Bruner and Tajfel considered that the former were liable to react rapidly even if their responses were wrong; but the latter were afraid of making wrong responses, and therefore adjusted slowly.

A fourth type of cognitive control was termed originally, by Klein and Schlesinger (1951), 'form-bounded' *versus* 'form-labile'. Later it was called *'tolerance of perceptual ambiguity'* (Gardner and Moriarty, 1968). It appeared in the perception of apparent movement phenomena. The more tolerant perceived apparent movement over a wider range of conditions. They also showed more free imagination in responses to the Rorschach ink-blots, whereas the less tolerant gave narrow and constricted responses limited to the more obvious characteristics of the ink-blots. The less tolerant were also less ready to perceive the distortions produced by viewing through aniseikonic lenses, and had lower thresholds for flicker fusion. Loomis and Moskowitz (1958) demonstrated a relationship between tolerance of perceptual ambiguity, or of unrealistic experiences, and constricted and flexible control. They exhibited a series of pictures in which a sheep was gradually modified to a landscape. Those who had shown constricted control on the Color Word test were less able than those with flexible control to see both the sheep and the trees of the landscape in the same picture. The constricted tended to restructure the ambiguities of the picture into something more definite and meaningful.

A variety of personality characteristics has been hypothesized to be related to these dimensions of cognitive control, but these appear to have varied somewhat in successive studies. Moreover, Gardner, Klein and their colleagues seemed to be more concerned to trace relationships with the unconscious characteristics postulated by Freudian theory, and particularly with the mechanisms of ego defence, than with conscious and overt motivational trends. Thus wide scanning, indicated by other experiments to appear in delayed and careful judgment and the tendency to obtain the maximum amount of information about a situation before responding to it, was considered to be related to ego defence through isolation and projection, as exhibited in Rorschach responses and the capacity to segregate cognitive processes from emotional associations

(Gardner and Long, 1962a). In stress conditions, wide scanners tended to increase scanning behaviour, whereas narrow scanners decreased it (Hoffman, 1968). Levelling was said to be related to ego defence through repression (Holzman and Gardner, 1959). Klein (1951) attributed form-boundedness, hence intolerance of perceptual ambiguity, to rigidity; but Loomis and Moskowitz (1958) did not accept this connection. There was apparently some association between field dependence and repression (Witkin *et al.*, 1962). But according to Gardner *et al.* (1968) it was more closely related to differences in objectivity and detachment from others and to personal autonomy. Messick and Fritsky (1963) also found a relationship between field independence and analytical categorizing, and the tendency to articulate together the discrete elements of forms.

Now it is difficult to understand why in ordinary circumstances in which no particular stress is involved there should be any connection between manner of perceiving and mechanisms of defence. It must be remembered, however, that according to Freudian theory the ego is continually obliged to defend itself, even during its ordinary interaction with the environment, against the onslaughts of the id. But to those not committed to belief in Freudian theory, it would appear more probable that manner of perceiving is associated with personality traits such as those suggested by Witkin. It would seem from Gardner's most recent publication (Gardner and Moriarty, 1968) that he also is now more dubious as to the significance of associations between perceiving and the mechanisms of defence. This book describes a study of cognitive controls and a large variety of personality characteristics in children aged nine to thirteen years. Though several of the controls appeared to operate consistently in perceptual experiments in these children, some, notably sharpening and levelling, were absent. Certain mechanisms of defence could be assessed from personality ratings, but there was little correlation between these and cognitive controls; except that there was a slight association between field articulation and repression. A more important relationship appeared between the former and a capacity to articulate experience generally, in activities other than perceptual. Another important control was adequacy of reality testing, associated with delayed response and good impulse control. Extensiveness of scanning, however, was unrelated to defence through isolation, or to other personality factors.

It was clear from these studies that the associations between modes of perceiving, as determined by cognitive controls, and personality qualities were more ambiguous and less straightforward, and more variable with age, than suggested by the earlier studies of Gardner and his colleagues. It would appear that the controls themselves may be fairly consistent in operation. Thus Gardner and Long (1960) found good test and re-test correlations in the size estimation test of scanning and the shifting squares test of levelling-sharpening. But as Gardner and Moriarty (1968) pointed out, there may be other important controls on modes of perceiving which they have not investigated; and other personality characteristics may be involved which they did not assess. Thus it would seem wise to regard with great caution the existence of limitations on speed and accuracy of perception imposed by personality factors, at least in normal observers.

XIII

Conclusions

It would seem difficult to draw any conclusions except of a very general nature from the experimental data discussed in this book. In many cases experimental investigations appear to have raised many more queries than they can answer. This is due in part to the lack of agreement on many points of different experimenters; and in part to the comparative neglect of certain important areas of enquiry. It is true that variation in experimental findings is to some extent a natural consequence of variation in the conditions of experiment and the stimulus material used. Sometimes quite small changes in these produce a large alteration in results, even a complete reversal; and such alterations may be difficult to explain because the fundamental factors in the situation have been inadequately gauged and defined. In particular, their impact on the observer and his understanding of and reaction to the situation have been insufficiently considered. There has frequently been a failure to take into account the schematic background on which the observer's perceptions are based; his equipment of knowledge, skills, established expectations. These factors may be operative to a greater extent in laboratory experiments than in ordinary perception in natural surroundings. The experimental situation is almost inevitably impoverished, and the observer is obliged to employ his perceptual processes in an unusual manner, to obtain information from partial cues and to attempt to infer from them the nature of the whole event. In natural surroundings, redundancy of information makes it possible for him to utilize those features which he perceives spontaneously and readily. Thus except with brief, sudden and unexpected events, or unless the surroundings are restricted by natural causes (as in very dim light, for instance), perception is usually sufficiently rapid and veridical to enable the observer to react quickly and appropriately. It is because of this fundamental difference between laboratory and natural surroundings that the value of observations made in the latter condition has been stressed. We need to know far more as to what aspects of the natural environment are selected in perception, how percepts of these are integrated and to what inferences and actions they lead.

It is undoubtedly true that considerable advances have been made in studying and understanding the origins and development of perception in children. Nevertheless there still exist many gaps in our knowledge. Thus, if perception begins with the responses of cell units in the visual mechanisms to lines in different orientations, how are these integrated into the patterns and configurations which, it has been recognized since the work of the Gestalt psychologists, are of fundamental significance in perception? We noted that infants appeared to perceive and differentiate patterns; but no data are available as to their responses to the types of configuration studied by the Gestalt psychologists. Do infants in fact perceive 'good' Gestalten more readily than the less 'good'? Here it is difficult to differentiate in infants the tendency to spend time in exploring patterns possessing a high degree of randomness or uncertainty, in order to discover their nature and structure; and the possible attraction of 'good' forms as such. There then arises a further problem, occurring in adult perception also: Can 'goodness' in the Gestalt sense be equated with redundancy and lack of uncertainty? Such an equation may be possible for qualities such as symmetry, regularity and simplicity, but appears improbable with regard to aspects such as continuity, completion and articulation of the parts within the whole. From what we know at present, it seems inevitable to suppose that there exists natural tendencies to perceive configurations as continuous coherent wholes. These appear to exert so strong an influence on perception as to give rise to illusory perception which it is impossible to overcome. Yet in spite of this, in certain respects the perception of form and pattern increases in accuracy with age, as the result of maturation and learning.

When we turn to consider the perception of objects, which constitutes the overwhelming bulk of our everyday life perception, it becomes even harder to trace any relationship to the perception of lines and even of complex non-representational forms. It cannot be supposed that object perception is innate, though it could be hypothesized that the infant possesses an innate tendency to perceive not only form but also the natural environment in terms of objects, and that this comes into operation as his experiences of objects develop. It might also be supposed that the infant has a natural tendency to perceive a spatial continuum within which objects are spatially related to himself and to each other. Nevertheless we have suggested that from infancy upwards the child builds up complex integrations, or schemata, by means of which what is perceived at any moment is related to memories and knowledge, particularly that obtained through the active experience of manipulating objects and moving through the environment. Furthermore, the processes of reasoning and of conceptual classification come to bear on these schemata, in such a manner that immediate perception is modified and corrected to give rise to more veridical impressions of the environment. In spatial judgments particularly an extensive system of concepts is involved to which immediate percepts are normally related. But in all complex stimulus situations cognitive processes of inference, reasoning and judgment may be employed in coding incoming information. It is likely that the outcome of this is labile and widely variable. On the other hand, object percepts in certain respects are stable; thus they resist modification through variation in background conditions, as is apparent in the property of 'constancy'. Yet even this is not universally operative, and may vary as the result of the observer's attitudes and judgments. And these again may differ in natural surroundings and in those of the laboratory experiment.

It would seem that perception and the other associated cognitive processes are integrated within schemata which develop maximally along particular lines in accordance with experience and sometimes through special training. Thus not only is perception likely to be the most rapid and accurate in relevant situations but also expectations are established such that attention is quickly aroused and effectively directed towards these situations as soon as they occur. Nevertheless from infancy upwards an innate tendency operates to respond to novel, incongruous and unexpected events by rapidly switching attention and directing it towards these events and sometimes proceeding to immediate appropriate action. However, more deliberate perception and inference may be necessary to gain a full understanding of the situation before action takes place. There can be little doubt that the ability to respond to a constantly varying environment is one of our most fundamental inborn tendencies.

Among the most frequent environmental variations is movement. We have noted that attentional response to and perception of movement as such appear almost from birth, and would seem to be innate. Nevertheless, just as particular static forms are schematized in the perception and identification of objects, so also certain movement patterns become associated with classes of objects and events. It might be supposed that there is an innate tendency to perceive movement patterns characteristic of living objects, including the expressive movements of people. Perception of smiling faces is an instance in point. However, it is difficult to be certain that learning through experience does not exert some influence even on the inception of these perceptions. Obviously they are again enormously refined and improved through learning.

We have noted that there is an important interaction between the perception of form and movement such that shapes which are ill-defined and imperfectly perceived when stationary may be spontaneously and readily identified when they are in movement. It would seem that two processes are at work. In the first place, a form moving across a stationary background stands out and is perceived, possibly through the arousal of responses in the cell units of the visual mechanism. Secondly, the constituent parts or aspects of a form are integrated together by their movements in relation to each other. It may be that here a schema comes into operation which coordinates the regular and inter-related modifications of form that occur with changes in orientation. Such schemata are acquired by the infant and young child in their manipulation and examination of objects.

We have seen that there may be an innate tendency to perceive the spatial characteristics of the surroundings; that is to say, the infant has an innate disposition not only to differentiate 'figure' from 'ground' but also to attribute spatial extension to the 'ground'. Probably also there is an innate though somewhat rudimentary appreciation of the position of the body in space, and particularly in relation to the gravitational coordinate. However, again the exact perception of these spatial relations can be acquired only through learning. It appears from the investigations into the effects of wearing distorting lenses that very powerful and complex schemata are developed involving all the sensory information available as to position and orientation, and that these are strongly resistant to modification, though some change may be effected through active learning.

A considerable proportion of this book has been devoted to the discussion of experimental work on the effects on perception of individual motivation and personality qualities, mainly in order to elucidate the very extensive findings of these experiments. Yet is has appeared that such effects may be inconsiderable except in highly restricted circumstances. It is the author's belief that their main effects are indirect, functioning through the varied acquisition by different individuals of particular knowledge and skills. These modify or even initiate the organization of schemata which direct selective attention and improved discrimination, identification and reaction along particular lines, yet without impairing the veridical perception of the environment which is essential for the maintenance of life in a constantly varying and challenging environment. Much further investigation is necessary to discover and define the nature and mode of operation of these schematic organizations.

References

ADAMS, G. K. (1923) 'An experimental study of memory color and related phenomena.' *Amer. J. Psychol.*, **34**, 359.

ADAMS, O. S., FITTS, P. M., RAPPAPORT, M. and WEINSTEIN, M. (1954) 'Relations among some measures of pattern discriminability'. *J. Exper. Psychol.*, **48**, 81.

ALLPORT, G. W. and PETTIGREW, T. F. (1957) 'Cultural influence on the perception of movement: the trapezoidal illusion among Zulus. *J. Ab. Soc. Psychol.*, **55**, 104.

ALLPORT, G. W., VERNON, P. E. and LINDZEY, G. (1951) *Study of Values*. Boston: Houghton Mifflin.

ALPERN, M. (1953) 'Metacontrast'. *J. Opt. Soc. Amer.*, **43**, 648.

AMBROSE, J. A. (1960) 'The smiling response in early human infancy'. *Unpublished Ph.D. Thesis*, University of London.

AMBROSE, J. A. (1961) 'The development of the smiling response in early infancy'. In B. M. Foss (Ed.), *Determinants of Infant Behaviour*, II. London: Methuen.

AMES, A. (1946) *Some Demonstrations Concerned with the Origin and Nature of Our Sensations*. Dartmouth Eye Institute.

AMES, A. (1951) 'Visual perception and the rotating trapezoidal window'. *Psychol. Monog.*, **65**, No. 7.

AMES, L. B. and LEARNED, J. (1948) 'The development of verbalized space in the young child'. *J. Genet. Psychol.*, **72**, 63.

AMES, L. B., LEARNED, J., METRAUX, R. and WALKER, R. (1953) 'Development of perception in the young child as observed in responses to the Rorschach Test blots'. *J. Genet. Psychol.*, **82**, 183.

ANDERSON, N. S. and LEONARD, J. A. (1958) 'The recognition, naming and reconstruction of visual figures as a function of contour redundancy'. *J. Exper. Psychol.*, **56**, 262.

ANSTIS, S. M. and GREGORY, R. L. (1965) 'The after-effect of seen motion: the role of retinal stimulation and of eye movements'. *Quart. J. Exper. Psychol.*, **17**, 262.

ARDIS, J. A. and FRASER, E. (1957) 'Personality and perception: the constancy effects and introversion'. *Brit. J. Psychol.*, **48**, 48.

ARNOLD, P., MEUDELL, P. R. and PEASE, K. G. (1968) 'Influence of meaning on fragmentation of visual after images'. *Percept. Motor Skills*, **27**, 965.

ARNOULT, M. D. and PRICE, C. W. (1961) 'Pattern matching in the presence of visual noise'. *J. Exper. Psychol.*, **62**, 372.

ARONFREED, J. M., MESSICK, S. A. and DIGGORY, J. C. (1953) 'Re-examining emotionality and perceptual defense'. *J. Pers.*, **21**, 517.

ASCH, S. E. and WITKIN, H. A. (1948a) 'Studies in space orientation, I: Perception of the upright with displaced visual fields'. *J. Exper. Psychol.*, **38**, 325.

ASCH, S. E. and WITKIN, H. A. (1948b) 'Studies in space orientation, II: Perception of the upright with displaced visual fields and with body tilted'. *J. Exper. Psychol.*, **38**, 455.

ASCH, S. E., CERASO, J. and HEIMER, W. (1960) 'Perceptual conditions of association'. *Psychol. Monog.*, **74**, No. 3.

ATTNEAVE, F. (1954) 'Some informational aspects of visual perception'. *Psychol. Rev.*, **61**, 183.

ATTNEAVE, F. (1955) 'Symmetry information and memory for patterns'. *Amer. J. Psychol.*, **68**, 209.

ATTNEAVE, F. (1957) 'Physical determinants of the judged complexity of shapes'. *J. Exper. Psychol.*, **53**, 221.

BABSKA, Z. (1965) 'The formation of the conception of identity of visual characteristics of objects seen successively'. *Monog. Soc. Res. Child Devel.*, **30**, No. 2.

BAGBY, J. W. (1957) 'A cross-cultural study of perceptual predominance in binocular rivalry'. *J. Ab. Soc. Psychol.*, **54**, 331.

BAHRICK, H. R., FITTS, P. M. and RANKIN, R. E. (1952) 'Effect of incentives upon reaction to peripheral stimuli'. *J. Exper. Psychol.*, **44**, 400.

BAIRD, J. C. (1963) 'Retinal and assumed size cues as determinants of size and distance perception'. *J. Exper. Psychol.*, **66**, 155.

BAKAN, P. (1955) 'Discrimination decrement as a function of time in a prolonged vigil'. *J. Exper. Psychol.*, **50**, 387.

BAKER, C. H. (1956) 'Biasing attention to visual displays during a vigilance task'. Cited in D. E. Broadbent, *Perception and Communication*. London: Pergamon.

BAKER, C. H. (1958) 'Attention to visual displays during a vigilance task, I: Biasing attention'. *Brit. J. Psychol.*, **49**, 279.

BAKER, C. H. (1959) 'Attention to visual displays during a vigilance task, II: Maintaining the level of vigilance'. *Brit. J. Psychol.*, **50**, 30.

BAKER, C. H. (1963) 'Further towards a theory of vigilance'. In D. N. Buckner and J. J. McGrath (Eds.), *Vigilance: A Symposium*. New York: McGraw-Hill.

BARRETT, G. V. and WILLIAMSON, T. R. (1966) 'Sensation of depth with one or two eyes'. *Percept. Motor Skills*, **23**, 895.

BARTHEL, C. E. and CROWNE, D. P. (1962) 'The need for approval, task categorization and perceptual defense'. *J. Consult. Psychol.*, **26**, 547.

BARTLETT, F. C. (1932) *Remembering*. Cambridge University Press.

BARTLETT, F. C. (1943) 'Fatigue following highly skilled work'. *Proc. Roy. Soc.*, *B*. **131**, 247.

BEAMS, H. L. (1954) 'Affectivity as a factor in the apparent size of pictured food objects'. *J. Exper. Psychol.*, **47**, 197.

BEATTY, F. S., DAMERON, L. E. and GREENE, J. E. (1959) 'An investigation of the effects of reward and punishment on visual perception'. *J. Psychol.*, **47**, 267.

BECK, J. (1961) 'Judgments of surface illumination and lightness'. *J. Exper. Psychol.*, **61**, 368.

BECK, J. (1965) 'Apparent spatial position and the perception of lightness'. *J. Exper. Psychol.*, **69**, 170.

BECK, J. (1966) 'Perceptual grouping produced by changes in orientation and shape'. *Science*, **154**, 538.

BECK, J. and GIBSON, J. J. (1955) 'The relation of apparent shape to apparent slant in the perception of objects'. *J. Exper. Psychol.*, **50**, 125.

BEELER, G. W., FENDER, D. H., NOBEL, P. S. and EVANS, C. R. (1964) 'Perception of pattern and colour in the stabilized retinal image'. *Nature*, **203**, 1200.

BEERY, K. E. (1068) 'Form reproduction as a function of complexity'. *Percept. Motor Skills*, **26**, 219.

BEIER, E. G. and COWEN, E. L. (1953) 'A further investigation of the influence of "threat-expectancy" on perception'. *J. Pers.*, **22**, 254.

BENDER, M. B. and TEUBER, H.-L. (1946) 'Ring scotoma and tubular fields'. *Arch. Neurol. Psychiat.*, **56**, 300.

BENNETT-CLARK, H. C. and EVANS, C. R. (1963) 'Fragmentation of patterned targets when viewed as prolonged after-images'. *Nature*, **199**, 1216.

BERLYNE, D. E. (1951) 'Atttention to change'. *Brit. J. Psychol.*, **42**, 269.

BERLYNE, D. E. (1957) 'Conflict and information-theory variables as determinants of human perceptual curiosity'. *J. Exper. Psychol.*, **53**, 399.

BERLYNE, D. E. (1958) 'The influence of complexity and novelty in visual figures on orienting responses'. *J. Exper. Psychol.*, **55**, 289.

BERLYNE, D. E. (1960) *Conflict, Arousal and Curiosity.* New York: McGraw-Hill.

BERLYNE, D. E. (1963) 'Complexity and incongruity variables as determinants of exploratory choice and evaluative ratings'. *Canad. J. Psychol.*, **17**, 274.

BERLYNE, D. E., CRAW, M. A., SALAPATEK, P. H. and LEWIS, J. L. (1963) 'Novelty, complexity, incongruity, extrinsic motivation and the GSR'. *J. Exper. Psychol.*, **66**, 560.

BERLYNE, D. E. and LAWRENCE, G. H. (1964) 'Effects of complexity and incongruity variables on GSR, investigatory behavior and verbally expressed preference'. *J. Gen. Psychol.*, **71**, 21.

BERLYNE, D. E. and LEWIS, J. L. (1963) 'Effects of heightened arousal on human exploratory behavior'. *Canad. J. Psychol.*, **17**, 398.

BERRY, J. W. (1968) 'Ecology, perceptual development and the Müller-Lyer illusion'. *Brit. J. Psychol.*, **59**, 205.

BEVAN, W., DUKES, W. F. and AVANT, L. L. (1966) 'The effect of variation in specific stimuli on memory for their superordinates'. *Amer. J. Psychol.*, **79**, 250.

BEVAN, W. and ZENER, K. (1952) 'Some influences of past experience upon the perceptual thresholds of visual form'. *Amer. J. Psychol.*, **65**, 434.

BEVERIDGE, W. M. (1935) 'Racial differences in phenomenal regression'. *Brit. J. Psychol.*, **26**, 59.

BEXTON, W. H., HERON, W. and SCOTT, T. H. (1954) 'Effects of decreased variation in the sensory environment'. *Canad. J. Psychol.*, **8**, 70.

BINDER, A. (1958) 'Personality variables and recognition response level'. *J. Ab. Soc. Psychol.*, **57**, 136.

BITTERMAN, M. E. and KNIFFIN, C. W. (1953) 'Manifest anxiety and "perceptual defense"'. *J. Ab. Soc. Psychol.*, **48**, 248.

BITTERMAN, M. E., KRAUSKOPF, J. and HOCHBERG, J. (1954) 'Threshold for visual form: a diffusion model'. *Amer. J. Psychol.*, **67**, 205.

BITTERMAN, M. E. and WORCHEL, P. (1953) 'The phenomenal vertical and horizontal in blind and sighted subjects'. *Amer. J. Psychol.*, **66**, 598.

BOARDMAN, W. K. (1957) 'Utilization of word structures in pre-recog nition hypotheses'. *J. Pers.*, **25**. 672.

BOLLES, R. C. and BAILEY, D. E. (1956) 'Importance of object recognition in size constancy'. *J. Exper. Psychol.*, **51**, 222.

BOOTZIN, R. R. and NATSOULAS, T. (1965) 'Evidence for perceptual defense uncontaminated by response bias'. *J. Pers. Soc. Psychol.*, **1**, 461.

BORING, E. G. (1930) 'A new ambiguous figure'. *Amer. J. Psychol.*, **42**, 444.

BORING, E. G. and TITCHENER, E. B. (1923) 'A model for demonstration of facial expressions'. *Amer. J. Psychol.*, **34**, 471.

BORRESEN, C. R. and LICHTE, W. H. (1962) 'Shape constancy: dependence upon stimulus familiarity'. *J. Exper. Psychol.*, **63**, 91.

BOWER, T. G. R. (1965) 'Stimulus variables determining space perception in infants'. *Science*, **149**, 88.

BOWER, T. G. R. (1966a) 'The visual world of infants'. *Scient. Amer.*, **215**, (6), 80.

BOWER, T. G. R. (1966b) 'Slant perception and shape constancy in infants'. *Science*, **151**, 832.

BOWER, T. G. R. (1967) 'Phenomenal identity and form perception in an infant'. *Percept. & Psychophys.*, **2**, 74.

BOYCE, P. R. (1967) 'Monocular fixation in human eye movement', *Proc. Roy. Soc.*, B, **167**, 293.

BOYCE, P. R. and WEST, D. C. (1967) 'A perceptual effect on the control of fixation'. *Optica Acta*, **14**, 119.

BOYNTON, R. M. and BUSH, W. R. (1956) 'Recognition of forms against a complex background'. *J. Opt. Soc. Amer.*, **46**, 758.

BRAND, H. (1954) 'Variability in perceptual dimensions'. *J. Pers.*, **22**. 395.

BRENNAN, W. M., AMES, E. W. and MOORE, R. W. (1966) 'Age differences in infants' attention to patterns of different complexities'. *Science*, **151**, 354.

BRENNER, M. W. (1956) 'The effect of meaning on apparent movement'. *J. Nat. Inst. Pers. Res.*, **6**, 125.

BRENNER, M. W. (1957) 'The developmental study of apparent movement'. *Quart. J. Exper. Psychol.*, **9**, 169.

BRICKER, P. D. and CHAPANIS, A. (1953) 'Do incorrectly perceived tachistoscopic stimuli convey some information?' *Psychol. Rev.*, **60**, 181.

BROADBENT, D. E. (1958) *Perception and Communication*. London: Pergamon.

BROADBENT, D. E. (1963) 'Possibilities and difficulties in the concept of vigilance'. In D. N. Buckner and J. J. McGrath (Eds.), *Vigilance: A Symposium*. New York: McGraw-Hill.

BROADBENT, D. E. and GREGORY, M. (1963) 'Vigilance considered as a statistical decision'. *Brit. J. Psychol.*, **54**, 309.

BROADBENT, D. E. and GREGORY, M. (1965) 'Effects of noise and of signal rate upon vigilance analysed by means of detection theory'. *Human Factors*, **7**, 155.

BROOKS, R. M. and GOLDSTEIN, A. G. (1963) 'Recognition by children of inverted photographs of faces'. *Child Develop.*, **34**, 1033.

BROWN, A. F. (1929) 'The relation of heterogeneous and homogeneous chromatic stimuli in the range of visual apprehension experiment'. *Amer. J. Psychol.*, **41**, 577.

BROWN, J. (1960) 'Evidence for a selective process during perception of tachistoscopically presented stimuli'. *J. Exper. Psychol.*, **59**, 176.

BROWN, J. F. (1931a) 'The visual perception of velocity'. *Psychol. Forsch.*, **14**, 199.

BROWN, J. F. (1931b) 'The threshold for visual movement'. *Psychol. Forsch.*, **14**, 249.

BROWN, J. F. and VOTH, A. C. (1937) 'The path of seen movement as a function of the vector field.' *Amer. J. Psychol.*, **49**, 543.

BROWN, L. B. and HOUSSIADAS, L. (1965) 'The perception of illusions as a constancy phenomenon'. *Brit. J. Psychol.*, **56**, 135.

BROWN, R. (1958) 'How shall a thing be called?' *Psychol. Rev.*, **65**, 14.

BROWN, R. H. and CONKLIN, J. E. (1954) 'The lower threshold of visible movement as a function of exposure-time'. *Amer. J. Psychol.*, **67**, 104.

BROWN, W. P. (1961) 'Conceptions of perceptual defence'. *Brit. J. Monog. Supp.*, **35**.

BRUCE, R. H. and LOW, F. N. (1951) 'The effect of practice with brief-exposure techniques upon central and peripheral visual acuity and a search for a brief test of peripheral acuity'. *J. Exper. Psychol.*, **41**, 275.

BRUNER, J. S. (1957) 'On perceptual readiness'. *Psychol. Rev.*, **64**, 123.

BRUNER, J. S. (1966) 'On cognitive growth'. In J. S. Bruner, R. R. Olver and P. M. Greenfield (Eds.), *Studies in Cognitive Growth*. New York: Wiley.

BRUNER, J. S. and GOODMAN, C. C. (1947) 'Value and need as organizing factors in perception'. *J. Ab. Soc. Psychol.*, **42**, 33.

BRUNER, J. S. and MINTURN, A. L. (1955) 'Perceptual identification and perceptual organization'. *J. Gen. Psychol.*, **53**, 21.

R

BRUNER, J. S. and POSTMAN, L. (1947) 'Emotional selectivity in perception and reaction'. *J. Pers.*, **16**, 69.

BRUNER, J. S. and POSTMAN, L. (1949) 'On the perception of incongruity'. *J. Pers.*, **18**, 206.

BRUNER, J. S., POSTMAN, L. and RODRIGUES, J. (1951) 'Expectation and the perception of color'. *Amer. J. Psychol.*, **64**, 216.

BRUNER, J. S. and POTTER, M. C. (1964) 'Interference in visual recognition'. *Science*, **144**, 424.

BRUNER, J. S. and RODRIGUES, J. (1953) 'Some determinants of apparent size'. *J. Ab. Soc. Psychol.*, **48**, 17.

BRUNEL, J. S. and TAJFEL, H. (1961) 'Cognitive risk and environmental change'. *J. Ab. Soc. Psychol.*, **62**, 231.

BRUNSWIK, E. (1928) 'Zur Entwicklung der Albedo-wahrnehmung'. *Zeit. f. Psychol.*, **109**, 40.

BRUNSWIK, E. (1935) *Experimentelle Psychologie*. Wien: Springer.

BRUNSWIK, E. (1944) 'Distal focusing of perception: size constancy in a representative sample of situations'. *Psychol. Monog.*, **56**, No. 1.

BRUNSWIK, E. (1956) *Perception and the Representative Design of Psychological Experiments* (2nd Ed.). University of California Press.

BRUNSWIK, E. and REITER, L. (1938) 'Eindruckscharaktere schematisierter Gesichter'. *Zeit. f. Psychol.*, **142**, 67.

BUCKNER, D. N. (1963) 'An individual-difference approach to explaining vigilance performance'. In D. N. Buckner and J. J. McGrath (Eds.), *Vigilance: A Symposium*. New York: McGraw-Hill.

BUGELSKI, B. R. and ALAMPAY, D. A. (1961) 'The role of frequency in developing perceptual sets'. *Canad. J. Psychol.*, **15**, 205.

BÜHLER, C. and HETZER, H. (1928) 'Das erste Verständnis für Ausdruck im ersten Lebensjahr'. *Zeit. f. Psychol.*, **107**, 50.

BURZLAFF, W. (1931) 'Methodologische Beiträge zum Problem der Farbenkonstanz'. *Zeit. f. Psychol.*, **119**, 177.

CANTOR, G. N., CANTOR, J. H. and DITRICHS, R. (1963) 'Observing behavior in preschool children as a function of stimulus complexity.' *Child Develop.*, **34**, 683.

CAPPON, D., BANKS, R. and RAMSEY, C. (1968) 'Improvement of recognition on a multi-modal pattern discrimination test'. *Percept. Motor Skills*, **26**, 431.

CAREY, J. E. and GOSS, A. E. (1957) 'The role of mediating verbal responses in conceptual sorting behavior of children'. *J. Genet. Psychol.*, **90**, 69.

CARLSON, V. R. (1960) 'Overestimation in size-constancy judgments'. *Amer. J. Psychol.*, **73**, 199.

CARLSON, V. R. (1962) 'Size constancy judgments and perceptual compromise'. *J. Exper. Psychol.*, **63**, 68.

CARMICHAEL, L., HOGAN, H. P. and WALTER, A. A. (1932) 'An experimental study of the effect of language on the reproduction of visually perceived form'. *J. Exper. Psychol.*, **15**, 73.

CARON, A. J. and WALLACH, M. A. (1959) 'Personality determinants of repressive and obsessive reactions to failure-stress'. *J. Ab. Soc. Psychol.*, **59**, 236.

CARON, R. F. and CARON, A. J. (1968) 'The effects of repeated exposure and stimulus complexity on visual fixation in infants'. *Psychonom. Sci.*, **10**, 207.

CARPENTER, B., WIENER, M. and CARPENTER, J. T. (1956) 'Predictability of perceptual defense behavior'. *J. Ab. Soc. Psychol.*, **52**, 380.

CARPENTER, G. C. and STECHLER, G. (1967) 'Selective attention to mother's face from week 1 through week 8'. *Proc. 75th Annual Convention, A.P.A.*, **2**, 153.

CARR, H. A. (1935) *An Introduction to Space Perception.* New York: Longmans Green.

CARTER, L. F. and SCHOOLER, K. (1949) 'Value, need and other factors in perception'. *Psychol. Rev.*, **56**, 200.

CASPERSON, R. C. (1950) 'The visual discrimination of geometric forms'. *J. Exper. Psychol.*, **40**, 668.

CATTELL, J. MCK. (1886) 'The inertia of eye and brain'. *Brain*, **8**, 295.

CHAPANIS, A. and MANKIN, D. A. (1967) 'The vertical-horizontal illusion in a visually-rich environment'. *Percept. & Psychophys.*, **2**, 249.

CHAPMAN, D. W. (1932) 'Relative effects of determinate and indeterminate *Aufgaben*'. *Amer. J. Psychol.*, **44**, 163.

CHARLESWORTH, W. R. (1966) 'Persistence of orienting and attending behavior in infants as a function of stimulus-locus uncertainty'. *Child Develop.*, **37**, 473.

CHASE, W. P. (1937) 'Color vision in infants'. *J. Exper. Psychol.*, **20**, 203.

CHEATHAM, P. (1952) 'Visual perceptual latency as a function of stimulus brightness and contour shape'. *J. Exper. Psychol.*, **43**, 369.

CHODORKOFF, B. (1956) 'Anxiety, threat and defensive reactions'. *J. Gen. Psychol.*, **54**, 191.

CHRISTENSEN, J. M. and CRANNELL, C. W. (1955) 'The effect of selected visual training procedures on the visual form field'. Cited in *Psychol. Abstr.*, (1956) **30**, 6714.

CLARK, H. J. (1965) 'Recognition memory for random shapes as a function of complexity, association value and delay'. *J. Exper. Psychol.*, **69**, 590.

CLARK, W. C., SMITH, A. H. and RABE, A. (1956a) 'The interaction of surface texture, outline gradient and ground in the perception of slant'. *Canad. J. Psychol.*, **10**, 1.

CLARK, W. C., SMITH, A. H. and RABE, A. (1956b) 'Retinal gradients of outline distortion and binocular disparity as stimuli for slant'. *Canad. J. Psychol.*, **10**, 77.

CLINE, M. G. (1956) 'The influence of social context on the perception of faces'. *J. Pers.*, **25**, 142.

COHEN, L. (1959) 'Rate of apparent change of a Necker cube as a function of prior stimulation'. *Amer. J. Psychol.*, **72**, 327.

COHEN, R. L. (1964) *Problems in Motion Perception.* Uppsala: Appelbergs.

COHEN, R. L. (1965) 'Adaptation effects and after effects of moving patterns viewed in the periphery of the visual field'. *Scand. J. Psychol.*, **6**, 257.

COHEN, R. L. (1967) 'On the relationship between phenomenal space and phenomenal velocity'. *Scand. J. Psychol.*, **8**, 107.

COHEN, W. (1957) 'Spatial and textural characteristics of the *Ganzfeld*'. *Amer. J. Psychol.*, **70**, 403.

COHEN, W. (1958) 'Apparent movement of simple figures in the *Ganzfeld*'. *Percept. Motor Skills*, **8**, 32.

COHEN, W. (1960) Cited in L. L. Avant, 'Vision in the *Ganzfeld*'. *Psychol. Bull.* (1965) **64**, 246.

COHEN, W., HERSHKOWITZ, A. and CHODAK, M. (1958) 'Size judgment at different distances as a function of age level'. *Child Develop.*, **29**, 473.

COLQUHOUN, W. P. (1961) 'The effect of "unwanted" signals on performance in a vigilance task'. *Ergonomics*, **4**, 41.

COMALLI, P. E. (1960) 'Studies in physiognomic perception, VI: Differential effects of directional dynamics of pictured objects on real and apparent motion in artists and chemists'. *J. Psychol.*, **49**, 99.

COOPERSMITH, S. (1964) 'Relationship between self-esteem and sensory (perceptual) constancy'. *J. Ab. Soc. Psychol.*, **68**, 217.

CORNWELL, H. G. (1963) 'Prior experience as a determinant of figure-ground organization'. *J. Exper. Psychol.*, **65**, 156.

COSTA, A. M. (1949) Cited by E. J. Gibson and V. Olum (1960) in P. H. Mussen (Ed.), *Handbook of Research Methods in Child Development.* New York: Wiley.

COULES, J. (1955) 'Effect of photometric brightness on judgments of distance'. *J. Exper. Psychol.*, **50**, 19.

COURTNEY, J., DAVIS, J. M. and SOLOMON, P. (1961) 'Sensory deprivation: the role of movement'. *Percept. Motor Skills*, **13**, 191.

COWEN, E. L. and BEIER, E. G. (1950) 'The influence of "threat-expectancy" on perception'. *J. Pers.*, **19**, 85.

COWEN, E. L. and BEIER, E. G. (1954) 'Threat-expectancy, word frequencies and perceptal prerecognition hypotheses'. *J. Ab. Soc. Psychol.*, **49**, 178.

COWEN, E. L. and OBRIST, P. A. (1958) 'Perceptual reactivity to threat and neutral words under varying experimental conditions'. *J. Ab. Soc. Psychol.*, **56**, 305.

CRABBÉ, G. (1967) 'Les conditions d'une perception de la causalité'. *Monog. Françaises de Psychologie*, **12**.

CRAIK, K. J. W. and VERNON, M. D. (1942) 'Perception during dark adaptation'. *Brit. J. Psychol.*, **32**, 206.

CRAIN, L. and WERNER, H. (1950) 'The development of visuo-motor performance on the marble board in normal children'. *J. Genet. Psychol.*, **77**, 217.

CRAWFORD, B. H. (1947) 'Visual adaptation in relation to brief conditioning stimuli'. *Proc. Roy. Soc.*, *B*, **134**, 283.

CROOK, M. N. (1957) 'Facsimile-generated analogues for instrumental form displays'. In J. W. Wulfeck and J. H. Taylor (Eds.), *Form Discrimination as Related to Military Problems*. Washington, D. C.: Nat. Acad. Sci.-Nat. Res. Counc.

CRUIKSHANK, R. M. (1941) 'The development of visual size constancy in early infancy'. *J. Genet. Psychol.*, **58**, 327.

DALLENBACH, K. M. (1928) 'The "range of attention"'. *Psychol. Bull.*, **25**, 152.

DAVIES, D. R. and HOCKEY, G. R. J. (1966) 'The effects of noise and doubling the signal frequency on individual differences in visual vigilance performance'. *Brit. J. Psychol.*, **57**, 381.

DAVIS, J. M., MCCOURT, W. F., COURTNEY, J. and SOLOMON, P. (1961) 'Sensory deprivation: the role of social isolation'. *Arch. Gen. Psychiat.*, **5**, 84.

DAVIS, J. M., MCCOURT, W. F. and SOLOMON, P. (1960) 'The effect of visual stimulation on hallucinations and other mental experiences during sensory deprivation'. *Amer. J. Psychiat.*, **116**, 889.

DAWSON, J. L. M. (1967) 'Cultural and physiological influences upon spatial-perceptual processes in West Africa'. *Internat. J. Psychol.*, **2**, 115.

DAY, R. H. (1962) 'The effects of repeated trials and prolonged fixation on error in the Müller-Lyer figure'. *Psychol. Monog.*, **76**, No. 14.

DAY, R. H. (1965) 'Inappropriate constancy explanation of spatial distortions'. *Nature*, **207**, 891.

DAY, R. H. and POWER, R. P. (1963) 'Frequency of apparent reversal of rotary motion in depth as a function of shape and pattern'. *Austral. J. Psychol.*, **15**, 162.

DAY, R. H. and POWER, R. P. (1965) 'Apparent reveral (oscillation) of rotary motion in depth'. *Psychol. Rev.*, **72**, 117.

DAYTON, G. O., JONES, M. H., STEELE, B. and ROSE, M. (1964) 'Developmental study of coordinated eye movements in the human infant, II: An electrographic study of the fixation reflex in the newborn'. *Arch. Ophthal.*, **71**, 871.

DEES, V. and GRINDLEY, G. C. (1947) 'The transposition of visual patterns'. *Brit. J. Psychol.*, **37**, 152.

DEESE, J. (1956) Cited by H. W. Hake, 'Form discrimination and the invariance of form'. In L. Uhr (Ed.), *Pattern Recognition* (1966). New York: Wiley.

DEFARES, P. B. and DE HAAN, D. (1962) 'The perception of movement modalities in "static" form changes'. *Acta Psychol.*, **20**, 210.

DELK, J. L. and FILLENBAUM, S. (1965) 'Differences in perceived color as a function of characteristic color'. *Amer. J. Psychol.*, **78**, 290.

DE LUCIA, J. J. and STAGNER, R. (1954) 'Emotional *vs.* frequency factors in word-recognition time and association time'. *J. Pers.*, **22**, 299.

DEMBER, W. N. and EARL, R. W. (1957) 'Analysis of exploratory, manipulatory and curiosity behaviors'. *Psychol. Rev.*, **64**, 91.

DENIS-PRINZHORN, M. (1960) 'Perception des distances et constance des grandeurs'. *Arch. de Psychol.*, **37**, 181.

DEREGOWSKI, J. B. (1968) 'Difficulties in pictorial depth perception in Africa'. *Brit. J. Psychol.*, **59**, 195.

DEWAR, R. E. (1967a) 'Stimulus determinants of the magnitude of the Müller-Lyer illusion'. *Percept. Motor Skills*, **24**, 708.

DEWAR, R. E. (1967b) 'Stimulus determinants of the practice decrement of the Müller-Lyer illusion'. *Canad. J. Psychol.*, **21**, 504.

DIETZE, D. (1955) 'The facilitating effects of words on discrimination and generalization'. *J. Exper. Psychol.*, **50**, 255.

DINNERSTEIN, D. (1965) 'Previous and concurrent visual experience as determinants of phenomenal shape'. *Amer. J. Psychol.*, **78**, 235.

DITCHBURN, R. W. and FENDER, D. H. (1955) 'The stabilized retinal image'. *Optica Acta*, **2**, 128.

DITCHBURN, R. W., FENDER, D. H. and MAYNE, S. (1959) 'Vision with controlled movements of the retinal image'. *J. Physiol.*, **145**, 98.

DITCHBURN, R. W. and GINSBORG, B. L. (1952) 'Vision with a stabilized retinal image'. *Nature*, **170**, 36.

DITCHBURN, R. W. and GINSBORG, B. L. (1953) 'Involuntary eye movements during fixation'. *J. Physiol.*, **119**, 1.

DITCHBURN, R. W. and PRITCHARD, R. M. (1956) 'Stabilized interference fringes on the retina'. *Nature*, **177**, 434.

DIXON, N. F. (1955) 'The effect of subliminal stimulation upon cognitive and other processes'. *Unpublished Ph.D. Thesis*, University of Reading.

DIXON, N. F. (1958a) 'The effect of subliminal stimulation upon autonomic and verbal behavior'. *J. Ab. Soc. Psychol.*, **57**, 29.

DIXON, N. F. (1958b) 'Apparent changes in the visual threshold as a function of subliminal stimulation'. *Quart. J. Exper. Psychol.*, **10**, 211.

DIXON, N. F. and DIXON, P. M. (1966) '"Sloping water" and related framework illusions'. *Quart. J. Exper. Psychol.*, **18**, 369.

DIXON, N. F. and HAIDER, M. (1961) 'Changes in the visual threshold as a function of subception'. *Quart. J. Exper. Psychol.*, **13**, 229.

DIXON, N. F. and MEISELS, L. (1966) 'The effect of information content upon the perception and after-effects of a rotating field'. *Quart. J. Exper. Psychol.*, **18**, 310.

DOANE, B. K., MAHATOO, W., HERON, W. and SCOTT, T. H. (1959) 'Changes in perceptual function after isolation'. *Canad. J. Psychol.*, **13**, 210.

DOEHRING, D. G. (1962) 'Value, frequency and practice in visual word recognition'. *Psychol. Rec.*, **12**, 209.

DONAHUE, W. T. and GRIFFITHS, C. H. (1931) 'The influence of complexity on the fluctuations of the illusions of reversible perspective'. *Amer. J. Psychol.*, **43**, 613.

DRAGUNS, J. G. and MULTARI, G. (1961) 'Recognition of perceptually ambiguous stimuli in grade school children'. *Child Develop.*, **32**, 541.

DULANY, D. E. (1957) 'Avoidance learning of perceptual defense and vigilance'. *J. Ab. Soc. Psychol.*, **55**, 333.

DUNCKER, K. (1929) 'Über induzierte Bewegung'. *Psychol. Forsch.*, **12**, 180.

DUNCKER, K. (1939) 'The influence of past experience upon perceptual properties'. *Amer. J. Psychol.*, **52**, 255.

EAGLE, M. (1959) 'The effects of subliminal stimuli of aggressive content upon conscious cognition'. *J. Pers.*, **27**, 578.

EAGLE, M., BOWLING, L. and KLEIN, G. S. (1966) 'Fragmentation phenomena in luminous designs'. *Percept. Motor Skills*, **23**, 143.

EAGLE, M. and KLEIN, G. S. (1962) 'Fragmentation phenomena with the use of the stabilized retinal image'. *Percept. Motor Skills*, **15**, 579.

EASTERBROOK, J. A. (1959) 'The effect of emotion on cue utilization and the organization of behavior'. *Psychol. Rev.*, **66**, 183.

EDWARDS, A. E. (1960) 'Subliminal tachistoscopic perception as a function of threshold method'. *J. Psychol.*, **50**, 139.

EGERTH, H. (1967) 'Selective attention'. *Psychol. Bull.*, **67**, 41.

EGERTH, H. and SMITH, E. E. (1967) 'Perceptual selectivity in a visual recognitive task'. *J. Exper. Psychol.*, **74**, 543.

EISSLER, K. (1933) 'Die Gestaltkonstanz der Sehdinge bei Variation der Objekte und ihrer Einwirklungsweise auf den Wahrnehmenden'. *Arch. f. d. ges. Psychol.*, **88**, 487.

EKMAN, P., SORENSON, E. R. and FRIESEN, W. V. (1969) 'Pan-cultural elements in facial displays of emotion'. *Science*, **164**, 86.

ELKIND, D., KOEGLER, R. R. and GO, E. (1964) 'Studies in perceptual development, II: Part-whole perception'. *Child Develop.*, **35**, 81.

ELKIND, D. and SCOTT, L. (1962) 'Studies in perceptual development, I: The decentering of perception'. *Child Develop.*, **33**, 619.

ELKIND, D. and WEISS, J. (1967) 'Studies in perceptual development, III: Perceptual exploration'. *Child Develop.*, **38**, 553.

ELLIOTT, R. (1961) 'Inter-relationships among measures of field dependence, ability and personality traits'. *J. Ab. Soc. Psychol.*, **63**, 27.

ELLIS, H. C. and MULLER, D. G. (1964) 'Transfer in perceptual learning following stimulus pre-differentiation'. *J. Exper. Psychol.*, **68**, 388.

ENGEL, E. (1956) 'The role of content in binocular resolution'. *Amer. J. Psychol.*, **69**, 87.

EPSTEIN, W. (1962) 'Apparent shape of a meaningful representative form'. *Percept. Motor Skills*, **15**, 239.

EPSTEIN, W. (1963a) 'The influence of assumed size on apparent distance'. *Amer. J. Psychol.*, **76**, 257.

EPSTEIN, W. (1963b) 'Attitudes of judgment and the size-distance invariance hypothesis'. *J. Exper. Psychol.*, **66**, 78.

EPSTEIN, W. (1967) 'Perceptual learning resulting from exposure to a stimulus-invariant'. *Amer. J. Psychol.*, **80**, 205.

EPSTEIN, W., BONTRAGER, H. and PARK, J. (1962) 'The induction of non-veridical slant and the perception of shape'. *J. Exper. Psychol.*, **63**, 472.

EPSTEIN, W. and DE SHAZO, D. (1961) 'Recency as a function of perceptual oscillation'. *Amer. J. Psychol.*, **74**, 215.

EPSTEIN, W., JANSSON, G. and JOHANSSON, G. (1968) 'Perceived angle of oscillatory motion'. *Percept. & Psychophys.*, **3**, 12.

EPSTEIN, W. and ROCK, I. (1960) 'Perceptual set as an artifact of recency'. *Amer. J. Psychol.*, **73**, 214.

ERICKSON, R. A. (1964) 'Visual search performance in a moving structured field'. *J. Opt. Soc. Amer.*, **54**, 399.

ERIKSEN, C. W. (1951a) 'Perceptual defense as a function of unacceptable needs'. *J. Ab. Soc. Psychol.*, **46**, 557.

ERIKSEN, C. W. (1951b) 'Some implications for TAT interpretation arising from need and perception experiments'. *J. Pers.*, **19**, 282.

ERIKSEN, C. W. (1952a) 'Location of objects in a visual display as a function of the number of dimensions on which objects differ'. *J. Exper. Psychol.*, **44**, 56.

ERIKSEN, C. W. (1952b) 'Defense against ego-threat in memory and perception'. *J. Ab. Soc. Psychol.*, **47**, 230.

ERIKSEN, C. W. (1953) 'Object location in a complex perceptual field'. *J. Exper. Psychol.*, **45**, 126.

ERIKSEN, C. W. (1955) 'Partitioning and saturation of visual displays and efficiency of visual search'. *J. Appl. Psychol.*, **39**, 73.

ERIKSEN, C. W., AZUMA, H. and HICKS, R. B. (1959) 'Verbal discrimination of pleasant and unpleasant stimuli prior to specific identification'. *J. Ab. Soc. Psychol.*, **59**, 114.

ERIKSEN, C. W. and BROWNE, C. T. (1956) 'An experimental and theoretical analysis of perceptual defense'. *J. Ab. Soc. Psychol.*, **52**, 224.

ETTLINGER, G., WARRINGTON, E. and ZANGWILL, O. L. (1957) 'A further study of visual-spatial agnosia'. *Brain*, **80**, 335.

EVANS, C. R. (1964) 'Pattern perception and the stabilized retinal image'. *Unpublished Ph.D. Thesis*, University of Reading.

EVANS, C. R. (1965) 'Some studies of pattern perception using a stabilized retinal image'. *Brit. J. Psychol.*, **56**, 121.

EVANS, C. R. and PIGGINS, D. J. (1963) 'A comparison of the behaviour of geometrical shapes when viewed under conditions of steady fixation, and with apparatus for producing a stabilized retinal image'. *Brit. J. Physiol. Opt.*, **20**, 1.

EVANS, C. R. and SMITH, G. K. (1964) 'Alpha-frequency of electroencephalogram and a stabilized retinal image'. *Nature*, **204**, 303.

EX, J. and DE BRUIJN, G. L. (1956) 'An experimental study of the influence of the mental set on the perception of identity and substitution'. *Acta Psychol.*, **12**, 198.

FANTZ, R. L. (1958) 'Pattern vision in young infants'. *Psychol. Rec.*, **8**, 43.

FANTZ, R. L. (1961) 'The origin of form perception'. *Scient. Amer.*, **204** (5), 66.

FANTZ, R. L. (1964) 'Visual experience in infants: decreased attention to familiar patterns relative to novel ones'. *Science*, **146**, 668.

FANTZ, R. L., ORDY, J. M. and UDELF, M. S. (1962) 'Maturation of pattern vision in infants during the first six months'. *J. Comp. Physiol. Psychol.*, **55**, 907.

FELEKY, A. M. (1924) *Feelings and Emotions*. New York: Pioneer.

FELLOWS, B. J. (1967) 'Reversal of the Müller-Lyer illusion with changes in the length of the inter-fins line'. *Quart. J. Exper. Psychol.*, **19**, 208.

FELLOWS, B. J. (1968a) *The Discrimination Process and Development*. Oxford: Pergamon.

FELLOWS, B. J. (1968b) 'The reverse Müller-Lyer illusion and "enclosure"'. *Brit. J. Psychol.*, **59**, 369.

FIEANDT, K. V. (1936) 'Dressurversuche an der Farbenwahrnehmung'. *Arch. f. d. ges. Psychol.*, **96**, 467.

FIEANDT, K. V. and GIBSON, J. J. (1959), 'The sensitivity of the eye to two kinds of continuous transformation of a shadow-pattern'. *J. Exper. Psychol.*, **57**, 344.

FILLENBAUM, S., SCHIFFMAN, H. R. and BUTCHER, J. (1965) 'Perception of off-size versions of a familiar object under conditions of rich information'. *J. Exper. Psychol.*, **69**, 298.

FISCH, R. I. and MCNAMARA, H. J. (1963) 'Conditioning of attention as a factor in perceptual learning'. *Percept. Motor Skills*, **17**, 891.

FISHER, G. H. (1967) 'Measuring ambiguity'. *Amer. J. Psychol.*, **80**, 541.

FISHER, G. H. (1968a) 'Gradients of distortion seen in the context of the Ponzo illusion and other contours'. *Quart. J. Exper. Psychol.*, **20**, 212.

FISHER, G. H. (1968b) 'An experimental comparison of rectilinear and curvilinear illusions'. *Brit. J. Psychol.*, **59**, 23.

FISHER, G. H. and LUCAS, A. (1968) 'Illusions in concrete situations'. *Ergo*, **11**.

FISHER, S. C., HULL, C. and HOLTZ, P. (1956) 'Past experience and perception: memory color'. *Amer. J. Psychol.*, **69**, 546.

FISS, H. (1966) 'The effects of experimentally induced changes in alertness on response to subliminal stimulation'. *J. Pers.*, **34**, 577.

FOLEY, J. E. and ABEL, S. M. (1967) 'A study of alternation of normal and distorted vision'. *Canad. J. Psychol.*, **21**, 220.

FOOTE, W. E. and HAVENS, L. L. (1967) 'Differential effects of stimulus frequency and graphic configuration in free- and forced-choice experiments'. *J. Exper. Psychol.*, **73**, 340.

FORGUS, R. H. (1966) *Perception*. New York: McGraw-Hill.

FORREST, D. W., GORDON, N. and TAYLOR, A. (1965) 'Generalization of perceptual defense'. *J. Pers. Soc. Psychol.*, **2**, 137.

FORREST, D. W. and LEE, S. G. (1962) 'Mechanisms of defense and readiness in perception and recall'. *Psychol. Monog.*, **76**, No. 4.

FOX, W. R. (1957) 'Visual discrimination as a function of stimulus size, shape and edge-gradient'. In J. W. Wulfeck and J. H. Taylor (Eds.), *Form Discrimination as Related to Military Problems*. Washington, D.C.: Nat. Acad. Sci.-Nat. Res. Counc.

FRAISSE, P. (1960) 'L'évolution génétique de différentes formes de l'illusion de Müller-Lyer'. Cited by E. Vurpillot (1963) in *L'Organization Perceptive*. Paris: Vrin.

FRAISSE, P. and ELKIN, E. H. (1963) 'Étude génétique de l'influence des modes de présentation sur le seuil de reconnaissance d'objets familiers'. *Année Psychol.*, 63, 1.

FRAISSE, P. and VAUTREY, P. (1956) 'The influence of age, sex and specialized training on the vertical-horizontal illusion'. *Quart. J. Exper. Psychol.*, 8, 114.

FRASER, D. C. (1935) 'The relation of an environmental variable to performance in a prolonged visual task'. *Quart. J. Exper. Psychol.*, 5, 31.

FRASER, D. C. (1957) 'A study of vigilance and fatigue'. Cited by D. E. Broadbent in *Perception and Communication* (1958). London: Pergamon.

FREEDMAN, S. J. and HELD, R. (1960) 'Sensory deprivation and perceptual lag'. *Percept. Motor Skills*, 11, 277.

FREEMAN, J. T. (1954) 'Set or perceptual defense?' *J. Exper. Psychol.* 48, 283.

FREEMAN, J. T. and ENGLER, J. (1955) 'Perceptual recognition thresholds as a function of multiple and single set and frequency of usage of the stimulus material'. *Percept. Motor Skills*, 5, 149.

FREEMAN, R. B. (1966) 'Function of cues in the perceptual learning of visual slant'. *Psychol. Monog.*, 80, No. 2.

FREUD, S. L. (1964) 'The physiological locus of the spiral after-effect'. *Amer. J. Psychol.*, 77, 422.

FUHRER, M. J. and ERIKSEN, C. W. (1961) 'The unconscious perception of the meaning of verbal stimuli'. *J. Ab. Soc. Psychol.*, 61, 432.

FULKERSON, S. C. (1957) 'The interaction of frequency, emotional tone and set in visual recognition'. *J. Exper. Psychol.*, 54, 188.

FURTH, H. G. and MENDEZ, R. A. (1963) 'The influence of language and age on Gestalt laws of perception'. *Amer. J. Psychol.*, 76, 74.

FUSTER, J. M. (1958) 'Effects of stimulation of brain stem on tachistoscopic perception'. *Science*, 127, 150.

GANTENBEIN, M.-M. (1952) 'Récherche sur la développement de la perception du mouvement avec l'âge'. *Arch. de Psychol.*, 33, 197.

GARDNER, R. W. (1961) 'Cognitive controls of attention deployment as determinants of visual illusions'. *J. Ab. Soc. Psychol.*, 62, 120.

GARDNER, R. W. and LOHRENZ, L. J. (1961) 'Attention and assimilation'. *Amer. J. Psychol.*, **74**, 607.

GARDNER, R. W., LOHRENZ, L. J. and SCHOEN, R. A. (1968) 'Cognitive control of differentiation in the perception of persons and objects'. *Percept. Motor Skills*, **26**, 311.

GARDNER, R. W. and LONG, R. I. (1960) 'The stability of cognitive controls'. *J. Ab. Soc. Psychol.*, **61**, 485.

GARDNER, R. W. and LONG, R. I. (1961) 'Selective attention and the Müller-Lyer illusion'. *Psychol., Rec.*, **11**, 317.

GARDNER, R. W. and LONG, R. I. (1962a) 'Control, defence and centration effect: a study of scanning behavior'. *Brit. J. Psychol.*, **53**, 129.

GARDNER, R. W. and LONG, R. I. (1962b) 'Cognitive controls of attention and inhibition: a study of individual consistencies'. *Brit. J. Psychol.*, **53**, 381.

GARDNER, R. W. and MORIARTY, A. (1968) *Personality Development at Preadolescence*. Seattle: University of Washington Press.

GARNER, W. R. (1962) *Uncertainty and Structure as Psychological Concepts*. New York: Wiley.

GARNER, W. R. and CLEMENT, D. E. (1963) 'Goodness of pattern and pattern uncertainty'. *J. Verb. Learn. Verb. Behav.*, **2**, 446.

GATES, G. S. (1923) 'An experimental study of the growth of social perception'. *J. Educ. Psychol.*, **14**, 449.

GELB, A. (1929) 'Die "Farbenkonstanz" der Sehdinge'. *Handbuch der normalen und pathologischen Physiologie*, **12**, 594.

GELLERMAN, L. W. (1933) 'Form discrimination in chimpanzees and two-year-old children'. *J. Genet. Psychol.*, **42**, 28.

GEMELLI, A. (1958) 'The visual perception of movement'. *Amer. J. Psychol.*, **71**, 291.

GEMELLI, A. and CAPELLINI, A. (1958) 'The influence of the subject's attitude in perception'. *Acta Psychol.*, **14**, 12.

GENGERELLI, J. A. (1948) 'Apparent movement in relation to homonymous and heteronymous stimulation of the cerebral hemispheres'. *J. Exper. Psychol.*, **38**, 592.

GESELL, A., ILG, F. L. and BULLIS, G. E. (1959) *Vision: Its Development in Infant and Child*. New York: Hoeber.

GHENT, L. (1956) 'Perception of overlapping and embedded figures by children of different ages'. *Amer. J. Psychol.*, **69**, 575.

GHENT, L. (1961) 'Form and its orientation: a child's-eye view'. *Amer. J. Psychol.*, **74**, 177.

GHENT, L. and BERNSTEIN, L. (1961) 'Influence of the orientation of geometric forms on their recognition by children'. *Percept. Motor Skills*, **12**, 95.

GIBSON, E. J. (1953) 'Improvement in perceptual judgments as a function of controlled practice or training'. *Psychol. Bull.*, **50**, 401.

GIBSON, E. J., BERGMAN, R. and PURDY, J. (1955) 'The effect of prior training with a scale of distance on absolute and relative judgments of distance over ground'. *J. Exper. Psychol.*, **50**, 97.

GIBSON, E. J., GIBSON, J. J., PICK, A. D. and OSSER, H. (1962) 'A developmental study of the discrimination of letter-like forms'. *J. Comp. Physiol. Psychol.*, **55**, 897.

GIBSON, E. J., GIBSON, J. J., SMITH, O. W. and FLOCK, H. (1959) 'Motion parallax as a determinant of perceived depth'. *J. Exper. Psychol.*, **58**, 40.

GIBSON, E. J., OSSER, H. and PICK, A. D. (1963) 'A study of the development of grapheme-phoneme correspondences'. *J. Verb. Learn. Verb. Behav.*, **2**, 142.

GIBSON, E. J., PICK, A. D., OSSER, H. and HAMMOND, M. (1962) 'The role of grapheme-phoneme correspondence in the perception of words'. *Amer. J. Psychol.*, **75**, 554.

GIBSON, J. J. (Ed.) (1947) *Motion Picture Testing and Research*. Army Air Forces Aviation Psychology Research Reports, No. 7.

GIBSON, J. J. (1950a) *The Perception of the Visual World*. Boston: Houghton Mifflin.

GIBSON, J. J. (1950b) 'The perception of visual surfaces'. *Amer. J. Psychol.*, **63**, 367.

GIBSON, J. J. (1951) 'What is form?' *Psychol. Rev.*, **58**, 403.

GIBSON, J. J. (1952) 'The relation between visual and postural determinants of the phenomenal vertical'. *Psychol. Rev.*, **59**, 370.

GIBSON, J. J. (1966) *The Senses Considered as Perceptual Systems*. Boston: Houghton Mifflin.

GIBSON, J. J. and CORNSWEET, J. (1952) 'The perceived slant of visual surfaces – optical and geographical'. *J. Exper. Psychol.*, **44**, 11.

GIBSON, J. J. and DIBBLE, F. N. (1952) 'Exploratory experiments on the stimulus conditions for the perception of a visual surface'. *J. Exper. Psychol.*, **43**, 414.

GIBSON, J. J. and GIBSON, E. J. (1955) 'Perceptual learning: differentiation or enrichment?' *Psychol. Rev.*, **62**, 32.

GIBSON, J. J. and GIBSON, E. J. (1957) 'Continuous perspective transformations and the perception of rigid motion'. *J. Exper. Psychol.*, **54**, 129.

GIBSON, J. J. and MOWRER, O. H. (1938) 'Determinants of the perceived vertical and horizontal'. *Psychol. Rev.*, **45**, 300.

GIBSON, J. J., OLUM, P. and ROSENBLATT, F. (1955a) 'Parallax and perspective during aircraft landings'. *Amer. J. Psychol.*, **68**, 372.

GIBSON, J. J., PURDY, J. and LAWRENCE, L. (1955b) 'A method of controlling stimulation for the study of space perception: the optical tunnel'. *J. Exper. Psychol.*, **50**, 1.

GIBSON, J. J. and ROBINSON, D. (1935) 'Orientation in visual perception: the recognition of familiar plane forms in differing orientations'. *Psychol. Monog.*, **46**, No. 3, 39.

GIBSON, J. J. and WADDELL, D. (1952) 'Homogeneous retinal stimulation and visual perception'. *Amer. J. Psychol.*, **65**, 263.

GILCHRIST, J. C., LUDEMAN, J. F. and LYSAK, W. (1954) 'Values as determinants of word-recognition thresholds'. *J. Ab. Soc. Psychol.*, **49**, 423.

GILCHRIST, J. C. and NESBERG, L. S. (1952) 'Need and perceptual change in need-related objects'. *J. Exper. Psychol.*, **44**, 369.

GILINSKY, A. S. (1951) 'Perceived size and distance in visual space'. *Psychol. Rev.*, **58**, 460.

GILINSKY, A. S. (1955) 'The effect of attitude on the perception of size'. *Amer. J. Psychol.*, **68**, 173.

GOGEL, W. C. (1954) 'Perception of relative distance position of objects as a function of other objects in the field'. *J. Exper. Psychol.*, **47**, 335.

GOGEL, W. C. (1956) 'The tendency to see objects as equidistant and its inverse relation to lateral separation'. *Psychol. Monog.* **70**, No. 4.

GOGEL, W. C. (1960) 'The perception of a depth interval with binocular disparity cues'. *J. Psychol.*, **50**, 257.

GOGEL, W. C. (1964) 'Perception of depth from binocular disparity'. *J. Exper. Psychol.*, **67**, 379.

GOGEL, W. C., HARTMAN, B. O. and HARKER, G. S. (1957) 'The retinal size of a familiar object as a determiner of apparent distance.' *Psychol. Monog.*, **71**, No. 13.

GOINS, J. T. (1958) 'Visual perceptual abilities and early reading progress'. *Suppl. Educ. Monog.*, *No.* 87.

GOLDBERGER, L. and HOLT, R. R. (1958) 'Experimental interference with reality contact (perceptual isolation)'. *J. Nerv. Ment. Dis.*, **127**, 99.

GOLDFARB, W. (1945a) 'Psychological privation in infancy and subsequent adjustment'. *Amer. J. Orthopsychiat.*, **15**, 247.

GOLDFARB, W. (1945b) 'Effects of psychological deprivation in infancy and subsequent stimulation'. *Amer. J. Psychiat.*, **102**, 18.

GOLDIAMOND, I. (1958) 'Indicators of perception, I: Subliminal perception, subception, unconscious perception'. *Psychol. Bull.*, **55**, 373.

GOLDIAMOND, I. and HAWKINS, W. F. (1958) 'Vexierversuch: The log relationship between word frequency and recognition obtained in the absence of stimulus words'. *J. Exper. Psychol.*, **56**, 457.

GOLDSTEIN, A. G. and MACKENBERG, E. J. (1966) 'Recognition of human faces from isolated facial features'. *Psychonom. Sci.*, **6**, 149.

GOLDSTEIN, M. E. (1960) 'Subliminal perception with optical illusions'. *J. Gen. Psychol.*, **62**, 89.

GOLDSTEIN, M. J., HIMMELFARB, S. and FEDER, W. (1962) 'A further study of the relationship between response bias and perceptual defense'. *J. Ab. Soc. Psychol.*, **64**, 56.

GOLDSTONE, S. (1955) 'Flicker fusion measurements and anxiety level'. *J. Exper. Psychol.*, **49**, 200.

GOLLIN, E. S. (1956) 'Some research problems for developmental psychology'. *Child Develop.*, **27**, 223.

GOLLIN, E. S. (1960) 'Developmental studies of visual recognition of incomplete objects'. *Percept. Motor Skills*, **11**, 289.

GOODENOUGH, D. R. and EAGLE, C. J. (1963) 'A modification of the embedded-figures test for use with young children'. *J. Genet. Psychol.*, **103**, 67.

GOODNOW, R. E. (1954) Cited by H. W. Hake, 'Form discrimination and the invariance of form'. In L. Uhr (Ed.) (1966), *Pattern Recognition*. New York: Wiley.

GORMAN, J. J., COGAN, D. G. and GELLIS, S. S. (1957) 'An apparatus for grading the visual acuity of infants on the basis of optokinetic nystagmus'. *Pediatrics*, **19**, 1088.

GOTTSCHALDT, K. (1926) 'Über den Einfluss der Ehrfahrung auf die Wahrnehmung von Figuren'. *Psychol. Forsch.*, **8**, 261.

GOTTSCHALK, J., BRYDEN, M. P. and RABINOVITCH, M. S. (1964) 'Spatial organization of children's responses to a pictorial display'. *Child Develop.*, **35**, 811.

GOULD, J. D. and SCHAFFER, A. (1965) 'Eye-movement patterns in scanning numeric displays'. *Percept. Motor Skills*, **20**, 521.

GRAHAM, C. H. (1951) 'Visual perception'. In S. S. Stevens (Ed.), *Handbook of Experimental Psychology*. New York: Wiley.

GRAHAM, F. K., BERMAN, P. W. and ERNHART, C. B. (1960) 'Development in preschool children of the ability to copy forms'. *Child Develop.*, **31**, 339.

GREEN, B. F. (1961) 'Figure coherence in the kinetic depth effect'. *J. Exper. Psychol.*, **62**, 272.

GREEN, P. C. and GORDON, M. (1964) 'Maternal deprivation: its effects on exploration in infant monkeys'. *Science*, **145**, 292.

GREEN, R. T. and HOYLE, E. M. (1963) 'The Poggendorff illusion as a constancy phenomenon'. *Nature*, **200**, 611.

GREENBAUM, M. (1956) 'Manifest anxiety and tachistoscopic recognition of facial photographs'. *Percept. Motor Skills*, **6**, 245.

GREGORY, R. L. (1958) 'Eye movements and the stability of the visual world'. *Nature*, **182**, 1214.

GREGORY, R. L. (1963) 'Distortion of visual space as inappropriate constancy scaling'. *Nature*, **199**, 678.

GREGORY, R. L. (1966a) 'Traditional theories of the illusions'. In B. M. Foss (Ed.), *New Horizons in Psychology*. Harmondsworth: Penguin Books.

GREGORY, R. L. (1966b) 'Comment on Dr. Vernon Hamilton's paper'. *Quart. J. Exper. Psychol.*, **18**, 73.

GREGORY, R. L. and WALLACE, J. G. (1963) 'Recovery from early blindness'. *Exper. Psychol. Soc. Monog.*, No. 2.

GROSS, F. (1959) 'The role of set in the perception of the upright'. *J. Pers.*, **27**, 95.

GRUBER, H. E. (1954) 'The relation of perceived size to perceived distance'. *Amer. J. Psychol.*, **67**, 411.

GRUBER, H. E. and CLARK, W. C. (1956) 'Perception of slanted surfaces'. *Percept. Motor Skills*, **6**, 97.

GRUBER, H. E. and DINNERSTEIN, A. J. (1965) 'The role of knowledge in distance-perception'. *Amer. J. Psychol.*, **78**, 575.

GRUBER, H. E., FINK, C. D. and DAMM, V. (1957) 'Effects of experience on perception of causality'. *J. Exper. Psychol.*, **53**, 89.

GRUEN, A. (1957) 'A critique and re-evaluation of Witkin's perception and perception-personality work'. *J. Gen. Psychol.*, **56**, 73.

GRUNEBAUM, H. U., FREEDMAN, S. J. and GREENBLATT, M. (1960) 'Sensory deprivation and personality'. *Amer. J. Psychiat.*, **116**, 878.

GUTHRIE, G. and WIENER, M. (1966) 'Subliminal perception or perception of partial cues with pictorial stimuli'. *J. Pers. Soc. Psychol.*, **3**, 619.

HAAF, R. and BELL, R. Q. (1967) 'A facial dimension in visual discrimination by human infants'. *Child Develop.*, **38**, 893.

HAHN, E. L. and BARTLEY, S. H. (1954) 'The apparent orientation of a luminous figure in darkness.' *Amer. J. Psychol.*, **67**, 500.

HAIDER, M. (1967) 'Vigilance, attention, expectation and cortical evoked potentials'. *Acta Psychol.*, **27**, 246.

HAIGH, G. V. and FISKE, D. W. (1952) 'Corroboration of personal values as selective factors in perception'. *J. Ab. Soc. Psychol.*, **47**, 394.

HAMILTON, V. (1960). 'Imperception of phi: some further determinants'. *Brit. J. Psychol.*, **51**, 257.

HAMILTON, V. (1966a) 'Size constancy and intelligence: a re-examination'. *Brit. J. Psychol.*, **57**, 319.

HAMILTON, V. (1966b) 'Susceptibility to the Müller-Lyer illusion and its relationship to differences in size constancy'. *Quart. J. Exper. Psychol.*, **18**, 63.

HAMMOND, K. R. (Ed.) (1966) *The Psychology of Egon Brunswik*. New York: Holt, Rinehart & Winston.

HANLEY, C. and ZERBOLIO, D. J. (1965) 'Developmental changes in five illusions measured by the up- and down-method'. *Child Develop.*, **36**, 437.

HANTON, V. D. (1955) 'The recognition of inverted pictures by children'. *J. Genet. Psychol.*, **86**, 281.

HARDING, G. F., GLASSMAN, S. M. and HELZ, W. C. (1957) 'Maturation and the spiral after-effect'. *J. Ab. Soc. Psychol.*, **54**, 276.

HARLOW, H. F. and ZIMMERMAN, R. R. (1959) 'Affectional responses in the infant monkey'. *Science*, **130**, 421.

HARPER, R. S. (1953) 'The perceptual modification of colored figures'. *Amer. J. Psychol.*, **66**, 86.

HARRIS, C. S. (1963) 'Adaptation to displaced vision: visual, motor or proprioceptive change'. *Science*, **140**, 812.

HARRIS, C. S. (1965) 'Perceptual adaptation to inverted, reversed and displaced vision'. *Psychol. Rev.*, **72**, 419.

HARTMAN, A. M. (1964) 'Effect of reduction on the relationship between apparent size and distance'. *Amer. J. Psychol.*, **77**, 353.

HASLERUD, G. M. and CLARK, R. E. (1957) 'On the redintegrative perception of words'. *Amer. J. Psychol.*, **70**, 97.

HASTORF, A. H. and MAYO, G. (1959) 'The effect of meaning on binocular rivalry'. *Amer. J. Psychol.*, **72**, 393.

HASTORF, A. H. and WAY, K. S. (1952) 'Apparent size with and without distance cues'. *J. Gen. Psychol.*, **47**, 181.

HATFIELD, R. O. (1959) 'The influence of an affective set on disyllable recognition thresholds'. *J. Ab. Soc. Psychol.*, **59**, 439.

HAY, J. and PICK, H. L. (1966) 'Visual and proprioceptive adaptation to optical displacement of the visual stimulus'. *J. Exper. Psychol.*, **71**, 150.

HAYNES, H., WHITE, B. L. and HELD, R. (1965) 'Visual accommodation in human infants'. *Science*, **148**, 528.

HEATON, J. M. (1968) *The Eye*. London: Tavistock.

HEBB, D. O. (1949) *The Organization of Behavior*. New York: Wiley.

HEBB, D. O. (1958) *A Textbook of Psychology*. Philadelphia: Saunders.

HECKHAUSEN, H. (1964) 'Complexity in perception'. *Canad. J. Psychol.*, **18**, 168.

HEIDER, F. (1958a) *The Psychology of Interpersonal Relations*. New York: Wiley.

HEIDER, F. (1958b) 'Perceiving the other person'. In R. Tagiuri and C. Petrullo (Eds.), *Person Perception and Interpersonal Behavior*. Stanford University Press.

HEIDER, F. and SIMMEL, M. (1944) 'An experimental study of apparent behavior'. *Amer. J. Psychol.*, **57**, 243.

HELD, R. and BOSSOM, J. (1961) 'Neonatal deprivation and adult re-arrangement'. *J. Comp. Physiol. Psychol.*, **54**, 33.

HELD, R. and FREEMAN, S. J. (1963) 'Plasticity in human sensorimotor control'. *Science*, **142**, 455.

HELD, R. and MIKAELIAN, H. (1964) 'Motor-sensory feedback versus need in adaptation to rearrangement'. *Percept. Motor Skills*, **18**, 685.

HELD, R. and REKOSH, J. (1963) 'Motor-sensory feedback and the geo-metry of visual space'. *Science*, **141**, 722.

HELD, R. and WHITE, B. (1959) 'Sensory deprivation and visual speed'. *Science*, **130**, 860.

HENLE, M. (1955) 'Some effects of motivational processes on cognition'. *Psychol. Rev.*, **62**, 423.

HERMAN, D. T., LAWLESS, R. H. and MARSHALL, R. W. (1957) 'Variables in the effect of language on the reproduction of visually perceived forms'. *Percept. Motor Skills*, **7**, 171.

HERNANDEZ-PEON, R., SCHERRER, H. and JOUVET, M. (1956) 'Modi-fication of electric activity in cochlear nucleus during "attention" in unanaesthetized cats'. *Science*, **123**, 331.

HERON, W. (1957) 'Perception as a function of retinal locus and atten-tion'. *Amer. J. Psychol.*, **70**, 38.

HERON, W., DOANE, B. K. and SCOTT, T. H. (1956) 'Visual disturbances after prolonged perceptual isolation'. *Canad. J. Psychol.*, **10**, 13.

HERSHENSON, M. (1964) 'Visual discrimination in the human newborn'. *J. Comp. Physiol. Psychol.*, **58**, 270.

HERSHENSON, M. (1967) 'Development of the perception of form'. *Psychol. Bull.*, **67**, 326.

HERSHENSON, M., MUNSINGER, H. and KESSEN, W. (1965) 'Preference for shapes of intermediate variability in the newborn human'. *Science*, **147**, 630.

HOCHBERG, C. B. and HOCHBERG, J. (1952) 'Familiar size and perception of depth'. *J. Psychol.*, **34**, 107.

HOCHBERG, J. (1968) 'In the mind's eye'. In R. N. Haber (Ed.), *Contemporary Theory and Research in Visual Perception.* New York: Holt, Rinehart & Winston.

HOCHBERG, J. and BROOKS, V. (1958) 'Effects of previously associated annoying stimuli (auditory) on visual recognition thresholds'. *J. Exper. Psychol.*, **55**, 490.

HOCHBERG, J. and BROOKS, V. (1960) 'The psychophysics of form: reversible perspective drawings of spatial objects'. *Amer. J. Psychol.*, **73**, 337.

HOCHBERG, J. and BROOKS, V. (1962) 'Pictorial recognition as an unlearned ability'. *Amer. J. Psychol.*, **75**, 624.

HOCHBERG, J., GLEITMAN, H. and MACBRIDE, P. D. (1948) 'Visual threshold as a function of simplicity of form'. *Amer. Psychol.*, **3**, 341.

HOCHBERG, J., HABER, S. L. and RYAN, T. A. (1955) '"Perceptual defense" as an interference phenomenon'. *Percept. Motor Skills*, **5**, 15.

HOCHBERG, J. and HARDY, D. (1960) 'Brightness and proximity factors in grouping'. *Percept. Motor Skills*, **10**, 22.

HOCHBERG, J. and MCALISTER, E. (1953) 'A quantitative approach to figural "goodness"'. *J. Exper. Psychol.*, **46**, 361.

HOCHBERG, J., TRIEBEL, W. and SEAMAN, G. (1951) 'Color adaptation under conditions of homogeneous visual stimulation (*Ganzfeld*)'. *J. Exper. Psychol.*, **41**, 153.

HODGE, M. H. (1959) 'The influence of irrelevant information upon complex visual discrimination'. *J. Exper. Psychol.*, **57**, 1.

HOFFMAN, H. E. (1968) 'Effect of stress on scanning'. *Percept. Motor Skills*, **27**, 891.

HOISINGTON, L. B. and SPENCER, C. (1958) 'Specific set and the perception of "subliminal" material'. *Amer. J. Psychol.*, **71**, 263.

HOLMES, A. C. (1963) 'A study of understanding of visual symbols in Kenya'. *Overseas Visual Aids Centre*, No. 10.

HOLWAY, A. H. and BORING, E. G. (1941) 'Determinants of apparent visual size with distance variant'. *Amer. J. Psychol.*, **54**, 21.

HOLZMAN, P. S. (1954) 'The relation of assimilation tendencies in visual, auditory and kinesthetic time-error and cognitive attitudes of levelling and sharpening'. *J. Pers.*, **22**, 375.

HOLZMAN, P. S. and GARDNER, R. W. (1959) 'Levelling and repression'. *J. Ab. Soc. Psychol.*, **59**, 151.

HONKAVAARA, S. (1961) 'The psychology of expression'. *Brit. J. Psychol. Monog. Suppl.*, No. 32.

HOTOPF, W. H. N. (1966) 'The size-constancy theory of visual illusions'. *Brit. J. Psychol.*, **57**, 307.

HOUSSIADAS, L. (1964) 'Effects of "set" and intellectual level on the perception of causality'. *Acta Psychol.*, **22**, 155.

HOWARD, I. P. (1961) 'An investigation of a satiation process in the reversible perspective of revolving skeletal shapes'. *Quart. J. Exper. Psychol.*, **13**, 19.

HOWARD, I. P., CRASKE, B. and TEMPLETON, W. B. (1965) 'Visuomotor adaptation to discordant exafferent stimulation'. *J. Exper. Psychol.*, **70**, 189.

HOWES, D. (1954). 'On the interpretation of word frequency as a variable affecting speed of recognition'. *J. Exper. Psychol.*, **48**, 106.

HOWES, D. and SOLOMON, R. L. (1951) 'Visual duration threshold as a function of word-probability'. *J. Exper. Psychol.*, **41**, 401.

HUBEL, D. H. and WIESEL, T. N. (1960) 'Receptive fields of optic nerve fibres in the spider monkey'. *J. Physiol.*, **154**, 572.

HUBEL, D. H. and WIESEL, T. N. (1962) 'Receptive fields, binocular interaction and functional architecture in the cat's visual cortex'. *J. Physiol.*, **160**, 106.

HUBEL, D. H. and WIESEL, T. N. (1963) 'Receptive fields of cells in striate cortex of very young, visually inexperienced kittens'. *J. Neurophysiol.*, **26**, 994.

HUBEL, D. H. and WIESEL, T. N. (1968) 'Receptive fields and functional architecture of monkey striate cortex'. *J. Physiol.*, **195**, 215.

HUDSON, W. (1960) 'Pictorial depth perception in sub-cultural groups in Africa'. *J. Soc. Psychol.*, **52**, 183.

HUDSON, W. (1967) 'The study of the problem of pictorial perception among uncultured groups'. *Internat. J. Psychol.*, **2**, 89.

HULL, J. and ZUBEK, J. P. (1962) 'Personality characteristics of successful and unsuccessful sensory isolation subjects'. *Percept. Motor Skills*, **14**, 231.

HUMPHREY, G., DAWE, P. G. M. and MANDELL, D. (1955) 'New high-speed electronic tachistoscope'. *Nature*, **176**, 231.

HUMPHREY, G. and SPRINGBETT, B. M. (1946) 'The after-image of the phi-phenomenon'. *Bull. Canad. Psychol. Assoc.*, **6**, 3.

HUNT, J. T. (1964) 'Luminous figures: influence of point of fixation on their disappearance'. *Science*, **143**, 1193.

HUTTENLOCHER, J. (1967) 'Discrimination of figure orientation: effects of relative position'. *J. Comp. Physiol. Psychol.*, **63**, 359.

HYMAN, R. and HAKE, H. W. (1954) Cited by H. W. Hake 'Form discrimination and invariance of form'. In L. Uhr (Ed.) (1966), *Pattern Recognition*. New York: Wiley.

ISCOE, I. and CARDEN, J. A. (1961) 'Field dependence, manifest anxiety and sociometric status in children'. *J. Consult. Psychol.*, **25**, 184.

ITTELSON, W. H. (1951) 'Size as a cue to distance: radial motion'. *Amer. J. Psychol.*, **64**, 188.

ITTELSON, W. H. (1960) *Visual Space Perception*. New York: Springer.

ITTELSON, W. H. and AMES, A. (1950) 'Accommodation, convergence and their relation to apparent distance'. *J. Psychol.*, **30**, 43.

JACKSON, C. W. and KELLEY, E. L. (1962) 'Influence of suggestion and subjects' prior knowledge in research on sensory adaptation'. *Science*, **135**, 211.

JACKSON, C. W. and POLLARD, J. C. (1962) 'Sensory deprivation and suggestion'. *Behav. Sci.*, **7**, 332.

JACKSON, D. N. (1954) 'A further examination of the role of autism in a visual figure-ground relationship'. *J. Psychol.*, **38**, 399.

JAHODA, G. (1966) 'Geometric illusions and environment: a study in Ghana'. *Brit. J. Psychol.*, **57**, 193.

JEFFREY, H. J. (1968) 'An enquiry into inappropriate constancy scaling'. *Quart. J. Exper. Psychol.*, **20**, 294.

JENKIN, N. (1958) 'Size constancy as a function of personal adjustment and disposition'. *J. Ab. Soc. Psychol.*, **57**, 334.

JENKIN, N. and FEALLOCK, S. M. (1960) 'Developmental and intellectual processes in size-distance judgment'. *Amer. J. Psychol.*, **73**, 268.

JENKIN, N. and HYMAN, R. (1959) 'Attitude and distance-estimation as variables in size-matching'. *Amer. J. Psychol.*, **73**, 68.

JENSEN, G. D. (1960) 'Effect of past experience upon induced movement'. *Percept. Motor Skills*, **11**, 281.

JERISON, H. J. (1963) 'On the decrement function in human vigilance'. In D. N. Buckner and J. J. McGrath (Eds.), *Vigilance: A Symposium*. New York: McGraw-Hill.

JOHANSEN, M. (1954) 'An introductory study of voluminal form perception'. *Nordisk Psykologi's Monog. Ser.*, No. 5.

JOHANSSON, G. (1950) *Configurations in Event Perception*. Uppsala: Almqvist & Wiksells.

JOHANSSON, G. (1954) 'Studies of movement after-effects'. *Reports from the Psychological Laboratory*, No. 4. University of Stockholm.

JOHANSSON, G. (1964) 'Perception of motion and changing form'. *Scand. J. Psychol.*, **5**, 181.

JOHANSSON, G. (1968) 'Vision without contours: a study of visual information from ordinal stimulation'. *Percept. Motor Skills*, **26**, 335.

JOHNSON, B. and BECK, L. F. (1941) 'The development of space perception, I. Stereoscopic vision in preschool children'. *J. Genet. Psychol.*, **58**, 247.

JOHNSON, M. L. (1953) 'Seeing's believing'. *New Biol.*, No. 15.

JOHNSON, R. C., FRINCKE, G. and MARTIN, L. (1961) 'Meaningfulness, frequency and affective character of words as related to visual duration threshold'. *Canad. J. Psychol.*, **15**, 199.

JONES, A. (1959) 'The efficiency of utilization of visual information and the effects of stress'. *J. Exper. Psychol.*, **58**, 428.

JONES, A. (1964) 'Drive and incentive variables associated with the statistical properties of sequences of stimuli'. *J. Exper. Psychol.*, **67**, 423.

JONES, A. WILKINSON, H. J. and BRADEN, I. (1961) 'Information deprivation as a motivational variable'. *J. Exper. Psychol.*, **62**, 126.

JONES, E. E. and BRUNER, J. S. (1954) 'Expectancy in apparent visual movement'. *Brit. J. Psychol.*, **45**, 157.

JOUVET, M. (1957) Cited in D. E. Berlyne (1960), *Conflict, Arousal and Curiosity*. New York: McGraw-Hill.

JOYNSON, R. B. (1958) 'An experimental synthesis of the Associationist and Gestalt accounts of the perception of size'. *Quart. J. Exper. Psychol.*, **10**, 65, 142.

JOYNSON, R. B. and NEWSON, L. J. (1962) 'The perception of shape as a function of inclination'. *Brit. J. Psychol.*, **53**, 1.

JULESZ, B. (1964) 'Binocular depth perception without familiarity cues'. *Science*, **145**, 356.

KAGAN, J., HENKER, B. A., HEN-TOV, A., LEVINE, J. and LEWIS, M. (1966) 'Infants' differential reactions to familiar and distorted faces'. *Child Develop.*, **37**, 519.

KAGAN, J., ROSMAN, B. L., DAY, D., ALBERT, J. and PHILLIPS, W. (1964) 'Information processing in the child'. *Psychol. Monog.*, **78**, No. 1.

KAHNEMANN, D., BEATTY, J. and POLLACK, I. (1967) 'Perceptual deficit during a mental task'. *Science*, **157**, 218.

KAISER, P. F. (1967) 'Perceived shape and its dependency on perceived slant'. *J. Exper. Psychol.*, **75**, 345.

KANIZSA, G. and METELLI, F. (1961) 'Récherches expérimentales sur la perception visuelle d'attraction'. *J. de Psychol.*, **58**, 385.

KATZ, D. (1935) *The World of Colour*. London: Kegan Paul.

KATZ, P. A. (1963) 'Effects of labels on children's perception and discrimination learning'. *J. Exper. Psychol.*, **66**, 423.

KAUFMAN, E. L., LORD, M. W., REESE, T. W. and VOLKMANN, J. (1949) 'The discrimination of visual number'. *Amer. J. Psychol.*, **62**, 498.

KEEHN, J. D. (1959) 'Increase in perceptual sensitivity as a function of learning in the test situation'. *Brit. J. Psychol.*, **50**, 37.

KEMPLER, B. and WIENER, M. (1963) 'Personality and perception in the recognition threshold paradigm'. *Psychol. Rev.*, **70**, 349.

KERPELMAN, L. C. and POLLACK, R. H. (1964) 'Developmental changes in the location of form discrimination cues'. *Percept. Motor Skills*, **19**, 375.

KIDD, A. H. (1965) 'Closure as related to manifest anxiety and rigidity'. *Percept. Motor Skills*, **20**, 1177.

KILBRIDE, P. L. and ROBBINS, M. C. (1968) 'Linear perspective, pictorial depth perception and education among the Baganda'. *Percept. Motor Skills*, **27**, 601.

KILPATRICK, F. P. (1954) 'Two processes in perceptual learning'. *J. Exper. Psychol.*, **47**, 362.

KING, H. E., LANDIS, C. and ZUBIN, J. (1944) 'Visual subliminal perception where a figure is obscured by the illumination of the ground'. *J. Exper. Psychol.*, **34**, 60.

KISSIN, B., GOTTESFELD, H. and DICKES, R. (1957) 'Inhibition and tachistoscopic thresholds for sexually charged words'. *J. Psychol.*, **43**, 333.

KLEIN, G. S. (1951) 'The personal world through perception'. In *Perception: An Approach to Personality*. New York: Ronald Press.

KLEIN, G. S. (1954) 'Need and regulation'. In M. R. Jones (Ed.) (1954), *Nebraska Symposium on Motivation*, 1954. University of Nebraska Press.

KLEIN, G. S. and SCHLESINGER, H. J. (1951) 'Perceptual attitudes towards instability, I: Prediction of apparent movement experiences from Rorschach responses'. *J. Pers.*, **19**, 289.

KLEIN, G. S., SCHLESINGER, H. J. and MEISTER, D. E. (1951) 'The effect of personal values on perception'. *Psychol. Rev.*, **58**, 97.

KLEIN, G. S., SPENCE, D. R., HOLT, R. R. and GOUREVITCH, S. (1958) 'Cognition without awareness: subliminal influences upon conscious thought'. *J. Ab. Soc. Psychol.*, **57**, 255.

KOFFKA, K. (1935) *Principles of Gestalt Psychology*. London: Kegan Paul.

KOHEN-RAZ, R. (1966) 'The Ring-Cube test: a brief time sampling method for assessing primary development of coordinated bilateral grasp responses in infancy'. *Percept. Motor Skills*, **23**, 675.

KÖHLER, W. and WALLACH, H. (1944) 'Figural after-effects: an investigation of visual processes'. *Proc. Amer. Philos. Soc.*, 88, 269.

KOLERS, P. A. (1957) 'Subliminal stimulation in problem-solving'. *Amer. J. Psychol.*, 70, 437.

KOLERS, P. A. (1963) 'Some differences between real and apparent visual movement'. *Vision Res.*, 3, 191.

KOLERS, P. A. (1964) 'Apparent movement of a Necker cube'. *Amer. J. Psychol.*, 77, 220.

KORCHIN, S. J. and BASOWITZ, H. (1954) 'Perceptual adequacy in a life stress'. *J. Psychol.*, 38, 495.

KORCHIN, S. J., BASOWITZ, H. et al. (1957) 'Visual discrimination and the decision process in anxiety'. *Arch. Neurol. Psychiat.*, 78, 425.

KORNER, A. F. and GROBSTEIN, R. (1966) 'Visual alertness as related to soothing in neonates'. *Child Develop.*, 37, 867.

KORTE, A. (1915) 'Kinematoskopische Untersuchungen'. *Zeit. f. Psychol.*, 72, 193.

KOTTENHOFF, H. (1957) 'Situational and personal influences on space perception with experimental spectacles'. *Acta Psychol.*, 13, 79.

KRAGH, U. (1955) *The Actual-Genetic Model of Perception-Personality*. Lund: Gleerup.

KRECH, D. and CALVIN, A. (1953) 'Levels of perceptual organization and cognition'. *J. Ab. Soc. Psychol.*, 48, 394.

KREMENAK, M. (1950) Cited by E. Brunswik (1956) in *Perception and the Representative Design of Psychological Experiments*, (2nd ed). University of California Press.

KRISTOFFERSON, A. B. (1957a) 'Visual detection as influenced by target form'. In J. W. Wulfeck and J. H. Taylor (Eds.), *Form Discrimination as Related to Military Problems*. Washington, D.C.: Nat. Acad. Sci.-Nat. Res. Counc.

KRISTOFFERSON, A. B. (1957b) 'Word recognition, meaningfulness and familiarity'. *Percept. Motor Skills*, 7, 219.

KRULEE, G. K. (1958) 'Some informational aspects of form discrimination'. *J. Exper. Psychol.*, 55, 143.

KÜLPE, O. (1904) *Ber. I Kongress exp. Psychol.*, Giessen. Leipsig.

KÜNNAPAS, T. M. (1955) 'An analysis of the "vertical-horizontal" illusion'. *J. Exper. Psychol.*, 49, 134.

KÜNNAPAS, T. M. (1957) 'The vertical-horizontal illusion and the visual field'. *J. Exper. Psychol.*, 53, 405.

KÜNNAPAS, T. M. (1958) 'Influence of head inclination on the vertical-horizontal illusion'. *J. Psychol.*, 46, 179.

LABERGE, D., TWEEDY, J. R. and RICKER, J. (1967) 'Selective attention: incentive variables and choice time'. *Psychonom. Sci.*, **8**, 341.

LACY, O. W., LEWINGER, N. and ADAMSON, J. F. (1953) 'Foreknowledge as a factor affecting perceptual defense and alertness'. *J. Exper. Psychol.*, **45**, 169.

LAMBERCIER, M. (1946) 'La configuration en profondeur dans la constance des grandeurs'. *Arch. de Psychol.*, **31**, 287.

LANDAUER, A. A. (1964) 'The effect of viewing conditions and instructions on shape judgments'. *Brit. J. Psychol.*, **55**, 49.

LANDAUER, A. A. and RODGER, R. S. (1964) 'Effect of "apparent" instructions on brightness judgments'. *J. Exper. Psychol.*, **68**, 80.

LANDIS, D., JONES, J. M. and REITER, J. (1966) 'Two experiments on perceived size of coins'. *Percept. Motor Skills*, **23**, 719.

LANGDON, J. (1953) 'Further studies in the perception of a changing shape'. *Quart. J. Exper. Psychol.*, **5**, 89.

LANSING, R. W., SCHWARTZ, E. and LINDSLEY, D. B. (1959) 'Reaction time and EEG activation under alerted and nonalerted conditons'. *J. Exper. Psychol.*, **58**, 1.

LAWRENCE, D. H. and COLES, G. R. (1954) 'Accuracy of recognition with alternatives before and after the stimulus'. *J. Exper. Psychol.*, **47**, 208.

LAWRENCE, D. H. and LABERGE, D. L. (1956) 'Relationship between recognition accuracy and order of reporting stimulus dimensions'. *J. Exper. Psychol.*, **51**, 12.

LAZARUS, R. S. and MCLEARY, R. A. (1951) 'Autonomic discrimination without awareness'. *Psychol. Rev.*, **58**, 113.

LAZARUS, R. S., YOUSEM, H. and ARENBERG, D. (1953) 'Hunger and perception'. *J. Pers.*, **21**, 312.

LEEPER, R. (1935) 'A study of a neglected portion of the field of learning – the development of sensory organization'. *J. Genet. Psychol.*, **46**, 41.

LEIBOWITZ, H. and BOURNE, L. E. (1956) 'Time and intensity as determiners of perceived shape'. *J. Exper. Psychol.*, **51**, 277.

LEIBOWITZ, H., CHINETTI, P. and SIDOWSKI, J. (1956) 'Exposure duration as a variable in perceptual constancy'. *Science*, **123**, 668.

LEIBOWITZ, H. and GWOZDECKI, J. (1967) 'The magnitude of the Poggendorff illusion as a function of age'. *Child Develop.*, **38**, 573.

LEIBOWITZ, H. and HARVEY, L. O. (1967) 'Size matching as a function of instructions in a naturalistic environment'. *J. Exper. Psychol.*, **74**, 378.

LEIBOWITZ, H. and JUDESCH, J. M. (1967) 'The relation between age and the magnitude of the Ponzo illusion'. *Amer. J. Psychol.*, **80**, 105.

LEIBOWITZ, H., POLLARD, S. W. and DICKSON, D. (1967) 'Monocular and binocular size-matching as a function of distance at various age-levels'. *Amer. J. Psychol.*, **80**, 263.

LEIBOWITZ, H., WASKOW, I., LOEFFLER, N. and GLASER, F. (1959) 'Intelligence level as a variable in the perception of shape'. *Quart. J. Exper. Psychol.*, **11**, 108.

LEUBA, C. (1940) 'Children's reactions to elements of simple geometric patterns'. *Amer. J. Psychol.*, **53**, 575.

LEVINE, R., CHEIN, I. and MURPHY, G. (1942) 'The relation of the intensity of a need to the amount of perceptual distortion'. *J. Psychol.*, **13**, 283.

LEWIS, M., KAGAN, J. and KALAFAT, J. (1966) 'Patterns of fixation in the young infant'. *Child Develop.*, **37**, 331.

LEWIS, M. M. (1936) *Infant Speech*. London: Kegan Paul.

LEWIS, M. M. (1957) *How Children Learn to Speak*. London: Harrap.

LICHTE, W. H. (1952) 'Shape constancy: dependence upon angle of rotation; individual differences'. *J. Exper. Psychol.*, **43**, 49.

LICHTE, W. H. and BORRESEN, C. R. (1967) 'Influence of instructions on degree of shape constancy'. *J. Exper. Psychol.*, **74**, 538.

LINDNER, H. (1953) 'Sexual responsiveness to perceptual tests in a group of sexual offenders'. *J. Pers.*, **21**, 364.

LINDSLEY, D. B. (1957) 'The reticular system and perceptual discrimination'. In H. H. Jasper *et al.* (Eds.), *Reticular Formation of the Brain*. London: Churchill.

LING, B. C. (1941) 'Form discrimination as a learning cue in infants'. *Comp. Psychol. Monog.*, **17**, No. 2.

LONG, E. R., REID, L. S. and HENNEMAN, R. H. (1960) 'An experimental analysis of set: variables influencing the identification of ambiguous visual stimulus objects'. *Amer. J. Psychol.*, **73**, 553.

LONGENECKER, E. D. (1962) 'Perceptual recognition as a function of anxiety, motivation and the testing situation'. *J. Ab. Soc. Psychol.*, **64**, 215.

LOOMIS, H. K. and MOSKOWITZ, S. (1958) 'Cognitive style and stimulus ambiguity'. *J. Pers.* **26**, 349.

LOVELL, K. (1959) 'A follow-up study of some aspects of the work of Piaget and Inhelder on the child's conception of space'. *Brit. J. Educ. Psychol.*, **29**, 104.

LOWENFELD, J. (1961) 'Negative affect as a causal factor in the occurrence of repression, subception and perceptual defense'. *J. Pers.*, **29**, 54.

LUCHINS, A. S. (1945) 'Social influences on perception of complex drawings'. *J. Soc. Psychol.*, **21**, 257.

LUCHINS, A. S. and LUCHINS, E. H. (1955) 'Influences on perception of previous experience with ambiguous and non-ambiguous stimuli'. *J. Gen. Psychol.*, **53**, 199.

LURIA, A. R. (1961) *The Role of Speech in the Regulation of Normal and Abnormal Behaviour.* Oxford: Pergamon.

LURIA, S. M. and KINNEY, J. A. S. (1968) 'Judgments of distance under partially reduced cues'. *Percept. Motor Skills*, **26**, 1019.

LYSAK, W. (1954) 'The effects of punishment upon syllable recognition thresholds'. *J. Exper. Psychol.*, **47**, 343.

MCCALL, R. B. and KAGAN, J. (1967) 'Attention in the infant: effects of complexity, contour, perimeter and familiarity'. *Child Develop.*, **38**, 939.

MCCLELLAND, D. C. and ATKINSON, J. W. (1948) 'The projective expression of needs, I: The effect of different intensities of the hunger drive on perception'. *J. Psychol.*, **25**, 205.

MCCLELLAND, D. C. and LIBERMAN, A. M. (1949) 'The effect of need for achievement on recognition of need-related words'. *J. Pers.*, **18**, 236.

MCFIE, J., PIERCY, M. F. and ZANGWILL, O. L. (1950) 'Visual spatial agnosia associated with lesions of the right cerebral hemisphere'. *Brain*, **73**, 167.

MCGHEE, J. M. (1963) 'The effect of group verbal suggestion and age on the perception of the Ames trapezoidal illusion'. *J. Psychol.*, **56**, 447.

MCGINNIES, E. (1949) 'Emotionality and perceptual defense'. *Psychol. Rev.*, **56**, 244.

MCGINNIES, E., COMER, P. B. and LACEY, O. L. (1952) 'Visual-recognition thresholds as a function of word length and word frequency'. *J. Exper. Psychol.*, **44**, 65.

MCGINNIES, E. and SHERMAN, H. (1952) 'Generalization of perceptual defense'. *J. Ab. Soc. Psychol.*, **47**, 81.

MCGRATH, J. J. (1963a) 'Irrelevant stimulation and vigilance performance'. In D. N. Buckner and J. J. McGrath (Eds.), *Vigilance: A Symposium.* New York: McGraw-Hill.

MCGRATH, J. J. (1963b) 'Some problems of definition and criteria in the study of vigilance'. *Ibid.*

MACK, A. (1967) 'The role of movement in perceptual adaptation to a tilted retinal image.' *Percept. & Psychophys.*, **2**, 65.

MACKAY, D. M. (1958) 'Perceptual stability of a stroboscopically lit visual field containing self-luminous objects'. *Nature*, **181**, 507.

MACKAY, D. H. (1965) 'Visual noise as a tool of research'. *J. Gen. Psychol.*, **72**, 181.

MCKENNELL, A. C. (1960) 'Visual size and familiar size: individual differences'. *Brit. J. Psychol.*, **51**, 27.

MCKINNEY, J. P. (1963) 'Disappearance of luminous designs'. *Science*, **140**, 403.

MCKINNEY, J. P. (1966) 'Verbal meaning and perceptual stability'. *Canad. J. Psychol.*, **20**, 237.

MACKWORTH, J. F. and TAYLOR, M. M. (1963) 'The d' measure of signal detectability in vigilance-like situations'. *Canad. J. Psychol.*, **17**, 302.

MACKWORTH, N. H. (1950) 'Researches on the measurement of human performance'. *Med. Res. Counc. Spec. Rep. Ser.*, No. 268.

MACKWORTH, N. H. (1965) 'Visual noise causes tunnel vision'. *Psychonom. Sci.*, **3**, 67.

MACKWORTH, N. H., KAPLAN, I. T. and METLAY, W. (1964) 'Eye movements during vigilance'. *Percept. Motor Skills*, **18**, 397.

MANDES, E. and GHENT, L. (1963) 'The effect of stimulus orientation on the recognition of geometric form in adults'. *Amer. Psychol.*, **18**, 425.

MANGAN, G. L. (1959) 'The role of punishment in figure-ground re-organization'. *J. Exper. Psychol.*, **58**, 369.

MANN, C. W., BERTHELOT-BERRY, N. H. and DAUTERIVE, H. J. (1949) 'The perception of the vertical, I: Visual and non-labyrinthine cues'. *J. Exper. Psychol.*, **39**, 538.

MAREK, J. (1963) 'Information, perception and social context'. *Hum. Rel.*, **16**, 209.

MARKS, E. S. (1943) 'Skin color judgments of Negro College students'. *J. Ab. Soc. Psychol.*, **38**, 370.

MATTHEWS, A. and WERTHEIMER, M. (1958) 'A "pure" measure of perceptual defense uncontaminated by response suppression'. *J. Ab. Soc. Psychol.*, **57**, 373.

MEFFORD, R. B. (1968a) 'Perception of depth in rotating objects, 4: Fluctuating stereokinetic perceptual variants'. *Percept. Motor Skills*, **27**, 255.

MEFFORD, R. B. (1968b) 'Perception of depth in rotating objects, 7: Influence of attributes of depth on stereoscopic percepts'. *Percept. Motor Skills*, **27**, 1179.

MEILI, R. and TOBLER, E. (1931) 'Les mouvements stroboscopiques chez les enfants'. *Arch. de Psychol.*, **23**, 131.

MEISENHEIMER, J. (1929) 'Experimente im peripheren Sehen von Gestalten'. *Arch. f. d. ges. Psychol.*, **67**, 1.

MENEGHINI, K. A. and LEIBOWITZ, H. (1967) 'Effect of stimulus distance and age on shape constancy'. *J. Exper. Psychol.*, **74**, 241.

MEREDITH, G. M. and MEREDITH, C. G. W. (1962) 'Effect of instructional conditions on rate of binocular rivalry'. *Percept. Motor Skills*, **15**, 655.

MESSICK, S. and FRITSKY, F. J. (1963) 'Dimensions of analytic attitude in cognition and personality'. *J. Pers.*, **31**, 346.

METZGER, W. (1930) Cited by K. Koffka (1935) in *Principles of Gestalt Psychology*. London: Kegan Paul.

MEYER, E. (1940) 'Comprehension of spatial relations in preschool children'. *J. Genet. Psychol.*, **57**, 119.

MICHELS, K. M. and ZUSNE, L. (1965) 'Metrics of visual form'. *Psychol. Bull.*, **63**, 74.

MICHOTTE, A. (1946) *La Perception de la Causalité*. Publications Universitaires de Louvain. Translated (1963) as *The Perception of Causality*. London: Methuen.

MICHOTTE, A. (1955) 'L'influence de l'expérience sur la structuration des données sensorielles dans la perception'. In A. Michotte, J. Piaget and H. Piéron (Eds.), *La Perception*. Paris: Presses Universitaires de France.

MICHOTTE, A., KNOPS, L. and COEN-GELDERS, A. (1957) 'Etude comparative des diverses situations expérimentales donnant lieu à des impressions causales d'entraînement'. In *Contributions à une Psychologie Humaine Dédiées au Professeur Buytendy'k*. Utrecht: Spectrum.

MIKAELIAN, H. and HELD, R. (1964) 'Two types of adaptation to an optically-rotated visual field'. *Amer. J. Psychol.*, **77**, 257.

MILLER, E. F. (1959) 'Effects of exposure time upon the ability to perceive a moving target'. *N.M. 1701 11 Report No. 2*. U.S. School of Aviation Medicine.

MILLER, G. A. (1956) 'The magical number seven, plus or minus two'. *Psychol. Rev.*, **63**, 81.

MILLER, G. A., BRUNER, J. S. and POSTMAN, L. (1954) 'Familiarity of letter sequences and tachistoscopic identification'. *J. Gen. Psychol.* **50**, 129.

MILLER, J. G. (1939) 'Discrimination without awareness'. *Amer. J. Psychol.*, **52**, 562.

MILLER, J. W. and LUDVIGH, E. (1960) Cited by L. L. Avant (1965) in 'Vision in the *Ganzfeld*'. *Psychol. Bull.*, **64**, 246.

MINARD, J. G. (1965) 'Response-bias interpretation of "perceptual defense"'. *Psychol. Rev.*, **72**, 74.

MINTURN, A. L. and REESE, T. W. (1951) 'The effect of differential reinforcement on the discrimination of visual number'. *J. Psychol.*, **31**, 201.

MOFFIT, J. W. and STAGNER, R. (1956) 'Perceptual rigidity and closure as functions of anxiety'. *J. Ab. Soc. Psychol.*, **52**, 354.

MOONEY, C. M. (1958) 'Recognition of novel visual configurations with and without eye movements'. *J. Exper. Psychol.*, **56**, 133.

MOONEY, C. M. (1960) 'Recognition of ambiguous and unambiguous visual configurations with short and longer exposures'. *Brit. J. Psychol.*, **51**, 119.

MORANT, R. B. and BELLER, H. K. (1965) 'Adaptation to prismatically rotated visual fields'. *Science*, **148**, 530.

MORTON, J. (1964) 'The effects of context upon speed of reading, eye movements and eye-voice span'. *Quart. J. Exper. Psychol.*, **16**, 340.

MOUNT, G. E., CASE, H. W., SANDERSON, J. W. and BRENNER, R. (1956) 'Distance judgment of colored objects'. *J. Gen. Psychol.*, **55**, 207.

MOWBRAY, G. H. (1952) 'Simultaneous vision and audition: the detection of elements missing from overlearned sequences'. *J. Exper. Psychol.*, **44**, 292.

MULHOLLAND, T. (1956) 'Motion perceived while viewing rotating stimulus-objects'. *Amer. J. Psychol.*, **69**, 96.

MUNSINGER, H. and GUMMERMAN, K. (1967) 'Identification of form in patterns of visual noise'. *J. Exper. Psychol.*, **75**, 81.

MURDOCK, B. B. (1954) 'Perceptual defense and threshold measurements'. *J. Pers.*, **22**, 565.

MURRAY, H. A. (1938) *Explorations in Personality*. Oxford University Press.

NEEL, A. F. (1954) 'Conflict, recognition time and defensive behavior'. *Amer. Psychol.*, **9**, 437.

NEISSER, U. (1954) 'An experimental distinction between perceptual process and verbal response'. *J. Exper. Psychol.*, **47**, 399.

NEISSER, U. (1964) 'Visual search'. *Sci. Amer.*, **210**, (6), 94.

NEISSER, U. (1967) *Cognitive Psychology*. New York: Appleton-Century-Crofts.

NELSON, T. M. and BARTLEY, S. H. (1956) 'The perception of form in an unstructured field'. *J. Gen. Psychol.*, **54**, 57.

NEWBIGGING, P. L. (1961) 'The perceptual redintegration of words which differ in connotative meaning'. *Canad. J. Psychol.*, **15**, 133.

NEWSON, E. (1955) 'The development of line figure discrimination in preschool children'. *Unpublished Ph.D. Thesis*, University of Nottingham.

NEWSON, J. (1958) 'Some principles governing changes in the apparent lightness of test surfaces isolated from their normal backgrounds'. *Quart. J. Exper. Psychol.*, **10**, 82.

NEWTON, K. R. (1955) 'A note on visual recognition thresholds'. *J. Ab. Soc. Psychol.*, **51**, 709.

NOBLE, C. E. (1952) 'An analysis of meaning'. *Psychol. Rev.*, **59**, 421.

NOBLE, C. E. (1953) 'The meaning-familiarity relationship'. *Psychol. Rev.*, **60**, 89.

NOELTING, G. (1960) 'La structuration progressive de la figure de Müller-Lyer en fonction de la répétition chez l'enfant et chez l'adulte'. *Arch. de Psychol.*, **37**, 311.

OLDFIELD, R. C. and WINGFIELD, A. (1964) 'The time it takes to name an object'. *Nature*, **202**, 1031.

OLUM, V. (1956) 'Developmental differences in the perception of causality'. *Amer. J. Psychol.*, **69**, 417.

OLVER, R. R. and HORNSBY, J. R. (1966) 'On equivalence'. In J. S. Bruner, R. R. Olver and P. M. Greenfield (Eds.), *Studies in Cognitive Growth*. New York: Wiley.

ONO, H., HASTORF, A. H. and OSGOOD, C. E. (1966) 'Binocular rivalry as a function of incongruity in meaning'. *Scand. J. Psychol.*, **7**, 225.

ORBACH, J. and SOLHKHAH, N. (1968) 'Size judgments of disks presented against the zenith sky'. *Percept. Motor Skills*, **26**, 371.

ORLANSKY, J. (1940) 'The effect of similarity and difference in form on apparent visual movement'. *Arch. Psychol.*, No. 246.

OSLER, S. F. and LEWINSOHN, P. M. (1954) 'The relation between manifest anxiety and perceptual defense'. *Amer. Psychol.*, **9**, 446.

OSTERRIETH, P. A. (1945) 'Le test de copie d'une figure complexe'. *Arch. de Psychol.*, **30**, 205.

OVER, R. (1967) 'Detection and recognition measures of shape discrimination.' *Nature*, **214**, 1272.

OVER, R. and OVER, J. (1967) 'Detection and recognition of mirror-image obliques by young children'. *J. Comp. Physiol. Psychol.*, **64**, 467.

OYAMA, T. (1960) 'Figure-ground dominance as a function of sector angles, brightness, hue and orientation'. *J. Exper. Psychol.*, **60**, 299.

PASSEY, G. E. (1950) 'The perception of the vertical, IV: Adjustment to the vertical with normal and tilted frames of reference'. *J. Exper. Psychol.*, **40**, 738.

PASTORE, N. (1949) 'Need as a determinant of perception'. *J. Psychol.*, **28**, 457.

PASTORE, N. (1952) 'Some remarks on the Ames oscillatory effect'. *Psychol. Rev.*, **59**, 319.

PEMBERTON, C. L. (1952) 'The closure factors related to temperament'. *J. Pers.*, **21**, 159.

PENROSE, L. S. and PENROSE, R. (1958) 'Impossible objects: a special type of visual illusion'. *Brit. J. Psychol.*, **49**, 31.

PERKY, C. W. (1910) 'An experimental study of imagination'. *Amer. J. Psychol.*, **21**, 422.

PETTIGREW, T. F., ALLPORT, G. W. and BARNETT, E. O. (1958) 'Binocular resolution and the perception of race in South Africa'. *Brit. J. Psychol.*, **49**, 265.

PFAFFLIN, S. M. (1960) 'Stimulus meaning in stimulus predifferentiation'. *J. Exper. Psychol.*, **59**, 269.

PHARES, E. J. (1962) 'Perceptual threshold decrements as a function of skill and chance expectancies'. *J. Psychol.*, **53**, 399.

PHILLIPSON, H. (1955) *The Object Relations Technique*. London: Tavistock.

PIAGET, J. (1936) *La Naissance de l'Intelligence chez l'Enfant*. Neuchâtel: Delachaux & Niestlé.

PIAGET, J. (1937) *La Construction du Réel chez l'Enfant*. Neuchâtel: Delachaux & Niestlé.

PIAGET, J. (1945) *La Formation du Symbole chez l'Enfant*. Neuchâtel: Delachaux & Niestlé.

PIAGET, J. (1946) *Les Notions de Mouvement et de Vitesses chez l'Enfant*. Paris: Presses Universitaires de France.

PIAGET, J. (1951) *Play, Dreams and Imitation in Childhood*. London: Heinemann.

PIAGET, J. (1952) *The Origins of Intelligence in Children*. New York: International Universities Press.

PIAGET, J. (1955) *The Child's Construction of Reality*. London: Routledge & Kegan Paul.

PIAGET, J. (1961) *Les Mécanismes Perceptifs*. Paris: Presses Universitaires de France.

PIAGET, J. (1963) 'Le développement des perceptions en fonction de l'âge'. In P. Fraisse and J. Piaget (Eds.), *Traité de Psychologie Experimentale*, **6**. Paris: Presses Universitaires de France.

PIAGET, J. and INHELDER, B. (1956) *The Child's Conception of Space*. London: Routledge & Kegan Paul.

PIAGET, J. and LAMBERCIER, M. (1943) 'La problème de a comparaison visuelle en profondeur (constance de la grandeur) et l'erreur systématique de l'étalon'. *Arch. de Psychol.*, **29**, 255.

PIAGET, J. and LAMBERCIER, M. (1951) 'La comparaison des grandeurs projectives chez l'enfant et chez l'adulte'. *Arch. de Psychol.*, **33**, 81.

PIAGET, J. and LAMBERCIER, M. (1958) 'La causalité perceptive visuelle chez l'enfant et chez l'adulte'. *Arch. de Psychol.*, **36**, 77.

PIAGET, J., MAIRE, F. and PRIVAT, F. (1954) 'Le résistance des bonnes formes à l'illusion de Müller-Lyer'. *Arch. de Psychol.*, **34**, 155.

PIAGET, J. and STETTLER-VON ALBERTINI, B. (1950) 'L'illusion de Müller-Lyer'. *Arch. de Psychol.*, **33**, 1.

PIAGET, J. and STETTLER-VON ALBERTINI, B. (1954) 'Observations sur la perception des bonnes formes chez l'enfant par actualization des lignes virtuelles'. *Arch. de Psychol.*, **34**, 203.

PIAGET, J. and VINH BANG (1961) 'Comparaison des mouvements oculaires et des centrations du regard chez l'enfant et chez l'adulte'. *Arch. de Psychol.*, **38**, 167.

PICK, H. L. and HAY, J. C. (1964) 'Adaptation to prismatic distortion'. *Psychonom. Sci.*, **1**, 199.

PICK, H. L., HAY, J. C. and WILLOUGHBY, R. H. (1966) 'Interocular transfer of adaptation to prismatic distortion'. *Percept. Motor Skills*, **23**, 131.

PICKREL, E. W. (1957) 'Levels of perceptual organization and cognition: conflicting evidence'. *J. Ab. Soc. Psychol.*, **54**, 422.

POLAK, P. R., EMDE, R. N. and SPITZ, R. A. (1964a) 'The smiling response to the human face, I'. *J. Nerv. Ment. Dis.*, **139**, 103.

POLAK, P. R., EMDE, R. N. and SPITZ, R. A. (1964b) 'The smiling response to the human face, II'. *J. Nerv. Ment. Dis.*, **139**, 407.

POLLARD, J. C., UHR, L. and JACKSON, C. W. (1963) 'Studies in sensory deprivation'. *Arch. Gen. Psychiat.*, **8**, 435.

PORTNOY, S., PORTNOY, M. and SALZINGER, K. (1964) 'Perception as a function of association value with response bias controlled'. *J. Exper. Psychol.*, **68**, 316.

POSTMAN, L. (1955a) 'Association theory and perceptual learning'. *Psychol. Rev.*, **62**, 438.

POSTMAN, L. (1955b) 'Review of *Personality through Perception*'. *Psychol. Bull.*, **52**, 79.

POSTMAN, L., BRONSON, W. C. and GROPPER, G. L. (1953) 'Is there a mechanism of perceptual defense?' *J. Ab. Soc. Psychol.*, **48**, 215.

POSTMAN, L. and BROWN, D. R. (1952) 'The perceptual consequences of success and failure'. *J. Ab. Soc. Psychol.*, **47**, 213.

POSTMAN, L., BRUNER, J. S. and MCGINNIES, E. (1948) 'Personal values as selective factors in perception.' *J. Ab. Soc. Psychol.*, **43**, 142.

POSTMAN, L. and CRUTCHFIELD, R. S. (1952) 'The interaction of need, set and stimulus-structure in a cognitive task'. *Amer. J. Psychol.*, **65**, 196.

POSTMAN, L. and LEYTHAM, G. (1951) 'Perceptual selectivity and ambivalence of stimuli'. *J. Pers.*, **19**, 390.

POSTMAN, L. and ROSENWEIG, M. R. (1956) 'Practice and transfer in the visual and auditory recognition of verbal stimuli'. *Amer. J. Psychol.*, **69**, 209.

POSTMAN, L. and SCHNEIDER, B. H. (1951) 'Personal values, visual recognition and recall'. *Psychol., Rev.*, **58**, 271.

POSTMAN, L. and SOLOMON, R. L. (1950) 'Perceptual sensitivity to completed and uncompleted tasks'. *J. Pers.*, **18**, 347.

POTTER, M. C. (1966) 'On perceptual recognition'. In J. S. Bruner, R. R. Olver and P. M. Greenfield (Eds.), *Studies in Cognitive Growth*. New York: Wiley.

POWER, R. P. (1967) 'Stimulus properties which reduce apparent reversal of rotating rectangular shapes'. *J. Exper. Psychol.*, **73**, 595.

POWESLAND, P. F. (1959) 'The effect of practice upon the perception of causality'. *Canad. J. Psychol.*, **13**, 155.

PRATT, K. C. (1960) 'The neonate'. In L. Carmichael (Ed.), *Manual of Child Psychology*, 2nd Ed. New York: Wiley.

PRENTICE, W. C. H. (1954) 'Visual recognition of verbally labelled figures'. *Amer. J. Psychol.*, **67**, 315.

PRESSEY, A. W. (1967) 'Field dependence and susceptibility to the Poggendorff illusion'. *Percept. Motor Skills*, **24**, 309.

PRITCHARD, R. M. (1961) 'Stabilized images on the retina'. *Sci. Amer.*, **204** (6), 72.

PRITCHARD, R. M., HERON, W. and HEBB, D. O. (1960) 'Visual perception approached by the method of stabilized images'. *Canad. J. Psychol.*, **14**, 67.

PUSTELL, T. E. (1957) 'The experimental induction of perceptual vigilance and defense'. *J. Pers.*, **25**, 425.

RADNER, M. and GIBSON, J. J. (1935) 'Orientation in visual perception: the perception of tip character in forms'. *Psychol. Monog.*, **46**, No. 6.

RANKEN, H. B. (1963) 'Language and thinking: positive and negative effects of thinking'. *Science*, **141**, 48.

RAPPAPORT, M. (1957) 'The role of redundancy in the discrimination of visual forms'. *J. Exper. Psychol.*, **53**, 3.

REECE, M. M. (1954) 'The effect of shock on recognition thresholds'. *J. Ab. Soc. Psychol.*, **49**, 165.

REESE, H. W. (1963) '"Perceptual set" in young children'. *Child Develop.*, **34**, 151.

REID, L. S., HENNEMAN, R. H. and LONG, R. (1960) 'An experimental analysis of set: the effect of categorical restriction'. *Amer. J. Psychol.*, **73**, 568.

RENSHAW, S. (1945) 'The visual perception and reproduction of forms by tachistoscopic methods'. *J. Psychol.*, **20**, 217.

RHEINGOLD, H. L. (1961) 'The effect of environmental stimulation upon social and exploratory behaviour in the human infant'. In B. M. Foss (Ed.), *Determinants of Infant Behaviour*, II. London: Methuen.

RIGBY, W. K. and RIGBY, M. K. (1956) 'Reinforcement and frequency as factors in tachistoscopic thresholds'. *Percept. Motor Skills*, **6**, 29.

RIGGS, L. A., RATLIFF, F., CORNSWEET, J. C. and CORNSWEET, T. N. (1953) 'The disappearance of steadily fixated visual test objects'. *J. Opt. Soc. Amer.*, **43**, 495.

RIVERS, W. H. R. (1905) 'Observations on the senses of the Todas'. *Brit. J. Psychol.*, **1**, 321.

ROBINSON, J. S., BROWN, L. T. and HAYES, W. H. (1964) 'Tests of effects of past experience on perception'. *Percept. Motor Skills*, **18**, 953.

ROBSON, K. S. (1967) 'The role of eye-to-eye contact in maternal-infant attachment'. *J. Child Psychol. Psychiat.*, **8**, 13.

ROCK, I. (1954) 'The perception of the egocentric orientation of a line'. *J. Exper. Psychol.*, **48**, 367.

ROCK, I. (1956) 'The orientation of forms on the retina and in the environment'. *Amer. J. Psychol.*, **69**, 513.

ROCK, I. (1957) 'The effect of retinal and phenomenal orientation on the perception of form'. *Amer. J. Psychol.*, **70**, 493.

ROCK, I. (1966) *The Nature of Perceptual Adaptation*. New York: Basic Books.

ROCK, I. and EBENHOLTZ, S. (1962) 'Stroboscopic movement based on change of phenomenal rather than retinal location'. *Amer. J. Psychol.*, **75**, 193.

ROCK, I. and FLECK, F. S. (1950) 'A re-examination of the effect of monetary reward and punishment on figure-ground perception'. *J. Exper. Psychol.*, **40**, 766.

ROCK, I. and HEIMER, W. (1957) 'The effect of retinal and phenomenal orientation on the perception of form'. *Amer. J. Psychol.*, **70**, 493.

ROCK, I. and KAUFMAN, L. (1962) 'The moon illusion'. *Science*, **136**, 1023.

ROCK, I. and KREMER, I. (1957) 'A re-examination of Rubin's figural after effect'. *J. Exper. Psychol.*, **53**, 23.

ROCK, I. and VICTOR, J. (1964) 'Vision and touch: an experimentally created conflict between the two senses'. *Science*, **143**, 594.

ROCKETT, F. C. (1956) 'Speed of form recognition as a function of stimulus factors and test anxiety'. *J. Ab. Soc. Psychol.*, **53**, 197.

ROSCA, M. (1959) 'The perception of incomplete pictures in normal and mentally retarded children'. Cited in *Psychol. Abstr.* (1965) 39-1, 4557.

ROSEN, A. C. (1954) 'Changes in perceptual threshold as a protective function of the organism'. *J. Pers.*, **23**, 182.

ROSENSTOCK, I. M. (1951) 'Perceptual aspects of repression'. *J. Ab. Soc. Psychol.*, **46**, 304.

ROSS, S., YARCZOWER, M. and WILLIAMS, G. M. (1956) 'Recognitive thresholds for words as a function of set and similarity'. *Amer. J. Psychol.*, **69**, 82.

ROSSI, A. M., FUHRMAN, A. and SOLOMON, P. (1964) 'Sensory deprivation: arousal and rapid eye movement correlates of some effects'. *Percept. Motor Skills*, **19**, 447.

ROSSI, A. M. and SOLOMON, P. (1965) 'Note on reactions of extraverts and introverts to sensory deprivation'. *Percept. Motor Skills*, **20**, 1183.

RUBIN, E. (1921) *Visuelwahrgenomme Figuren: Studien in Psychologische Analyse.* Kobenhavn: Gyldendal.

RUCKMICK, C. A. (1921) 'A preliminary study of the emotions'. *Psychol. Monog.*, **30**, No. 3.

RUDEL, R. G. and TEUBER, H.-L. (1963) 'Discrimination of direction of line in children'. *J. Comp. Phsyiol. Psychol.*, **56**, 892.

SALAPATEK, P. and KESSEN, W. (1966) 'Visual scanning of triangles by the human newborn'. *J. Exper. Child Psychol.*, **3**, 155.

SALTZMAN, I. J. and GARNER, W. R. (1948) 'Reaction time as a measure of span of attention'. *J. Psychol.*, **25**, 227.

SALZEN, E. A. (1963) 'Visual stimuli eliciting a smiling response in the human infant'. *J. Genet. Psychol.*, **102**, 51.

SAMPAIO, A. C. (1962) 'La translation des objets comme facteur de la permanence phénoménale'. In A. Michotte *et al.*, *Causalité, Permanence et Réalité Phénoménales.* Publications Universitaires de Louvain.

SAMUELS, I. (1959) 'Reticular mechanisms and behavior'. *Psychol. Bull.* **56**, 1.

SAMUELS, M. R. (1939) 'Judgment of faces'. *Char. & Pers.*, **8**, 18.

SARBIN, T. R. and HARDYCK, C. D. (1955) 'Conformance in role perception as a personality variable'. *J. Consult. Psychol.*, **19**, 109.

SAUGSTAD, P. (1966) 'Effect of food deprivation on perception-cognition'. *Psychol. Bull.*, **65**, 80.

SAUGSTAD, P. and LIE, I. (1964) 'Training of peripheral visual acuity'. *Scand. J. Psychol.*, **5**, 218.

SAYONS, K. (1964) 'Kinetic frame effects, II: Vista motion'. *Percept. Motor Skills*, **18**, 857.

SCHAFER, R. and MURPHY, G. (1943) 'The role of autism in a visual figure-ground relationship'. *J. Exper. Psychol.*, **32**, 335.

SCHAFFER, H. R. (1958) 'Objective observations of personality development in early infancy'. *Brit. J. Med. Psychol.*, **31**, 174.

SCHAFFER, H. R. and PARRY, M. H. (1969) 'Perceptual-motor behaviour in infancy as a function of age and stimulus familiarity'. *Brit. J. Psychol.*, **60**, 1.

SCHIFF, W., CAVINESS, J. A. and GIBSON, J. J. (1962) 'Persistent fear responses in Rhesus monkeys to the optical stimulus of "looming"'. *Science*, **136**, 982.

SCHIFFMAN, H. R. (1967) 'Size-estimation of familiar objects under informative and reduced conditions of viewing'. *Amer. J. Psychol.*, **80**, 229.

SCHILLER, P. H. and WIENER, M. (1963) 'Monoptic and dichoptic visual masking'. *J. Exper. Psychol.*, **66**, 386.

SCHLESINGER, H. J. (1954) 'Cognitive attitudes in relation to susceptibility to interference'. *J. Pers.*, **22**, 354.

SCHLOSBERG, H. (1941) 'A scale for the judgment of facial expressions'. *J. Exper. Psychol.*, **29**, 497.

SCHUCK, J. R., BROCK, T. C., and BECKER, L. A. (1964) 'Luminous figures: factors affecting the reporting of disappearances'. *Science*, **146**, 1598.

SCHULTZ, D. P. (1965) *Sensory Restriction: Effects on Behavior.* New York: Academic Press.

SCHWITZGEBEL, R. (1962) 'The performance of Dutch and Zulu adults on selected perceptual tasks'. *J. Soc. Psychol.*, **57**, 73.

SECORD, P. F. (1958) 'Facial features and inference processes in interpersonal perception'. In R. Tagiuri and L. Petrullo (Eds.), *Person Perception and Interpersonal Behavior.* Stanford University Press.

SECORD, P. F. and BEVAN, W. (1956) 'Personalities in faces, III: A cross-cultural comparison of impressions of physiognomy and personality in faces'. *J. Soc. Psychol.*, **43**, 283.

SECORD, P. F., BEVAN, W. and KATZ, B. (1956) 'The Negro stereotype and perceptual accentuation'. *J. Ab. Soc. Psychol.*, **53**, 78.

SECORD, P. F., DUKES, W. F. and BEVAN, W. (1954) 'Personalities in faces, I: An experiment in social perceiving'. *Genet. Psychol. Monog.*, 49, 231.

SECORD, P. F. and MUTHARD, J. E. (1955a) 'Personalities in faces, IV: A descriptive analysis of the perception of women's faces'. *J. Psychol.*, 39, 269.

SECORD, P. F. and MUTHARD, J. E. (1955b) 'Individual differences in the perception of women's faces'. *J. Ab. Soc. Psychol.*, 50, 238.

SEGALL, M. H., CAMPBELL, D. T. and HERSKOVITS, M. J. (1963) 'Cultural differences in the perception of geometric illusions'. *Science*, 139, 769.

SEGALL, M. H., CAMPBELL, D. T. and HERSKOVITS, M. J. (1966) *The Influence of Culture on Visual Perception*. Indianapolis: Bobbs-Merrill.

SEGUNDO, J. P., ARANA, R. and FRENCH, J. D. (1955) 'Behavioral arousal by stimulation of the brain in the monkey'. *J. Neurosurg.*, 12, 601.

SEMMES, J., WEINSTEIN, S., GHENT, L. and TEUBER, H.-L. (1955) 'Spatial orientation in man after cerebral injury.' *J. Psychol.*, 39, 227.

SHEEHAN, M. R. (1938) 'A study of individual consistency in phenomenal constancy'. *Arch. Psychol.*, No. 222.

SHIPLEY, W. C., KENNEY, F. A. and KING, M. E. (1945) 'Beta apparent movement under binocular, monocular and interocular stimulation'. *Amer. J. Psychol.*, 58, 545.

SHOR, R. E. (1957) 'Effect of preinformation upon human characteristics attributed to animated geometric figures'. *J. Ab. Soc. Psychol.*, 54, 124.

SHRAUGER, S. and ALTROCHI, J. (1964) 'The personality of the perceiver as a factor in person perception'. *Psychol. Bull.*, 62, 289.

SIEGMAN, A. W. (1956) 'Some factors associated with the visual threshold for taboo words'. *J. Clin. Psychol.*, 12, 282.

SIGEL, I. E. (1933) 'Developmental trends in the abstraction ability of children'. *Child Develop.*, 24, 131.

SILVER, C. A., LANDIS, D. and MESSICK, S. (1966) 'Multidimensional analysis of visual form: an analysis of individual differences'. *Amer. J. Psychol.*, 79, 62.

SILVERMAN, L. H. and LUBORSKY, L. (1965) 'A note on the relationship between perceptual blocking and inhibition of drive expression'. *J. Pers. Soc. Psychol.*, 2, 435.

SIMON, B. (Ed.) (1957) *Psychology in the Soviet Union*. London: Routledge & Kegan Paul.

SINGER, J. L. (1952) 'Personal and environmental determinants of perception in a size constancy experiment'. *J. Exper. Psychol.*, 43, 420.

SLACK, C. W. (1956) 'Familiar size as a cue to size in the presence of conflicting cues'. *J. Exper. Psychol.*, **52**, 194.

SLEIGHT, R. B. (1952) 'The relative discriminability of several geometric forms'. *J. Exper. Psychol.*, **43**, 324.

SMITH, D. E. P. and HOCHBERG, J. (1954) 'The effect of "punishment" (electric shock) on figure-ground perception'. *J. Psychol.*, **38**, 83.

SMITH, G. J. W. and HENRIKSSON, M. (1955) 'The effect on an established percept of a perceptual process beyond awareness'. *Acta Psychol.*, **11**, 346.

SMITH, K. R., PARKER, G. B. and ROBINSON, G. A. (1951) 'An exploratory investigation of autistic perception'. *J. Ab. Soc. Psychol.*, **46**, 324.

SMITH, K. U. and SMITH, W. M. (1962) *Perception and Motion*. Philadelphia: Saunders.

SMITH, O. W. and SMITH, P. C. (1966) 'Developmental studies of spatial judgments by children and adults'. *Percept. Motor Skills*, **22**, 3.

SMITH, S. and LEWTY, W. (1959) 'Perceptual isolation using a silent room'. *Lancet*, ii, 342.

SMOCK, C. D. (1955) 'The influence of psychological stress on the "intolerance of ambiguity"'. *J. Ab. Soc. Psychol.*, **50**, 177.

SMOCK, C. D. (1956) 'The relationship between test anxiety, "threat expectancy" and recognition threshold for words'. *J. Pers.*, **25**, 191.

SMOCK, C. D. and RUBIN, B. M. (1964) 'Utilization of visual information in children as a function of incentive motivation'. *Child Develop.*, **35**, 109.

SOLLEY, C. M. and MURPHY, G. (1960) *Development of the Perceptual World*. New York: Basic Books.

SOLOMON, R. L. and HOWES, D. W. (1951) 'Word frequency, personal values and visual duration thresholds'. *Psychol., Rev.*, **58**, 256.

SOLOMON, R. L. and POSTMAN, L. (1952) 'Frequency of usage as a determinant of recognition thresholds for words'. *J. Exper. Psychol.*, **43**, 195.

SOMMER, R. (1957) 'The effects of rewards and punishments during perceptual organization'. *J. Pers.*, **25**, 550.

SPEARS, W. C. (1964) 'Assessment of visual preference and discrimination in the four-month-old infant'. *J. Comp. Physiol. Psychol.*, **57**, 381.

SPENCE, D. E. (1957) 'A new look at vigilance and defense'. *J. Ab. Soc. Psychol.*, **54**, 103.

SPERLING, G. (1960) 'The information available in brief visual presentations'. *Psychol. Monog.*, **74**, No. 11.

SPIKER, C. C., GERJUOY, I. R. and SHEPARD, W. O. (1956) 'Children's concept of middle-sizedness and performance on the intermediate size problem'. *J. Comp. Physiol. Psychol.*, **49**, 416.

SPITZ, R. A. and WOLF, K. M. (1946) 'The smiling response'. *Genet. Psychol. Monog.*, **34**, 57.

SQUIRES, P. C. (1959) 'Topological aspects of apparent visual motion'. *Psychol. Forsch.*, **26**, 1.

STAPLES, R. (1932) 'The responses of infants to color'. *J. Exper. Psychol.*, **15**, 119.

STAVRIANOS, B. K. (1945) 'The relation of shape perception to explicit judgments of inclination'. *Arch. Psychol.*, No. 296.

STEWART, E. C. (1959) 'The Gelb effect'. *J. Exper. Psychol.*, **57**, 235.

STIRNIMAN, F. (1944) 'Über das Farbempfinden Neugeborener'. *Ann. Paediat.*, **163**, 1.

STRATTON, G. M. (1896) 'Some preliminary experiments on vision without inversion of the retinal image'. *Psychol. Rev.*, **3**, 611.

STRATTON, G. M. (1897) 'Vision without inversion of the retinal image'. *Psychol. Rev.*, **4**, 341, 463.

STRITCH, T. M. and SECORD, P. F. (1956) 'Interaction effects in the perception of faces'. *J. Pers.*, **24**, 272.

STROOP, J. R. (1935) 'Studies of interference in serial verbal reactions'. *J. Exper. Psychol.*, **18**, 643.

SUEDFELD, P. (1964) 'Conceptual structure and subjective stress in sensory deprivation'. *Percept. Motor Skills*, **19**, 896.

SYLVESTER, J. (1960) 'Apparent movement and the Brown-Voth experiment'. *Quart. J. Exper. Psychol.*, **12**, 231.

TAJFEL, H. (1957) 'Value and the perceptual judgment of magnitude'. *Psychol. Rev.*, **64**, 192.

TAJFEL, H. and CAWASJEE, S. D. (1959) 'Value and accentuation of judged differences'. *J. Ab. Soc. Psychol.*, **59**, 436.

TAUBER, E. S. and KOFFLER, S. (1966) 'Optomotor response in human infants to apparent motion: evidence of innateness'. *Science*, **152**, 382.

TAUSCH, R. (1954) Cited by W. H. N. Hotopf (1966) in 'The size constancy theory of visual illusions'. *Brit. J. Psychol.*, **57**, 307.

TAYLOR, A. and FORREST, D. W. (1966) 'Two types of set and the generalization of perceptual defence'. *Brit. J. Psychol.*, **57**, 255.

TAYLOR, D. W. and BORING, E. G. (1942) 'The moon illusion as a function of binocular regard'. *Amer. J. Psychol.*, **55**, 189.

TAYLOR, J. A. (1956a) 'Effect of set for associated words on duration threshold'. *Percept. Motor Skills*, **6**, 131.

TAYLOR, J. A. (1956b) 'Physiological need, set and visual duration threshold'. *J. Ab. Soc. Psychol.*, **52**, 96.

TAYLOR, J. G. (1962) *The Behavioral Basis of Perception.* Yale University Press.

TEICHNER, W. H., KOBRICK, J. L. and WEHRKAMP, R. F. (1955) 'The effects of terrain and observation distance on relative depth discrimination'. *Amer. J. Psychol.*, **68**, 193.

TEPAS, D. L. (1962) Cited by L. L. Avant (1965) in 'Vision in the Ganzfeld'. *Psychol. Bull.*, **64**, 246.

TERWILLIGER, R. F. (1963) 'Pattern complexity and affective arousal'. *Percept. Motor Skills*, **17**, 387.

TEUBER, H.-L. (1960) 'Perception'. In J. Field and H. W. Magoun (Eds.), *Handbook of Physiology and Neurophysiology*, III. Washington, D.C.: American Physiological Society.

TEUBER, H.-L. (1966) 'Alterations of perception after brain injury'. In J. C. Eccles (Ed.), *Brain and Conscious Experience.* Berlin: Springer.

TEUBER, H.-L. and WEINSTEIN, S. (1956) 'Ability to discover hidden figures after cerebral lesions'. *Arch. Neurol. Psychiat.*, **76**, 369.

THIÉRY, A. (1896) Cited by W. H. N. Hotopf (1966) in 'The size-constancy theory of visual illusions'. *Brit. J. Psychol.*, **57**, 307.

THOMAS, H. (1965) 'Visual-fixation responses of infants to stimuli of varying complexity'. *Child Develop.*, **36**, 629.

THOMPSON, J. (1941) 'Development of facial expressions of emotion in blind and seeing children'. *Arch. Psychol.*, No. 264.

THOULESS, R. H. (1931a) 'Phenomenal regression to the real object, I'. *Brit. J. Psychol.*, **21**, 338.

THOULESS, R. H. (1931b) 'Phenomenal regression to the real object, II'. *Brit. J. Psychol.*, **22**, 1.

THOULESS, R. H. (1933) 'A racial difference in perception'. *J. Soc. Psychol.*, **4**, 330.

THURSTONE, L. L. (1944) *A Factorial Study of Perception.* University of Chicago Press.

TOCH, H. H. and ITTELSON, W. H. (1956) 'The role of past experience in apparent movement'. *Brit. J. Psychol.*, **47**, 195.

TOLMAN, E. C. (1935) 'Review of Brunswik, E.: *Wahrnehmung und Gegenstandswelt: Grundlegung einer Psychologie vom Gegenstand her.*' *Psychol. Bull.*, **32**, 608.

TOLMAN, E. C. and BRUNSWIK, E. (1935) 'The organism and the causal texture of the environment'. *Psychol. Rev.*, **42**, 43.

TULVING, E. and GOLD, C. (1963) 'Stimulus information and contextual information as determinants of tachistoscopic recognition of words'. *J. Exper. Psychol.*, **66**, 319.

TURNURE, E. C. and WALLACH, L. (1965) 'The influence of contextual variation on the differentiation of parts from wholes'. *Amer. J. Psychol.*, **78**, 481.

VAN DE CASTLE, R. L. (1960) 'Perceptual defense in a binocular-rivalry situation'. *J. Pers.*, **28**, 448.

VANDERPLAS, J. M. and GARVIN, E. A. (1959a) 'The association value of random shapes'. *J. Exper. Psychol.*, **57**, 147.

VANDERPLAS, J. M. and GARVIN, E. A. (1959b) 'Complexity, association value and practice as factors in shape recognition following paired-associate training'. *J. Exper. Psychol.*, **57**, 155.

VENABLES, P. H. and WARWICK-EVANS, L. A. (1967) 'Cortical arousal and two flash threshold'. *Psychonom. Sci.*, **8**, 231.

VENGER, L. A. (1964) 'The development of visual matching of form in preschool children'. Cited in *Psychol. Abstr.* (1965) **39**, 1298.

VERNON, J. A. and HOFFMAN, J. (1956) 'Effect of sensory deprivation on learning rate in human beings'. *Science*, **123**, 1074.

VERNON, J. A. and MCGILL, T. E. (1960) 'Utilization of visual stimulation during sensory deprivation'. *Percept. Motor Skills*, **11**, 214.

VERNON, M. D. (1931) *The Experimental Study of Reading*. Cambridge University Press.

VERNON, M. D. (1937) *Visual Perception*. Cambridge University Press.

VERNON, M. D. (1940) 'The relation of cognition and phantasy in children'. *Brit. J. Psychol.*, **30**, 273.

VERNON, M. D. (1946) 'Learning from graphical material'. *Brit. J. Psychol.*, **36**, 145.

VERNON, M. D. (1947) 'Different types of perceptual ability'. *Brit. J. Psychol.*, **38**, 79.

VERNON, M. D. (1950) 'The visual presentation of factual data'. *Brit. J. Psychol.*, **20**, 174.

VERNON, M. D. (1952) *A Further Study of Visual Perception*. Cambridge University Press.

VERNON, M. D. (1957) 'Cognitive inference in perceptual activity'. *Brit. J. Psychol.*, **48**, 35.

VERNON, M. D. (1961) 'The relation of perception to personality factors'. *Brit. J. Psychol.*, **52**, 205.

VERNON, M. D. (Ed.) (1966) *Experiments in Visual Perception*. Harmondsworth: Penguin Books.

VITZ, P. C. (1966) 'Preference for different amounts of visual complexity'. *Behav. Sci.*, **11**, 105.

VOGEL-SPROTT, M. (1963) 'Influence of peripheral visual distraction on perceptual motor performance'. *Percept. Motor Skills*, **16**, 765.

VON HOLST, E. (1957) Cited by W. H. N. Hotopf (1966) in 'The size-constancy theory of visual illusions'. *Brit. J. Psychol.*, **57**, 307.

VOOR, J. H. (1956) 'Subliminal perception and subception'. *J. Psychol.*, **41**, 437.

VURPILLOT, E. (1963) *L'Organisation Perceptive: Son Rôle dans l'Évolution des Illusions Optico-Géométriques*. Paris: Vrin.

VURPILLOT, E. (1964) 'Perception et représentation dans la constance de la forme'. *Année Psychol.*, **64**, 61.

VURPILLOT, E. and BRAULT, H. (1959) 'Etude expérimentale sur la formation des schèmes empiriques'. *Année Psychol.*, **59**, 381.

VURPILLOT, E. and ZOBERMAN, N. (1956) 'Rôle des indices communs et des indices distincts dans la différentiation perceptive'. *Acta Psychol.*, **24**, 49.

WADE, N. J. and DAY, R. H. (1968) 'Development and dissipation of a visual spatial after effect from prolonged head tilt'. *J. Exper. Psychol.*, **76**, 439.

WAGMAN, I. H. and BATTERSBY, W. S. (1959) 'Neural limitations of visual excitability, II: Retrochiasmal interaction'. *Amer. J. Physiol.*, **197**, 1237.

WAGNER, R. (1941) 'On the perception of shadowless objects'. Cited in *Psychol. Abstr.* (1946) **20**, 4076.

WALK, R. D. and DODGE, S. H. (1962) 'Visual depth perception in a 10-month-old monocular human infant'. *Science*, **137**, 529.

WALK, R. D. and GIBSON, E. J. (1961) 'A comparative and analytical study of visual depth perception'. *Psychol. Monog.*, **75**, No. 15.

WALL, H. W. and GUTHRIE, G. M. (1959) 'Academic stress and perceptual thresholds'. *J. Gen. Psychol.*, **61**, 269.

WALLACH, H. (1948) 'Brightness constancy and the nature of achromatic colors'. *J. Exper. Psychol.*, **38**, 310.

WALLACH, H. (1963) 'The perception of natural colors'. *Sci. Amer.*, **208** (1), 107.

WALLACH, H. and GALLOWAY, A. (1946) 'The constancy of colored objects in colored illuminations'. *J. Exper. Psychol.*, **36**, 119.

WALLACH, H. and KARSH, E. B. (1963a) 'Why modification of stereoscopic depth perception is so rapid'. *Amer. J. Psychol.*, **76**, 413.

WALLACH, H. and KARSH, E. B. (1963b) 'The modification of stereoscopic depth-perception and the kinetic depth-effect'. *Amer. J. Psychol.*, **76**, 429.

WALLACH, H., KRAVITZ, J. H. and LINDAUER, J. (1963b) 'A passive condition for rapid adaptation to displaced visual direction'. *Amer. J. Psychol.*, **76**, 568.

WALLACH, H., MOORE, M. E. and DAVIDSON, L. (1963a) 'Modification of stereoscopic depth-perception'. *Amer. J. Psychol.*, **76**, 191.

WALLACH, H. and O'CONNELL, D. N. (1953) 'The kinetic depth effect'. *J. Exper. Psychol.*, **45**, 205.

WALLACH, H., O'CONNELL, D. N. and NEISSER, U. (1953) 'The memory effect of visual perception of three-dimensional form'. *J. Exper. Psychol.*, **45**, 360.

WALLACH, M. A. and KOGAN, N. (1965) *Modes of Thinking in Young Children*. New York: Holt, Rinehart & Winston.

WALTERS, R. H. (1958) 'Conditioning of attention as a source of autistic effects in perception'. *J. Ab. Soc. Psychol.*, **57**, 197.

WALTERS, R. H., BANKS, R. K. and RYDER, R. R. (1959) 'A test of the perceptual defense hypothesis'. *J. Pers.*, **27**, 47.

WEBSTER, R. G. and HASLERUD, G. M. (1964) 'Influence on extreme peripheral vision of attention to a visual or auditory task'. *J. Exper. Psychol.*, **68**, 269.

WEINER, M. (1955) 'Effects of training in space orientation on perception of the upright'. *J. Exper. Psychol.*, **49**, 367.

WEINER, M. (1956) 'Perceptual development in a distorted room'. *Psychol. Monog.*, **70**, No. 16.

WEINSTEIN, N. and HABER, R. N. (1965) 'A U-shaped backward masking function in vision'. *Psychonom. Sci.*, **2**, 75.

WEINSTEIN, S., FISHER, L., RICHLIN, M. and WEISINGER, H. (1968) 'Bibliography of sensory and perceptual deprivation, isolation and related areas'. *Percept. Motor Skills*, **26**, 1119.

WEINSTEIN, S., SERSEN, E. A., FISHER, L. and WEISINGER, M. (1964) 'Is re-afference necessary for visual adaptation?' *Percept. Motor Skills*, **18**, 641.

WEIR, M. W. and STEVENSON, H. W. (1959) 'The effect of verbalization in children's learning as a function of chronological age'. *Child Develop.*, **30**, 143.

WEISBERG, P. and FINK, E. (1968) 'Effect of varying and non-varying stimulus consequences on visual persistence in twenty-month-old infants'. *Percept. Motor Skills*, **26**, 883.

WENDT, R. H., LINDSLEY, D. F., ADEY, W. R. and FOX, S. S. (1963) 'Self-maintained visual stimulation in monkeys after long-term visual deprivation'. *Science*, **139**, 336.

WERNER, H. (1948) *Comparative Psychology of Mental Development*. New York: International Universities Press.

WERNER, H. and THUMA, B. D. (1942) 'A deficiency in the perception of apparent motion in children with brain injury'. *Amer. J. Psychol.*, **55**, 58.

WERTHEIMER, M. (1912) 'Experimentelle Studien über das Sehen von Bewegung'. *Zeit. f. Psychol.*, **61**, 161.

WERTHEIMER, M. (1923) 'Untersuchungen zur Lehre von der Gestalt'. *Psychol. Forsch.*, **4**, 301.

WEXLER, D., MENDELSON, J., LEIDERMAN, H. and SOLOMON, P. (1958) 'Sensory deprivation'. *Arch. Neurol. Psychiat.*, **79**, 225.

WHITE, B. L. and CASTLE, P. W. (1964) 'Visual exploratory behavior following postnatal handling of human infants'. *Percept. Motor Skills*, **18**, 497.

WHITE, B. L., CASTLE, P. W. and HELD, R. (1964) 'Observations on the development of visually-directed reaching'. *Child Develop.*, **35**, 349.

WIENER, M. (1955) 'Word frequency or motivation in perceptual defense'. *J. Ab. Soc. Psychol.*, **51**, 214.

WIENER, M. and SCHILLER, P. H. (1960) 'Subliminal perception or perception of partial cues'. *J. Ab. Soc. Psychol.*, **61**, 124.

WIESEL, T. N. and HUBEL, D. H. (1963) 'Single-cell responses in striate cortex of kittens deprived of vision in one eye'. *J. Neurophysiol.*, **26**, 1003.

WIESEL, T. N. and HUBEL, D. H. (1966) 'Spatial and chromatic interactions in the lateral geniculate body of the rhesus monkey'. *J. Neurophysiol.*, **29**, 1115.

WILLIAMS, L. G. (1967) 'The effects of target specification on objects fixated during visual search'. *Acta Psychol.*, **27**, 355.

WILLIS, E. J. and DORNBUSH, R. L. (1968) 'Preference for visual complexity'. *Child Develop.*, **39**, 639.

WINGFIELD, A. (1967) 'Perceptual and response hierarchies in object identification'. *Acta Psychol.*, **26**, 216.

WINKLER, M. (1951) Cited by E. Brunswik (1956) in *Perception and the Representative Design of Psychological Experiments*, 2nd Ed. University of California Press.

WISPÉ, L. G. and DRAMBAREAN, N. C. (1953) 'Physiological need, word frequency and visual duration thresholds'. *J. Exper. Psychol.*, **46**, 25.

WITKIN, H. A. (1949a) 'Perception of body position and of the position of the visual field'. *Psychol. Monog.*, **63**, No. 7.

WITKIN, H. A. (1949b) 'The nature and importance of individual differences in perception'. *J. Pers.*, **18**, 145.

WITKIN, H. A. (1950) 'Perception of the upright when the direction of the force acting on the body is changed'. *J. Exper. Psychol.*, **40**, 93.

WITKIN, H. A. and ASCH, S. E. (1948) 'Studies in space orientation, III: Perception of the upright in the absence of a visual field'. *J. Exper. Psychol.*, **38**, 603.

WITKIN, H. A. and ASCH, S. E. (1948) 'Studies in space orientation, IV: Further experiments on perception of the upright with displaced visual fields'. *J. Exper. Psychol.*, **38**, 762.

WITKIN, H. A., DYK, R. B., FATERSON, H. F. GOODENOUGH, D. R. and KARP, S. A. (1962) *Psychological Differentiation: Studies of Development.* New York: Wiley.

WITKIN, H. A., LEWIS, H. B., HERTZMAN, M., MACHOVER, K., MEISSNER, P. B. and WAPNER, S. (1954) *Personality through Perception.* New York: Harper.

WITTREICH, W. J. (1952) 'The Honi phenomenon: a case of selective personal distortion'. *J. Ab. Soc. Psychol.*, **47**, 705.

WOHLWILL, J. F. (1963) 'Overconstancy in distance perception as a function of texture of the stimulus field and other variables'. *Percept. Motor Skills*, **17**, 831.

WOHLWILL, J. F. and WIENER, M. (1964) 'Discrimination of form orientation in young children'. *Child Develop.*, **35**, 1113.

WOODWORTH, R. S. (1938) *Experimental Psychology.* New York: Holt.

WORTHINGTON, A. G. (1964) 'Differential rates of dark adaptation to "taboo" and "neutral" stimuli'. *Canad. J. Psychol.*, **18**, 257.

WRIGHT, N. A. and ABBEY, D. S. (1965) 'Perceptual deprivation tolerance and adequacy of defenses'. *Percept. Motor Skills*, **20**, 35.

WRIGHT, N. A. and ZUBEK, J. P. (1966) 'Use of the multiple discriminant function in the prediction of perceptual deprivation tolerance'. *Canad. J. Psychol.*, **20**, 105.

WULF, F. (1922) 'Über die Veränderung von Vorstellungen'. *Psycho Forsch.* **1**, 333.

WYATT, D. F. and CAMPBELL, D. T. (1951) 'On the liability of stereotype or hypothesis'. *J. Ab. Soc. Psychol.*, **46**, 496.

WYATT, S. and FRASER, J. N. (1929) 'The effects of monotony in work'. Indust. Fat. Res. Board, Report No. 56.

WYATT, S. and FRASER, J. N. (1937) 'Fatigue and boredom in repetitive work'. Indust. Health Res. Board, Report No. 77.

WYKE, M. and ETTLINGER, G. (1961) 'Efficiency of recognition in left and right visual fields'. *Arch. Neurol.*, **5**, 659.

YELA, M. (1952) 'Phenomenal causation at a distance'. *Quart. J. Exper. Psychol.*, **4**, 139.

YENSEN, R. (1957) 'The perception of a rotating shape'. *Quart. J. Exper. Psychol.*, **9**, 130.

YOUNG, H. H. (1959) 'A test of Witkin's field-dependance hypothesis'. *J. Ab. Soc. Psychol.*, **59**, 188.

ZEIGLER, H. P. and LEIBOWITZ, H. (1957) 'Apparent visual size as a function of distance for children and adults'. *Amer. J. Psychol.*, **70**, 106.

ZUBEK, J. P. (1963) 'Counteracting effects of physical exercises performed during prolonged perceptual deprivation'. *Science*, **142**, 504.

ZUBEK, J. P. (1964) 'Behavioural changes after prolonged perceptual deprivation (no intrusions)'. *Percept. Motor Skills*, **18**, 413.

ZUBEK, J. P., AFTANAS, M., KOVACH, K., WILGOSH, L. and WINOCUR, G. (1963) 'Effect of severe immobilization of the body on intellectual and perceptual processes'. *Canad. J. Psychol.*, **17**, 118.

ZUBEK, J. P. and MACNEILL, M. (1966) 'Effects of immobilization: behavioral and EEG changes'. *Canad. J. Psychol.*, **20**, 316.

ZUBEK, J. P. and MACNEILL, M. (1967) 'Role of the recumbent position'. *J. Ab. Psychol.*, **72**, 147.

ZUBEK, J. P., PUSHKAR, D., SANSOM, W. and GOWING, J. (1961) 'Perceptual changes after prolonged sensory isolation (darkness and silence)'. *Canad. J. Psychol.*, **15**, 83.

ZUBEK, J. P., SANSOM, W. and PRYSIAZNIUK, A. (1960) 'Intellectual changes during prolonged perceptual isolation (darkness and silence)'. *Canad. J. Psychol.*, **14**, 233.

ZUBEK, J. P. and WELCH, G. (1963) 'Electroencephalographic changes after prolonged sensory and perceptual deprivation'. *Science*, **139**, 1209.

ZUCKERMAN, M. (1955) 'The effect of frustration on the perception of neutral and aggressive words'. *J. Pers.*, **23**, 407.

ZUCKERMAN, M., ALBRIGHT, R. J., MARKS, C. S. and MILLER, G. L. (1962) 'Stress and hallucinatory effects of perceptual isolation and confinement'. *Psychol. Monog.*, **76**, No. 30.

ZUCKERMAN, M., PERSKY, H., LINK, K. E. and BASU, G. K. (1968) 'Response to confinement: an investigation of sensory deprivation, social isolation, restriction of movement and set factors'. *Percept. Motor Skills*, **27**, 319.

Index of Authors

U

Index of Subjects